White Flags of Surrender

Lili Hahn

WHITE FLAGS OF
SURRENDER

Robert B. Luce, Inc.   Washington–New York

Copyright © 1974 by Lili Hahn

Library of Congress Catalog Card Number   73-9055

ISBN 0-88331-062-7

Translated by Sibyl Milton

Contents

To Julius, my husband,
without whose help, inspiration
and encouragement I never would
have finished this book.

Author's Note

If I add yet another volume to the immense number of books already written about the Third Reich, it is because the grass-roots experience of an average citizen in the Nazi drama has been neglected.

We have many statements by leading National Socialists from their perspective at the top. They were inspired to prove that they personally knew nothing and never had anything to do with atrocities. But even during the bitterest war years, they lived in a brown paradise like maggots in bacon, satiated, warm, and untouched. Or we can read a history of the Third Reich written by men who lived outside Germany; men who never stood for two hours in the cold and snow for a quarter pound of sausage and whose knowledge was based on partly falsified documents. We also have access to books which describe heartrending individual histories which spotlight only a small sector of the whole.

In contrast, I had the dubious privilege of living in Germany from the beginning to the bitter end of the Third Reich, and participated in the daily life under a growing dictatorship — a small grass root among the others. The fact that I was born of a mixed marriage, with an Aryan father and a Jewish mother, granted me an insight into both camps.

My first childhood memories are filled with hunger and a longing for a father I did not know. He was away in a field-gray uniform in a foreign land. I also remember that my parents' house was filled with music. The melodies of Schubert, Beethoven, Brahms, and Mozart wafted up to my room as a child and sang me to sleep.

After the end of World War I, my father returned home, gloomy and depressed. He was a patriotic, conservative German, and our loss of the war almost broke his heart. He returned to his post as medical superintendent of a Frankfurt hospital; and our life gradually resumed its normal course.

In contrast to my taciturn father, my mother was small and graceful with an unpredictable and exuberant temperament. Although outwardly she could not deny her Jewish origins, inwardly she was a fanatic Christian. For hours at a time she had "significant conversations" with my older sister Katherina.

Katherina was a convert to Catholicism. She rejected all worldly matters and surrounded herself with a circle of old-maidish and pious girl friends. Since her proposed entry into a convent precipitated a breach with my father, she decided instead to become a social worker.

My brother Wolf, ten years my senior, was my idol, confidant, and protector. He was the only family member to whom I was intimately and deeply attached. It was very hard on me when he decided to emigrate to America in 1929, after completing his studies in engineering. Conditions in economically depressed postwar Germany offered him few opportunities.

Towards the end of my school years, my father inquired about my plans for a career. He was disappointed and irritated that I wished to become a journalist or a music critic. But after lengthy arguments, he grudgingly gave his consent and I attended lectures at the university and the music academy.

In the autumn of 1932, midway through my preparations for a career, father mentioned that he belonged to the Fighting League for German Culture. The League needed someone to write reviews of concerts broadcast on Southwest German Radio; and he had suggested me for the job. I would begin by writing for the *Frankfurter Post,* a small nationalist newspaper. In my ignorance of what the Fighting League for German Culture represented, I began my career at the brink of the Thousand Year Reich in a Nazi organization.

The *Frankfurter Post* belonged to Mr. Hoffman, an advertisement salesman, and Mr. Löbcke, a bankrupt printshop proprietor: both were unencumbered by education, expertise, or experience. The paper was located in what had been a small apartment, one room of which served as the printing office. The editorial staff consisted of several free-lance journalists and an editor-in-chief named Langer. Langer write news stories and editorial commentar-

10

ies. He also did the paper's makeup and served as his own secretary. He guided me patiently into my new job, which soon included more than reviews of radio concerts.

In this atmosphere, I received my initiation into journalism. Just as I was starting my career, I experienced the consequences of the *Schriftleitergesetz* (Editorial Control Law). Permission to write for a newspaper depended on being on the editors list of the Reichs Association of the German Press. Germans who had previously belonged to the Communist or the Socialist party, Jehovah's Witnesses, and many other organizations were blackballed. Moreover, everyone had to produce Aryan credentials dating back to January 1, 1800. The smallest genealogical blemish disqualified one from membership.

Despite many assertions to the contrary, Hitler and his restrictive laws did not suddenly appear on the German political scene. With promises of jobs and bread, Hitler was duly elected by a people who had one-third of the population unemployed or working part time. The fifteen catastrophic years which followed defeat in the First World War predisposed the Germans to believe the lies and blandishments, that they would once again be able to live in a secure and carefree future.

Hitler was not a genius, just a mediocre bourgeois; but he came at the right moment and told the people what they wanted to hear. Then, once in power, he did what he wanted. The charges that the German people abetted Hitler are equally valid for any nation that uncritically and trustingly follows the promises of its politicians and its government.

Immediately after entering the cabinet, Hitler and his followers began to terrorize their actual and alleged opponents, but it was only with the death of President von Hindenburg that he received a free hand. He proclaimed new laws and decrees which gradually gave him full power. He relentlessly persecuted all "enemies of the state." In his obsession with the purity of the Aryan race, Hitler sought to render harmless all people who were in any way related to Jews. The promulgation of the National Citizenship Law, also known as the Nuremberg Laws, at the party congress in Nuremberg in September 1935 gave Hitler legal grounds for these actions.

According to this law, Jews were not citizens and therefore could no longer vote. Half-Jews, raised as Jews, were to be considered Jews. In addition, almost all professions were organized. Doctors became members of the Reichs Medical Chamber; lawyers

11

belonged to the Reichs Legal Chamber. Actors, writers, artists, and musicians belonged to the Reichs Chamber of Culture, or one of its subsidiary organizations. Artisans were organized in workers' chambers; civil servants were respectively mobilized in their own organizations. All members were required to show proof of Aryan ancestry, traced back to their grandparents. Innumerable lives were ruined as solid citizens discovered with horror that one of their ancestors was a Jew.

When it finally dawned on a significant part of the nation what National Socialism really meant, it was too late. The people were wrapped up in a web of insecurity, mistrust, and fear. Old friendships broke up; relatives became enemies. In many families, parents feared to utter a critical word in the presence of their own children, who were poisoned from infancy in the Nazi Hitler Youth and reported their parents' misdeeds to their superiors. Intimate friends were no longer trusted. All groups were infiltrated with spies, making organized opposition impossible.

Aside from the indescribable misery which Nazism heaped on the Jews, I will not forget those Germans of impeccable personal lineage and political past who were similarly persecuted because they listened to their conscience. The Gestapo purged any criticism of personalities or institutions in the national socialist state. Those who were not instantly sentenced to death, perished in prison or concentration camp. The Gestapo did not require courts of law in their administration of justice: they were simultaneously lethal prosecutors and judges.

Not all Germans who died for their convictions are known, only a few of the martyrs were as famous as Hans and Sophie Scholl, Mayor Gördeler, or Count von Stauffenberg. But they all remain alive in my memory, and taught me that no nation is all good or all evil.

1.   Prologue

The 30th of January began like any other day. In the afternoon I went to the editorial offices. About an hour after I arrived, we heard the cries of "special edition" coming from the street, but we could not understand what was being shouted. Hoffmann, who had just arrived, ran downstairs and returned breathlessly with a paper which read: ADOLF HITLER APPOINTED REICH CHANCELLOR. Von Hindenburg had yielded to the pressure of the Nazis who had become the strongest party.

The events of the following hours exceeded all imagination. Naturally, our only telephone was constantly busy. If Langer was not speaking with some news agency, our readers called in, as did the leading figures in the German National Party. Some of our editorial staff appeared sporadically. They rapidly wrote a few news communiqués or background sketches and then dashed off again. Our normally quiet office had become chaotic.

Then we saw the first flags being displayed in the neighborhood. There were small and large flags; some had the swastika insignia, others the black-white-red pre-Weimar colors. During a brief pause for breath, I went downstairs to Mainzer Landstrasse, a few steps away. Wherever one looked, flags were draped in every window. Everyone seemed to be on the move. Small groups of SA men — Storm Troopers — were standing everywhere, alongside them civilians. Trucks filled with jubilant Storm Troopers singing and shouting, rattled towards the city; swastika flags waved in the breeze of the moving vehicles.

Langer decided to print a thin special edition, which would carry the most important news. More detailed stories would appear in the main edition. Singing and shouts came from the streets below. The printers, confirmed communists, arrived with sullen expressions.

It was long past midnight when I left the office. Despite the late hour, no one seemed to be sleeping. The trams were as full as during daytime hours. The line of a gigantic torchlight parade, with people singing and marching in unison, moved through the streets from the main railroad station to Hauptwache Square. The black night skies glowed with reddish smoke. Crowds of people stood jammed together on the sidewalks, gesturing, calling, waving, and cheering the marchers on. Where there was no parade, Frankfurt's orderly citizens ran in all directions across the trolley tracks. The pauses between the marching songs were filled with cries of *"Sieg Heil!"* The marchers included the brown-uniformed SA ("Storm Troopers"), the black-uniformed SS ("Protection Detachment"), and party members in civilian clothing. The trolley moved forward at a snail's pace, until we left the center of the city.

I finally reached home, and am much too agitated to sleep. My ears still reverberate to the sounds of thousands of jackbooted marchers parading on the pavements of Frankfurt in counterpoint to the songs of raw male voices. Even in our quiet residential district, one hears an occasional Sieg Heil! This same scene occurs at this hour in all cities, large and small, throughout Germany.

February 19, 1933

Father, who originally arranged for my job with the *Post*, told me that after January 1st, the *Frankfurter Volksblatt* — the local Nazi newspaper — wants to print my radio commentaries. My only association with the *Volksblatt* was to mail carbon copies of my reviews to them. I never once checked whether they had printed my column or not.

Yesterday I received a telephone call from the *Volksblatt*. The new editor-in-chief, Norbert Bruchhäuser, wanted to speak to me. I went to the *Volksblatt* this afternoon. The usual salutation there is Heil Hitler!, which seems utterly idiotic to me.

Bruchhäuser was very nice and said that we had to clarify something about my radio commentaries. He took a review I had written a few days before. It concerned a broadcast of piano music for four hands, performed by the duo-pianists Hans Rosbaud and Erich Itor Kahn. The latter pianist is permanently employed by the

14

radio station. I emphasized their excellent technique, and the perfect harmonic balance of both artists. I also elaborated on the great sensitivity of their musical interpretation.

Bruchhäuser was rather cautious and made it clear that although he did not want to criticize my review, I ought to have written that Aryans could have performed it better.

I swallowed first, breathed deeply, and said with a pleasant smile; "No, Herr Bruchhäuser, I am truly sorry, but I could not have written that, much as I would like to please you."

"Really not? Then I believe it would have been better if you had not written anything about this program."

I can only hope that what I have experienced is not an omen of what the future will bring.

February 28, 1933

Bruchhäuser called me several days ago. After saying hello he asked, "You are surely aware that your reviews have not appeared for several days?"

"No."

"Oh? Well, so that you would not be surprised, I wanted to inform you that we will have to do without your contributions. I am truly sorry...." Somehow, he got stuck midway through the sentence.

"That is all right. The *Frankfurter Post* is still printing my columns."

May 1, 1933

Today I experienced my first May Day. The old Socialist May 1st celebration was elevated and rechristened the National Holiday of Labor. The news service provided a Berlin parade plan which showed how fully organized everything was; organized, so to speak, down to the last man. Naturally, Frankfurt was not inferior to Berlin in this respect.

Every firm had a placard with its name, carried by an employee in the front row. Other company employees marched behind. Attendance was mandatory.

Our meeting point was on the corner of Mainzer Landstrasse and Hohenzollern Anlage. Closely packed masses of people were visible as far as the eye could see. Those assembled at our rendezvous were only a minute part of what was being staged in Frankfurt and throughout Germany.

Bands were set up in the parks. They played marching music, and police horses pranced along rhythmically. The spectators stood jammed together on the crowded pavements. All the houses were decorated with flags. The sun streamed from a blue sky. Everyone talked and laughed in a joyous mood. Langer and I also laughed, but for other reasons. It is said that comical figures are never lost from view, even in a dense throng. Our bosses and their wives stood out. Short, plump, rosy Mr. Löbcke was next to thin, colorless Mr. Hoffmann. They looked like Laurel and Hardy.

Suddenly the crowd was silent. The German national anthem "Deutschlandlied" was played, followed by the "Horst Wessel" song. Everyone sang along. I gazed around me, and saw many brown uniforms in the assembly. They were electrified and fervent! They had jobs again, could live and make plans for the future. They were ready to follow their Führer blindly.

The first party orator appeared on the rostrum. The loudspeaker in our vicinity was out of order. Langer leaned towards me and said, "Come, let us go!" We slowly shoved our way to the sidewalk and were submerged in the crowds of onlookers. We advanced with great difficulty to the Café Excelsior, located a few steps away.

We found an empty table upstairs. Langer moved his hand over his forehead and eyes. Gesturing towards the street, he said, "That is really frightening, is it not?"

For quite some time, Langer had complained to me about various matters, and now told me that he had finally made up his mind to leave the *Post*. The newspaper was in financial difficulties; and as Langer said, "We are only an uncultured bourgeois newspaper." The National Socialist German Workers Party (NSDAP) stated on January 30th that every employed party member must subscribe to at least one National Socialist newspaper, and whenever possible recruit two new readers. Langer had observed developments at the *Post* for awhile; and the situation is deteriorating instead of improving. He will go to Berlin in mid-May, since he thinks the chances for success are more favorable in the capital.

It was almost time for us to rejoin our marching colleagues. We heard cries of "Sieg Heil!" from the street below, indicating the last of a parading unit.

Langer knew the restaurant where we would celebrate May Day. General cheers greeted our arrival since we had been "separated from the others in the crush." Three tables were placed together in the shape of a horseshoe, adequate space to seat the whole staff of the *Post*. There was potato salad, sausage, and a huge amount of beer. Finally, this social gathering came to an end too, in a state of mild intoxication.

May 15, 1933

Yesterday was Langer's last day at the *Post*.

My new duties include going at 9 A.M. to police headquarters. Police rookie Gabbusch reports on Frankfurt's criminal events: major burglaries, safecrackings, major traffic accidents and on occasion, a murder. The briefings seldom exceed a half hour, and the time passes in a lively manner with jokes and laughter. Gabbusch is frequently the butt of the joke, but he takes it in good humor. He has the comical habit of ending practically every sentence with "ne, ne, ne." This apparently stands for *nicht*—no. For example, "So you see that is so, nenene ne." We are all starting to imitate him.

June 20, 1933

The Frankfurt press corps was invited to a conference at the radio station. At 3 P.M. we were to welcome the Reichs Broadcasting Commissioner Eugen Hadamowsky—or he would welcome us.

Apparently the *Post's* upper management thought it would make a better impression if I did not go alone. Thus, Mr. Hoffmann accompanied me for the sake of appearances. We were led into the large conference room of the broadcasting station. It was furnished with a very long table surrounded by chairs.

All the press representatives were assembled promptly at 3 P.M.. Normally the Nazis are very punctual, but today something had gone wrong. We began to converse among ourselves. Hoffmann, who seemed totally out of place, did the best he could — he remained silent.

A party bureaucrat came and apologized for Hadamovsky, who was delayed on the way here and, consequently, behind schedule. A kindly soul appeared and placed silver boxes with cigarettes and cigars and ashtrays on the table. Some of us remained seated, others went out to grab a breath of fresh air.

We had been waiting for an hour when the bureaucrat

17

reappeared. A thousand apologies. The commissioner was not far from Frankfurt and would arrive in about a half hour. Slowly we reassembled. We had smoked and chatted for a total of nearly two hours when the news came: Mr. Hadamowsky was here. He would be with us in a few minutes.

Suddenly two high-level party functionaries entered the room. One can recognize their rank by gold emblems on their brown party uniforms. One was a member of Hadamowsky's entourage; the other was our regional propaganda chief Müller-Scheld.

Müller-Scheld looked at the ashtrays full of cigarette butts and scrutinized us closely. He is a handsome man; but his face was distorted by rage. His greeting was curt and cold. And then he let loose. In the future, when high party dignitaries come, the press is to send editors-in-chief and not third- or fourth-rank underlings! He expects more respect at such affairs. And the way we sit around and smoke is outrageous! Moreover, he demanded that in the future, the press listen to and report in detail on book reviews, given on radio, of works written by party members. Following the speech by Reichs Broadcasting Commissioner Hadamowsky, a book review of this type would be on the air. We should remain on the spot and listen to it.

Hoffmann squirmed uncomfortably in his chair while he squinted at my shorthand notebook. Hadamowsky's escort looked distinctly uncomfortable. Several of my colleagues had utterly expressionless faces; others looked as if they would explode at any moment. And then Hadamowsky arrived in person. Without an inkling of what had just happened, he greeted us affably and kindly. It was clear that he wanted to win us over.

He spoke about the importance of radio and the press. For heaven's sake—the man didn't have to make a special trip from Berlin for this! At the end of his speech, Hadamowsky closed with a "Heil Hitler!" He then asked us whether we wished to discuss anything else. (No, we wanted to return to our offices after we had already wasted so much time!) A few timid souls stood around indecisively because of the book-review broadcast which would follow. Hadamowsky's gold-epauletted escort was our rescuer; he gave everyone a blurb of the program.

We left.

Hoffmann walked quickly with me along the Eschersheimer-landstrasse in the direction of the tower. I noticed that he looked at me repeatedly and made several attempts to speak.

18

All of a sudden he burst out with a question, "What did you make of it?"

"Of what?"

"Of what Müller-Scheld said?"

"Oh, I believe he went too far."

"Do you really think so?"

"Yes."

"I noticed you took stenographic notes."

"Yes."

"But you couldn't possibly print them!"

"Why not?"

"That will not do!"

"Why? We have the exact text."

"Yes but..."

"But what? Mr. Hoffmann, we were invited to a press conference, correct? Normally that is done in order to inform the press what they should publish."

"Do you really mean that?"

"Yes, I really mean that. We will print Mr. Müller-Scheld literally, in his exact words."

My colleague Tilly von Waldensheim waddled in fromt of us, all two- or three-hundred pounds of her. Although Mr. Hoffmann was very upset by my intention to print the speech, I observed how he gaped at Tilly in total fascination. Suddenly he blurted out, "I would like to see that woman naked!"

I roared with laughter.

The next morning when the *Frankfurter Post* appeared, it was the only newspaper which mentioned Müller-Scheld's tirade and also printed exactly worded excerpts from his speech.

When I arrived in the office that afternoon, Löbcke greeted me, beaming with joy. *Frankfurter Zeitung* had called. They had heard that we printed the Müller-Scheld story. They wanted to know if it was true and requested that we send them two copies of the story. Mr. Müller-Scheld had gone on vacation for the time being.

June 29, 1933

The first time I met Karl was at a political rally which he covered as a representative of *Frankfurter Zeitung*. From them on,

19

our paths crossed frequently. His tall figure, rushing about with long rapid strides, his dark coat wide open, has become a familiar picture. If I miss seeing him, I am somehow disappointed.

After a while he began to notice me and our glances met more frequently. We became magnetically drawn to each other. He became an important—perhaps the most important—part of my life.

He simplified my life in a practical way by arranging for Günther Rund, a police reporter to pick me up in the morning. Günther arrives punctually every morning in front of our house to give me a lift on his motorbike. As a result of this commuter arrangement, Günther and I have developed a pleasant comradely relationship, despite his once spilling me at the feet of the traffic cop at Opernplatz. He did this so very gently that even the policeman had to laugh. Günther Rund, and many other colleagues who know the questionable circumstances under which I receive my journalistic education, helps me whenever I make a blunder. And I am sure I pull more boners than I am conscious of.

Yesterday morning, when we arrived at police headquarters, Günther, as usual, allowed me to precede him into Gabbusch's office.

I said in a loud and friendly voice, "Good morning!"

"Heil Hitler! is the correct form—ne ne ne," answered Gabbusch.

I began to grin, and Gabbusch asked me whether I found him funny.

"But of course not! What do you think, Mr. Gabbusch? Excuse me. It doesn't have anything to do with you."

"Then perhaps it is the German greeting?"

Feeling the eyes of the Nazi reporters looking at me, I glanced at Günther and said, "No, Mr. Gabbusch—actually I wanted to save Mr. Rund's honor as a motorcyclist. He dumped me in the street on the way here; and I was still laughing about it."

A sigh of relief went through the room, followed by laughter and questions: How—where—why?

As we were leaving, still on police headquarters stairs, Günther began to reprimand me. "Now listen here, Lili. There is nothing to laugh about! You should take everything that has to do with the Nazis in dead earnest. If, for example, someone asks me whether I have heard this or that political joke; I answer no. I simply do not know Nazi jokes! You must always reckon with the possibility that someone wants to trap you."

20

August 14, 1933

I have been promoted! Langer's successor wants me to cover more symphony concerts and events of that kind in the future. Since he considers himself unfamiliar with artistic matters, I will be editor of the art section with a by-line after the first of October.

This should make me happy—if I did not constantly have that uncertain feeling of insecurity; a dark premonition of the future, which is casting a shadow over my life, muting all the bright colors of joy.

October 19, 1933

For the first time since I have known Karl, I called him. I wanted to be sure that he would be going to the Cafe Hauptwache this evening. He said that whatever happened I should wait for him.

It was nearly midnight when he came. Well-meaning colleagues have warned me that Karl drinks. But until now I have only seen him in high spirits. This time he was groggy. He must have drunk a considerable amount before we met. He was not in high spirits, but seemed depressed.

"What is it?" he asked.

"The Editorial Control Law."

"Yes—it is bad! Do you understand clearly the full extent of the law?"

"Yes."

"Do you have a press identity card? I do not mean one from the *Post*, but from the State Association."

I nodded.

"Then don't be nervous for the time being. In any case it will be several months before the law goes into effect. In the interim I'll speak with Dörenfeld and we will be able to work something out."

November 24, 1933

Father makes his daily rounds through the wards with the interns in his wake. Recently during the large senior-staff rounds, his head physician, Dr. Kunz, wore an SA uniform, including jackboots, under his white medical coat. Not only that—he kept his smock wide open so everyone could see his uniform. After rounds,

21

father took him aside and told him quietly that he should change his clothing for rounds. Father, as always, wants to leave politics out of the hospital. Kunz exploded and explained that he had "emergency party duty" immediately afterwards and had no time to change. Father, who still has a weakness for the Nazis, remained friendly. He advised Kunz in a fatherly fashion, "My dear colleague, simply excuse yourself from rounds on such occasions." Kunz responded immediately in a mildly threatening manner. He said he would, naturally, have to report this incident to his superior. As fate would have it, his superior is Colonel Beckerle, currently the Frankfurt police chief.

Father was thoroughly put off balance by this encounter. He could not comprehend that by remaining true to his old principles, he can run into difficulties. It was also a bitter human disappointment which hurt him deeply. "That chap wore frayed trousers and was half-starved when I hired him as an intern. Now he is well clothed, well fed, and clatters through the neighborhood on his heavy motorcycle—that treacherous character!"

I could have cried! I was deeply sorry for father. But what could one say?

Our rescuing angel was Karl. He knows Beckerle from the years before the Third Reich when Beckerle was just a detective superintendent in the criminal police. Karl has a gift of dealing with people. They like him—even when they are totally opposed to him politically. I don't know what he said to Beckerle. He only told me the matter was settled. Father has nothing to fear for the present; but for heaven's sake, he should be more careful.

January 28, 1934

On the 20th of January the meeting of the Rhein-Main regional Association of the Reichs Association of the German Press took place. After the usual annual business report, the chairman, Otto Dörenfeld drew our attention to the new Editorial Control Law and its requirement for proof of Aryan identity, retroactive to January 1, 1800. I must admit that I have no idea what else was said. It was clear to me that my fate was sealed when Dörenfeld said "January 1, 1800." As long as it was a question of only one Jewish grandparent, a modest hope still remained. Now I had to go back to my great-grandparents, which means I have one and a half Jewish grandparents. Then it would be discovered that the pure

22

Aryan Lieutenant General von Kusserow married the pure Jewish Miss Oppenheim.

As we left the meeting, Karl saw me. On the street, he linked his arm under mine while his fingertips stroked the back of my hand. "Now do not lose your courage darling. We will find some kind of twist to obtain an exception for you. We still have almost a full year's time."

"Yes Karl—only it is hopeless! I had never thought further back than my Jewish grandfather. But since we must go back to 1800 it will become know that grandfather married a half-Jewess."

"Oh!"

"Perhaps the best chance would be if Uncle Heinz hires me until a decision is final."

"Who?"

"Uncle Heinz, H.S. [Dr. Heinz Simon]. He is my mother's cousin."

"You never told me that."

"Why? I barely know him. My parents have never made much use of our relationship because of political differences."

I arrived home just in time for lunch. Instinctively mother felt something was wrong. With her characteristic obstinacy, she questioned me until I finally answered.

Father accepted the news with some composure, apparently still convinced that the disease of National Socialism would be outgrown before the year was out. Mother was completely indignant. She had grown up in a Christian family. Her father was baptized as a very young man and had married a Christian; furthermore, grandmother Oppenheim had converted before she married grandfather von Kusserow; and she went on and on.

She simply did not understand—or did not want to comprehend—that under Hitler it is a question of race, not religion.

Father withdrew during this endless and familiar tirade to take his afternoon nap. However, mother continued. She wanted to prove to me that she has nothing to do with Jews. Finally I ran out of patience and said mercilessly, "You know, I wish that Jews were colored. Then you would at least know where you belong!"

February 11, 1934

On top of this, my life is complicated further, since the *Post* is encountering increased financial difficulties. Mr. Schätzlein is no longer there, and Mr. Löbcke has taken over his work. Apparently Schätzlein had at least seen that the money was justly distributed. Now Löbcke and Hoffmann have first claims on any money. Then come the printers, since without them our plant would be idle. What remains is irregularly divided between the young female bookkeeper, the editor-in-chief, and myself. Since the end of last year we no longer receive our full salary at the end of the month. Our earnings are paid in installments spread out over the full month, and even then it is not the entire salary. If Hoffmann brings in more advertising, Mrs. Löbcke and Mrs. Hoffmann come to the office a short time later to collect. Since I still have a roof over my head and can eat at the family dinner table, it is not a total calamity for me. The chief editor's situation is more distressing. He lives as a lodger in a widow's home, and appears to pay his rent by giving lessons to her son and supervising his school assignments. This cannot continue for any of us.

March 23, 1934

I had an unpleasant quarrel with Löbcke today. He has not paid me for several weeks, except an occasional eight or twelve marks.

Finally I was forced to tell him, "I'm sorry Mr. Löbcke, but I can not continue to work under these circumstances. With the small change I am receiving, I can just pay the trolley fare; but I cannot cover all possible meetings and events if I am to pay the taxi out of my own pocket."

Löbcke was rigid for a moment. He then answered me in a sneering tone of voice which increased in volume: "Miss Schroeder, if it does not suit you here, then go to another newspaper." He paused and emphasized the following words, "That is, if another paper will have you in your situation."

"Don't worry about me, Mr. Löbcke. As things stand now you still owe me six hundred marks. Perhaps you would prefer to tell me how you will settle this?"

Löbcke's red face turned a shade darker. His potbelly shook as he began to laugh. "Six hundred marks? Well—." He laughed even more. "You will have to figure out how to get them!"

"Just as you wish, Mr. Löbcke." I paused deliberately for effect and to give him the chance to change his mind. But as he only continued to laugh, I added, "Then goodby, that is, until we meet in court."

Naturally my first conversation after leaving the *Post* was with Karl. The situation is not very promising since I am not carried on the editors list. Karl thinks I should take a week's vacation. In the interim he will speak again with Dörenfeld.

April 15, 1934

I spent two restful and sunny weeks at Aunt Annemarie's estate in Simssee. She is Uncle Heinz's sister and anticipates the trend of the times with sober clarity. I found in her the understanding totally missing in my mother.

But even in this idyllic spot, my father's influence was felt and casts a dark shadow over me.

Since my father is so fully occupied with the hospital, private practice, national insurance, nursing courses, etc., there is very little time for us to talk together. Thus I was surprised to receive a lengthy letter from him. The contents astonished me even more than the letter itself; so much so that I read it twice. Even then I did not fully grasp the contents. Father is concerned about me—not about my botched future, which he still views as an unpleasant interlude, but about my personal attitude. He wrote that he understands that I am driven into political opposition out of spite, which is natural considering my youth. However, I should not go to extremes. The Nazis are correct in many respects, despite their momentary exaggerations.

He continued that although it is sad for Aunt Annemarie, it was to be expected that Uncle Heinz would have to leave Germany. He was typical of the intellectual Jew who have a destructive and demoralizing influence. Uncle Heinz had gotten himself into a precarious situation, practically all by himself. The letter continued with an outpouring of specific criticisms of Jewish morals and customs.

Had father been deluded by my mother's Christianity, although he normally had a very acute and logical mind for scientific questions? How could he write this, a man married to a Jewess? Is reason absent in politics? He always spoke with respect and admiration about his Jewish teacher Professor Lichtheim in Königsberg. Had father forgotten him? I was thunderstruck. What could one expect from the average citizen when a man like my father, edu-

25

cated, cultured, and intelligent could write such dangerous nonsense?

April 23, 1934

My vacation is over. I started to look for a new job. Since I have colleagues in all the other newspaper offices, I did not need a special introduction. But every conversation ended with the question: "Are you registered on the editors list?"

"No, I only have a temporary listing."

"I'm sorry, Miss Schroeder. I could really use a staff member like you. Please come again as soon as you get your final license."

Even at the *Neuen Zeitung,* a branch of the *F.Z.* located in the same building, things didn't go any better. Uncle Heinz, so to speak, is sitting on packed suitcases, ready to leave Germany any day. He no longer comes to the *F.Z.* editorial offices.

May 1, 1934

Spring weather this year is more beautiful than I can ever remember. Everything is already in full bloom. Yesterday was warm enough for me to sit with friends until midnight in an outdoor restaurant. Nature is apparently trying to compensate for the cruelty of human beings.

On April 24th, I went to the Labor Court hearing; it was short and surprising. Löbcke could not produce any pay vouchers for the period I was not paid; whereas I presented several clippings from the art section of the newspaper with my by-line to prove that I had been working.

The judge was about to sentence him to pay the six hundred marks in question when Löbcke suddenly recovered his speech. "You know, Your Honor, I actually employed her out of pity." The judge looked inquiringly at Löbcke, who hemmed and hawed. Ill at ease, he added, "There's something wrong with her family tree."

The judge exclaimed in utter contempt, "Do you also plan to tell me, perhaps, that you gave her the responsibility of art editor out of pity?"

June 3, 1934

An old friendship has fallen apart. A few days ago we had our

26

regular evening of chamber music. After playing, the evening ended with the usual social hour. Tea with rum was served.

The conversation began about new literary publications and then turned to musical events. Mrs. Rapp related that Klemperer had a horrible mishap.

Someone asked what happened.

"He fell backwards off the podium while conducting."

While we expressed our regrets, Mrs. Gräber exclaimed, "I wish he had broken his neck!"

For a moment, silence and consternation reigned. Totally flabbergasted, someone asked, "But... why?!"

And Mrs. Gräber replied, "Because he is a Jew!"

In the awkward silence that followed, mother said in a voice choked with emotion, "You don't seem to know that my beloved father was also a Jew!"

Mrs. Gräber was visibly embarrassed, and hedged. She had not meant it personally. Mother stood up with a crimson face and left the room, fighting back tears.

What irony. Mrs. Gräber achieved with one sentence what I had tried in vain to explain to mother in so many words. For the first time it hit home that, although a Christian, she was also affected. But how long will this realization last?

July 5, 1934

My head is buzzing! My brain is like a theater where panic has broken out. My thoughts are confused and disorderly, like people fighting for an exit. I have difficulty expressing my thoughts in accurate words and sentences.

As far as I can judge, the consequence of a controlled press is a wild proliferation of rumors and speculations. All Germany is talking about Röhm and the "Röhm putsch."

The official version of the story is that the SA Chief-of-Staff Ernst Röhm had staff quarters in the Pension Hanselbauer in Bad Wiessee. He allegedly held wild homosexual orgies there. The Führer got wind of it and surprised Röhm and his friends in the middle of such an orgy.

Mother was filled with moral indignation about 'these conditions'; it was unheard of! And how horrible for Hitler to experience this, from a person whom he had trusted!

In contrast, father beamed. "You see, things are being directed into normal channels. Hitler himself took a strong hand when he discovered such a deplorable state of affairs. It is only natural that rivalries will take place in such a movement. These are part of the childhood diseases of a revolution. Even von Papen intimated that such a turning point must come."

July 29, 1934

Despite the political hubbub, life at home continues in the same pattern as far back as I can remember. Mother's birthday was celebrated yesterday as usual. The chamber music evening was postponed. A few more friends were invited to dinner. In the early afternoon, since confusion and excitement reigned, I made myself scarce.

My refuge is still the Cafe Hauptwache. On Saturday afternoons, in contrast to other days, the fat pastry-gobbling ladies leave earlier because their husbands expect them home sooner. So I walked into a relatively empty Hauptwache. I glimpsed Arni Stein and Gerhard Straube seated at a table. Stein saw me and waved. The usual teasing and banter flew back and forth. None of us was in a rush to return home. After a while, Willi Becher arrived. He is a colleague of mine who has worked for a communist paper, no longer published. Naturally, he can not find a job anywhere. Karl has smuggled him into the *F.Z.* as a proofreader.

"Heil Hitler!" said Becher ironically. "You surely hold my views, the poor man must be *geheilt*. I am meeting my wife here. May I sit with you while I wait for her?"

After a while, Mrs. Becher arrived; and then, contrary to expectation, Karl.

He bowed deeply. "If you ladies and gentlemen have arranged a large gathering, you could have at least called me."

He forced a chair between Stein and me. While our hands touched, Stein said. "We knew our thoughts would draw you here."

Karl's slender hand passed over his forehead and he pushed back his hair. He shook his head; "I am sick—sick!" When Karl is drunk, he always speaks very slowly and distinctly. "You can all sit here and laugh?" he wondered.

Stein said in a smooth voice, "As long as we can still laugh, everything is not lost."

"... as long as we can still laugh...." Karl raised his voice

28

threateningly, "Stein, do you know for how much longer?"

"Psst!" hissed Willi. "Not so loud, Karl!"

Since Karl had not noticed the waiter, I ordered an open-faced sandwich and coffee for him.

With the obstinacy of a man slightly drunk, Karl continued unperturbed. "This Hitler has declared that law and order are restored. What kind of law and order? Does he believe that if he murders several hundred people, that is law? Is it not obvious what that means? He has also been congratulated for these murders. If you, or you"—he pointed to Stein and Straube—"say a wrong word, or what the Gestapo assumes to be a treasonous word—anything that offends this so-called order—then at the very least you will be put in prison."

Straube turned around cautiously and ascertained with relief that the tables close to us were empty.

I cut up the roll which the waiter brought, into small bitesize pieces. Absentmindedly Karl took the pieces, and with the same inattention, washed them down with coffee. His voice gradually returned to normal and became more subdued. He said urgently, "Let us not delude ourselves. The creation of the People's Court with its special tribunals has been initiated to muzzle people like us!"

"Who is muzzling whom?" questioned an agitated voice behind us.

Max Fuchs stood there. Nicknamed "Maxe," he was a freelance sports reporter. He was huge and corpulent like an elephant. Although a diabetic, he could never resist the sight of a cake at the counter. In his huge paw he juggled a plate containing a torte topped with whipped cream.

"One should place a muzzle on you," said Stein reproachfully. "Let a doctor prescribe one for you."

"Why should he pay his doctor when Hitler will wrap one around him gratis?" asked Becher sarcastically.

"You weren't speaking about me with a muzzle, were you?"

We laughed and Willi Becher took a chair from the next table and said, "Come sit down, Maxe."

When I entered the dining room at home, everybody at the table was very lively. Among our old friends was the internationally known physician and researcher Professor Sjöderbloom. In pronounced contrast to my father, nationalist and conservative,

29

Sjoderbloom is an absolute cosmopolitan. Their mutual professional esteem and common interest in chamber music has brought them closer through the years.

After the first toasts to the "birthday child," the usual light conversation and jokes turned to politics. While Aunt Elly, full of information gleaned from the daily press, spoke of Hitler as if he were a personal acquaintance. Sjöderbloom interjected, "Don't you think we are recently rather plentifully blessed with corpses?"

This comment put Aunt Elly in an embarrassing situation. Basically she admires Hitler. On the other hand, she has continued the old friendship of her parents into the following generation and has become attached to mother with oldmaidish enthusiasm. She knows mother's situation; and Hitler's anti-Semitism is a fact.

Father came to her help. "I consider what happened a routine struggle for power. We do not know which one of these men had unfulfilled expectations. It is, after all, the first time since the collapse of the monarchy that a strong personality has sought to unite Germany."

August 6, 1934

During the afternoon of July 31st, Karl called me at home and asked me to come to the editorial offices that evening. When I appeared at the prearranged hour, I saw a secretary with a shorthand pad just leaving the room.

"What is it, Karl?"

"Nothing special." Suddenly he looked at me sharply. "I did not want to frighten you! There are so many things going on that I simply had to see you. I will be finished in a half hour, then we can leave together."

We drank a glass of beer and strolled slowly to Holzhausen park. After reaching the park we sat on a bench. It was a warm summer night; the sky sparkled with stars. The bushes, shading the streetlights, cast long shadows on the lawn. From time to time sleepy birds softly twittered. Both our hearts were heavy. Our professional futures are more than risky; every new day takes away a little more hope.

We sat silently together for a while. After a deep sigh, Karl said, "I am afraid. Not personally afraid, but I fear what lies ahead for all of us: you, me, our friends, all of those who are different and think differently from those now in power." He fell back into a brooding silence, and suddenly spoke aloud, completing his chain of thoughts. "And after the Röhm affair? Psychologically, this would be the right time for Hindenburg to leave the stage."

Two days later, newsboys shouted on every street corner: "Hindenburg is dead." The radio constantly eulogized him and broadcasted high tributes to his memory.

A large part of the population was stunned. Although they had elected Hitler as their Führer, they knew that Hindenburg always stood in the wings. Hindenburg was the "loyal Eckehard," the hero of Tannenberg. Whatever they held against the old man, whatever bad jokes they made about him to prove his senility, were forgotten in one stroke. Many people were overcome with a feeling of uncertainty. They sensed that Hindenburg's death marked the end of an era. What would take its place?

Hitler permitted neither doubts nor questions about what path Germany would take in the future. He abolished the office of president. The German army took an oath of allegiance to Hitler personally. Yesterday, Sunday, August 5th, Hitler gave Hindenburg a huge state funeral.

Mother spoke with moist eyes about the loss of the guardian of Germany. For the first time I had the feeling that father's optimism gave way to a mild depression. Bursting with questions which my parents could not answer, I left the house yesterday evening in the hope of meeting a few colleagues in Cafe Hauptwache.

I had drunk coffee alone for over an hour, read the newspapers and was just about to leave when Karl came. He looked about for company then came to my table.

We went to Einmuth's wine tavern.

Karl asked, "Are you aware that Hindenburg's hour of death is the true birthday of the Third Reich?" Drinking at a disquieting pace, he suddenly opened the newspaper that he had under his arm. "Look closely at the date. On August 1st, this criminal officially decided to become master of Germany. One day *before* Hindenburg's death he enacted laws giving himself unlimited power!"

We had already opened a second bottle of wine. Karl continued, "This Führer—a raging petty bourgeois—an unscrupulous upstart. He does not have any new ideas, but he has an unbelievable advantage. The times are ripe for him. The stupidity of the Allies and his German predecessors paved the way for him. If von Papen had not been so concerned with morality, but had done something for the unemployed; if General von Schleicher had not continued in von Papen's worn-out tracks, Hitler would never have made it. Hitler is not an aristocrat. He comes from nowhere but has a special flair. He knows what the people want to hear. He speaks the language of the man in the street."

The second bottle of wine was almost empty. Karl had now reached the stage where nothing could restrain him. Raising his hand, he called the headwaiter, "Plaum!"

The man appeared in a waiter's jacket, a white napkin draped over his forearm.

"Bring another bottle, Plaum!" As the waiter was about to go, Karl held him back. "Wait a minute! Have you heard what our Führer said at the burial of our revered General Field Marshal von Hindenburg?"

"I don't know what in particular you mean." The intelligent eyes of the experienced headwaiter perceived the situation. He bowed to Karl. "Whatever it was, please, not so loud. Both of us want to enjoy our freedom for a while longer, right?"

Karl nodded slightly and said somewhat more softly but still distinctly, "Our Führer said, 'Now the Reichspresident and General Field Marshal von Hindenburg, the victor of Tannenberg, enters Valhalla as immortal Commander-in-Chief.'"

Plaum replied, "I also read that in the newspaper."

"Well?" asked Karl. "Did you never ask yourself whether perhaps someone helped our hero to enjoy the pleasures of Valhalla somewhat earlier than fate originally intended?"

I shoved my hand through Karl's arm and squeezed him lightly.

Plaum looked at Karl. "Naturally one wonders, after all that happened." And turning to me, he said with an almost unnoticeable smile, "Don't worry, I am married to a Jewess."

He went to fetch the next bottle of wine.

Karl's restless hands suddenly found a task. With his right forefinger he slowly drew a large *N* on the dark, polished wooden tabletop. He murmured, "In history, *N* stands for Napoleon." Then he wet his finger in the wineglass, dipped it in the cigarette ashes and drew a large *H*. He looked at me out of the corner of his eye. "Will this *H* play as catastrophic a role in world history as the *N*?"

The waiter returned with the bottle of wine. With his head inclined he looked at the large dirty *H*. With an apologetic smile, he

wiped the tabletop with his white napkin so that it shone as spot-
lessly as before.

2.   The Third Reich

September 14, 1934

Professionally I am still dangling between heaven and earth. To be sure, no prohibition has been pronounced against me, but silence reigns about the entry of my name in the professional register.

I go occasionally at noon to the table reserved for our regulars at the Cafe Hauptwache, although new faces slowly appear. Two new colleagues come daily with studied nonchalance. The normal, unburdened atmosphere of mutual trust has given way to a wary vigilance since we surmise the two men are Nazi spies. However, my old friends stick together and whenever we can get rid of the two questionable figures, the old candor returns.

A few days ago Gerhard Straube of the *General-Anzeiger* hurriedly stood up as I began to leave the Hauptwache. A few steps away from the table he said, "Lili, you should go to see Fritz Peters, our 'Letter-box Uncle.' He expects you."

Peters is a man of about fifty, with small crafty eyes and blond graying hair. He always plays the blunt, rough clod so that no one would suspect him of having a compassionate heart. However, his sensitive mouth with finely formed lips gives him away.

After I introduced myself, he smiled and nodded to me good-naturedly across the desk. "So you are Lili Schroeder, the girl Straube had in mind." He was somewhat embarrassed. "Do you have enough time to help me with my correspondence?" He indicated a large batch of letters. "I am receiving so much mail just now that I can no longer answer them all alone. Straube told me your father is a doctor. Perhaps you can answer the medical questions, and also a few household problems. For example, how does

35

one make homemade cheese?" Peters had apparently already prepared everything for me and handed me several bundles of letters.

At home, as I placed my new work on the desk, the newspaper clippings under the paperweight caught my eye. I read the following lines: "On the 5th, the National Party Congress was held at the Bürgerkeller in Munich. One of the leading Nazis said, 'No further revolution will take place in Germany for the next thousand years'."

Evil tongues now speak of the Thousand Year Reich.

October 3, 1934

Katherina has found a job! She is a parish assistant at Maria Hilf Church, a small chapel which belongs to the Gallus congregation and is located out near the airport in the Altenheiner district. The residents there are mostly simple people and the majority of them is poor. Katherina assists the priest with house calls, office hours, clerical work and suchlike. The community has grown so much during the years that a small chapel was built where Katherina now works. She is therefore not in the focus of attention as she would be in the main church. Moreover, she is employed directly by the church, and perhaps no one will care about her working there. After all, last month one of the oldest SA leaders was married in full pomp of the Catholic church. I wonder if he fears God's punishment or if it is only eyewash to show that the Nazis are not anticlerical.

October 24, 1934

Our neighbors across the street have left Germany with their deaf-mute daughter under cover of night. They learned from some underground source that Lisa would be hauled off and sterilized in a few days in compliance with the law against hereditary diseases.

Apparently not all cases are handled the same way. Not everyone receives a written summons to appear at a certain time and place. So far as we can determine, families with this kind of problem are placed in some form of detention. In many cases the "hereditary diseased" are simply hauled off, taken to a hospital, and operated on.

November 1, 1934

During the plebiscite of August 19th the German people were asked, as usual belatedly, for their approval of the consolidation of the jobs of Reichspresident and Reichschancellor. The answer was ninety percent yes, ten percent no. However, this offended our Führer, who wanted all the votes; the whole German people should stand one hundred percent behind him. So he appealed to the party to win and convince this ten percent.

Everything is being done to win these last opponents: taxes are lowered, exemptions from taxes given, housing constructed and salaries adjusted. However, what makes me feel uncertain are all of the "battles" fought by the Nazis. On October 7th the "battle" against wasting raw materials began. Ostensibly each year 20,000 tons of fat are poured out with the dishwater in seventeen million households. The motivation for greater thrift is that Germany depends on its own resources and therefore cannot afford wastefulness. I find this attitude understandable and in no way alarming. However, it was reported on October 23rd that "after the grease battle follows the battle for raw materials!" Cast iron shall replace bronze; aluminum will be substituted for copper. Deeply disturbed, I asked Karl for his opinion.

He looked at me silently for several minutes before he replied, "Don't you remember the election poster which read 'Hitler means war'? These are the first preparations."

November 27, 1934

One evening as I sat alone in the Hauptwache, Kreutzer came in. He is the young man who covers local events for the *Post*. He saw me and asked if he could join me. We chatted about the *Post*, its publishers, and other harmless subjects until Ulrich Reiss appeared. Reiss is a young, talented organist whom I have known for a long time. He joined us. Reiss, in his characteristic way which borders on naivete went right to political themes. Though he knows me, he could scarcely know on which side I stand—not to mention the fact that Kreutzer was a total stranger to him. Reiss simply assumes that anyone capable of clear thought must be "anti." To my greatest amazement he was correct. Kreutzer, who is somewhat

37

shy, forgot all caution. After a short time the three of us had unreservedly given vent to our feelings.

After this I have met them regularly. Tall, slender, and serious Kreutzer has smooth, parted, dark brown hair and light brown eyes; Reiss, barely medium-sized, leans toward plumpness and has thick wavy blond hair, blue eyes, a naturally happy temperament, and an infectious laugh. Reiss's Jewish girl friend Myriam Schnabel is a violinist. Like Kreutzer, his girl friend Gerti Grunbaum, also Jewish, is a chemistry student. She comes from a well-to-do family and is always extremely elegantly dressed.

After several meetings in one or another restaurant, we went one evening to the Toska, a small nightclub. We were unexpectedly joined by Dr. Goldschmidt, the uncle of a former classmate of mine. We are all in our early or middle twenties, while Dr. Goldschmidt is a confirmed bachelor in his mid-fifties. He is the legal consultant to the British consulate, and young in heart. From this evening on, he belonged to our circle.

One day Dr. Goldschmidt, an enthusiastic pianist, suggested we meet at Andree's Music House. One can rent a room with two pianos by the hour. Since then we meet once a week for our musical soirees. Together with Reiss, he performs compositions for two pianos. Frequently Reiss improvises. He is extremely talented at this. Dr. Goldschmidt accompanies him, extemporizing on the other instrument.

After I was sure that my friends would not bring musical dishonor to our home, I asked my parents' permission to meet fortnightly at my house, which was allowed. On alternate weeks we meet and play at Andree's.

Mother greeted the guests, listened a while and then left us alone. However, she is incorrigible. She said one evening, "But, Lili dear, this Dr. Goldschmidt is certainly much too old for you!"

December 10, 1934

A few days ago all the National Socialist newspapers carried the same story. "Assistant headmaster Dr. Schulte von der Winrich in Marienburg was summarily dismissed without pension because he refused to collect on the street for the Winter Relief campaign. In consequence of his behavior, he excluded himself from the community."

Previously a summary dismissal without pension took place

only when a civil servant committed a serious criminal offense. Now, if one refuses to go on the street with a collection box, one forfeits membership in the community. Apparently this is a crime. I will concede that the Winter Relief campaign is based on an excellent idea if it really is as the Nazis claim. I only hope that poor Dr. Schulte von der Winrich will not have to provide for a family. It is a warning to others in similar situations. In contemporary Germany, character is something that can all too easily be paid for with hunger.

January 2, 1935

Christmas, a holiday of tearful sentimentality, is once more happily done with. New Year's Eve was as always spent together, celebrated with punch, card games, and casting horoscopes with melted lead.

Outside the four walls of our home, party and national bigwigs made speeches about peace and equal rights. Everyone is smoking a peace pipe. However, the more peace is spoken of, the more those who think and observe, fear war. Former French Minister Jouvenal spoke to a French war veterans' association and said, "As long as we old soldiers are alive, no new war can begin." This optimistic comment was reprinted in headlines in all the German newspapers. Do the Nazis require reinsurance from the French to continue their preparations without interruption?

January 14, 1935

For the 250th birthday of Johann Sebastian Bach, March 21st, I sold a Bach article to the *Rhein-Mainische Volkszeitung*, a paper reputed to have very high standards. Generally I write about non-political things that I observe or hear. These articles appear occasionally in some newspaper or other, but rarely carry a by-line.

I met with Karl frequently throughout the Fall. We saw each other either in the Hauptwache, the Deutsche Bund, or in his office.

When I went to bed the first night of the new year I stared sleeplessly into the darkness and tried to imagine what the new year would have in store for me. Unavoidably, Karl appeared in my mind's eye. He had become a vital part of my life. I could flee to him when I have fear and do not know how to go on. It is absurd, bordering on superstition, but one always seeks specific dates to make a resolution. That night I resolved to break off my friendship with Karl. As long as he is married we can not think of a common future and, taking political considerations into account, I am a handicap to him. Naturally I thought for many days what I would say to him. But I finally reached the conclusion that I have to make this break, regardless of how difficult or painful it will be.

It is now long after midnight, and a few hours ago I sat opposite Karl at his *F.Z.* desk. He was, against his better judgment, depressed by yesterday's voting results in the Saar region. Ninety-one percent of the people want to return to the German empire.

I reached across the desk and grasped Karl's hand. "You know, dearest, when I saw you for the first time, you quoted Heine: *'Doch schon beim nächsten Morgenlicht,...'*"

He interrupted me, "But, my child, you do not understand! Before the next dawn comes, we must go through such a horrible night that it may be compared to the apocalypse."

Then Karl was silent. He stared through me and through the wall behind me, at something in the distance which was hidden. After a while he glanced back at me. "Only a few see what is coming and are not influenced by all the claptrap. For the majority it is like religion. Most people need a crutch, they are all too willing to believe. So they have chosen this mediocre, narrow-minded hypocrite as their god and hero. They are on a slippery path towards a dictatorship and will have no notion of what is happening until it is too late." Karl's voice was filled with bitter scorn. "Discipline and order will be restored; the troublesome elements—the Leftists—will be brought to account and punished. It has not dawned on the bourgeoisie that this is only a precursor of things to come. They will be next—their letters will be read and telephones tapped to be sure they are good citizens. And before they know it they will live under a dictatorship."

We drank a glass of beer in the Deutsche Bund, then Karl accompanied me home. The trees in Holzhausen Park stretched their dark, naked branches into the cold wintry sky.

With a pounding heart, and somewhat hesitantly, I said, "Karl, lately I have thought a great deal about us."

"Yes?"

"And I have come to the conclusion that we should not see each other any more."

He stopped and turned to face me. "Why?"

"Do I really have to explain in detail? You know as well as I how wrong and senseless it all is. And I think our lives are already complicated enough."

He pulled me towards him as if he didn't ever want to let me go. His fingertips touched my face as if he were blind and wanted to hold the memory in his hands. "Whatever you wish, my little one. I must leave this decision to you. But promise me that if you ever should be in serious trouble, you will call me! Promise me that— please!"

March 4, 1935

I no longer remember today what Sjöderbloom said and how I answered him, since it took place many months ago. It must have been in October. I only remember that he said he was going into seclusion for several months and when he returned he wanted to speak to me in private. And so it came about. That was the last evening of chamber music with him for a long time and another of my father's colleagues substituted as second violin.

Last Wednesday Sjöderbloom resumed his place. Apparently he had solved his research problem.

After the music came a pause. Steinbach poured only a little tea in his cup, sprinkled in a very small amount of sugar, and filled it to the brim with a large portion of rum. While he did this he muttered a magic formula: "Rum must, sugar can, water not required." Then he turned to Sjöderbloom and in his innately amiable way said, "Welcome, second violin!"

Sjöderbloom raised his teacup and said in a melancholy voice, "I have missed these evenings. Without music, life is only half lived."

According to an unspoken agreement between the doctors, there was no shoptalk on musical evenings. Instead, politics was discussed! After exchanging several unimportant remarks, Marietta could no longer keep quiet. She asked Sjöderbloom, "Tell me, my dear professor, what do you really think of the political situation?"

Sjöderbloom's mischievous boyish smile appeared on his face.

41

"Not much, dear lady." He continued more seriously, "It strikes me as a repetition, a remnant from the age of migrations—or the Inquisition."

He fell silent, while Etta said almost breathlessly, "What do you mean?"

"Under the Inquisition one burned witches. Now is the time for Communists and Jews. They are not burned yet; for the time being they are only locked up."

"For God's sake," Etta cried out, "have we not finally passed that stage?"

"Do you really think so?" asked Sjöderbloom politely. "We have a world war behind us, with all of its misery and suffering. But what have we learned? Has a new idea been born from this pain?" He then turned to all of us. "Please tell me, is there one new idea which has been tried? Hitler seems to me a member of the great society of the spiritually half dead—hundreds of years after his time. Dear friends, we are witnesses to the last revival of the past, with its absolute power on the one hand and suppression on the other. At the moment here it is a question of power against impotence, the master race against 'subhumans.' Across the ocean in the New World, in America, it is capitalism against poverty. But what is new? Two thousand years of Christianity with bloodshed and suppression. This doesn't seem to be especially original."

"No," said father. "Either this Mr. Christ expressed himself unclearly or his supporters have misunderstood him."

"But Bärchen," cried mother, shocked.

"I believe we should return to our Hayden, or it will be too late," interjected Steiba.

It is my job to let the guests out if Lenchen, the maid, has already gone to bed. The Steinbachs still talked with my parents in the music room, so I found myself alone with Sjoderbloom in the stairwell.

"Signorina." He brought this form of address back from his last trip to Italy. It sounds less formal than the stiff German *Fräulein*. "Signorina, if I send my car on Friday at eight o'clock, will you come to my place?"

"Yes, Signore," I said, in the same tone.

March 10, 1935

Sjöderbloom sent his car at the agreed hour. The chauffeur let me off in front of his elegant flat in the West End. The maid opened the door and led me into the study where Sjöderbloom greeted me with outstretched hands. A moment later I heard a panting noise. A boxer came from underneath the desk to sniff at me. To the satisfaction of his master the dog accepted me.

The large, tastefully furnished room with dark furniture, bookshelves, a wine-red rug, and small scuptures bathed in the light of floor lamps, captivated me.

We first conversed about music, then the conversation turned to *Fasching* which had just ended. Sjöderbloom had spent one day in Cologne, while I was in the Steinerne Haus. I told him that several interns from the Bürgerhospital had talked me into going with them.

Sjöderbloom wanted to know, "Did you have fun?"

"No, actually not. But I had an interesting experience. Several men, apparently career military officers in their mid- to late-forties, made a mildly drunken allusion to a revolution. One of them went so far as to hint about preparations of an army putsch.

"When I confronted him with 'How could you be so reckless? You don't know who I am!' he roared. 'Do you know, then, who *I* am?'

"I replied, 'Yes, an officer who talks too much.'

"Then he began to justify himself. 'What do you want? I have not said anything at all'."

Sjöderbloom was amused. *"In vino veritas.* That certainly is a peculiar way to plan a coup d'etat."

"Yes, but quite apart from that, it was grotesque. There were all these costumed people, some even masked, paper streamers, subdued colored lights, music and laughter. In this atmosphere of gaiety and merriment, these officers were plotting a revolution at a carnival ball!"

Sjöderbloom reflected a moment, then asked abruptly, "And you are a journalist?"

"Yes."

"A dangerous profession."

"How so?" I asked, surprised.

"A lying journalist is dangerous for the public; one who writes the truth is dangerous for the government; and occasionally even dangerous for himself."

He offered me a cigarette and continued, "However marvelous Gutenberg's invention was, he most certainly had no notion what a Pandora's box he opened."

43

I agreed. "We are just beginning to get a taste of it: how newspapers can be used and misused as a political instrument."

"There always have been unscrupulous people who used the news media to their own advantage; for example, Baron von Rothschild. He set up his own news service and with it spread the word that Napoleon was victorious. This led to a catastrophic fall in stock exchange prices and Rothschild bought gigantic quantities of securities dirt cheap. After he completed the transactions the truth became known."

Since I didn't know what to answer, he continued, "In almost every country, only a small group of people holds the power. It matters not whether the government is called a monarchy or a republic, whether it is labeled communist or fascist, or claims to be a democracy. In reality, with the exception of Scandinavian countries or the Swiss, the people are a herd of sheep who do what is commanded from the top. They swallow all the lies without doubting for a moment."

"Do you believe that is generally so?" I asked. "I always thought it was typically German. After all we coined the wonderful word *Kadavergehorsam* (corpselike obedience)."

Sjöderbloom smiled. "As far as I am informed, it is not any different in America. Pulitzer and Hearst unleashed the Mexican War with their 'yellow press' and false news stories. It's too bad that you are a journalist."

"Why?"

"If you were not one I would tell you, Signorina, do not believe a word of what is printed in the papers. Try to read between the lines and even then be suspicious of that!"

I had to laugh. "Since politics is not my department, I can only take your words to heart, Signore."

March 30, 1935

I spent two days in Basel to offer our old guest book for publication. The net proceeds would go into a Swiss bank account in case....

My parents had weighed the pros and cons for a long time. I convinced father, in a weak moment, that it would not be bad to have a small reserve fund in a country like Switzerland, which had hitherto always remained neutral and maintained bank secrecy. We agreed that his parents' guest book was the most suitable

44

object to offer. It contained an immense number of great names from the world of music, painting, and literature, stretching from the middle of the nineteenth to the beginning of the twentieth century. It also included some musical notes, sketches, and poems. It would thus be of general interest.

Before I started the long trip I consulted my half-French friend and colleague, Dr. Walter Gross. I asked him if he could recommend me to someone there.

"Certainly," said Walter. "My brother-in-law, Dr. Klotz, is editor of the *Basler Nachrichten*. I will alert him. Call him when you are in Basel. He will have time for you."

I arrived in Basel so early in the morning that I could not telephone my acquaintances. To kill an hour I sat at the railroad station and ordered breakfast. My suitcase stood beside me.

The coffee had not yet been served when a man sat down next to me. At a cursory glance he gave the impression of a harmless middle-class citizen. He was inconspicuously dressed, and was neither young nor old. Without circumlocutions he asked directly, "Are you from Germany?"

"Yes."

"Are you staying here any length of time?"

I must have looked utterly taken aback. It was completely clear to me that he was not looking for an adventure. His questions must have another motive. Upon closer inspection I noted his well-formed forehead; exceptionally alert, intelligent eyes peered through his eyeglasses and seemed to read my mental reservations.

In a soothing tone he said, "You do not have to answer me. I only wanted to warn you. Many Nazi spies are roaming about here. Be constantly aware of that if you speak with a stranger. In any case, however short or long you may be here, I wish you a pleasant time." He then stood up and left.

Suddenly the Spring morning no longer seemed so radiant and sunny.

My entire journey to Basel stood under an unlucky star. Dr. Klotz received me in a friendly manner. He looked through the guest book with interest, found it very unusual, but felt it was still too early to publish it. Perhaps in thirty or fifty years...

My hosts were charming and took me out to dinner. Here I discovered that German and Swiss butter and mayonnaise are quite different from each other. I could not eat much and on returning home, my hosts helped me fight nausea with plum brandy.

The next day I met my cousins Thea and Lili. Both have their doctorates. Thea, petite, with blond hair and radiant dark blue eyes, is like a volcano. Lili, a tall girl with auburn hair and bright eyes, is, by comparison, colorless, the prototype of the decadent Jewess. She had studied theology and plans to go as a missionary to Palestine, to convert small Jewish children into ardent Christians.

Through a haze of nausea and pain I wondered what was wrong with our family. I cast sidelong glances at Lili, a pallid figure in a black velvet dress, planning to bring Christianity to Palestine, and thought of my sister Katherina endlessly running to the church. Is Lili, my mother's godchild, afraid of life, and fleeing into the arms of the Christian church like Katherina? However we did not discuss such things, but took a stroll to show me something of Basel. It may have been pleasant for my cousins, but I fought against a constant feeling of nausea, acute pain and a pronounced longing for bed. I have been examined and x-rayed. My appendix is healthy. What could it possibly be?

On the return trip home I shared my compartment with a dainty Jewish woman. Her eyes were ringed in red and she sought in vain to check a flood of tears. Premature gray had crept into her dark hair. In her helplessness she reminded me of Elizabeth Bergner in a particular role, where the actress brilliantly expresses the tragedy of human conflicts. There was no other apparent similarity between the two women.

Although I felt wretched and sorry for myself, I could not sit by and watch her despair. I spoke to her. "What is it? Can I do something for you?"

In response she made a tired motion with her hand and began to sob uncontrollably.

I felt helpless and could do nothing but wait.

Finally she spoke. "I went to visit—Adolf Busch. And now—I must return to Germany."

I thought it over. "Could you not remain there?" She shook her head and a fresh flood of tears fell from her eyes. I persisted. "Isn't there any possibility that you can remain in Switzerland? Even without Busch's help?"

"No. I can't desert my mother. I must return to my work."

I was silent. Then suddenly I got an idea. "If you visited Busch, this will interest you!"

I stood up and while I lifted my suitcase out of the luggage rack, she said, "Oh, it was all so wonderful! The music—it was as it used to be in former times."

I opened the suitcase and took out the guest book. Sitting next to her I said, "Look here, this is a family guest album which my grandparents kept."

After a few pages her tears dried up. She was totally distracted and had a chance to regain her composure. During the remaining hours we talked. She is a secretary at Ullstein Publishing House in Berlin, and seems to see the future as clearly as I do. Only she does not have an Aryan father. She had experienced in Switzerland, perhaps for the last time, what it was like to live as a human being without fear.

April 3, 1935

Father is a little bit disappointed about the rejection of the guest book. However, he is not taking it too tragically since he still has not recognized the direct danger in which we live. Thus he does not see the necessity of a financial reserve abroad.

I did not say anything about my physical miseries in Basel.

April 6, 1935

Tonight Ulrich Reiss called me. He goes once a week to the Educational Training Institute in Weilburg, with Karl Müller, the organist at the Peterskirche. Both of them teach music there to teachers in training for work in elementary schools.

After saying hello in a manner that appeared somewhat constrained, Ulrich said, "Lili, you did tell me that the Bishop of Ermland set up a home for unwed mothers from the Labor Service?"

"Yes."

"I was in Weilburg today and Mr. Müller had brought his wife along. We talked politics as usual during lunch. I told him the story about a home for unwed mothers."

"Yes, and what else, Ulrich?"

"Mrs. Müller visited an acquaintance who is in the Labor Service there. She asked the director of the Labor Service whether the story about the home was true. She hadn't believed it."

He stopped again and this time I must admit that I waited with pounding heart.

He continued. "The director was furious and wanted to know where she heard the story. Mrs. Müller gave my name."

"What?" I exclaimed aghast. "That just is not possible!"

"Yes, really." We were both silent for a moment. Then Reiss continued somewhat hesitantly, "The director said she wanted to pursue this rumor. She will ask me what my source of information was. What should I do?"

"In what way?" I asked in disbelief. And after a moment I added, "Don't you really know?"

"No, I think..."

I thought in a flash that this good friend would sell me out in any case. "But Ulrich," I said ironically, "it is really very simple! Since I was the one who told you, give her my name."

"Really?"

"Yes, certainly!"

On the other end of the telephone line Ulrich said with relief, "Then I can give your name? Many thanks. Well then, see you soon."

April 15, 1935

Because of my press job and having been schooled by Karl, I do not even try to delude myself with regard to Reiss and the Labor Service. My nights are restless. Naturally my thoughts force me to Karl for help and advice. But there is plenty of time for that. For the moment I have been making my plans and waiting — waiting until the noon mail brought me a summons to appear before the regional director of the Women's Labor Service for Hessen-Nassau. The headquarters are in the local health-insurance building.

Father had his monthly meeting of the Association for Commerce, Industry, and Science this evening. After he left the house, I went to mother. "I must discuss something with Katherina and I would like you to be present."

We entered Katherina's sanctum where a pot of holy water is next to the door and a crucifix on the whitewashed wall. Katherina offered me a chair.

"Thanks," I said but remained standing while she and mother sat on a small sofa.

"Katherina, you told us a while ago about homes for unwed mothers from the Labor Service, which the Bishop of Ermland set up in his diocese in East Prussia?"

"Yes," said Katherina.

"I told the story to friends and have been denounced."

"Good Lord," Katherina exclaimed and stood up. Mother remained seated utterly flabbergasted.

"Now don't get yourself all upset," I said. "Until now nothing has happened."

"But who denounced you?" she wanted to know.

"For the time being that is unimportant. Who started this story?"

"One of our assistant priests. I no longer know who it was. During a mothers' program he openly warned about the dangers their daughters face in the Labor Service, and illustrated his warning with the example of the home in the Ermland diocese."

"Katherina, do you positively know that it was said and that it is true?"

"Yes. He sought to warn the mothers about the dangers to their daughters. I was not present that evening, but Reverend Schaller told me about it the next morning. During office hours, mothers repeatedly inquired about the unwed mothers' home."

After a short pause for reflection, I urgently asked once again, "You are positive it was said and that it is the truth?"

Katherina answered without hesitation, "Yes, definitely!"

I paced back and forth in the room and then said, "Do you think that under these circumstances it would be difficult to establish who gave this warning? I have been given a period of only two weeks before I must appear."

Katherina was silent.

Mother, who had followed our conversation with impatience, could no longer restrain herself and said, "Lili dear, what actually has happened?"

I told her exactly. At first she was furious with Mrs. Müller. "That vindictive person!"

It was ludicrous, but I attempted to defend that dumb cow. "Mrs. Müller did not grasp what was at stake. She did not want to entrap anyone. Moreover, she is typically German and must prove to higher authorities how German she is and that she could not give credence to such slander."

The next object of mother's and Katherina's wrath was Reiss.

"I will admit that Reiss is a weakling. He seems to be typical of the German man! But do not forget he is practically engaged to a Jewess and I do not want Myriam to be dragged in too. My mistake

49

was not distrusting my friends, as every German must these days."

Mother stood up, horrified, and said, "But Lili dear! You are exaggerating as usual. We can trust our friends. You can not throw the baby out with the bath water!"

Mrs. Gräber's hate-filled face appeared like a ghost in my mind's eye as she said, "Klemperer should have broken his neck because he is a Jew!" Ignoring mother's rebuke, I said, "Katherina, would you be so kind! I would like to know by tomorrow evening who told this story publicly. And one more thing, for the moment let us spare father this whole story."

The next evening, while father sat over his medical journals, we again gathered in Katherina's room. Despite all her efforts she could not find out who had warned the women at the program. It was simply impossible. But I should go to the priest at Marien Hospital. Perhaps he knows something. If not, he could at least advise me, since he is experienced in such matters.

For the time being Katherina will not be mentioned. I will first comply with the summons and then decide how to proceed.

April 27, 1935

In the interim I visited the priest at Marien Hospital. He did not deny knowing about such homes. However, I was astonished to discover that to his best knowledge and conscience he could not remember what had been said. Warnings had been given to mothers about the dangers of the Labor Service for Women and the home for unwed mothers had been referred to. It exists without doubt. He knows of it. But it isn't within the scope of his duties. Names? He was not interested in them at the time the story was told. He was honestly distressed not to be able to help me, and concluded his unctuous speech with the suggestion that I write to the Catholic Charity Organization in Freiburg. Perhaps I could get a confirmation that would exonerate me. In case I did not get a reply in time, I should play down the whole affair at the hearing and act as if it was a well-known fact which "the sparrows are twittering from all the rooftops."

Yesterday was the big day. I went to the health-insurance office in Sachsenhausen. I will not make any excuses. I was nervous and filled with a primitive fear. The outfit was located upstairs. In my agitation I could not find the stairs and had to take the freight elevator. Let us not pretend: I was not born to be a hero.

I was seated opposite the Regional Director, a very solid Aryan individual flanked by two secretaries who almost cringed with respect and probably functioned as witnesses.

After my personal data were written down, I was questioned about my relationship with Reiss and the Müllers. Were there other people present when I told Reiss about the homes?

"No, we were completely alone." (As usual the six of us were there.)

"From whom had I learned the rumor?"

"I do not remember anymore."

"Really not?"

"No."

"You should think it over again!"

"I am sorry, but I cannot remember. It surprises me that you have not yet heard about it. It is as widespread as if "the sparrows were twittering it from all the rooftops.""

The Regional Director almost had a stroke. With the statement that I would hear more about this matter, I was dismissed with a "Heil Hitler!"

I made a silent bow.

May 4, 1935

Hanns Schrader called and asked if I were willing to go with him to visit Erich's parents. Naturally I said yes.

Erich Köhlhofer, Schrader's friend, is a communist as are his brothers Alwin and Paul. Erich and Alwin are professional musicians. Paul is a writer. Erich is the smallest and physically most delicate of all of them. He was arrested a while ago on a charge of communist activities. I believe he had posted some handbills. We will probably never learn specifically what happened to him after his arrest. However, the fact is, he was so horribly tortured that he finally revealed the names of his brothers and several friends. They all landed in the penitentiary with the exception of Paul, who is a sick man and had just entered a tuberculosis sanitorium.

Schrader was deeply shocked by what had happened. I will never forget friends like Schrader. Although neither racially nor politically persecuted, they remain true to their less-fortunate friends because of pure human feelings for justice and human dignity, and despite the danger of getting themselves into difficulties.

51

Who can know after all, if Köhlhofer's parents' home is kept under surveillance.

Father Köhlhofer is a shoemaker, a small artisan and philosopher. Though careworn and griefstricken by everything that has befallen him, he is not about to give in or yield his political convictions. The mother, a warmhearted, solicitous woman, immediately made coffee for us and never lamented or shed tears. Naturally, they are indescribably worried about their sons, especially Erich, who probably suffers more from the forced betrayal than from sitting in the penitentiary. They appreciated our visit and we felt their unstated pleas to "help our Erich when he is out again."

Alwin will survive the arrest as many who share his fate. But Erich will be burdened for the rest of his life with a feeling of guilt — an innocent culprit.

May 16, 1935.

Two days ago I received a summons from the Gestapo [Secret State Police] to appear on May 20th.

Mother and I went to see Katherina in her room. She explained immediately that despite her best efforts she could not discover who started the story. She was almost hysterical when she approached me. "Lili, you must believe me. The story is true. Everyone knows about the unwed mothers' homes, but no one can tell me which priest warned the mothers on that particular evening.

Her voice began to quiver and rose appreciably in pitch when she added. "You can simply say that I told you! You don't know any of these priests. What do they want of you?" Then her voice broke. "I will be put in prison!" she wailed.

Mother stood helpless and somewhat concerned between us. Both looked expectantly at me. I raised my hand. "I would like to suggest that we consider this affair less emotionally and more factually. For heaven's sake, Katherina, don't be so theatrical! We must be very conscious about one thing. Our family is already politically incriminated by the story about father. You surely remember the fuss with the resident who wore his party uniform during hospital rounds. We are also possibly already on a blacklist someplace. Now my name is definitely in the files." I turned to both of them. "Do you really believe that we will be doing ourselves a favor if Katherina appears as number three? I am much more convinced that we should leave her completely out of this since I am already so deep in hot water.''

Katherina breathed with relief. However, she did say hesitantly, "But I did tell you—"

At the end of my patience I told her, "You don't know who said it. Apparently no one knows who could have said it. It is quite clear that I will be stuck with it. If I open my mouth and say that I heard it from you, that you told us during supper — then we are all involved. Each of us could have repeated it to others. We will all be suspected and you and I will only have dragged father and mother into this wretched mess.''

"She is right," interjected mother, to my astonishment.

"All right. Then it is clear. I don't know from whom I heard this story. And Katherina, for God's sake, do not do anything stupid! You have absolutely nothing to do with it!" Since no more contradictions followed, I added, "Now we can not avoid telling father.''

We walked downstairs and went into the dining room where father sat alone at the large circular polished table. To his right stood a full glass and a bottle of wine. His hands automatically played solitaire while his thoughts were occupied with a totally different problem. We sat down silently.

"Dear Bär," said mother softly.

His large eyes looked up a moment before he noticed us. "Yes, dearest?"

"We must discuss something with you." She got stuck.

"Yes?" he asked absentmindedly. "What is it?"

"I am the scapegoat, daddy," I said in a light tone.

"So?"

"Yes," I continued bravely. "I am accidentally involved in a rather stupid story. I said something political and was denounced.''

"Good God," said father, "what did you say?"

I told him briefly what had occurred, without mentioning the first hearing at Women's Labor Service.

He shook his head. "And how do you know that you were denounced?"

"Because I received a summons to appear before the Gestapo.''

"Hmmm." He thought about my answer while all our eyes focused on him. "A beastly story," he said indignantly to himself.

53

"But my dear, do not worry yourself unnecessarily. Things are not as black as they look."

Father dear, I thought, it will be worse than it looks. You have never dealt with the kind of people who could convince you of that.

Yesterday the six members of the "club of lost souls" agreed to meet. I called Reiss and urged him to come a half-hour earlier so we could be alone.

He said, "I wanted to call you. Today I received a summ---."

I interrupted him brusquely. "We'll see each other soon." Apparently It hasn't yet gotten through to Reiss that telephone conversations can be tapped.

Reiss and I met as agreed in the Hauptwache during one of its quietest hours.

"You wanted to tell me that you received a summons from the Gestapo?" I opened the conversation.

"Yes, how did you know?"

"Because I also received one."

"What will we do now?" he asked helplessly.

"What do you mean 'we'? You surely don't have to get upset about it. Say that I told you and with that you are totally out of the picture."

"But what if they ask me where you learned it?"

"Where *I* got the story? How should you know that? Ulrich, let's be sure not to leave anything unclear. If I ever told you where I got the story, it was a lie which you have long since forgotten. You heard this rumor from me. Period. If you go beyond that I promise you I will let you take the whole rap. I can still do that. In your position, I would rather rack my brains about how to answer them if they ask you why you repeated it. What was your motive in relating the story?"

He looked at me thunderstruck.

I added, "And in the event there is another hearing, a fact we must assume, stick to what you tell the Gestapo. Absolutely no contradictions! Always tell the same story!"

We tried to fill the remaining time until the others arrived with lighter conversation, but it did not quite come off. The old frankness was destroyed. Our relationship had cooled.

After a while, Kreutzer arrived. He seemed a bit self-conscious. He made apologies for his girl friend, who was tied up

54

with a chemical experiment. Myriam, who appeared at almost the same time as Dr. Goldschmidt, was as usual warm and natural. I had the feeling that Reiss had spoken with Kreutzer, and that all of them were informed about the situation with the exception of Dr. Goldschmidt. He greeted us with innocent enthusiasm and seemed full of new ideas.

He then looked around the group in surprise. "Is something wrong?"

An awkward silence followed. Finally I said, "Ulrich has spread a story which I told in our circle about homes for unwed mothers from the Labor Service. He apparently told it to very unreliable people and I received a summons to appear before the Gestapo."

Goldschmidt was speechless for a moment. I had the uneasy feeling of growing mistrust in our group.

"Reiss?" said Dr. Goldschmidt. "Is that true?"

Reiss nodded embarrassed.

Goldschmidt was dismayed. After some hesitation he asked me, "But how were you brought into it if Reiss spread the tale?"

The Hauptwache was filling up; the table next to us was occupied.

I placed the money for coffee on the table and reached for my gloves. "Excuse me, doctor, but we can't discuss it any further here. Too many people are coming in. And I think this is the end of our social gatherings. The way things are, I am afraid we appear to be a somewhat dangerous group." I left.

May 22, 1935

At the Gestapo I knocked on the door with the number my summons indicated. I had hardly entered the room and had not recognized the official who sat with his back against the bright window when a familiar voice asked, "What kind of a mess have you gotten yourself in, ne nene ne?"

"Mr. Gabbusch!" I exclaimed with relief.

We shook hands. He had been transferred from the criminal police to the Gestapo, as had many other officials, some not even party members.

"What kind of business is this with Reiss?"

"Absolutely nothing," I replied. "Simply a harmless friendship."

"Well, a pretty friendship, you know! Ne nenene ne."

He cross-examined me thoroughly. Finally he said, "It's too bad that you don't remember where you got the story!"

"Really Mr. Gabbusch—I would tell you confidentially. But you know, one meets so many people."

"Yes, I understand." He looked at me warily. "Miss Schroeder, we are not quite as uninformed as you assume, nenene. We know that you have nothing to do with Catholic circles. However, your sister is more concerned. She is a Catholic, and this slander comes from Catholic circles. You learned it from your sister! Think it over."

"My sister!" I said in utter amazement. "She of all people!" I began to laugh. "That old zealot! No, Mr. Gabbusch," I concluded with conviction, "she would be the last person for whom I would pull chestnuts from the fire!"

"Hmmm," Gabbusch muttered. "I would gladly help you," he said reflectively, "because we have known each other for so long. But if only you hadn't said this 'sparrows from the rooftops' nenene..."

The interrogation seemed to be over. As I stood up, I asked, "And what happens after this?"

"I'll do my utmost for you, but I must transmit my report to the assistant district attorney for further consideration. I wish you the best of luck. You can use it."

I was already in the doorway when he remembered the German greeting. "Heil Hitler!" he shouted briskly.

I waved to him and quietly closed the door.

June 4, 1935

For several months my column had appeared once a week on the letters-to-the-editor page of the *General Anzeiger*. It was two, often three columns with the heading "HOW CAN I BECOME...?"

One day Peters asked me, "Tell me, how many more professions can you write about before you come to the academicians? I have thought things over and spoke to somebody here. I believe there might be a chance for you to get a position in our Berlin office. Officially you will be a secretary; actually you'll be able to work there as a journalist, but not under your own name." He looked at me inquiringly and blinked nervously.

"Do you really think it would be possible that I could work as a journalist in Berlin?" I asked breathlessly.

He looked at his hands, which were clasped together on the desk in front of him, while a smile played around his lips. "It is possible. Since you would be engaged as a secretary, that would satisfy the people in Berlin. And here — who can determine who our Berlin reporters are?"

"Dearest Peter, I would like to hug you!"

"But you can't do that—not with all the stenographers around. They would tell my wife!"

Then I turned to practical matters. "When should I go?"

He suggested that I leave towards the end of June. If things do not work out smoothly right away, I can get acquainted with Berlin.

My parents accepted the Berlin offer with mixed feelings. On the one hand they are happy that I have a chance to get on firm professional footing again. On the other hand I am still so young and Berlin is such a bewildering city. Finally, however, they gave me their blessings.

June 26, 1935

On Sunday afternoon Sjöderbloom drove me to the sunny Taunus foothills. His mood conformed to the weather. He was almost boisterous, full of humor, light-hearted and animated.

For supper we went to the Forsthaus. I was astonished to recognize the waiter who served us as one of those young men who before Hitler's accession to power daily sat in Holzhausen Park and killed time with his unemployed fellow sufferers.

Slowly Sjöderbloom became more serious. "Do you really want to leave us, Signorina?"

"I don't want to, Signore, but I probably have no other choice."

"I will visit you," he said firmly. "My tailor is in Berlin." He winked at me. "You can not imagine how many suits I will order; and then I must go for fittings."

Parting from Sjöderbloom takes away some of my happiness at going to Berlin and having a job.

July 6, 1935

I am really in Berlin! I have a first-rate room on the ground floor of an elegant house in the Keithstrasse. It is filled with large baroque furniture and the couch cover is made of silk. My landlady, a Jewish widow, rents several rooms of her giant apartment and runs a millinery shop for ladies.

As agreed upon in Frankfurt, I called Dr. König in the Berlin editorial offices of the *General Anzeiger*. He was expecting me; and since the office is almost deserted because of vacations, he proposed we meet later that afternoon at the Romanischen Cafe. He described the table where I would find him.

July 10, 1935

As I strolled lonely and lost through Berlin, I considered writing General von Seeckt. Why should I wait? I learned from the newspapers that he had returned from China and lived in Berlin. Our friendship ended several years ago on a discordant note; however, the worst that could happen is that he would not answer me.

In February 1931, I had communicated my worries about my ancestry to him and he had answered immediately. Among other things, he wrote, "Our German nation would be bad off if it were not able to absorb and amalgamate non-German elements. The so-called pure descendancy seldom stands up to criticism. The exaggeration of the so-called 'Folk' I reject however as unhistorical, narrowminded and onesided."

So my friend, I thought, let us see how you think today. I wrote him that I was in Berlin, had some problems, remembered his earlier comforting letters, and wondered if he could give me advice.

The answer came promptly, "...although you flatly broke off our relationship, I was happy to hear from you again. I wish that the reason was more pleasant. Lately I have frequently thought of you. I well remember your small cares and anxieties of those days and our relationship which grew from them. I can also imagine how heavily the current conditions must weigh upon you. You can be sure that my views have not changed, even if things have taken a totally different course than I anticipated."

He suggested a meeting.

July 14, 1935

The reunion with Seeckt was somewhat frosty. It was clear that he knew why I broke with him and he was cautious not to drive me away with an indiscreet word. However, I was cool and on guard, not to say mistrustful. He could not give me any positive advice, but wanted to gather more information.

58

Berlin is an exciting city. If I could work here as a journalist I would scarcely miss Frankfurt. My friends come here anyway. If I do not see them as often here, I have them at least all to myself.

A few days ago I met Dr. König as agreed at the Romanische Cafe. We discussed the plan devised for me. He seemed to agree in principle, but he explained that the man responsible for hiring personnel was on vacation; and since even in Berlin absolutely nothing was happening, he couldn't hire me under the pretext of a crisis.

König's wife and children are also on holiday. Since this gives him free time, he suggested that we meet at the cafe in the afternoons. This way my future boss can sound me out. He is a sympathetic, sociable, somewhat cautious person. Although he is evidently no friend of the Third Reich, he never expresses himself clearly in this respect, nor does he commit himself. The whole situation is somewhat grotesque for me. He is alone for the time being and up to a point grateful for companionship. I barely know anybody in Berlin, cannot work yet and am happy to have the opportunity to talk with Dr. König. Under normal circumstances, neither of us would have deigned to give the other a second look. What brings us together for the moment is loneliness.

Meanwhile, Walter Gross was here and we spent one day together. Have I ever mentioned Walter? We owe our acquaintance to the regular journalists' table at the Cafe Hauptwache. After that we met occasionally and maintained a stimulating friendship. He is an Alsatian, more French than German; moreover he is Jewish. He values everything that appeals to the senses: fine cuisine, selected wines, fine kirsch and — women. Any woman in Walter's company has the feeling of being special.

A young man when the war broke out, Walter was drafted into the German army. Lying on a hillside, he was hit by a shell in his upper thigh. Walter criticizes the doctor in the military hospital. "I believe the butcher could have saved my leg. It was not that bad. But perhaps it was too much work. The wound was full of soil and filth. An amputation was probably faster and simpler."

We stood on the escalator which took us to the platform of the Wannsee train station. I had linked my arm under Walter's and he turned to me. His wide-awake eyes looked directly at me through his light horn-rimmed glasses. On his intelligent forehead two wrinkles appeared. "These escalators seem to have been invented for people like me. Climbing stairs is really a torture. That butcher could scarcely have removed the leg higher up than he did. Now I have a constant inflammation of the stump."

I did not know how I should answer.

After a brief pause, he continued, "By the way, if you ever want anything taken across the border: gold, jewelry or the like, give it to me. I'll stick it under the pad of my prosthesis. Isn't that a good hiding place?"

His bitter humor cut me to the quick.

"Why don't you say anything Lili? Don't you find my idea excellent? Just think, when I come to a border and the customs man asks me if I have anything to declare, I can say, 'Don't you want to examine my artificial leg? I, a Jew, lost my leg for you in the war!' What do you think, Lil?"

I looked at him. "Walter, please. . ."

Our hands met.

"Sorry," he said, "but sometimes. . ." He caught himself and from then on was the charming host I knew from the past. We spent a sunny harmonious day at Wannsee.

Walter was in Berlin to write about the preparations for the Olympics. He was highly amused by the efforts the German government makes to create a favorable impression abroad.

"Since I have worked in Germany for such a long time and have friendly connections with several colleagues, it is no problem for me to also get ahold of the unofficial press directives."

While he lovingly turned the wineglass in front of him and observed the lights it threw on the tablecloth, Walter said amused, "The Nazis are so very sensitive! They prefer to let one Jew slip through rather than offend a foreigner. Apart from that, don't underestimate the economic advantages of this international meeting. You surely know how urgently Germany needs foreign exchange. Every foreigner who visits the Olympics brings it with him."

"I hadn't thought of that at all. But Walter, do you really believe that Jews will also come?"

"I don't know. Maybe a few will come to get a personal impression of what's going on. But the warning, 'rather let a Jew slip through,' refers to something else. All the Latin-Americans, Italians, Spaniards, etc. could be mistaken for Jews by uneducated ruffians. Many of these people have dark eyes, dark wavy hair, and frequently a large nose: the things that Streicher depicts as characteristic of Jews. The joke is that many of these non-Nordic people are convinced anti-Semites. Thus, these Olympics will be a special attraction for them because of Hitler. These games should be run under the motto 'Anti-Semites of the World Unite.'"

When we said good-bye, I asked, "When will we see each other again, Walter?"

"I will be here to see the Olympics next year. Perhaps I'll be in Frankfurt in the fall. Will you be here?"

"Who knows? When you are in Frankfurt you can always check with my parents."

August 1, 1935

Today I called on Aunt Therese, Uncle Heinz's mother. We have never seen each other before, and she seemed eager to meet me. She invited me for lunch.

Forewarned by Aunt Annemarie's description, I arrived at her house with hat and gloves. A servant—I later learned, a lady's maid —received me and led me into the parlor.

The drawing room is a large room with heavy, dark furniture, small tables, and innumerable photographs of famous people. The dignified old lady was seated in a high-backed armchair. She extended her hand graciously, inspected me critically, and got up cumbersomely. Her thick lips stretched into a smile as she placed one ringed hand on my shoulder while the other grasped me under the chin and turned my face to the light. Pleased by what she saw, she exclaimed, "How much you resemble Gustav, my favorite cousin!"

The conversation now ran freely and unhindered. She had taken me to her heart because of my resemblance to Grandfather Simon; on the other hand she appealed to me because of her likeness to Uncle Heinz.

When her personal maid announced dinner, Aunt Therese got up with difficulty, extended her arm, and let me escort her to the dining room while the maid held the door open.

It was difficult to eat and make conversation because I was so astonished. The table was arranged as if for a party rather than for just two people. The silver, which glittered on the white damask tablecloth, was apparently polished daily. There was soup, a meat

61

course, and dessert. The maid stood behind us during the entire meal and seemed to follow our every gesture. One needed only to lift one's hand and her arm extended to push the saltshaker closer, refill the wineglass, or offer another portion. This silent person behind us made me nervous, while Aunt Therese ignored her completely and conversed freely about family affairs.

How many Jews, including Uncle Heinz, have already been forced to leave Germany because of the Nazis. How many of us — full or half-Jews—encountered the greatest difficulties or were thrown out of our professions. And here sits Aunt Therese, the grande dame, living like society ladies lived before the turn of the century. Behind her front door, time stops: there is no Hitler and no pogroms. The servants are still "primitive people"; they do not count, and see and hear nothing.

After the meal was finished, we moved back to the parlor where, after a short time, tea and cakes were served. When I said good-bye, Aunt Therese gave me her cheek for a farewell kiss and invited me for a drive in a few days. I could not refuse. She is a fascinating character: a remnant of the last century. I cannot imagine how the drive will be but I do not want to miss the experience.

August 7, 1935

As agreed upon, I called Seeckt shortly after our meeting and visited him again. He cannot help me. However, he suggested I name him as a reference in the event someone is interested.

His book *Thoughts of a Soldier,* is to be reprinted in a new edition. The publishers have requested two additional chapters. Since he has no secretary, he asked if I were interested in taking his dictation in shorthand and typing up the notes at home. I accepted.

I went to his home several days for dictation. Obviously it was up to me to set the tone between us. I was factual and businesslike. Occasionally I had the feeling that a personal question was on the tip of Seeckt's tongue, but he always refrained from asking.

When his essay, "The Meaning and Essence of Soldiery" lay completed and typed in front of him, he asked me hesitantly if I would also do the next section when he had finished it. I agreed and now await his call.

August 8, 1935

Several nights ago I awoke with my old familiar pain, so severe this time that I could scarce endure it. For the first time it became clear to me what it means to be alone in a strange city, no longer surrounded by my parents' protection and care. While I sought to find a tolerable position, I considered whether I could awaken the landlady, Frau Pächter, or someone else in the middle of the night. I did not even know a doctor I could call. How simple this was at home. If I was seriously ill, I had only to call father. Then mother came quietly, gave me the medicine, and always found the right things for me to eat or drink, to get me back on my feet again.

The next morning the pain was gone and the sun shone, while only the memory of a nightmare remained. That too disappeared when I took my afternoon drive with Aunt Therese.

I went to her house and guided her downstairs. Dressed totally in black with long kid gloves and a large straw hat, she nodded graciously to the chauffeur. He stood ready at the door of a large black limousine. Respectfully, he asked where her ladyship wanted to be driven. He always spoke to her in the third person. We then moved slowly down Heeresstrasse. The moment the driver pressed the gas pedal just a little, Aunt Therese's energetic voice was heard, "Not so fast!"

With upright head she looked from the window at the passers-by, strolling on the sidewalk in front of Wertheim's department store. I almost expected the people to stand still and cheer. In a friendly fashion she pointed out this or that building, or explained to me about various streets. Otherwise, I had the feeling of being a companion to a royal highness. The drive bordered on unreality and produced in me a mixture of utter astonishment and highest amusement. I realized that this egotistical despot was not touched in any way by the happenings of our time. She could ask without comprehension why her son had hastily fled Germany. "Why? He hadn't done anything!"

On the way home I thought to myself, My dear Aunt Therese, I hope you will be permitted to take your illusions to your grave. May a kind fate protect you in your last days and keep you unacquainted with raw reality! Involuntarily I thought of Tucholsky's words, "Learn to laugh without crying."

August 10, 135

Yesterday evening I went to Hilprich's for supper as I often did. Their large menu always has something to offer to people of modest means like myself. On these warm summer evenings I sat with pleasure at a table on the Kurfürstendamm, from where I could see the elegantly dressed people who leisurely sauntered past.

However, this time something disturbed me. At first it was not clear what did not fit the picture. Then all at once I saw it. At first, only isolated individuals, then larger groups of young people with rolled-up shirt-sleeves appeared. Normally this type did not turn up on Kurfürstendamm. And suddenly as if on a signal, all hell broke loose.

The young people on the sidewalks were joined by similarly clothed youngsters in open trucks. Then the sound boomed over the Kurfürstendamm as the choruses chanted: *"Juda verrecke"* (Jews must die). "Bedbugs are also animals, but they must be crushed underfoot! Jews are also people. *"Juda verrecke."*

The trucks traveled constantly around the green divider strip of the boulevard. Everything roared and hooted, until a shrill whistle rang out and the raucous crowd disappeared into nothingness. At that moment the police arrived. They, likewise, drove back and forth a few times and left. Scarcely had they gone when the vans reappeared.

Slowly dusk, the harbinger of night, fell over Berlin. The headlights stared out in front of the lorries and the lights produced a reflection of the troublemakers' white shirts in the elegant shopwindows.

While one side roared contemptuously, "Bedbugs are also animals, but they must be crushed underfoot," the opposite side shouted, full of hate, "Jews are also people, but they must be destroyed."

"Juda verrecke!"

"To hell with the Jewish louse!"

A shrill piercing whistle silenced the choruses. The Nazis disappeared and the police again arrived on the scene.

I do not know how many times this game was repeated. I sat there turned to stone, my eyes and ears wide open, not to miss anything. I still had no explanation for this uproar. Then farther down the street a large crowd formed. The solution to the mystery became clear. On the same street as Hilprich's was the Union movie theater, showing a rerun of the Jewish film 'Plüsch and Plümowski.' It was obviously too much for the Nazis; people were paying good money to see this "miserable Jewish concoction." At the end of the show when the unsuspecting audience left the movie theater, they were jostled and threatened by the furious Nazis. The police, however, came just in time and calm was soon restored. It was an alarming kind of quiet, since Kurfürstendamn, usually so alive day and night, became deserted.

I went home feeling deeply discouraged and defeated. My ears still rang with the merciless, hate-filled shout: "Juda verrecke!" It made me shudder. What can we expect? I suddenly imagined Aunt Therese in her bedroom, an old woman from a well-known Jewish family, being helped to undress by her maid.

I paced back and forth restlessly in my room. I could not read or sleep. I had to tell my impressions to someone who would understand. That same night I sent Walter, in Strassburg, a description of the atmosphere and the scene I had witnessed.

August 19, 1935

Dr. König told me that a large legal convention is taking place, and that I should go with him to Telchow, where he was meeting a gentleman from Butzbach. Butzbach is not far from Frankfurt, but is known to me only because of its penitentiaries.

We sat on Telchow's narrow balcony and looked down on Potsdamer Platz with its constantly moving throngs of cars and people.

"I think," Dr. König said, "that's Dr. Pfeifer over there." He stood up and went over to an inconspicuous man in his fifties who was standing in the doorway, glancing over the terrace. Dr. Pfeifer sat down at our table but did not order anything because he had to leave almost immediately. He discussed something with Dr. König in a concise and businesslike manner.

As he was about to leave, I inquired, "Do you live in Butzbach?"

"Yes, I am the director of a penitentiary there."

As we accompanied him to the door I said, "If I should be locked up, I'll try to land in your prison."

He was already on the staircase, but turned around and said with a smile. "That wouldn't be possible, I have only male inmates."

Dr. König and I returned to our table. We were not alone very long. A tall slender man, whose brown hair was just beginning to gray at the temples, nodded to Dr. König and came over to join us.

65

Dr. König barely had time to whisper, "He's Dr. Hartmann, an attorney." Then he introduced us.

"Berlin is really filled with lawyers," commented Dr. König, trying to start a conversation.

"I almost missed the meeting this time," replied Hartmann.

"Were you away?"

"Yes—in Silesia."

"In Silesia?" König repeated in astonishment. "Did you represent someone there?"

Hartmann shrugged and said, "However you choose to interpret it."

I felt that Hartmann wanted to tell König something but my presence hindered him.

"You can speak freely in front of Miss Schroeder," König said. "We're trying to find a place for her on our editorial staff. Because of racial grounds, she can't work anymore with the Frankfurt press."

For the first time, Dr. Hartmann looked directly at me and asked for details. He then spoke to both of us. "I spent several fantastic evenings in a spa in Silesia. There is a Catholic priest there who usually dresses in civilian clothing. He makes it his business to supply Aryan ancestors for Jewish converts to Catholicism."

I looked at him skeptically and asked, "How does he do that?"

"He searches through the regional parish registers for identical or similar names and compiles information for birth and baptismal certificates."

König said reflectively, "I've also heard about various relief actions performed by Catholic clergymen. Some of them really seem to have courage." He shook his head in amazement.

I asked Hartmann, "Are these catholicized Jews converted because of religious faith or merely out of a feeling of self-preservation?"

"Miss Schroeder, who can see into someone else's heart?"

I nodded silently.

"One Jew I met there," Hartmann continued, "seemed to be genuinely captivated by Catholicism and ready to make any material sacrifice."

"Were there others?" König asked.

"Yes," replied Hartmann. "There was one other unbaptized Jew who was absolutely committed to Judaism." He laughed involuntarily. "Both Jews came from Berlin and stayed in the same guesthouse in this godforsaken corner of the world. Naturally they

66

ended up talking to each other. The converted Jew came to this so-called health resort because the priest had to locate Aryan papers for him. The other Jew was on the run. He could hide there and rest for awhile without official controls. The three of them — the well-educated, intelligent, fanatic Catholic priest, the Catholic-Jew, and the Jewish-Jew — met every evening at the inn for a glass of wine and argumentative discussions. I was present on three such evenings.

"The dialogue between the Catholic priest and the unbaptized Jew had gone on for many evenings before my arrival. The two of them were evenly matched in education and intelligence. The priest had been an instructor of theology.

"When I stepped into the taproom on the first evening to join the three gentlemen at the table, I felt as if I had entered, rather belatedly, the auditorium of a small theater. Imagine a dimly lit, smoky tavern containing several rough, solid and well-scrubbed wooden tables with simple chairs. Since it was a weekday, only our table was occupied. Even the place behind the bar was vacant. A pale priest of average build was seated at the table, wearing a large gray woolen sweater. His bright eyes peered through rimless eyeglasses; his lenses reflected the subdued lighting of the room with every move of his head. His bald pate was framed by a wreath of gray hair resembling a halo. The unbaptized Jew sat directly opposite him. He was a slender man, in his mid-thirties, with luxuriant black hair and large intense lively eyes. The convert sat between them: an insignificant man of uncertain age, tending to fat. I never heard him utter a single word during these discussions." Hartmann added, "I also was silent.

"Midway through what appeared to be a lecture, the priest said, 'From time to time, God sends a Nero or a Hitler to chasten us. Hitler is the scourger, God's agent to punish us, so that people will return to the Church.' He stopped and raised his head. His chin jutted out triumphantly.

"In a pleasant sounding voice, the Jew asked, 'Really? What has the Church done during its two thousand years of domination in the West? Europe has torn itself apart in hatred and wars.'

"The priest interrupted him gently, gesturing defensively with his pale hand. 'That's what atheists say. Without the Church, there would not be a Europe today!'

"The Jew interjected ironically, 'So you believe that the Church has prevented the collapse of Europe.'

"'That's precisely what I mean. The Church is the custodian

of humanity.' He continued a bit louder, almost ecstatically, 'The Church watches over God's priceless holy shrine, over God's creatures.'

"The Jew observed the priest soberly. He missed neither the emotional connotations, nor the physical gestures used by the priest. He said coolly, a bit amused, 'What you're saying is a ghastly distortion of the truth. It is also utterly illogical. The majority of mankind is not christian, and therefore should have become extinct long ago, since it lacked the blessings of your church.'

"The well-trained churchman added soothingly, 'We don't know the inscrutable ways of God. You're trying to explain with reason what can only be understood through faith.' With prophetic radiance he added with conviction, 'God will let his scourge, Hitler, flagellate Europe until the people recognize from their deepest anguish that no earthly power can ever triumph over godly omnipotence. In order to find peace, they will stammer out long forgotten prayers in despair; freed and purified they will then return to their Lord and Master.'

"For a moment, stupefied silence prevailed. The Jew then asked affably but very distinctly, 'And the Jews?'

"'The Jews?' echoed the preacher in astonished repetition. 'For thirty pieces of silver they betrayed God's son.' His pale, powerless hand was raised threateningly. 'Their children and grandchildren will be punished unto the last generation! The time when our heavenly Father, in his unfathomable wisdom, will remove this curse from the Jews, shall remain hidden from us mortal human-beings.'

"'The son of God?' questioned the Jew ironically. 'We Jews betrayed the son of God?'

"As the agitated and enraged priest started to reply the Jew raised his strong and manly hand to stop him. 'Please let me finish. I've listened to you and your interpretations. The Judas myth was created by imaginative illiterates and is a crime. My dear reverend, you can consider this one of the largest debit items against the Catholic Church.' He stared at the priest without changing expression, then continued. His voice rose. 'I thus write off Hitler the scourge as your fault.'

"The priest responded indulgently, 'It is not granted to everyone to see God. Today you are among the defeated. God will forgive your words.' Rising to leave he added unctuously, 'I'll pray for your salvation daily!'"

Dr. König and I were both silent, completely captivated by the story. We asked almost simultaneously, "What happened next?"

"The next evening, after nearly twenty-four hours to recover his patience and to arm himself against the expected verbal assaults, the priest began smoothly. 'Yes, I have prayed for you and will continue to do so every day from now on until God grants you illumination. God, our heavenly Father, never expects us to understand Him. Whatever you may care to say and however much you may scorn Him, God is the one who decides life and death. Still, death is not the end. The soul, freed from the body, lives in eternal peace with God.'

"'Yes, certainly,' replied the Jew. 'I've already heard that story. Anyhow, according to you, God created the world. As the climax of his work, this God created people. So far as I am informed, he made man in his own image. Since this Christian God is also the God of the western world, he must be Caucasian. This is really amazing since, after all, the majority of mankind is colored. At the summit of his creation, God made people and also microbes. So far as my knowledge goes, germs are older than mankind. However, the Bible doesn't mention bacteria, although it contains a great deal about the devil in it.'

"The priest pushed his wineglass back and forth on the table. He stared at the wine as if it could preach the truth. He replied almost absentmindedly, 'Satan is a fallen angel.'

"'Was he also created by God?' exclaimed the Jew, utterly amazed. 'He probably made Satan before man became his goal, isn't that right?"

"Since the debate had barely started and the priest had come with the best intentions, his reply was mild. 'Since God gave man his own image, he certainly also gave it to the angels.'

"Silence reigned for a few minutes.

"Then the Jew asked thoughtfully, 'Isn't there something basically erroneous in your reasoning concerning heavenly omnipotence? Your infallible all-powerful God created Satan. He let this abysmally evil creature roam freely in the world — and you believe that this was unintentional.' He continued speaking reflectively and slowly, almost hesitantly. 'Something went very wrong since he was to have been a perfect angel.' He suddenly spoke very sharply, almost mercilessly, 'Why don't you hold your God responsible for Satan and his foul deeds?'

"The priest's pale complexion grew sallower as he murmured

almost inaudibly, 'God forgive them, for they know not what they do.'

"The Jew, noticing the priest's dismay, continued unerringly, 'Your God must be held as responsible as the average person when he causes damage and harm to others.' He continued warily, 'Isn't it true, Reverend, that you demand of your believers that they admit to their smallest faults in the confessional? To whom or before whom is your God held responsible for his indescribable atrocities? Since your God let an unpunished Satan loose on his creations, I am equally convinced that He will let Hitler rage unpunished.'

"His face completely white, the priest controlled himself with supreme effort. He said in an emotion-laden voice, 'May God forgive you, I can't. The Lord sends evil, whether it is Satan or Hitler, to tempt us human sinners, to test our strength and our belief in him and his omnipotence.'

"The Jew made a sound halfway between a laugh and a sob. He raised his arm, his elbow level to his face and said defensively, almost threateningly, 'Don't ask me to listen to that sort of God! This alleged omnipotence contains neither reason nor responsibility.' Stopping a moment to catch his breath, he continued, '—and your God certainly does not deserve faith!'

"The preacher's hand gripped the stem of the wineglass. I held my breath, expecting any minute to hear the glass shatter.

"The Jew stood up, tall and elegant, and looked down with derision. 'I believe it would be better for you to pray for him, your master! He is in urgent need of forgiveness from his creatures, since he sent them the scourge Hitler.' He turned on his heel and left."

Dr. König, lost in thought, played with a few bread crumbs. My eyes wandered over Potsdamer Platz without seeing anything. The sun was shining but my thoughts were still in that small, dark, smoky inn room. The rattle of a cup at the next table brought us suddenly back to the present.

Overwhelmed, I turned to Dr. Hartmann and said, "That's simply incredible! What happened afterwards?"

Absentmindedly, Dr. Hartmann glanced down at his watch. "Dear me! I should have been at Kempinski's a half hour ago! I must leave quickly!" He stood up.

"You know, Hartmann," König said slowly, "you should turn this into a theater piece."

"I don't think this cast of characters would be in vogue at the moment. Moreover, König, do you realize how many potential theater pieces I experience during a year? They usually begin in my office. As a rule they reach their climax in the courtroom, or they end in jail. If I wanted to make scenarios of them all, I'd be forced to give up my law practice."

He reached into his pocket and placed some money on the table for the waitress. With the hint of a bow to me and a farewell wave to König, he departed hurriedly.

August 31, 1935

Somehow it seems that fate is not very kind to me. There is a hitch with my proposed job at the *General Anzeiger*. Dr. König did not explain the details but apparently certain formalities must still be met — or suppressed. Whatever it is, I am worse off here than in Frankfurt, where at least I occasionally got into print.

Day before yesterday I received a letter from mother telling me that I had been summoned before the Special Court on September 27.

To climax everything, a few days ago I could scarcely drag myself home after lunch. Apart from the horrible pain, I was also terribly sick. This time I asked Mrs. Pächter to call a doctor, and I went to bed at noon in broad daylight.

Mrs. Pächter came to my room. "What is it? What's the matter with you?"

"I don't know. I have an awful pain."

"Who should I call?

"Anyone! Do you have a doctor?"

"Yes, but he is Jewish."

"Oh, really?"

"Yes." She had to laugh. "Dr. Block."

This Dr. Block finally came, a rather short, sympathetic man with large gray-blue eyes and sparse gray hair. He touched me cautiously while Mrs. Pächter stood in the background like a worried clucking hen. He shook his head and was not exactly sure what was wrong; but he had an idea about what it was, gave me a morphine injection and promised to come again in a few hours. A period of sleep was followed by semiconsciousness, pain, morphine, sleep, semiconsciousness — until I was once again awake and without pain.

Dr. Block's diagnosis was kidney-stone. An examination by a

71

specialist would be necessary. When I told him that my father is an internist at a hospital, he suggested, "You surely will get much better care there than here and it will be free. As soon as you can travel, take a train and go home."

Dr. Block and I understood and liked each other. When I inquired about his practice, he replied. "I'm leaving Germany in four weeks."

"Where will you go?" I asked astonished.

"To America. Chicago. Everything is arranged. Friends expect me there. I must take exams once again and work for one year in a hospital, then I'll settle there."

"I sincerely wish you the best of luck!"

"I feel only relief at the thought of being able to leave Germany with my family. I believe you need the luck more than I!" He smiled encouragingly at me. "First of all get well. Then see if you and your parents can't also get across the borders of our esteemed Fatherland. Mrs. Pächter told me your mother is Jewish."

We parted on this note.

Two days later, I took the train and returned to Frankfurt.

September 12, 1935

Father felt sorry about my bad luck and was also a bit concerned about my condition but not overly pessimistic. It was probably the jolting of the train that triggered off a new violent intestinal attack.

My examination by an urologist confirmed Dr. Block's diagnosis. But Dr. Dessecker wants to give me a chance with conservative treatment before resorting to surgery.

Since I am back in Frankfurt and the 27th of September draws nearer every day, I must consider how I should act in this unpleasant denunciation procedure. This evening, Katherina came to see me in my room to ask me how I felt.

"I can't complain at the moment. Even cigarettes taste good again."

We sat face to face for awhile until I broke the silence. "The kidney stone causes me far less discomfort than the hearing deadline."

Katherina stared at my desk and was silent. I lost my patience and pressed for an answer. "Have you learned nothing about this home for unwed mothers? After all, this information does come from your Catholic circles."

72

"No, and I have almost given up hope," she said, staring hard at the toes of her shoes. "The person who spoke on that mothers' evening seems to have disappeared from the surface of the earth. Nobody, *no* one can remember who it was," she said almost tearfully.

"Mmm," I considered aloud, "that is fatal."

"Couldn't the Catholic Charity Organization in Freiburg give you any information?"

"Oh, surely! They were very helpful. They know about as much as you do — namely nothing!"

"But what did they reply?"

"They wrote at first that it was probable that a home was located in Ermland. Since I couldn't do anything with this stupid answer, I wrote to them again. I requested that they be more specific, since I stood under indictment because of this statement. They should inform me how many such homes the Bishop of Ermland opened and how many unwed mothers from the Labor Service found admission there. And do you know what? 'None,' they replied. Suddenly not even the smallest home was there!" I laughed, stood up, lit a cigarette and paced back and forth in my room.

Katherina, who followed me with her eyes, was noticeably more nervous. Suddenly she almost shouted, "Yes, but what will happen now?"

I stopped and stood directly in front of her. "Happen, Käthe? I think what has happened is already more than enough. Since neither you nor any of your Catholic friends know the nameless phantom who put the story in circulation on that mothers' evening, it is clear that I will be condemned for slander. I can't rid myself of the feeling that one person in your camp is covering up for the other." Before she could answer, I said, "Please excuse me now. I must telephone someone." With that, I left the room.

I dialed Reiss's number.

An audible sigh of relief that I was back in Frankfurt escaped him. "I have received a summons."

I interrupted him. "Yes, that's what I wanted to know."

"But what should I do?"

"I only wanted to make sure of that, Ulrich. I will call you in a few days, then we can meet and talk the matter over." I hung up.

Then I telephoned the *F.Z.* "Is Mr. X still there?"

"One moment please," came the answer. And then, "Yes, Mr. X is still here. I will connect you."

73

Karl identified himself by name. I was dazed to hear his voice again after so long a time.

"Hello," he said impatiently, "is someone there?"

I answered and after a few words of greeting I continued, "I must speak to you at once."

He only asked, "Can you come now?"

I hesitated. "Tomorrow morning would be better. And in your office."

September 14, 1935

When I entered Karl's office, he stood up and awkwardly stroked my cheek with the back of his hand. Then he looked at me searchingly. "You've lost weight and are pale." With mild sarcasm he asked, "Did the Berlin air disagree with you?" He had, therefore, learned that I was in Berlin.

We sat opposite each other as we so often did in the past, separated by his desk piled with bundles of newspapers, manuscripts, notes, and teletype sheets.

Karl pulled himself together. "I don't assume that you came to tell me about Berlin, although I would like to hear something about that too. How can I help you?"

"I have been denounced."

His eyes opened wide. "By whom?"

"By a friend — from pure stupidity."

He pinched his lips together and his expression hardened. "Would you please give me an exact account, from the beginning, with all the details you can remember?"

I told him about my circle of friends, Reiss's trip to Weilburg, my discussions with Katherina, the hearing at the Women's Labor Service. Gabbusch's interrogation at the Gestapo, and the newest summons from the Special Court.

He listened tensely, occasionally interjected a question, and finally remarked that matters had gone pretty far. With his hand to his forehead and with half-closed eyes, he carefully considered the whole matter. Suddenly he looked at me. "I know that you won't like this but your best bet is to try to lie your way out of it. You must admire the general concern shown for these young women." He began to be amused by the situation that forced me to praise the Nazis. "You must emphasize how wonderful you think it is that

74

even the Bishop of Ermland, etc." He laughed mockingly. "You understand how I think you must act?"

I nodded.

"Nevertheless, as a precaution I would get in touch with a reliable attorney," Karl said. "Do you know someone?"

I thought it over. "Yes, perhaps Dr. Jelkmann. He represented our neighbor Dr. Fränkel's son. You know, in that 'racial disgrace' trial."

"The one where the father wasn't the father after all?" Karl remembered. "All right, you should consult Jelkmann tomorrow. I will have thought the matter over again by then. Be sure to call me tomorrow."

I then had to tell him about Berlin and my abrupt departure.

When I wanted to leave, he embraced me silently and we stood together like two lost children, who sought mutual consolation.

September 17, 1935

So much has happened that I scarcely know how I should begin. The best solution is probably chronological.

The next morning I telephoned Jelkmann, who granted me a half hour that same afternoon. He greeted me with charming old-school amiability. He is a tall, good-looking man, about father's age, with almost white hair, a fresh complexion, and childlike eyes. He filled me with absolute confidence. The only thing I kept secret was where I got the rumor.

He briefly tried to break my silence on this point when he said in an emphatic but friendly manner, "But my dear girl, you could surely free yourself from the whole indictment if you would name your source."

"I know that, Dr. Jelkmann, but I really would not be happy to send someone else to prison in my place. Can't we agree that I don't know it? Would you please oblige me and accept my forgetfulness in this respect as a fact?"

He agreed with an almost fatherly understanding. "Since you are apparently clear about the consequences, I will not make the effort to," he looked for the right word, "assist your memory."

We smiled at each other.

After I told him everything that had occurred until then, including Karl's proposal to lie my way out of things with praise for

75

the Nazi's public welfare, Jelkmann explained to me that the 27th of September was not the date for a court trial, but only for an interrogation by the examining magistrate. We also discussed various details, and Jelkmann dismissed me with the understanding that we would speak again after the pretrial hearing date.

I went directly from Jelkmann's office to Karl's. We met on the steps.

"I was just going to get a quick cup of coffee," he said. "Do you want to come too? Then we can return to my office."

On the way I told him about my visit with Jelkmann.

After we were in his office, Karl questioned me about Reiss. "Can you rely on him to do what you will request?"

"I can only hope so, Karl. Basically he is a coward. If he weren't, he wouldn't have behaved the way he did. Taking this small character defect into consideration, and given a corresponding dose of fear which I can throw into him, he will play along."

"What are you thinking of?"

"I believe I should remind him that he should avoid doing anything that would direct too much attention to himself, and could give room for doubts. I will tell him if certain authorities begin to show an interest in his personal life, his Jewish girl friend would come to light. Karl, I am genuinely worried that her name could surface. That probably would be fatal for her."

Karl's voice was sharp. "Yes, especially after the latest events."

Preoccupied with my own problems, I had neither read the newspaper nor heard the news on the radio today.

Karl stood up as I glanced at him questioningly. "What has happened?"

"My dearest, new laws have been passed." He fished a newspaper from his desk and gave it to me. "I must go to a brief editorial conference. It won't last long. Meanwhile, you can read this." He stroked me lovingly across the shoulder and left the room.

I knew that the party rally was being held in Nuremberg, but I had no idea what would be proclaimed, although it was certain to be something contrived during long conferences. The relevant paragraphs were headlined NATIONAL CITIZENSHIP LAW.

While I brooded about what this law meant, not only for me but for countless other people in Germany who are in any way related to Jews, I heard Karl's footsteps in the corridor.

76

He looked at me and said only, "The law won't go into effect until the end of November."

I nodded silently. "What difference does it make if it is now or in two months, since the law will be implemented in any case? It is a catastrophe."

After a while we turned again to the most urgent problem, namely my court appearance.

"Can you still get along amicably with this Reiss?" I looked at him blankly. He explained, "I have thought the whole thing over very thoroughly and reached the conclusion that it would make a good impression if you could act totally naturally, as if your friendship was still completely intact. This would furnish one more proof that neither of you has a guilty conscience.

"You told him the story of these homes in an approving manner. He most probably heard and repeated the story in the same way. Based on your positive attitude, it never occurred to him that he could harm you. You must bring this old maid in trousers, this sad sack of a man, to the point where he confirms that you hadn't the faintest intention of disparaging any institution of the Third Reich. That this or that girl in the Labor Service becomes pregnant — good grief! Such things happen everywhere. You must make light of it and minimize its importance."

I thought over Karl's proposal.

"The important thing is that this chap lie with you," said Karl emphatically. "When will you see him?"

"He is waiting for my phone call."

"Then give him one more day's time. By then the probability will be greater that he will have read the Nuremberg Laws before you meet him. I should think that would only make him even more willing to wriggle out of the jam he is in."

"Yes, and I will make the job easier for him with a warning to avoid everything that could drag his girl into this wretched mess."

"Naturally I'll expect your report about this idyllic reunion. Where will you meet him?"

"I think I'll let him come to my home. Perhaps I'm beginning to suffer from a persecution complex but to hold such a meeting in a cafe appears somewhat risky."

Yesterday I called Reiss. He appeared promptly in the afternoon and understood quickly what I expected of him. With forced ease he tried to meet me as he formerly had, and I must admit he played his part well. I can only hope that he will appear as convincingly before the Special Court. I considered yesterday a dress rehearsal for the performance before the special tribunal.

September 29, 1935

On the afternoon of the 26th I went once more to see Karl. We discussed the most important points for the last time and Karl drummed into me that I should avoid at any price telling the examining magistrate about my racial origins. His refrain was "Lie your way out. Lie your way out. You need not have any scruples with these criminals." His fear and anxiety for me showed in his eyes.

On my way home in the tram, the familiar pain began to be intermittently noticeable. The pain grew into a massive abdominal attack in the course of the night. I complained, "They will think at the tribunal that I am feigning something."

"Don't worry, child. Sleep, Lili dear, sleep," mother murmured soothingly while her cool hands gently and reassuringly stroked my hot, clammy forehead. I lapsed gratefully into oblivion.

It was bright day when I came around. The more I woke up the more intense the pain became. Mother, who was in the next room, heard me moving restlessly back and forth through the partly opened door and came immediately. With her appearance, my memory also returned.

"Mummy, what have you done about the Special Court hearing?"

"Don't get upset. We telephoned Dr. Jelkmann early this morning. He has taken all the necessary steps."

I tried to think clearly. There was still something important. Suddenly I knew what it was. "Would you please call Mr. X at the *F.Z.* and tell him what has happened?"

After about thirty-six hours I recovered enough to call Dr. Jelkmann. The hearing date was postponed until October 1. Mr. Reiss had been informed and would also appear then. The whole fear and agitation was prolonged by several days.

October 1, 1935

Today was the hearing before the examining judge. With hindsight, it is easy to see that we did not really have to get all worked up about it. No risky questions were asked. The procedure was very similar to Gabbusch's, only at a higher level of authority.

Reiss and I had arranged to meet at the Konstabler Wache and we went together to the District Court, in which the Special Court was only one department. We waited in the hall, talked together, and behaved like the best of friends — in front of everyone, including the examining magistrate.

The examining judge, no longer a young man, took a very humane attitude. He was concerned about my health, and wanted to receive my assurance that I was physically up to the interrogation and was comfortably seated. Conscious of his duty, he repeatedly asked me about the source of the rumor which I had spread. Apart from that, I tried to convince him how deeply moved I was by the care with which the Third Reich looked after these 'wayward girls,' who a short while ago were punished by the contempt of society. Much as I should like to, I could not remember who had told me the story about the Bishop of Ermland.

The judge shook his head very gently, somewhat sadly. Because of the type of questions he asked, I suddenly had the feeling that he began to suspect Reiss. He seemed to think we were lovers, and I had sacrificed myself for him by accepting full responsibility. The situation was not without humor.

After my interrogation was finished, I waited in the corridor for Reiss. He appeared after a while, evidently very relieved. He was so relieved that he was gay and laughed about the whole "ceremony." He could well laugh, since he was only a witness and not incriminated. Perhaps he was also too naive to realize the full consequence of these proceedings.

I went to see Karl late in the afternoon. I had to report the smallest detail to him, and I concluded, "Karl, I had the feeling that the examining magistrate was sorry for me."

"That is quite possible. The Nazi machinery isn't yet running altogether smoothly. Don't forget: not yet."

"What do you mean?" I asked uncomprehendingly. "The Special Court is certainly not an unimportant cog in the machinery."

"The Special Court — yes," said Karl bitterly. "But the Nazis don't have enough trained people from their own ranks. They have probably thrown out everyone who is suspicious, or pensioned them off. However, in many administrative bodies — for example, the courts — there are still people who are neither 'suspicious characters' nor Nazis. They are tolerated temporarily because of the lack of fully trained party members. Among all these high civil servants, there may still be many who feel more inclined to the left than to the right, but who do not commit themselves; and there are people who are absolutely unpolitical and thus 'uncompromised' in Nazi eyes."

He continued somewhat sarcastically, "It could be that your examining magistrate is one of those unsuspicious, uncompromised figures who have been put on Special Courts, and whose conscience is moved when he recognizes what an honorable task has been given to the half-hearted." Karl's voice became hard and bitter. "Namely, to deliver his fellow human beings — disrespectful citizens like yourself — to the knife."

Karl paced nervously up and down in his small office. "You know, my child, in my eyes these wishy-washy individuals are just as bad as the high party comrades who are sadists and take joy in persecuting the so-called enemies of the state. They either drive them out of the country or place them behind bars."

After a long silence, I asked, "Karl, and what should these men do if they must support a family?"

"You are asking that?" Karl was completely taken aback. "My child, has anyone asked you if you will exchange your grandparents to remain a journalist? Did anyone ask Willi Becher, the Kolhöfers or all of the many Jewish, socialist, or communist human beings or give them a choice? They all must somehow scrape through with their families."

He ended a tour around the room and stopped in front of me. Lifting his index finger and shaking his fist, Karl said in a hard and choppy voice, emphasizing every single word, "Concern for family should never be a reason for a man to sell his decency and conscience!"

He turned around and walked to the door, where he stopped, lost in thought. Facing me he said more softly, "I don't know if I could have respected my father when I was young if he had had his price." Half to himself, he wondered, "What kind of generation is growing up? Children who have enough to eat and will recognize one day that their father is an unprincipled pig." He wiped his hand over his eyes and forehead. "It is appalling!"

October 6, 1935

It is a strange feeling to anticipate an operation. I am occasionally depressed because of my inactivity and the hopelessness of my situation and would welcome a decent way out. On the other hand, I often get mad at myself. I will not believe that my life has reached an impasse and that I have nothing more to hope for or expect. I laugh at myself: already resigned at the age of twenty? Ridiculous! I must stick it out. The Thousand Year Reich will not even outlast a part of my life. And yet, all the same . . . .

With these mixed feelings I await the operation. If things should turn out badly? Perhaps, then I have not lost anything. If I pull through?

As matters stand I will try to forget the Third Reich, straighten up my desk, take my diaries to my friend Siegrid with the request that she burn them if necessary, write a few letters, and make a few visits. My aunts Elly and Anna were delighted by my last visit. I sat, as in the good old days, between these two oversized old maids; and I could see the glass-fronted cabinet full of knickknacks and figurines, and the ashtray supported by three brown salamanders that I so admired as a child.

October 7, 1935

This time Sjöderbloom did not wait for the maid to knock on the door, but immediately came to meet me. In contrast to the bottle of wine, the servant brought a large teapot to the table. After I received an enthusiastic reception from Bonzo, we again sat together under the subdued light of the floor lamps and talked. The dog stretched out at our feet.

Sjöderbloom asked me about my Berlin experiences, my professional prospects, and future plans. I fought with myself. Should I tell him about my difficulties? I lit a cigarette to gain time and decided to let the conversation drift. I told him that in Berlin I only waited and waited.

"And now?" asked Sjöderbloom. "Will you return to Berlin after you have recuperated from the operation?"

"I really don't know, Signore. Events, or rather national socialist policies, bring us incessant surprises. At the moment, I can't see how the Nueremberg Laws will affect me."

"Yes, the Nueremberg Laws," he said seriously. "They are as cruel as they are unrealistic."

Sjöderbloom stood up and went to his library. On the lowest shelf, where the bookcase was wider, lay several books. Selecting one with many strips of paper between the pages, he held the single volume out; it was Hitler's *Mein Kampf.* Looking through the marked pages, he said, "Here it is. Hitler said, 'Thus, I believe

81

today that I am acting in the meaning of the Almighty God: in so far as I resist the Jews, I am fighting for God's work.' Do you now understand what I mean?"

I nodded and said reflectively, "Yes, Mr. Hitler is evidently not only elected, but, on top of that chosen."

Sjöderbloom smiled suddenly. "Signorina, the idea just occurs to me. If this man had been born in another time, he certainly would have been a great prophet! He is made of the material from which prophets come: he can electrify and possess the masses, and unleash mass hysteria." He shook his head. "Formerly prophets whipped up the masses for good or for evil; today politicians do it. Strictly speaking, both are charlatans. Quite a phenomenon is occurring before our eyes!"

He lifted his teacup as I suddenly blurted out, "I expect to be arraigned before the Special Court." His hand with the teacup remained motionless in front of his mouth. "And this may cause certain changes in my life."

"Before the Special Court?" he asked, while he placed the cup noisily in its saucer.

Then I told him the unpleasant story, while I considered with a throbbing heart if this fresh incrimination of my character would mean the end of our friendship.

Although I had omitted any allusion to Katherina, Sjöderbloom seemed to surmise correctly. When I finished speaking, he asked, "Your source must surely know in what a precarious position you have been placed?"

I nodded. "Yes."

"And she — I mean the source — does nothing to exonerate you?"

I felt the blood rushing to my face. "Signore, it is all somewhat involved. It was my own free decision to answer for what I said. No one could force me to do it. Let's just say — I didn't want more names to be dragged in."

"Well done, Signorina!" A large cloud of smoke followed his words.

I bent down and patted Bonzo, who uttered a contented sigh and stretched himself.

"Signorina, will you do me a favor?"

I sat up. "Yes?"

The dog got up and rubbed his large damp nose against my hand; and, lost in thought, I automatically stroked his short soft coat.

Sjöderbloom continued, "For the time being, please don't think of anything else but that you must get well. Everything else has time . Agreed?"

November 6, 1935

I have been at home again for a few days and I will try to record everything that has happened, before I forget it.

The first days after the operation were not pleasant but they passed. Mother had a couch placed in my room and did not leave me for a moment. I never heard her, but as soon as I awakened and wanted anything, she was there.

I recovered rapidly, and after a week the stitches were removed. In the early afternoon I felt a mild pain in the top of my lungs with every breath.

Mother sat in an easy chair next to the bed and read. From time to time she smiled at me. Suddenly she bent closer. "Is something wrong?"

"Please don't get alarmed. However, ask if Dr. Dessecker is on call. I have pain when I breathe."

Mother literally flew out of the room and returned in a moment with the floor nurse. Dr. Dessecker appeared a half hour later. He examined me: nothing. False alarm! Then father came, startled out of his noon nap: not a false alarm — pulmonary embolism.

Day and night with an oxygen tank in the room, day and night during which I desperately fought for air to breathe. I saw no one except my parents, doctors, and nurses — with one exception.

A small red sign was fastened to my door, which forbade visitors. In spite of this a minister came! The Reverend Marold, the hospital clergyman, felt the prohibition of visitors did not apply to him. If someone was so ill, he especially needed religious solace — before departing for the hereafter.

In impotent rage, I had to tolerate his presence in the room. I was too weak to speak or show him the door — and mother would never turn a minister out. I only hoped that I would be on my feet at his next visit.

November 7, 1935

Finally the day came when the oxygen tank disappeared from the room. Visitors were allowed and mother brought me a letter

83

from my brother Wolf. She rejoiced, "Ah, Lili dear, just think —
he is coming!"

"Who is coming?" I asked without understanding.

"My — our dearest Wolf is coming to visit us!"

"Really?" I said in disbelief. "When?"

"He will celebrate Christmas with us. Isn't it wonderful!"

Walter Gross was one of my visitors. We talked about Berlin.
Then Walter said, "Your letter about the pogrom on Kurfürsten-
damm was excellent! I printed it exactly as you wrote it in the
French newspaper, naturally without your name. Don't be afraid."

I returned home on November 3rd. A gigantic bouquet of car-
nations from Sjöderbloom greeted me. I had returned in time for
an evening of chamber music.

Draped in a blanket I lay on the large blue sofa in the music
room, thoroughly enjoying being surrounded again by music and
familiar faces, away from the unhealthy hospital atmosphere where
temperatures, pulses, and bodily functions form the focus of life.

November 12, 1935

In a few days I will go to Mittelberg near Oy to convalesce; but
I will return not later than December 15th to be here when my
brother Wolf arrives. I can't describe what it means to me to be
able to see him again! He is the only person in the world with whom
I can be completely myself. I can confide everything to him without
reserve, and speak from my heart about my fears and doubts. Even
if he can't give me practical help, he will surely understand and
sympathize with me. I can afford to tell him that I am afraid. In
front of my big brother, I can remove my mask of nonchalance and
unaffectedness.

The house is already in an uproar although it is still more than
a month until he will be here. Painters are coming to repaint his old
room. Mother and Etta speak of him incessantly and even Katherina is excited. The anticipated joy should contribute substantially
to my recovery, despite all the other unpleasantnesses of life.

Every afternoon after lunch I have to lie down and usually I
sleep. When I awoke yesterday, mother stood in the room.

She looked lovingly at me. "Now, Lili dear, have you slept
well?" Drawing near, she touched my face. "But child! You are

84

very hot! Do you have a fever?"

I shook my head. "No — only a horrible dream." I tried in vain to shake off the memory.

"I dreamed I was down town. Suddenly, a man I recognized as the examining magistrate pointed at me from across the street and shouted something. I began to run, but he followed me, and every policeman who saw us joined in the pursuit. They all chased me to drag me to the Special Court. I ran and ran and felt my strength fail me — and then I woke up."

Mother looked at me a moment thoughtfully. With a sigh, she said, "How strange that you should have that dream. While you were asleep, the Special Court called. They wanted to know whether you were sufficiently recovered to establish the date for the hearing."

As a result of these events I called Jelkmann and was at his office this afternoon. Mother accompanied me.

He patted my hand and observed that I was still very thin and looked pale.

In an almost fatherly warm-hearted way he said, "Ladies, I would suggest that Miss Lili first take a rest and recuperate. When she returns, I am in favor of getting a court date as soon as possible, as a guarantee against all eventualities."

While I wondered what he really meant by this expression, mother asked, "What do you mean, Dr. Jelkmann?"

He said reassuringly, "Now ladies, please don't get alarmed. But as a lawyer one must consider all the possibilities. It is normal for a defendant sentenced by the Special Court to be hauled off from the court immediately and taken to prison."

"For heaven's sake!" mother exclaimed.

"Ma'am," Jelkmann said almost imploringly. "Your daughter isn't even before the court. Only to be on the safe side, I consider it advisable that we should aim for an early hearing. Then if we have bad luck and Miss Lili should be condemned, I could immediately file an objection against imprisonment, on grounds of her health. Please understand, ladies, I only want to win time, since I expect an amnesty on Hitler's birthday."

November 22, 1935

I am in Mittelberg. The Pension Angerer is one of those typical wooden houses, where one hears the mice turning somersaults between the ceiling of one's room and the floor of the room above.

Mother Angerer, a plump woman whose goodness shines from her eyes, is in charge of the kitchen. She provides simple, solid, and very tasty cooking. Father Angerer is a tall lean man whose rough hands can produce sensitive watercolors and play chamber music with his three children.

The scenery is not entirely to my liking. The small village is located on a high plateau where one can see the mountains, but not easily reach them. Before I arrived it had snowed and thawed again, so white spots are lying around like pieces of laundry forgotten on the lawn.

Since it is not the holiday season, it is very quiet here. Father Angerer is cock of the roost, surrounded by the fair sex. A teacher, accompanied by her mother, is here in the hope that mountain air will improve her asthma. Another inconspicuous woman is recuperating from some illness. I looked forward to a rather gloomy time, when three days after my arrival, a new guest arrived, a Mrs. von Töbelmann from Berlin. She has a thin elegant appearance and is only slightly older than I. In the natural course of events, we started taking small walks together and helped each other pass the time. I do not know what she is doing in this solitary place. She seems to be in good health.

November 29, 1935

Mrs. von Töbelmann and I told each other something of our lives. Her trip here was practically a flight to find time for thought and to put her life and marriage in order.

Naturally I told her that after my return I expected my brother from America. My happiness must have been visible on my face, since she asked how long we had been apart, how we related to each other, and more of the same. She cautiously said, "I hope you won't be disappointed."

"But why?" I asked stupefied. "We have corresponded all these years and nothing seems to have changed."

Mrs. von Töbelmann laughed a bit. "Excuse me for saying it; but if a person like your brother has lived for over six years in that unscrupulous country, a little bit of it must have stuck to him."

"How do you come to this conclusion?" I asked somewhat skeptically.

86

"I believe emigrants have something in common with converts. Their new home is the most perfect country in the world; if they were previously not nationalistic, they suddenly espouse that feeling. Do you understand what I mean?"

With a heartfelt sigh, I replied, "Probably better than you can imagine! My sister converted from Protestantism to Catholicism."

"Oh!" Mrs. von Töbelmann laughed. "Then you do know what I mean."

I hesitated. "Actually not, when I think of my brother. According to what he has written, the American political system appears to be very different from ours; and I must say, especially compared to what we have now, it really sounds quite appealing. I can well imagine how, under these circumstances, he was captivated and discovered a patriotic feeling." I was silent and thought about the differences between the country of freedom on the other side of the ocean and the oppressive life in a totalitarian state.

Mrs. von Töbelmann interrupted my thoughts. "From a distance all that may seem very alluring. America asserts that it is a democratic country. The oldest known democracy was Athens. In Athens ten thousand landed gentry controlled everything. Only those who had a definite amount of land could vote. The poorer people who possessed no land couldn't, and therefore could not participate in national decisions. In America, it is not the gentry; there it is the millionaires. A few families like the Woolworths, Vanderbilts, Rockefellers, are decisive. There, in the so-called democracy, these few hold the well-being and woe of millions of people in their purses. The little man has absolutely nothing to say, and he is deluded into believing he has a say by extremely adroit propaganda."

I was speechless. After I recovered, I said, "But there are still two parties in America: the Republicans and the Democrats. Doesn't one keep a careful watch on the other?"

Mrs. von Töbelmann shook her head. "Two parties? That all belongs to the process of hoodwinking. In reality there is one party with a conservative and a liberal wing, where 'liberal' is a wild exaggeration. Basically it is a state that is as capitalistic as it is corrupt; where lots of money, bargained in secret, will buy power."

December 22, 1935

I returned home on the 15th, and Wolf arrived three days

87

later. The whole family went to the station and the joy of the reunion was boundless.

We sit together, talking and explaining. He is a convinced American and happy he lives in the States. We try to make what is going on here clear to him. He does not understand and is surprised at our attitude. Shaking his head, he said that it would be utterly inconceivable in America to speak of the president in the derogatory way we do of Hitler. He pointed to the positive sides of National Socialism. He was deeply impressed by a Nazi proclamation, "A German Christmas" for all citizens. Our Führer wants it so. If ever, it should be true now that no one will be hungry or cold in Germany!"

I can only hope that if Wolf remains here a bit longer he will see behind the scenes. I had been so indescribably happy about his coming. Now? With sinking heart I remember Mrs. von Töbelmann's warning.

When one hears Wolf speak of the American president, one could believe that at the very least he is referring to a demigod. Though it is nice for people to venerate their head of state - what would happen if one day a madman, or a criminal, or a combination of both is at the head of their government? Will they then also speak of him uncritically and full of respect and admiration? Since I have no reason to doubt Wolf's words, I must assume that the Americans are at least as large a flock of sheep as the Germans. A 'free people' without their own opinions.

December 28, 1935

Christmas, the holiday of tears, is behind us. On the 25th, the Aunts Olbricht came for lunch. For as long as I can remember, they have always shared Christmas and the Christmas goose with us. One of Katherina's girl friends also stayed with us during the holidays. Because she works for a private welfare organization, Wolf asked her a thousand questions. He will probably be able to visit several welfare institutions with her help, or that of her employer.

Something slowly dissolves between Wolf and me. We had no quarrels but I suspect that as I doubt the accuracy of his views, he rejects many of mine. After strolling through town, he explained that in America 'Keep smiling' is a general principle. Whatever happens, people keep a smiling face. He told us about a natural disaster: a heavy sandstorm in Illinois which caused great destruction and claimed several lives. With smiling faces, the Americans rebuilt their homes, buried their dead, and attended to the Sisyphean task of removing the fine sand from all the house-joints and clothing. They did it without complaint — smiling. He noticed how serious, almost sullen, the people here look on the street.

Yes, brother dear, although you are here, we couldn't be farther apart if you were still in America. Keep smiling! Probably I will go to prison; isn't that a cause for laughter? A gentle smile hardly suffices for that. Are these Americans such empty shells that a feeling of deep sorrow or pain does not affect them, or how else are they constantly able to smile? Or are they so trained that they continually carry a smiling mask? How nerve-racking! When I see a face I want to know what is going on in the person. To hide behind a perpetually smiling mask is a lie, for which only three explanations are possible: a total vacuum, cowardice, or the fear of being discovered. Whatever the reason to keep smiling, it does not please me. You are charmed by it. Thus our spirits part. Our opposing views on this seem to me a symbol of all the other problems which we view so differently.

January 4, 1936

The new year was welcomed in the family circle. We toasted each other while I foolishly wished that time could stand still and I could escape a future I fear. Mother looked deeply in my eyes, embraced me lovingly, and said, "My dearest Lili, may God watch over you and protect you from all harm!"

Her words brought me immediately down to earth. I am convinced that the man with the long beard who lives someplace above the clouds is relatively indifferent to what becomes of me.

Immediately after my return from Mittelberg I reported to Jelkmann, who asked sympathetically how I felt.

"Thank you, very well, but the final word rests with my doctor."

"Can I then set the date?"

After I had agreed, he said he would get in touch with the Special Court right away.

Yesterday the summons came. The date is January 15th.

January 12, 1936

Katherina's girl friend kept her promise and Wolf obtained entry into all kinds of welfare institutions: welfare kitchens, Winter Relief sewing rooms and collection points, and everything else he could find. He was simply enthusiastic. Moreover, he reads the newspapers carefully for materials related to this subject.

I certainly do not want to belittle the merits of the Nazis with respect to what they do for the unfortunate people, who have fallen into incredible misery through no fault of their own, but thanks to their megalomaniac and immoral Kaiser. I am trying to understand what kind of an impression all these organizations in a socialist state make on a person with a pronounced sense of justice, a person who lives in a capitalist state where everyone looks out for himself, and where the contrast between poverty and wealth exceeds our imagination.

Since Wolf allowed himself to become intoxicated only by the positive side, and is not willing to see all the horror and unmercifulness, he apparently thinks something is wrong with us. We belong among the perpetual "alarmists and grumblers" whom the Nazis scorn. I no longer see any possibility of a meeting of minds between us.

January 15, 1936

The Special Court hearing was today at eleven.

My parents sent me on my way with their best wishes; and I felt that they—especially father—viewed the whole matter as nothing more than an inconvenience which could scarcely have serious consequences.

Before we entered the court room, Reiss and I stood in the huge stone corridor, where every step echoes. We listened one last time to Jelkmann's instructions.

With almost fatherly pride, he inspected me and said encouragingly, "You look splendid, my dear child. You'll do all right. And don't forget that I'm here to help you." He shook my hand and nodded coolly to Reiss.

In the courtroom Reiss and I sat down next to each other. The first thing which impressed me was the judge's appearance. A cap sat on his small head with sharp features. Gray hair peeked out from under it. A pair of grayish-green eyes above high cheekbones looked over the courtroom. His black robe only emphasized the picturesqueness of his appearance. I had the feeling of looking at a Rembrandt's model who had come alive and climbed out of its frame.

"What a picture!" I whispered to Reiss.

"What?" he whispered back. "What?"

At the moment, the Special Court was in session with the case against a young Catholic priest. He had maintained that the girls in the Labor Service became pregnant, and that homes were already set up to receive these unwed mothers until their children were born. We only heard the end of the proceedings and the verdict. The young priest was condemned to six months in prison.

My thoughts turned somersaults. Six months, I thought, six months! I was stunned when the priest was marched off before our eyes.

My hopes clung to Jelkmann — and the judge. District Court Judge Rehorn's cousin is my father's colleague and knows us. Even though we do not mix socially, we have met frequently.

Judge Rehorn asked his questions and Reiss and I answered according to our agreement. Everything went without a hitch until the district attorney cross-examined me. Surely as a journalist I had to know what I had said. Surely, in my case it was not simply a matter of a young woman thoughtlessly spreading some rumor. The jurors moved their heads almost imperceptibly in agreement.

"It must especially be taken into consideration that the accused is an editor, and holds a responsible position in a responsible profession," said the young district attorney.

It was repeatedly asked what I had thought when I made my statement. I could say nothing but that I admired how excellently the unwed mothers from the Labor Service were cared for.

I must admit that Judge Rehorn gave me every opportunity to place the entire blame on Reiss; however, I did not react to this. Or if I would give my source, the proceeding against me would be dismissed since the court was under the impression that I had not spread the stated rumor with malicious intent.

The young district attorney, who probably wanted to earn his first laurels, was however of another opinion. Referring to the condemned priest, he indicated that "we already have had such a sad case." He strongly favored that the activities of slanderers be stopped. I assume that it is juridically inadmissible in a trial to point to the guilt of a defendant in another trial. But whether admissible or not, my case was before the Special Court.

Finally the court withdrew for deliberation.

Jelkmann motioned me to come to him. Beaming, he said, "I think everything went very well. I am convinced we'll get an acquittal!"

After a while the court returned. The courtroom became quiet. My head swam as some of the words reached me. The court emphasized that the plaintiff is conscious of the damaging character of her statements; however, no subversive views could be determined. Therefore, she will receive a prison sentence of only two months.

Two months! I thought. Two months: sixty days. Thoughts swirled through my head like the colors in a kaleidoscope. What would my parents say? . . . My career? . . . Sjöderbloom? . . . Would my parents be angry? . . . Berlin. . . . Two months behind bars! . . . I did not hear what else was said until Jelkmann suddenly stood up, walked up to the bench, and spoke to Rehorn. He moved for a postponement of arrest because of the state of my health and the operation I had just undergone. Without batting an eye, Judge Rehorn agreed to the motion and postponed carrying out the sentence until the medical examiner would determine my ability to undergo imprisonment.

Jelkmann felt completely defeated. He had been convinced of an acquittal. Shaking his head, he said, "And I had the feeling that the judge was well-disposed toward you. I simply don't understand it." With a concealed side-glance at Reiss he said, "Please be sure to call me tomorrow morning in my office." We parted.

On the street in front of the courthouse I said good-bye to Reiss. "As far as you are concerned the case is closed."

Reiss was visibly shocked. "I hadn't expected this," he said helplessly.

"Really not? But I had, my friend. You can thank Myriam. If it wasn't for her, you would be in my place."

Notwithstanding what had occurred, my parents were taking their afternoon nap. Only Wolf, pipe in hand, waited for me in the dining room.

"Hi kitten!" he greeted me. "How did it go?"

"I got two months."

"You're kidding?" An uncertain smile appeared on his face. "Tell me truthfully. You weren't really convicted?"

"I am not joking, Wolf," I said stonily. "I am sentenced to two months imprisonment."

He turned a shade paler and stared at me aghast. "Two months! God, what will you do?"

"Do?" I looked at him uncomprehendingly. "In all probability I'll go to jail for two months. And Wolf, I will neither be the first nor the last to whom this happens. I know it isn't customary for people in our class to sit in prison; but we will get accustomed to that."

It is evening and I try unsuccessfully to bring my thoughts into focus.

Two months prison was the sentence of the Special Court. And I was lucky. Yes, lucky! I was tempted to laugh when I remembered the deadly question of the judge "Are you a member of the Reichs Association of the German Press?" Without answering him I placed my old press credentials in front of him.

How would my sentence have been if he had known about my ancestry?

It was luck.

My thoughts turn like a merry-go-round, steadily in circles. And every thought ends with the refrain: two months prison.

January 16, 1936

Dr. Bernd called.

"You sound exactly the same as before," he said relieved. "Miss Schroeder, I have been asked to send you greetings from all of your acquaintances here at the radio station. We are sorry about what happened, and we think of you."

"How?" I asked bewildered. "How did you find out so quickly?"

"It is in the *Volksblatt*."

On the way to Jelkmann's office I bought the *Volksblatt*. Under the title SLANDERS CONDEMNED stood the full story complete with my name.

I placed the paper on Jelkmann's desk. He only said, "Delay it, delay as long as possible! There will be an amnesty on Hitler's birthday. Let Dr. Dessecker issue a certificate attesting that medically you are not able to undergo imprisonment. I will then take all the necessary steps and send the appropriate brief."

On the way back I went to the *F.Z.* and entered Karl's office without being announced.

He jumped up and put his arms around me. "My dearest . . . my dear . . . it is simply horrible."

I had to give him a detailed report about the trial and ended, "Jelkmann is simply defeated and doesn't understand how it could happen. He felt that Rehorn was well-disposed toward me."

Karl asked reflectively, "How long did the Catholic priest get?"

"Six months."

"Since both of you were convicted of practically the same thing, you received a relatively light sentence." He was silent for a moment. "It is very possible that Rehorn did feel kindly towards you. People like you, who say anything against the glorious institutions of the Third Reich, and are not convicted by the Special Court, are frequently picked up by the SA at the door of the courtroom to be further 'educated' in a concentration camp. Perhaps Rehorn wanted to prevent that."

February 26, 1936

Max Fuchs, the sports reporter who belonged to our regular journalists' table in the Hauptwache, is in prison. The Gestapo learned that he, a Jew, is engaged to an Aryan. His friends pressed him to leave Germany. When he applied for a passport, they made no difficulties for him as he was a war veteran.

Karl told me how he urgently warned Max on the evening before he picked up his passport, not to return home. "Go directly to the station, take the next train and disappear."

But Max Fuchs went home. The Gestapo surprised him in bed with Felicitas a short time later and arrested him. Felicitas was summoned as a witness. She never tried to deny her relations with her fiancé. Max got six months in prison and was immediately hauled off.

Karl continued, "When Felicitas was about to leave the courtroom, I grabbed her roughly under the arm and spoke sharply to her within hearing of the SA men. "Come with me! We still have things to straighten out!" The SA people probably thought I was a Gestapo official in civilian clothing, and stepped silently aside."

March 13, 1936

The day before yesterday I received a letter from the Rhine-Main chapter of the National Association of the German Press. It informed me that I had been struck off the professional membership list, effective immediately, because I had been convicted by the Special Court and because of my faulty Aryan identity certificate. I returned my press card.

Today the summons came for a physical examination by Professor Haye at the Medical Examiners' Institute on March 20th.

Irrespective of what happens to me personally, time goes on. After the last conversation with Karl, I imagine hearing a very soft ticking. The ticking which precedes the moment when the flame runs along the fuse to be followed by a horrible explosion.

March 20, 1936

Dr. Dessecker wrote a medical certificate for Professor Haye, which I took along with me.

Professor Haye sat at a cheap old desk in a large empty whitewashed room. Without moving a muscle in his pale face, he took Dr. Dessecker's certificate and read it slowly. His cold blue eyes were then directed at me, and he asked several questions: among them, "Do you still have any pain?"

"Yes."

"Where?"

I answered, while my right hand touched my waistline, "Here."

Haye's face turned red and he roared, "Do you want to make a fool of me?" In a rough voice, emphasizing each syllable, he commanded, "Go into the next room," and he pointed at an open door. "Get completely undressed and lie down on the examination table."

I went into the adjoining room, which Haye could partly see from his desk and began to undress, took my shoes and stockings off and stood with bare feet on the cold floor. I was filled with disgust, when I saw the examination table, covered with a dirty spotted sheet. I closed my eyes, overcome with a feeling of nausea.

Professor Haye stepped behind me. "Lie down!" He stood at the foot of the table. His eyes slid slowly over me. He came closer.

95

As he bent over me, his white smock opened and I saw the party emblem pinned on the lapel of his suit.

I stared at the ceiling and felt his hands sliding along my scar, until he gruffly said, "Spread your legs." While his hand pushed my knee up, he roared, "Open! Spread them all the way open!"

It seemed to me an eternity passed before he finally said, "Get up."

Several minutes later I was dressed again, and had survived the ordeal.

I do not know how I reached home. I was numbed with shock. I only remember that I immediately took a hot bath and put on fresh underwear.

March 25, 1936

Father came late for lunch. Mother and I waited for him. Wolf had already gone out.

Father looked at me and suddenly said, "I went to the prison today and spoke with the director."

Words failed me. I looked at him speechless. He had never said much about my misfortune, but had apparently brooded over it.

Father continued, "He was really a very nice, understanding person. I got a good impression of him. And he assured me that we shouldn't worry about you."

"But, daddy — what made you do that?" I asked overwhelmed, while my eyes began to burn.

"My dear," he answered hesitantly, almost embarrassed. "I had to know where you're going."

Alone in my room that evening I thought about our conversation again. Naturally I was moved by father's anxiety; on the other hand, the whole incident seemed absolutely ridiculous, and illustrated father's utter naiveté. As if he wanted to enroll me in a girls' boarding school, he went to the prison.

March 28, 1936

The afternoon mail brought the news that I was to report for imprisonment on April 1.

"Admittance to prison occurs only on weekdays between 8 A.M.

and 5 P.M., and on days before Sundays and holidays only until noon. This summons must be submitted when you report."

This eventful day is Wolf's last one with us. I have the feeling that he still has not really understood what is going on in Germany, not even now. Even though he has not said it, I feel a silent reproach. No, he does not shake his head and say, "How could you! The institutions which are opened by the head of state are simply not to be made fun of." But I feel I can read his thoughts. We who were once so close can no longer understand each other. But I still feel sad about his departure. Now and then my memories of him overlap with my current impressions. Maybe my grief is caused by bitter disappointment at his lack of understanding.

March 31, 1936

The day before yesterday, another plebiscite was held. With my arrest warrant in my pocket, I voted for the first time in my life, and wrote a large NO on my ballot.

The radio announced the great victory that evening: 99 percent said yes to everything our Führer did. So I belong to the disgraceful one percent. Of course it has been rumored for some time that election results are falsified.

Tomorrow before I go to prison, Siegrid will pick up my diary as a precaution. So I will say good-bye to my sincerest friend, who silently accepts my thoughts and worries. Perhaps I am very unfair, my dear diary, in the last analysis you are only made of paper and will never answer when I so urgently need advice.

Before I start to become sentimental, I will conclude my last entry in freedom.

April 28, 1936

I am home again, sitting in my room surrounded by a sea of flowers. The showpiece stands in the middle of the table: a large green container with a gigantic bouquet of red tulips. A small card stuck in it reads, "Welcome Signorina!" The tulips are surrounded by innumerable nosegays, containers with cyclamen, primroses, and everything nature conjures up. There are flowers on the desk, on the bookcase, and on the large cabinet in the corner.

On my way to Siegrid's this morning, a few steps away from

97

the house a complete stranger walked straight across the street towards me. This middle-aged man said, "Congratulations, Miss
Schroeder."

I stopped short for a moment, and then thanked him with a
happy smile.

Who was this man? Did he mean it honestly or was he sent to
lure me into a trap? I don't know; and I now have a constant companion—mistrust—which follows me like a shadow.

But I want to return to April first, when mother accompanied
me to prison.

Father had called the director once more, and they agreed that
I should report to his office when my prison term started.

After the iron bars closed behind me I was escorted to Director
Hensel's office. A young man in his thirties stood before me.
Despite all his efforts, his jet-black hair fell constantly over his
forehead and stood in striking contrast to his intense dark blue
eyes.

With an extended hand, he greeted me like an old friend.
"There you are Miss Schroeder! I expected you much sooner!"

In the course of our brief conversation, it was obvious that
Director Hensel is opposed to the Nazis. Apparently he was trying
to smooth over my fear of going to prison.

Then he stood up. "I must now take you to the women's
wing."

The female prison staff appeared immediately. Four coarse
hands reached for me and frisked me from head to foot. Then they
took me into another room. The dying light of an unfriendly April
day fell through the barred windows. A long table ran across the
length of a dirty-gray room; it contained pieces of laundry. Gray
metal cabinets with open doors stood along the walls.

"Undress!" the order rang out.

It took me a moment before I understood that the command
was directed to me.

A sharp woman's voice repeated, "Can't you hear? Get undressed! Everything, also your underwear!"

When my lingerie landed in a bundle on the table, it sunk in
that I had been turned over to these hyenas. I stood naked and
helpless between them. I was a number, a criminal — otherwise I
would not be in prison.

Suddenly everything appeared gray, colorless and unreal. The attendants who fitted me with underwear and prison clothing no longer had faces. A smoke screen came between them and me.

They made a list of my property, which I signed automatically. The only thing my senses noticed was the penetrating odor of disinfectant. After countless washings the coarse undershirt was no longer white. It was rough from constant chlorine treatment and chafed my skin.

I spent the first evening mainly feeling sorry for myself. I sat on a straight chair and stared in front of me, when I wasn't crying. A single light bulb screwed in the middle of the ceiling kept me company, until it was turned off at nine o'clock.

The so-called bed was a thick level wooden board on which an old straw mattress and several horse blankets lay. I shivered. Although by nature a night owl, I was obliged, throughout the early evening, to lie on the hard bed, surrounded by monotonous blackness. Finally, I fell asleep.

When I awoke it was still night. In the darkness, I listened to the strange noises reaching me from the corridor: the jangling of metal keys and subdued conversations between the matrons who patrolled the long halls.

Day finally came.

The bucket was collected, the water pitcher was filled, and I received my breakfast and looked around at my new home. There was a peephole in the cell door; opposite, high above the ground, was a barred window. In one corner stood the bucket which served as a toilet and was emptied once a day.

Bored, I sat down on the chair. My glance fell on the wooden tabletop which was scratched with initials and the inevitable hearts with arrows through them. I stood up and looked more closely at the walls. Initials were also there, as well as curses, calendars with small x's crossing off the days, and here and there a vulgar word.

I stood in the middle of my cell and tilted my head to see the sky through the grated window. It seemed to be windy; gray tattered clouds rushed past, between them an occasional blue patch. I tried to forget my surroundings and to recall familiar voices and sounds. Lost in thought, I heard the cell door being unlocked and turned around.

A slender young girl entered, holding a sheaf of blue lined paper under her arm and pencils in her hand. With a friendly smile, she said softly, "Good day, Miss Schroeder. I hope you have already adjusted a bit." She continued loudly, "Here is some stationery. After twenty-four hours in custody you are permitted to write home, and after that once a month."

She placed a sheet of notepaper and a pencil on the rickety table. "The mail will be picked up after supper," she said — then added in a whisper, "Do you want me to send a message?"

I shook my head and tried to hold back my tears.

Katherina had suggested Miss Hoffmann as a messenger. She belongs to a group of Catholic friends and was completing her probationary period as a social worker in the prison.

The heavy bunch of keys jangled against the cell door. I was alone again, pacing back and forth, trying to dry my tears. Six steps to the door, six steps back to the window, six steps . . .

I felt like a sheep with the staggers — and then I became angry with myself. I thought about Erich and Alwin Kohlhöfer in the penitentiary, of Max Fuchs in the men's wing and all the others I had heard about. I realized that I was behaving like a silly goose— and my tears dried up.

Sometime or other I received something to eat; I no longer remember what. About an hour later a matron with a sly look came and gave me a quick inspection. "Come to the courtyard."

The yard, a dismal place surrounded by prison walls, served as the exercise area. The inmates ran around this square for a half hour, in single file at a prescribed distance from each other. Since the prison was evidently well occupied, we had to go in two shifts.

A young person in front of me slowed down, came closer to me and whispered, "Why are you here?"

"Political," I whispered back.

She then quickened her steps.

In about three minutes everyone was in the know.

The woman in front of me seemed to trip. She had apparently already developed a routine for collecting news. "How long?"

"Two months," I murmured.

While the news of a new "political" was making the rounds, a lanky woman of about forty was called from our ranks. She was not wearing prison clothes but had on a gray suit. This meant, I learned, that she was in detention pending trial. After a relatively short time she returned, without change of expression as far as I could see. However, the whole courtyard buzzed with conjecture.

In my cell again I picked up the lined blue paper with the return address "Penal Institution, Frankfurt am Main—Preungesheim" and wrote:

100

Dear Parents:

I am well. I even slept the first night, although not very softly. The food is sufficient; in any case, I am not hungry. I am alone and therefore have time to meditate — which is perhaps not the purpose of my present whereabouts.

Today, during exercize in the prison courtyard, a woman was called out. She was informed of her sentence: five years in the penitentiary for criminal abortions.

Don't worry about me. I am in the best of company.

With my fondest regards,
your Lili.

The second night was not much better than the first. Because of the enforced early bedtime I awoke between three and four in the morning, and then waited until my water jug was filled around five o'clock.

I had repeatedly deciphered everything scratched on the walls and sat in front of my table looking at the initials for the umpteenth time. I was trying to imagine exactly who my predecessors might have been and why they were here, when the key rattled in my cell door.

I stood up and faced a small lean woman who barely reached my shoulder. A pair of piercing eyes were concealed behind glittering eyeglasses. Her gray hair, parted in the middle, was held together on the back of her head in a modest knot.

"I am Mrs. Schäfer, the head matron," she said and reached into a pocket which was concealed in the folds of her black dress. She held my letter to my parents in her hand.

"Schroeder, you wrote a letter which we can't allow to go through. You are in prison as a prisoner — not to write editorials. It is completely incomprehensible how you could have learned all this. You will get another sheet of paper."

While leaving, she turned around again. "Moreover, in the future, you will no longer go into the yard with the others."

A while later, a matron appeared to take me to the doctor. She pushed me into the room and disappeared, closing the door behind her.

The physician, Dr. Strüder, rose and greeted me with a friendly handshake. He asked how I felt.

101

Somewhat insecure, I replied, "Thank you. Considering the circumstances, very well."

"Miss Schroeder" — yes, he put 'Miss' before my name — "you can trust me. I know about you and I assure you I will do everything in my power to make your situation easier. Please tell me how I can help you."

I hesitated a moment before answering. "Dr. Dessecker, my attending physician, warned me against chills. I am freezing. It is cold in this building."

He nodded. "You will get warmer underwear and I will prescribe a diet for you. I am sorry that I can't do more."

I looked at him astonished.

"Your case has caused a lot of discussion. After all, your father's name means something in Frankfurt."

The days and nights crawled by. I was like a dog running back and forth without aim or purpose. Suddenly I discovered the magic of a silent soliloquy: a kind of dialogue of jumbled thoughts and ideas. At that moment the four dreadful walls which encircled me crumbled. The monotony of confinement lost its power, contrary to the intention of my persecutors. And I discovered that if I walked in a figure eight, the cell lost its narrowness and my thoughts no longer bounced back at me from the walls. The caged-dog attitude of reconciling myself to the inescapable disappeared.

My first question was: Who has the right to issue laws which are contrary to the essence of life?

Had not God already said "Thou shalt and thou shalt not"?

Forgotten incidents from former years returned as if they had just occurred. Time intervals disappeared; actions and events were joined together without interruption.

I was back at the Saalbau, leaning against a pillar during intermission, when my glance fell on this curious couple. He was barely of medium height with crafty gray eyes, a gray beard, and a potbelly. She was so much younger she could easily have been his daughter. Her flaxen hair was wound around her head in pigtails. From the pink-cheeked face her inquisitive eyes looked at me while he observed me partly amused, partly concerned, obviously giving her his comments about me. I knew this couple, having met them for months during the concerts and I seemed always to be the focus of their interest.

Even remembering them made me laugh now. Mr. Pötz—

which was his name—made me think of an ageing chubby faun, on whose words the young, healthy Gretchen hung, as if they were revelations. Sporadically I met both of them or Pötz alone. What he did professionally remained a secret for me. At any rate, he was a philosopher, had a considerable knowledge of history at his disposal, held very outspoken political views, and was not religious.

One day we were seated in the Kakao Stube at the Katharinenpforte and he leaned back importantly in his chair, his jacket open and his thumbs hooked into his old suspenders. "In what language, my dear friend, do you believe God was speaking?"

His head was tilted back and a mocking smile played around the corners of his mouth. "What did this God say to the Neanderthal man or to the African caveman who could scarcely have known more than ten or fifteen sounds? Did he say 'ugh-ugh'? The translation of God's original sounds into our contemporary speech is truly remarkable! And what did this God look like? We have, to be sure, an absolutely authentic tradition that God created man out of clay in his own image. According to what we know today about our ancestors, our heavenly Father must have been a hairy giant."

Moving his hand through his gray hair, he said reflectively, "A mystery which I simply cannot fathom is why did he equip his image with reproductive organs? Why did he have to create two sexes? These two sexes required the invention of a snake, an apple, and a fig leaf. Was the fall of man perhaps nothing else than the beginning of deceit from higher ups? Or did this originate as a fantasy of a psychopathic prophet?"

Sitting back again, Pötz looked at me with a somewhat indulgent smile. "This kind father of mankind demanded that Abraham slaughter his son — naturally, only in order to test him. This all-powerful, all-knowing God was made from the mold of tyrants — the first of an endless chain of merciless tyrants, who invented wicked lies to make faithful slaves of their followers."

After a longer silence, he concluded aloud, "The prophets took shelter behind the word *God* to indulge in their pathological ideas of power."

As Pötz disappeared like a shadow through the no longer existing walls, I thought to myself that Hitler is nothing new. He only found an economically depressed people whom he taught to believe in the idea of the Thousand Year Reich. Hitler is only half a Messiah, half a Christ. He speaks of a Thousand Year Reich, whereas Christ supposedly said, "My kingdom is a thousand years and no more than a thousand years"? Is that to say we approach the end of the intolerant, bloody Christendom? Would we . . .

A matron unlocked my cell door to fetch me for my solitary walk in the courtyard.

The first day I marched around the square, bored and alone. On the second day a face appeared behind a barred basement window. A pair of brown eyes in a pale face, framed with red curls, followed me. On the third tour I smiled at her; on the fourth, she opened the window (we had a pole with a hook for this purpose) and asked my name; and the fifth time around I knew her name was Alice. Alice then expected me every day. I presume she shoved her table against the window and placed the chair on top of it to see out. She was a prostitute imprisoned for fourteen days because of a violation: she had solicited a man instead of waiting for his approach.

My thoughts often returned to my home. I imagined the endless telephone conversations between Etta and mother. The temperamental Etta was deeply outraged but at the same time she tried to calm mother.

And father? — What were his thoughts now?

A few years ago he had read to me from the *Völkischen Beobachter* parts of Hitler's speeches. In his opinion Hitler was confronting the Allies in the right way.

Germany is rising out of the ashes and father is witnessing the resurrection of his country. A few weeks before my imprisonment, the Third Reich celebrated Armed Forces Day. The garrison officers were received in the Römer, where an emperor was once crowned. In the evening there was a great torchlight tattoo in Opernplatz. Possessed by patriotic hysteria, Frankfurt's and its suburbs' population enthusiastically cheered this event. Instead of participating in this great day with pride in his heart, father remained at home with his Jewish wife and his 'convict' daughter.

And now Father is proud because Germany is again a military power. Will he never understand that borders are made by man and are unnatural? Does he really believe that the German on this side a few steps away from the frontier is better than the Frenchman on the other side? The clouds which sail through the skies above us know no boundaries. The flowers do not care whether they bloom on German or French soil — or on the middle of the border.

While these thoughts went through my head I kept pacing my cell in a figure eight.

Mother had often told me how depressed father was about Germany's losing the war.

I don't understand it. Wasn't he depressed by the mass murder and the terrible mutilation? How can a doctor, a scientist, be for militarism and war? He who has pledged the Hippocratic oath to do everything in his power to save life . . . Does a physician not break his pledge if he condones war?

A few months ago Father started a new project; he wants to find a means to destroy the tuberculosis bacillus. A great idea which could save countless lives. Why then does he not reject the idea of war — which extinguishes the lives of millions of young healthy people? Why fight against tuberculosis?

Mother tried to raise me as a good Christian; father wanted to make me a good German. I felt like laughing at the irony in the result of their efforts.

Father probably no longer had any illusions about my patriotic feelings.

Why was I in prison? Was I being punished because I said the truth or because I spread a lie? How would I ever find out? With every step I repeated, "Truth? — Lie? — Truth? — Lie?" Finally I sat down on the chair exhausted.

I reflected that it was all a bad joke. Probably everyone locked up here knew why. The short fat woman in the next cell, whom I saw in the morning when our water jugs were filled, is here because of theft. Alice because of soliciting. Even the pale young woman who managed the prison library knows why she will spend the next three years here. She was an active communist until recently. But I? Is it because of the truth or because of a lie?

One morning the head matron appeared and pulled a letter out of the pocket of her pleated skirt. The letter was from my parents and already opened.

"Here, Schroeder — because it is your birthday. I wish you well for your next year." She became silent. Whatever else she wanted to say she kept to herself.

Living somewhat timelessly, I had forgotten that it was my birthday.

While I sat at the table, my hand covering my forehead and

105

eyes in order to think undisturbed, I heard the faint noise of metal grating against metal. I looked at the door, but the peephole was shut. How long had I been secretly observed? I stood up again and began pacing my cell.

What would my next birthday be like? Would I spend the future years as an outsider, debarred from my profession — perhaps from any career? How many hateful eyes, expressly schooled in the Third Reich, would find peepholes to spy on me, so as to denounce me and then to convict me? Would I have to be constantly on my guard like a hunted animal?

My thoughts ran into emptiness. I had reached a dead end. My fantasy deserted me and I stared into a monotonous gray nothingness.

Automatically I reached for mother's letter which the matron had brought. The large, undisciplined, barely readable handwriting of my small dainty mother gushed forth on the paper with meaningless and exaggerated assertions of love. God's blessings and the suffering and love of Christ were emphasized. Father added in clear small letters, "We are thinking of you. Be brave!"

The humor of mother's perception of me in contrast with my real personality overwhelmed me.

I fought against an almost hysterical fit of laughter when I suddenly imagined Pötz, the aging faun complete with the gray beard which gave prominence to his receding chin and his small eyes which could narrow to slits then open wide for theatrical effect.

I remembered his asking, "Do you really understand my dear young friend how closely the military is related to the church?"

He slid his thumbs from under his suspenders, the slits of his eyes opened. "No? Haven't you noticed that from all the sins which the church invented, it intentionally omitted one: the sin against peace? No? You see! You surely know the military was created to preserve peace. But in the two thousand years of Christianity the military has never upheld peace, but only conducted wars. And the more civilized, the more sophisticated we become as well. The army of mercenaries has been replaced by the people's army, where it is every man's privilege to be armed and fight.

"While the Church is very strict concerning sins and the Ten Commandments, she has special interpretations when her position is endangered. For these special cases, she does not flatly command 'Thou shalt not kill'; but changes it to 'Thou shalt not kill, except in war.' Mass murder is permitted. The Church blesses the weapons for a bloodbath. The generals, these masters of mass murder, enjoy the respect and prestige of the church fathers and society in general. However, if all the dead the generals have on their conscience were to putrefy right in their brains, the generals would stink from their nostrils like vultures."

I shuddered involuntarily.

His hand reached across the table towards me, without touching me. With an indulgent smile, he said, "Don't look at me so aghast. One can't learn history in a romantic mood."

"Whoever created this world permitted himself a cynical joke with the invention of Christianity ... two thousand years of hypocrisy and lies, of celibacy and whoring, of charity and mass murder — in the name of God or f o r God, as in the Crusades and the 'holy wars.' Hand in hand the church and the military wander on the paths of destruction. They personify the shadow of death, which hovers over mankind." Suddenly he laughed noiselessly, "And all that is done to please God."

Father Dietz, the Catholic prison chaplain, visited me. He is a mild old man with white hair, who did not make the slightest effort to speak in a religious manner. He said only that he came to see me.

During the few minutes he spent in my cell, I asked, "Do you know Max Fuchs?"

He nodded.

"How is he?"

"He's fine." He saw my doubtful expression and smiled reassuringly. "Really."

"Would you," I asked hesitantly, "deliver my greetings?"

"I will," the old man said. "He will be glad."

Alone again, I continued pacing my cell like a polar bear. At first I thought about Max. What kind of crazy people could lock up someone because he loves? What does love or the heart have to do with race? Who could dare to act as a judge in these matters? Who can maintain that one race is superior and the other inferior? Probably one had to be a stunted German like the brown-haired Hitler with his somewhat Slavic cheekbones, or be a little Mickey Mouse like Goebbels, whose inferiority complex combined with envy inspired him to promote the Germanic race and a breed of supermen.

I began to brood more and more, and ended up as I so fre-

107

quently did, with the question: Why was I in prison? Because I have different opinions from the current rulers?

To lock people up because of their convictions is not only medieval but stupid and shortsighted. The best method to increase contempt and hatred is political arrest. Today's dictators should have reached this conclusion long before now. They should have learned from their own experience that imprisonment is not a means of political persuasion, but often produces the opposite results.

I thought about today's rulers, while walking around my cell in a figure eight, about the current German rulers and the heads of state in other countries. What is the difference? Monarchy, republic, democracy, or whatever the country is called, with very few exceptions the rulers are dictators who force their subordinates into spiritual straitjackets. They determine what is moral and immoral, and why one should be sent to prison, penitentiary or concentration camp, and where one dies, for what flag and when. These "servants of the people," paid by the people, have long ago forgotten the pretty promises they made to reach their goal. Once in power they maintain their positions whatever happens. The doubters who believe that they can demand their money's worth from their servants must be rendered harmless. The skeptics are placed behind locks and bars, or their existence destroyed through defamation. Doubt and skepticism are extremely dangerous and could shake the whole power structure.

But despite this, we cannot be robbed of our thoughts; thoughts have wings and can overcome everything. They can pass through the thick walls of this cell, which for me are the symbol of our rulers.

I paced my figure eight faster and faster. On this day a new me was born. For the first time in my life I felt a deep hatred rise in me. Sentimentality and self-pity finally evaporated. During those hours I realized that I should save my feelings for matters of the heart. The struggle for life as it appears now required toughness and a cool head.

It certainly was an unfortunate coincidence that just the next morning the supervisor appeared in my cell. A short, plump woman who did her duty impersonally, she explained that since I was in solitary I would probably welcome something to do. I could go to the sewing room and do needlework for the Winter Relief.

108

Standing straight up so that I grew a bit taller, I felt my heart beat faster. I must have looked like an apparition when I said with a rigid expression, "You don't seem to know why I am here. I will not move a finger for the Winter Relief!"

The woman looked at me just as rigidly; something like fury glittered in her eyes. "In the event you change your mind, you can have me called."

"Thank you," I said icily. "I definitely will not trouble you to come here any more."

She looked perplexed for a moment and then left.

From then on, my prison term continued uneventfully. During the day I was alone with my thoughts; and at night, with my dreams, which often grew into nightmares.

I remembered that one of Wolf's last admonitions was "Keep smiling."

Involuntarily I began smiling as I paced my endless figures eight repeating "Keep smiling — keep smiling!"

Finally I sat down and rubbed my aching face. "How crazy can you be!" I said aloud. My thoughts wandered back to what Wolf told me about Madison Avenue with its gigantic advertisement agencies, something we do not have here. Apparently all kinds of techniques to influence public opinion are available to these giant firms. Newspapers, magazines, and radio stations are used to hammer their opinions into the empty heads of the American population. They are the ones who are responsible for elevating the man favored by influential circles to the presidency, whereas the man with character and his own initiative would certainly die a political death.

I began to think about the phenomenon of Madison Avenue. I moved faster in my cell to keep pace with my thoughts.

There are two great centers in this world — a secular and a clerical. One has its headquarters on Madison Avenue, the other is located in the Vatican. The main task of both of them seems to be to hold the masses in a state of stupidity. They are successful — only too successful. Their techniques are completely different, but the result is the same. The worldly power drums political slogans into the people, until it becomes second nature to them and they believe all the nonsense preached to them in so many variations. The clerical power reaches its goal with threats of sin and eternal purgatory. When the unfortunate believer does something

109

which does not fit into the religious concept he has committed a sin. This sin is the first step on the road to purgatory. It is fantastic how hunger for power has developed all these perverse methods.

I thought about Hitler who, with fanatical intensity, makes all kinds of promises to a believing people. How easy it is to influence the masses. Examined more closely, it is a matter of herd mentality: in one case a smiling and in the other a very serious herd of sheep. I suddenly remembered that in America there is a certain day proclaimed when all the men wear straw hats to inaugurate summer. What would happen, I reflected, if Hitler — or even Goebbels — moved onto Madison Avenue? I imagined millions of smiling Americans marching in brown uniforms, with right hands extended in salute, shouting a friendly "Hi."

I looked through the window at the sky and thought about the city. I wondered if Karl was now in the Hauptwache. I saw him before me with his smoothly combed hair that fell over his forehead during lively conversations, his bright eyes able to command and beg, and his sensitive, expressive hands, which always reminded me of hands in Gothic paintings. Then suddenly Sjöderbloom rose between Karl and me. Sjöderbloom is as tall as Karl and so much older than I that he probably feels this a handicap.

I stood still in the middle of my cell. Can one be in love with two men at the same time? Didn't I have time, here in isolation, to make up my mind? Then, all of a sudden, both disappeared as I realized that Hitler would also make this decision for me. An ice-cold feeling crept into my heart.

A prison matron who ocasionally came into my cell for a short chat, reminded me of Hitler's birthday and the prospect of an amnesty. That was what Jelkmann expected too. However, April 20 came and went, and nothing happened. The days really began to creep by. With every new morning my hopes shrunk and gave way to a slight depression.

On Saturday the 25th, after supper, I decided to resign myself to the inevitable and rather forget about Jelkmann's forecast of an amnesty. Saturday was the worst day as far as food was concerned, and I had so hoped not to experience another one in jail. We were given potatoes boiled in a net still covered with earth. Every prisoner received in his cell such a dirty slippery net with a herring, an entire fish with head, tail and entrails.

After I had choked down the meal and cleaned the stinking fish off the plate as well as I could manage, I endeavoured to forget

110

that there ever was a chance for me to escape these walls earlier than the court had decided. I had to overcome this impasse so as not to lose my inner resiliency.

Suddenly a matron unlocked the cell door. "Come along."

I went to the door.

"No," she said. "Take your things with you, but hurry. You have been released."

Later I sat in the study with my parents and Katherina. Somehow the evening seemed unreal like a dream.

Although the room was familiar, a strange phenomenon occurred. I perceived all colors and odors with great intensity. They all were exaggerated. The soap smelled overly perfumed, the wine had such a sweet aroma that it sickened me. I tried to smoke a cigarette but put it out after several drags because it tasted simply awful. Moreover, Katherina's presence gave me a vague feeling of uneasiness. I wondered if I had already developed a psychosis and was seeing ghosts everywhere.

I grew increasingly monosyllabic, which led father to the comment that I was probably overtired. Thankfully I withdrew and crawled into bed exhausted. Somehow I was disappointed by my first night at home, feeling like a guest in my own room.

The next day the flowers arrived and I learned that Sjöderbloom had called twice a day since amnesty was announced on the 20th, with the impatient question, "Still nothing new?"

April 30, 1936

This evening after supper I was seated at my desk when Katherina came in. She asked lovingly how I was. We exchanged a few insignificant words.

And then my darling sister said with a shaky, emotion-laden voice, "Pastor Perabo from St. Gallus sends greetings, and said he was so sorry you had been in prison. If he had only known, he would have gone to the Gestapo himself and said that he had spread the rumor. If you want, you should come to visit him. He would be pleased."

For a moment I felt dizzy because it hit me like a blow. Naturally this Pastor Perabo had known that I was sentenced by the Special Court; and of course Katherina had known all the time who the mysterious priest was on that evening.

111

I breathed deeply and said in a choked voice, "Tell your Pastor Perabo that he should be happy and thank his creator if I don't visit him. If I came, the walls would come crashing down!"

I went to the door, opened it and exclaimed, "Go!" Then said to the door, closed behind her, "You god-damned pig! You have sacrificed your own sister for your priest!"

May 5, 1936

Yesterday morning I received a call from the Gestapo. Officer Mohr, whom I had casually met during my years as a journalist, asked me politely to come for a talk.

However courteously such an invitation from the Gestapo is phrased, one does not respond with a counter question. One goes.

So today at 11 A.M. I was at the Gestapo. My senses, grown more acute, caused me to observe that on the left side of the room a door to another office stood ajar.

I walked up to Mohr. He is a tall slim man with short light-blond hair, the prototype of the ideal Germanic male. He was seated at his desk, his back against the window so that one could scarcely see his face while he could not miss the slightest change of expression on his victim's.

After we exchanged a few friendly comments, he said, "Miss Schroeder, we have received instructions to ask you once more about the source of your rumor."

"So?" I wondered and stared at him. "About the source?"

"You know the source."

I nodded thoughtfully and then replied, "Mr. Mohr, I thought this question was settled by the Special Court."

"Not for us. The court may have taken your statements at face value and based its judgment on them. But we don't." Insidiously he added, "We believe that your sister spread the rumor. She is, after all, the Catholic in your family. So admit it! It was she, wasn't it?"

"Oh, do you really believe that? Mr. Mohr, if I actually knew it, do you seriously believe that having been to prison, I would afterwards satisfy your curiosity?" I laughed openly.

Mohr and I stood up simultaneously. We stood facing each other with the cheap office desk between us. He opened its middle drawer and removed a revolver which he held threateningly in his hand. "I can do otherwise."

112

I nodded. Staking everything on one card, I said ironically, half laughing, "Naturally you can shoot me, but dead people don't talk!"

At that moment a sympathetic baritone voice sounded behind me, "Mohr, put the gun down!"

I turned around and looked into a pair of gray eyes. Our gaze caught and held each other. He was of medium height, with blondish gray curly hair, wearing a grayish-green sport suit with knickers, gray socks, and brown crêpe-soled shoes.

"All right, who was it?" the newcomer asked. "It was certainly your sister!"

"I think I have answered this question sufficiently already and apparently you have also heard our conversation."

"But you know who it was," he said positively. "Won't you tell us?"

"I had enough time in prison to ponder. Even there I could not remember."

Mohr interrupted, "Commissioner, should I?"

The commissioner made a defensive gesture while we looked at each other.

"You won't tell us?" he asked almost doubtfully.

I shook my head. "I no longer remember."

He considered the matter briefly and apparently struggled with himself. "Very well, Miss Schroeder. You can deceive a court, but not us. I will tell you who it was—your sister."

He paused, while I was seized with a feeling of panic. I thought about my incorrigible father with his regular cronies, about the telephone conversations and about . . .

I do not know what this Gestapo commissioner read in my face, because he continued, "You don't say either yes or no? Silence is also an answer." He turned to Mohr. "Close the file. The interrogation has resulted in nothing new."

I was then dismissed.

I returned home just in time for lunch. On the stairs I heard father on the telephone making an extremely disparaging remark about "brown nurses." [i.e. belonging to the Nazi Nurse Association]

An icy hand clasped my throat as I went to the wardrobe to hang up my coat. I heard father say, "Thanks, Mr. Bergenhoff. Yes, well until Tuesday evening. Good-bye."

113

I forced myself to smile when I greeted father with a kiss and said, "Please, please be careful on the telephone."

"But why?" he asked utterly astonished.

"We never know who is listening in."

"Nonsense. You're seeing ghosts, little one."

Am I seeing ghosts? The lawyer Bergenhoff, whose Jewish wife suffers from melancholia under the Third Reich, is one of father's regular cronies. There is also the president of the Senate, a leading German Nationalist party member, known as an enemy of the Nazis, and four or five other gentlemen friends. They sit every Tuesday evening in the Thomas Bräu and curse the Nazis. Who would know if a Gestapo official was seated at the next table? Father has learned nothing from his earlier difficulties in the hospital and from my arrest. It is simply unimaginable for the head doctor of a leading hospital to feel threatened by the little street rowdies.

I picked at my food and tried to sit up straight, although I had such severe stomach cramps that I would have rather curled up on my couch.

May 14, 1936

Sjöderbloom had written father that he was no longer able to participate in our chamber-music evenings. So as we sat, as we often did, in his large peaceful study, I tried to solve the mystery.

"Signore, why won't you come to our musical evenings any more?"

His friendly face became serious, almost hard. "Do you know that your mother wrote a letter to me on my birthday?"

"Yes. She told me that she wrote and sent you tea roses."

"Did she also tell you what she wrote?"

I shook my head.

He struggled with himself for a moment. Then he said, "She is after all your mother. Anyway, I will never again set foot in your parents' home."

After a long pause I interrupted the silence. "I'm terribly sorry, Signore, but I fear I could scarcely change anything in this situation."

"Will you still come to visit me despite this?" I saw the doubt in his eyes.

"What does my mother's letter have to do with me, Signore?"

114

He lifted his glass and we drank to each other. The subject had been firmly closed.

"Would you tell me something about your 'vacation'?"

"Certainly. What do you want to know? What the daily routine was? Or how I converted myself into an ardent Nazi?"

"Yes, everything."

I gave him a short concentrated description.

He had listened attentively and said, "So you are of the opinion that imprisonment — whether jail, penitentiary, or concentration camp — can not change a person's outlook?"

"Absolutely certain. It can not. Until I went to prison, I found the system only unjust and brutal. Since I had so much time to think undisturbed, I have learned to hate from the bottom of my heart. I have understood the absurdity of putting people behind bars because of their convictions. If before such an arrest, one had hidden doubts, they would be left behind bars. Only a coward could be converted to conform to the demands of such a government and cowards are usually cautious enough not to land in prison or to be enticed into such awkward situations. As far as I am concerned I can only say that I left prison a convinced opponent."

Thoughtfully he exhaled a cloud of smoke. "What you have said, Signorina, is very plausible." He pensively inhaled the smoke again. "Have you ever thought about what right the government has to force its convictions on you?"

"Yes, Signore, I have given it much thought and concluded that a totalitarian state, in any case, takes the right of absolute control over the lives of its citizens. A monarchy only determines where, when, and for what, one had to die or be crippled for life. Under National Socialism, in addition to this, the citizen is even ordered whom he may or may not love."

I am busy collecting the ruins of my life, to try to put things together into a half way workable structure. The only marketable item I have to offer is my competence as a typist. I looked around for independent secretarial work where I did not have to produce any Aryan identification. Even I.G. Farben demands an Aryan identification from their newly hired secretaries; although not as far back as 1800, it goes only up to one's grandparents.

I found my first job through an advertisement. Thus, I wrote for many hours daily: "Dear Sirs! The problem of clogged water pipes should not be unfamiliar to you. We however have . . ." I wrote this to hospitals, sanatoriums, industrial firms, and so on. My employer represents a firm which sells chemicals and filters to prevent calcium deposits from accumulating in water pipes.

Pastor Walde asked if I would take down in shorthand several theological essays which would appear collectively in book form.

This is a way of killing time and also earning some money. Although without help from my parents, I could not cover my living expenses. With a sinking heart I have to admit to myself that I cannot continue this way for long. I must decide on something else. The Third Reich will certainly be with us for many more years.

June 5, 1936

Several days ago, Pötz called to arrange a meeting at the Kakao Stube.

He looked at me attentively, his eyes seemed to examine every feature of my face. He nodded silently, leaned against the back of his chair, and anchored his thumbs under his suspenders. "What have your parents said about your somewhat unusual sojourn?"

"They were terribly worried about me."

"So?" He repeated the statement with a mild irony: "They were worried about you. Tell me, my dear, didn't your parents also worry about you before you were born? You don't know? Have your parents ever asked you if you wanted to come into this world? No? Naturally not, parents are egotists. They want to have children. They fulfill their personal, selfish wish without ever considering that perhaps the child does not want to have them as parents, and does not want to come into this world anyhow."

With raised eyebrows, he smiled at me in a superior fashion, "I will divulge something else to you, my friend, you don't owe your parents anything. It is just the other way around. You have fulfilled your parents' wish and have appeared. Your parents owe you an apology every day for the life they imposed on you and for which you didn't ask."

He waited silently for the effect of his words.

"But is it not a law of nature to propagate, in order to preserve the species?"

"Yes, it is a law of nature, but there are many objections. I will give you only a few. It is maintained that man differs from animals in so far as he can think. I honestly doubt that, if he could think, he

116

would learn from the animals." Pötz suddenly leaned towards me. "Have you ever heard that a bird comes from a rich or a poor home? Is it ever known in any animal family that the young have greater chances for a good future because their father is someone special or has special connections? No, in the animal world, there is no order of precedence and the young all have equal chances in life.

"Mankind, however, has divided society into classes. With few exceptions, the rich high-ranking people produce fewer children, while the poor breed more than they can feed. Without thinking or understanding they multiply until space is too crowded and existence put into question. And thus we come to my second objection: When people have multiplied enough, and there is an excessive supply available, then war is initiated to eliminate the surplus. I have never heard that animals of the same species fall into rank and file to mutually murder each other. This is reserved for humans. Man, who is intellectually superior to animals, has not even understood the most primitive laws of life."

He let go of his suspenders, ran one hand through his gray hair, and smoothed his goatee with the other. His mouth curled into a smile, while his head moved back and forth. "You are so wonderfully young that one can still read your face. You have not yet learned to wear a mask. And somehow you recognized during your forced isolation that Pötz sometimes has very sensible ideas. That is no reason to blush, my child. Anyway, do you not agree with what I said about parents?"

As I nodded silently, he asked amiably, "If one had given you the choice to live through the Third Reich — and I hope that you survive it — or to slumber on the petal of a waterlily in the pond from which babies are fished, would you have picked this life?"

I hesitated before I responded, "I don't think so."

"You don't think so? But you have never thought about it? Naturally not. You have not even considered that you can thank your parents for the Third Reich. Weren't your parents the ardent royalists, the patriotic and the dedicated opponents of socialism? Am I mistaken?"

I looked at the table and shook my head involuntarily.

"You see. Your parents are ostensibly educated, intelligent people; but like the whole class to which they belong, they have neither understood nor drawn advice from the lessons of history. They merely decided to become parents, like Hitler decided to become a politician. Your parents, my dear, didn't have the responsi-

117

bility to ask the question if this world offered their child any kind of future or if it would be better that the unborn remained unborn."

After a short silence, he asked, "Would you like to have children?"

"No, I would not have the courage — I am not willing to produce cannon fodder. Apart from that, in times like these, when race is such an important factor . . . ." I broke off.

Pötz folded his hands over his stomach, looked at me with large eyes, and ended the sentence for me, "In times such as these, you think you shouldn't burden a child with a Jewish descent. Very well. As I said before, one has left you no choice with regard to your parents. If you could have decided yourself, who knows? Perhaps you would have picked as a father a man who is today a Gauleiter?" He laughed soundlessly.

He was silent, his eyes narrowed to slits. "A day will come, when the youth will no longer be led by the nose, but will soberly face their parents and ask: 'Why have you placed us in this miserable world? That we are alive was your pleasure. We have nothing to thank you for, but will go our own way. Continue to amuse yourself. Hold firmly to your outmoded values — and be damned!' "

June 10, 1936

Yesterday, I kept my promise and called Alice, my friend from prison. While her voice came to me over the telephone, I imagined her large brown eyes and red curls.

Slightly embarrassed, she said that she couldn't see me, since she was extremely busy. It was National Artisan's Day. In my middle-class milieu, I had never given any importance to this day, nor considered the horizontal consequences for street walkers in the railroad district.

My interest in Artisan's Day aroused, I fetched yesterday's newspaper from the rack. Frankfurt has been declared City of German Handicraft. Like everything that the Nazis do, they staged this event with great pomp.

After the official ceremonies, a flood of craftsmen poured into the city. In all the wine taverns and saloons, they sat and drank to the Führer. They were filled with new self-esteem and did not doubt for a moment their importance and greatness. Mastercraftsman Piefke, who had tried in vain to be a pillar of society in some god-forsaken place, was suddenly pronounced an important person by the heads of government. Bombastic and feeling important, filled with sweet wine, intoxicated by the Thousand Year Reich, far from wife and child, the mastercraftsmen kissed all the prostitutes they could find and fell into their beds.

June 12, 1936

Today, in the late afternoon, while I was waiting for a tram at the Hauptwache, Karl came up to me. "You'll surely drink a glass of wine with me?"

He grasped me by the arm, turned me around, and pushed me in the direction of Eschenheimer Gasse.

We entered Einmuth's wine tavern. The head waiter Plaum, with his knowing smile, offered us a table in a niche.

"What have you been doing with yourself?"

"I sought temporary employment as a typist."

"As a typist?"

I nodded and he did not press me further.

"And what are you doing Karl?"

"I must recover from the craftsmen's day." He took a large gulp from the glass that Plaum had placed in front of him. "Those mad bums!" And then he was silent again.

"In addition to observing the events in general, I made several nightly visits to saloons in the old town and talked with the people. God!" His slender nervous hand moved over his forehead and eyes. "Were they drunk! They live in a permanent state of intoxication brought about by self admiration and enthusiasm for the Führer and the Reich. It is frightening to see what the Nazis, in so short a time, have made of these basically simple modest people." Karl stared at the glass in front of him, and then emptied it.

He again became aware of my presence and with typical gentle irony continued his comments. "Do you know that Hitler has revived the sixteenth century because he can't understand the twentieth century." He began to laugh.

I laughed with him, but then I said, "Wasn't it time that artisans were set on their feet again?"

"Absolutely. The appalling thing is the psychology the Nazis use to obligate everyone. Inwardly, even the small artisan from Podunk knows that without the Nazis he would fall back to his old social position. He will thus do everything in his power to support the system and preserve it." Karl emptied his second glass. Plaum took it and looked at him inquiringly. Karl's thoughts raced ahead and he nodded absentmindedly. "Rearmament is occurring on all fronts, including the production of children. The decline of the birthrate is labeled as racial suicide. Every healthy citizen must consider it a holy task to produce a sufficient number of children."

"The production of German people shall be brought into full swing?" I asked.

"Hitler requires cannon fodder and the assurance that replacements are ready for those who will be destroyed in his war. Moreover, he probably has the tactics of the Catholic Church in mind. What the Catholic Church alleges as a religious reason against contraception is hogwash. They want to have as many Catholic children as possible, to have the numerical superiority to overpower the others. Hitler plans the same thing. He will convert the German woman into a breeding machine and persuade her to be proud of this. He needs at least a million new people. . . ."

"Karl." I grasped his hand which nervously moved back and forth over the table with a cigarette between its fingers.

"You don't believe me?" he asked irritably. "You will find out! Unfortunately mankind has not yet understood that by being blessed with children they are feeding power-hungry ambitious men. Women will thus produce children with the same pride with which the craftsman forges iron or the Nordic German puts on an SS uniform."

He smoked a few puffs before he stubbed out his cigarette. Staring at the glowing ashes, he continued, "Somebody told me about a play that was produced in Munich shortly after the war. I believe it survived only three performances. The young author made a statement which I now remember frequently. 'Whom the gods love, they shower with gifts of stupidity; and whom they hate, they punish with intelligence.'" He clasped his forehead and muttered, "I believe that now, you, I, and our friends are hated by the gods."

June 29, 1936

My work for Pastor Walde is finished. I have also written all the letters about the calcified water pipes.

For a week now I have worked mornings for father. He dictates his medical reports for the National Insurance Company and letters to scientists and IG Farben, which is beginning to be interested in his tuberculosis research.

After father's vacation, at the end of August, I will be trained in the laboratory of the Bürgerhospital, and when I have also received my driving license, I plan to look around for a position as a medical aide.

July 24, 1936

While my parents are on vacation, I take care of the house and Dr. Strüder watches over the Bürgerhospital. As long as I can remember, father had always entrusted the wards to his head assistant. But this year, taking this opportunity to help a friend, he found it absolutely essential to find a substitute. Since Dr. Strüder's name was included in the official list of replacements, father was able to place the internal medicine division in his hands for four weeks.

Feeling that this might be the last time, for a long while, when I could be lazy, I make myself comfortable. Apart from Siegrid, whom I saw frequently, I occasionally met one or another of my somewhat neglected friends.

Occasionally on the weekend, I had dates with Stephani, a Butzbach penitentiary director. We usually meet halfway between Frankfurt and Butzbach, in Bad Nauheim, Bad Homburg, or Giessen. I travelled by tram or by train, while he drove up in his small D.K.W. He let me take over the steering wheel and gave me instructions, when I told him that I had to get a driver's license.

September 1, 1936

My parents returned refreshed, recovered, and far removed from thoughts of the Third Reich.

After the Olympic flame was extinguished on August 16th, our Führer apparently forgot that he had spoken about a festival of peace and understanding between peoples when he opened the games. One week after the Olympics ended, he decided that military service would be extended from one to two years.

Reading the news and shaking my head, I wondered how many good German citizens would wonder why Hitler waited with this decision until the last Olympic guest had left Germany.

On Saturday, I met Stephani again. After supper, we sat in the Homburg casino over a glass of wine, watched the dancing couples, and chatted together.

I no longer remember what caused Stephani's comment. "I am certainly not in favor of the way Hitler treats the Jews. My feelings as a jurist revolt against this. But," he leaned towards me with a crooked smile, "to be honest, I don't like Jews either."

I nodded and fell silent. My thoughts turned topsy-turvy. How would he react if I explained my ancestry to him? Should I have told him at the start of our acquaintance? Was I obliged immediately to warn every man I met? It became intolerable for me to remain in his company any longer.

He had apparently said something, since he touched my arm lightly, "Didn't you hear?"

I suddenly woke up. "Oh," I said and touched my forehead, "Excuse me, I am getting a splitting headache."

Concerned, he asked, "Would you rather go home?"

"Yes."

On arriving at home I wrote him a letter that same night, explaining my regret at not having known his attitude sooner, since it meant the end of our friendship.

This afternoon's mail brought his answer. He thanked me for my honesty and made several polite comments about the time we spent together. However . . .

I could not help it; I had to laugh aloud.

The next moment the door opened and mother came into the room. I stood leaning against the desk, holding in my hand the pages with the handwriting which was familiar to her.

I still continued to laugh, while mother looked from me to the letter and from the letter to me. "What is it, Lili dear?"

"He doesn't want to have me as the mother of his children!"

"What?" she asked me disconcerted.

"He is an anti-Semite."

"My poor love!" said mother and came towards me.

I made a defensive gesture. "Don't worry! My ancestry saved me from an extremely embarrassing situation. We never made allusion to marriage, let alone that I would be the mother of his children."

September 15, 1936

Slowly I am being initiated into the secrets of the medical laboratory. The small delicate nurse in charge of father's laboratory instructs, with angelic patience, not only me but also the young doctors completing their residences and the new interns fresh from the university. Frequently three of us sit bent over our microscope to count white and red blood corpuscles or to seek bacteria and cocci on dyed slides.

I forgot to mention that I had received my driver's license two weeks ago.

October 1, 1936

Yesterday I spent the evening with Sjöderbloom.

We were conversing about recent books and records, when he suddenly asked, "Tell me, Signorina, how is Mrs. Steinbach doing? You still see her, don't you?"

"Yes, frequently." Knowing to what he alluded, I continued, "The poor woman is possessed by a panicky fear about her sons. The extension of the military service hasn't contributed to her peace of mind."

"How old are the sons?"

"I don't know exactly. The oldest, who was born during the war, was just inducted into the army, and the younger one must join the Labor Service in the near future."

Sjöderbloom inhaled the smoke of his cigarette thoughtfully. "This is up to a point a way of fighting unemployment. But in practice, three years are stolen from the lives of young people." He shook his head.

"Signore, do you believe that only three years will be stolen from them?"

"No," he replied in a resigned manner. "I too believe that this is only the beginning."

He got up abruptly, his hands buried in the pockets of his gray-striped housecoat. "It is a frightening idea that in all probability we must endure this insanity for a second time. Everything will be repeated — all the folly, enthusiasm, murder. It is ghastly." He moved back and forth in the room, the sound of his steps muffled by the carpet. Bonzo lifted his head, yawned and got up drowsily. Sjöderbloom petted his dog's head, "Yes. It's all right, old friend," and sat down again in his chair.

"You were too young during the war . . ." He paused, "You were already born?"

"Yes, just."

"I was a grown man then and was very conscious of the pre-

123

vailing chauvinism and as an Alsatian, with more than mixed feelings. Naturally, the young were in a flush of victory before the first shot fell — if we disregard the one in Sarajevo. They travelled singing to the front in freight cars, decorated with garlands of leaves and flowers. At every train station they were greeted by girls with flower bouquets. They believed they were immortal and victorious." He was silent for a moment and filled our glasses again. "You know, Signorina, Hitler is preparing the people for the same jingoism. And since the majority of the people can't think, they will again be led obediently like lambs to slaughter. However, those who bring this boundless misfortune, sit safe and sound in secure places and speak of sacrifice. Those who shout the loudest about the obligation to fight and sacrifice are always the people who have the assurance that they will not be affected personally, because of their age and position."

When he was silent, I said: "One should let the few heads of state, who are so willing to make war, fight against each other. Perhaps, they would then be somewhat more cautious."

November 4, 1936

On Wednesdays, father has his free afternoon, and I can also dispose of my time independently. Coming from the movies, I strolled through a fog, which gave the streetlamps halos. Everything appeared subdued and mysterious.

At the Eschensheimer Tower I heard rapid steps overtaking me. I turned as Karl put his arm around my shoulder. "What kind of a mousehole have you crawled into? One doesn't see you any more."

"I spend my time in the Bürgerhospital," I answered and added with a laugh, "learning how one can help suffering mankind."

Karl said approvingly, "That is indeed a gigantic task!" After a short silence, he added, "Probably your services will be needed urgently in the near future."

"Karl, do you really believe that we will have war soon?"

"Yes, now more than ever. Don't you know what is happening in Spain?"

"Certainly. There is a revolution there. I wondered how Hitler could send German warships to Spain without anybody objecting."

"The affair with the warships already belongs to the past.

Hitler attempted to find out how far he could go with impunity. Since nothing has happened, he chose Spain as his area for maneuvers."

"I don't understand."

Karl touched his forehead. "I forgot that you are no longer with the press. Have you never heard of the Condor Legion?"

"No."

"But you know that the condor is a large bird?"

I nodded.

"The Condor Legion also flies — but what they drop are bombs."

"They are bombing Spain?" I exclaimed in disbelief.

"Yes, my child. Hermann Göring, the ace fighter pilot in the war, was not empowered, by chance, on the 18th of October to undertake rearmament. So the Germans bomb from the air, and the Italians try out their newest tanks. According to the scanty reports that we receive, it must be horrible. But it is probably harmless compared to what lies ahead for us."

We silently walked on. I asked, "In case of war, would Mussolini fight on Hitler's side?"

"Yes. And if Franco is successful, which he will be with this support, then an apocalyptic triumvirate will be formed. In the end, they will certainly perish, but after what destruction and sacrifice! The munition kings are already rubbing their hands in anticipation of great times soon to come. Steel is now the multiplication table of death."

We walked into Holzhausen Park. The bare wet branches looked ghostly next to the streetlamps, and the bushes glistened darkly. A white fog hung over the lawn becoming grayish on the paths. Our steps and voices seemed held in a damp web.

Karl laughed once briefly and harshly, "Isn't it horrible? Hitler and his politics can't leave us alone even during the meagre minutes we are together. The horror is with us day and night. One can't escape it."

We reached the end of Holzhausen Park, where we could see my parents' house.

"Aren't you coming to the editorial offices again?"

I shook my head silently.

"Why?"

I hesitated, "Karl, what I told you once long ago, is still valid."

125

He tilted his head. "That, my love, is your decision."

Kissing me farewell, he said with a smile that did not allow any doubt: "However much you try to fight against it, we will never really be free of each other."

As I walked towards the house, I turned around once to waive to him before his figure disappeared in the fog.

December 25, 1936

A part of the miserable Christmas holiday is already behind us. With every passing year it grows harder for me to please my parents by celebrating Christmas Eve with them.

I stared obediently at the Christmas tree, but I am afraid that it aroused feelings and thoughts in me contrary to those of the rest of the family. The Lord's birthday is celebrated, although nobody can prove that he actually existed. The holiday of love which was celebrated drove me to compare it with Fasching. Willi Reichert labelled Fasching bottled gaiety. On the prescribed day, the corks are removed and joyfulness explodes at a scheduled time. Yesterday, we celebrated the feast of love in just the same way.

At 6 P.M. on December 24th every Christian is moved to tears and love for all mankind, even if he can't stand them during the rest of the year. The Catholics more than other sects exhibit this love profusely, and hold matins at midnight in all their churches. Their godly love will be poured out over the German people with a special intensity, since all the leading Nazis are Catholics: Hitler, Göring, Goebbels, and Himmler. Following in the footsteps of their Catholic church fathers, they have lodged all those who do not share their convictions in prisons, penitentiaries, and concentration camps. The only soul-saving church which, in the course of time, murdered over nine million people as heretics, witches, and suchlike, serves the Nazis as a shining example. An indefinite doubt makes me wonder whether the Nazis intend to break this record in the name of their master.

December 29, 1936

Christmas Eve fell on a Thursday this year and the holidays were followed by a Sunday. On Monday morning, I appeared impatiently at the breakfast table earlier than the rest of the family.

While drinking my first cup of coffee, my eye automatically

126

wandered over the morning paper, which lay folded at father's place. A black cross stood out boldly from the front page and the name . . .? No, that could not be! I got up and bent over the newspaper. On the upper right-hand corner was a small two-column box captioned General von Seeckt. Under the name it read: "On Sunday night died quite unexpectedly after a brief illness. . . ."

I crawled back to my room and locked the door behind me. In my last letter to him I had expressed, among other things, my fear of an impending war. He had not replied.

I took his letters out of the lower drawer of my desk. Did he die unexpectedly? No, he had prepared me many times for the approaching farewell, but I had not understood. Now I was deeply affected by his death. The chain of self-reproach which began with the words "if only I had," would not stop. Yes, I would have done things differently, had I known the meeting at the train station was the last I would have.

Someone knocked on my door. "Yes?" I said irritably, and realized that I had locked the door. I opened it impatiently.

Mother stood before me with an unhappy look. "Lili dear!"

Before she could even say anything, I interrupted her, "Mother, would you do me a favor? Please don't speak about it."

December 31, 1936

Sjöderbloom asked, "Wasn't General von Seeckt a friend of yours?"

I nodded.

"How did you become acquainted with him?"

I told him about the time I spent in the Odenwald school and my first letter to Seeckt.

"So that's how it was. I always wondered how someone with your point of view could be friends with a general."

"Conversations about certain political views were absolutely tabu. What I liked about him, and what made him a charming friend, was his sensitivity, his fine sense of humor, his love for Mozart, his honesty, and his human warmth. But now . . ." I stopped abruptly and Sjöderbloom looked at me astonished.

As I remained silent, he asked: "What did you want to say?"

"That I reproach myself a thousand times. I had grown fond of him. Strictly speaking, I had the same feelings towards him that I had for my favorite uncle. Probably I simply represented youth

127

for the old man. And he was indescribably lonely. Now all of the 'if only I had's' haunt me."

Sjöderbloom said with a comforting smile, while he placed his hand lightly on my arm, "Signorina, fate doesn't burden us with more than we can carry. If you had given your friend the Sphinx, more than you really felt for him, he would perhaps have been disappointed. Most of our dreams are woven from unfulfilled wishes."

After a brief silence, he asked, "Tell me one more thing: was Seeckt on good terms with the Nazis?"

"No. He loathed them and they made use of him only if they needed him. Otherwise they viewed him with absolute distrust. Why do you ask?"

"Because he was given a state funeral. You surely noticed the flags at half-mast on all public buildings. To an impartial observer, it would look as if all of Germany mourned him."

"I don't know who in Germany mourns his passing. Hitler and his comrades certainly don't. They are probably pleased. Perhaps they express their thanks that their opponent was removed by giving him a state funeral. They also gave Hindenburg a state funeral."

January 3, 1937

Today's Sunday meant the end of a long, comparatively peaceful holiday. Even the Nazis were outwardly relatively inactive for a short time. But that will again be different tomorrow. The people were presented with the Four Year Plan on the 1st of January as a New Year's greeting; in any case, it was already drawn up before Christmas.

January 8, 1937

I came home a while ago. Every time I spend an evening with Sjöderbloom, I am much too awake to go to sleep. I am therefore putting my thoughts on paper. When I close my eyes, I see him before me; this tall, heavy man with gray hair and a childlike smile, who can make the most cutting remarks amiable in his soft voice.

As we sat in his study, Sjöderbloom looked thoughtfully at his wineglass. He turned it playfully several times with his thumbs and forefinger on the stem, took a sip, and said, "The cult of heroes and saints makes the world a play-ground for fanatics and fools. In this

128

government, we have a mixture of both. Fanaticism is, however, sometimes dangerous — for others."

"Without doubt, Hitler has done a great deal for the unemployed—or should we say for the army of poverty stricken and hopeless. However, I still view him as an unimportant little bourgeois who constantly reveals his true self. Strictly speaking, I consider him a historical accident."

Sjöderbloom impulsively raised his glass and drank to me. "Well put, Signorina!" Thoughtfully, he repeated, "A historical accident, a very unfortunate historical mishap." He leaned towards me and said in high spirits: "Do you realize that Hitler is in reality an opportunist?" He smiled in a way that gave something youthful to this tall man with graying hair.

I probably looked at him blankly since he explained, "The Kaiser received his power through birth; Hitler received his from the unemployed."

January 31, 1937

Hitler's mandate was extended yesterday for four more years, which means that he can rave for four more years without a veto. Surely, nothing else was expected; but nevertheless, somehow one always hopes against one's better judgment.

My parents, seated in the music room, listened to his words. When the Führer speaks, mother would not for the world miss a single word of what her gallant Führer says. Father keeps her company. I had a short argument with mother, who urged me to listen with her.

Not understanding, she asked: "Why don't you want to hear his speech?"

"Because, dearest mother, this megalomaniac fool has already destroyed enough of my life. His voice alone makes me physically ill. Moreover, it exceeds my understanding that you can still manage to listen for hours to the empty tirades of your greatest persecutor."

Father made a mollifying gesture, but I continued, "He always says the same thing! He begins with 'fourteen years' since even now, apparently he is surprised that he finally succeeded after that fourteen-year struggle. After this introduction, he indulges in dark threats against one group or another; then he intoxicates himself and his listeners about what has been accomplished and what will still be achieved. Now tell me, after four years of this, do you still seriously expect something new?"

129

"Yes," she replied hesitantly, "it could be." She became rattled.

Because of our conversation, we missed the triumphant entrance of Hitler and his faithful followers. Subdued sounds reached us: "Heil Hitler! Sieg Heil! We thank our Führer! Heil to our Führer!" Father turned the volume up. Hitler's voice sounded clear and distinct, "German men and women!"

I just closed the door, when he said, "Fourteen years . . ."

February 5, 1937

It was already midnight. I was still sitting in the dining room with mother eating a sandwich, when father returned from his regular get-together with his cronies. His right hand clenched into a fist, opened and closed again. He stared gloomily in front of him and shook his head.

"What is it?" asked mother anxiously.

"Ach," he said irritably, "those grumblers at the pub. Several of them paint such a gloomy picture. Küppers believes he sees preparations for war."

"But that is impossible!" mother exclaimed.

"Nothing is impossible," I said curtly, caught myself and added soothingly, "I'm sorry; but this blind cult for a criminal grates on my nerves."

An awkward silence followed until mother pulled herself together and asked almost shyly, "Tell me, child, don't you think you're somewhat harsh in your judgment?"

"In what way?" I looked at them. "Not harsh enough! Look around for once and observe what is happening. Haven't you read about the Adolf Hitler Schools?"

"Certainly," she said astonished.

"Aren't you fully aware of the kind of person they are trying to create? The elite from the Hitler Youth are educated in these schools free of charge for six years, beginning at twelve; afterwards, a career in the state or the party is open to them."

"But isn't it wonderful, if they otherwise couldn't afford it financially?" asked mother näively.

I had to laugh. "Haven't you ever heard how those 'elite' children behave towards their parents, if they aren't Nazis?" She stared at me with frightened eyes. "No?" I continued mercilessly. "Haven't you heard anything yet about parents who no longer dare open their mouths in the presence of their Hitler Youth children, because their sweet little ones would denounce them in cold blood to their leaders. The Youth leader gives these reports to the district leader. You have seen in my case, what happens then."

"But that is really horrible!" said mother shocked.

"It is."

Father intervened, "You know, little one, after everything you have experienced, I understand your negative outlook. But often I think you are inclined to extremes. You must give them more time."

I shook my head. "Dad, they have been in power for four years. How much more time do you expect? Only a few days ago, they placed civil servants under loyalty oath. I only remember that the Führer came first and then the Reich. How many of these officials, if they have families, possess the strength of character to refuse this oath? Don't you see what is happening? Our esteemed Führer has made the Germans a people of liars, hypocrites, and informers."

While I stood up to leave the room, I turned to father, "I don't believe that this is the nation of poets and thinkers you carry in your heart."

March 4, 1937

Several weeks ago I completed my laboratory training in the Bürgerhospital and looked for work. It was not as simple to find a job as I had imagined. I was extremely depressed when week after week passed without result, although I diligently answered all the advertisements.

Finally, a doctor in Oberrad hired me. I will start work on March 15th.

April 7, 1937

I have been working almost a month at my new profession. The first days were somewhat difficult, but I have long since adjusted. The site of my new activity is on the second floor of a converted three-room apartment. The large kitchen is arranged as a laboratory; the window overlooks a backyard, where a noisy automobile repair shop is located. I take my brief coffee breaks in this room.

On the first day when I unwrapped my sandwich, surrounded

by test tubes of urine and other waste products of man, I was momentarily overwhelmed by a feeling of hopelessness. From outside came an indescribable noise of a motor running at high-speed. I swallowed a few tears along with my bread. The doctor's office reminded me faintly of the *Frankfurter Post* editorial offices — of another life and a different career to which my heart clung.

Meanwhile, everything has gone well. The patients are nice, simple people, mostly craftsmen and gardeners. Politics does not seem to form the center of their lives. They are more concerned with doing a good job, and that their gardens and fields produce the desired harvest.

Father asked me to come to the Bürgerhospital four mornings a week, on the days I have afternoon duty in Oberrad. He wants me to write his reports, as I did before. Thus, my days are fairly full.

When I returned home today shortly before supper, I met Etta in the doorway, who had had a lengthy afternoon tea with mother.

She greeted me with her characteristic cordiality. After a few questions about my job, she asked about my relationship with my new employer.

"Something is not quite right," I answered half laughing. "I have no idea if he knows something about me and therefore I avoid personal conversations. But every time he appears for office hours with a scowl on his face, which happens frequently, I think that he knows. He has heard I was in prison, or that I am a half-breed, or both. Now he will fire me!"

Taken aback, she was quiet for a moment. Then she said, "For heaven's sake Lili! You ought not to let such thoughts become part of you! You'll destroy yourself and your life this way!"

I looked at her in astonishment, "Do you really think so, Etta? You usually think so clearly and keenly. My life won't be destroyed by my thoughts, but by facts — by the reality of the Third Reich."

June 7, 1937

My diary has been neglected because of all my work. Also, there is very little to record. The Nazis continuously proclaim new decrees and laws, which increasingly persecute and suppress their opponents. Goebbels commands that, on every suitable and unsuitable occasion, all houses and dwellings display flags. Since the number of unemployed has sunk to under a million, most Germans remain enthusiastic. Those who have lost their livelihood and the few who use their brains keep silently aloof.

Recently, we discussed the Nazi pigs at dinner. To avoid any misunderstanding: pig farms have been placed around the cities. Food scraps and garbage are to be collected and fed to these pigs.

Mother found the idea of this "food aid" simply splendid.

June 20, 1937

Dr. Münzer had planned for a long time to take a trip to the Mediterranean for his vacation. All the preparations were made with the exception of one small oversight. He had not looked around for a substitute in time. Now, whomever he called, was occupied.

He raced through the office like a madman. "I simply can't get a replacement. I must cancel everything! I can't go!

"Perhaps I know someone," I said timidly.

He looked at me astonished, while I added hesitantly, "Of course, I don't know, if you would approve."

"Naturally, I agree," he interrupted me, "if it is a doctor who can substitute for me."

After I telephoned, I pointed to one of the last names on the list of substitutes. "Here, Dr. Strüder is available."

Today Dr. Strüder sat in Münzners place and for the first time, I felt relatively light hearted. I am secure in my job for at least the next three weeks.

July 8, 1937

Office hours have been quiet because many patients wait until their regular doctor returns.

Dr. Strüder and I sat opposite each other in the office.

"How is director Hensel doing?" I asked.

"I rarely hear from him, but I assume, that he has settled down." When he saw my astonished face, he asked, "Don't you know that he directs Fuhlsbüttel penitentiary near Hamburg?"

"No."

We were silent and our thoughts reverted to Preungesheim Prison.

Unexpectedly Dr. Strüder said: "The prisons and penitentiaries are being filled with members of religious orders."

I nodded.

Dr. Strüder, a Catholic, knew why I was in prison and possibly

133

for whom. He asked cautiously, "What do you think about all these trials concerning the morals of the monks?"

I looked at him searchingly. "To be honest, when the first trial began against the Franciscans — or whatever order it was — I believed it was genuine. Please don't misunderstand me, I don't want to offend you. But I feel that the clerical law of celibacy is both unnatural and incomprehensible. If your church is so concerned about fulfilling God's wishes, it shouldn't compel its servants to live against their creator's will. I believe that somewhere the Bible states that man must leave his mother and father and cleave to his wife. The Bible doesn't say to lock men in one cloister and women in another, and if the flesh weakens, it is a sin!"

Dr. Strüder laughed involuntarily, as I continued: "Consequently when the first sex trial began, I thought these men were only human; they were healthy normal men. But it seems unbelievable that all monks in all German monasteries are homosexuals. I now believe this is one of the typically sly Nazi methods to get rid of religious orders. Since one can't really accuse the monks of being communists and apparently no other incriminating material could be found in the cloisters, it was determined that they were sexual offenders.

"Only inferior, morally sick people grasp at such methods, to throw filth on the innocent in order to render them harmless! What a corrupt mentality to pose as pure and morally fit, to expose and punish filth with reluctance and a heavy heart, as was done in Röhm's case. They knew all along that he was a homosexual. When they wanted to get rid of him, this fact became a deadly crime. In any case, no means are too base to be used against enemies of the state."

Strüder looked thoughtfully at his desk. "But why? What did the monks do to them?"

"What did they do to the Nazis? Well, apart from the fact that in many Catholic circles there is open opposition, there are still some von Papen supporters at work. These so-called sex trials are probably a warning shot. Goebbels or Himmler, or whoever staged this action, wanted to prove that the Nazis would not be deterred from using a strong hand in an emergency. A few innocent monks are sacrificed to this end; such trifles are insignificant in the Nazis' eyes."

"That is probably the idea behind the trials," confirmed Strüder seriously. "All opponents are systematically exterminated

134

or muzzled. A machinist from Essen made 'subversive remarks' in his pub and was dismissed by the firm after twelve years employment. A weaver in a Plauen curtain factory was given his dismissal notice, because he gave nothing to the Winter Relief Fund. A husband was divorced in Halberstadt, because he grumbled and criticized his wife's membership in the Nazi Women's League and didn't want his son to use the German salute as a greeting. Whatever is considered an offense by today's rulers is punished. They see to it that the sinner makes amends and serves as an example and a warning to others. What family man can afford to lose his livelihood?"

"It seems monstrous to me that people are punished because someone wants their job or because they are opposed to the regime. Take the case of a radio announcer, who never was a communist but whose desk drawer contained communist literature which he had never seen before. He lost his job. Another of my friends, an implacable foe of the Nazis whom they couldn't catch, is now in the penitentiary as a transvestite. During a house search they found women's shoes and clothing in his closet. The Gestapo had brought the evidence they indignantly found during the house search, along with them. The sole purpose is to remove every possibility that these enemies of the state could influence others. These methods aren't new. Monsieur Fouchè developed them brilliantly; and before him the Tzarist regimes used them. Actually it is of no consequence who had the idea first, since it produces the desired results."

Strüder's powerful, reliable hands clenched into fists, "One is so helpless as an individual against this system of fear and terror."

August 13, 1937

Already I have been in my Hinterstein for one week! Fourteen days vacation.

The mountains, with their familiar profiles towering to the sky, are unchanged; as unchanged as are the inhabitants: upright, inflexible, and free, as only mountain people are. They simply do not take National Socialism seriously, but seemed to find it an inexhaustible source of humor.

According to an old habit of mine, I climbed to one of the high Alpine pastures long before the other vacation guests awoke. Surrounded by silent mountains, my thoughts returned to the populated lowlands. While drinking in all the beauty, I asked myself what it is in certain human beings that ignites the wish to destroy.

135

My thoughts reverted to the past, when as a small child I was torn from my sleep and carried to the cellar. We strained our ears for the occasional humming of a lone airplane, which threatened us with death from the sky. I remembered how I watched Wolf with fascination, as he balanced on a ladder and painted the electric bulbs and the skylight blue.

Extensive air-raid drills are now taking place. The darkened city is being checked by airplanes. Block wardens inspect all the streets to see whether any windows have a gap through which light might leak. On September 1st, the great attic cleanup begins. All inflammable objects are to be cleared away from garrets and storage places. Simultaneously, as an air-raid precaution, it is required that air-raid shelters be installed, when rebuilding or adding to houses.

I remembered scraps of conversation. "Göring said that we must be prepared in the event of an attack."

"Certainly, but why does he need bombers? One doesn't drop bombs on one's own country!"

"Our Führer certainly doesn't want war!"

"Why is the whole population equipped with gas masks?"

"No cause for alarm! It is a means to provide work, simply an employment scheme!"

"We are a people without sufficient space. We are entitled to live — even if we must arm ourselves and fight."

The Germans feel so strong and superior, they cannot imagine that war could bring blood and misery. After all, we are so powerful, so secure, we can only win. In similar fashion as we systematically control the enemies within our country, so shall we cope with the enemies across the border!

My thoughts returned to my dead friend.

"Tell me," I asked his ghost, "How can a man be a career soldier? How could you educate people to kill?"

A white cloud sailed over the blue summer sky and disappeared behind a mountain peak.

"You only instruct them to defend their homeland? Do you really believe that, my friend? To keep the instruments of war cleaned and oiled is senseless. The cabinetmaker wants to make furniture, the locksmith to produce an iron-grating, and the soldier? You train these brainless puppets to kill until they master the art to perfection. When your tin soldiers stand in rank and file, they will also find an enemy, however imaginary it is.

"You won't admit it? Then tell me, my friend, what have the

French done to you Germans? What did they have to do with the shot at Sarajevo? You are silent. I shouldn't speak to you so harshly, but concern myself with more pleasant things? Why? Because I am young? Is my youth a shield against future horrors? You smile?"

My glance was caught by a dwarf fir tree. Its foliage seemed to change into a grinning skull. It was difficult for me to breathe, when I said: "I only knew a peaceful old man who was saddened by Mozart's music.

"Tell me, General von Seeckt, how many thousands of human lives do you have on your conscience? How could you ever again eat, drink, listen to music, laugh, and love? Didn't you build up the hundred-thousand man army after the war? For what? For defense? Who ever wanted to attack this defeated people and shattered land?"

The more I saw through the web of thoughts of the leading soldier, the more the death's-head lost its horror for me. My eyes ranged over the mountain meadow to the valley down below, where the tiny houses and barns disappeared in the gray dawn and re-appeared in flashes of the sunlight.

I said thoughtfully, "No, my friend, in the depth of your heart you neither thought about defense nor attack. You only wanted to have your plaything back, your army — the regular army, which Hitler could use as a basis for rebuilding the great German military machine — to bring renewed misfortune over the world. Why else does one need an army or an air force, which Göring's fingers itch to put into action? You laid the foundation for all of this."

In response, a deep rumble sounded behind the mountains. I looked up and saw the first dark thunderclouds shoving across the blue sky.

"I'm very sorry, my friend. Right now I understand it for the first time. A soldier, especially a general, is born. He can't help being what he is. Like the chess player, who pushes his pieces back and forth on the chessboard, the general moves his troops back and forth on the map, and forgets, except for infrequent moments, that he is playing with human lives. Just as foreign as the concept of war and killing is to me, so is it your second nature, the essence of your life."

While I hurried for protection to the Alpine cabin, dazzling flashes of lightning illuminated the almost darkened landscape. I felt a certain relief. "For once I had to express it, my old friend. If you loved me for my youth, you also had to suffer pain because young people think and feel differently—the eternal rotating dance of generations."

For a moment, an icy gust of wind embraced me in my thin summer dress. I was a few steps away from the cabin. "I will try to preserve you in my heart as I knew you — not because of what you were."

The first large raindrops fell as the herdsmen opened the door of their warm protective hut.

September 13, 1937

Of late, I seldom saw Sjöderbloom, although we spoke to each other almost every morning on the telephone. I cannot describe what a shock it was, when the day before yesterday, his secretary answered instead of his familiar voice. She said that the professor was in Berlin for an operation, and he had written to me. I could not learn anything more from her; she replied to all my questions that I should wait for his letter.

I lived through hell until his letter arrived. Sjöderbloom wrote that he has tuberculosis. He had the choice of spending two years in Davos or having an operation. In accordance with his temperament, he decided to have an operation.

Mother stood in the room, "Lili," she called, "you have overslept!"

It was Wednesday and I had morning duty. I jumped out of bed, into my clothes and rushed out of the house.

After office hours, when all the patients had gone, I placed several laboratory results on the desk in front of Dr. Münzner. He looked up suddenly. "Tell me, do you know something about Professor Sjöderbloom? I heard . . ."

He raised his eyebrows as tears fell from my eyes.

With a choked voice, I answered, "I know nothing."

September 29, 1937

Many many years ago I used to walk part of the same way to school, which now leads me to work. During a long time I covered this distance with my favorite teacher. He was the first love of my twelve-year-old life; in any case, he was the first man who had an appreciable influence over me.

138

We came from different directions, met at the Eschersheimer Turm, and walked to school in the morning air through the city and over the Main River bridge. In winter the sky stretched over us heavy and gray; and in the summer, it was still fresh and cool, before the dust danced in the hot sun. My favorite time was autumn. The sunbeams broke through the Main River fog, gilded the fruits on the street vendors' handcarts and shone on the autumn flowers along the riverbank. He walked next to me, a tall and slender man, a bit bent over with his arms dangling and hands open at his sides. His dark brown, melancholy eyes drank in the beauty and he pointed out the interplay of light, shadow, and color. He taught me to see. Moreover, he taught me to be honest and upright, and to stand by my convictions. He detested evasions and empty phrases. I knew I could believe him, could always rely on his word; I made him my idol.

My heart withstood the sorrow of his marrying, and our friendship lasted even after I left school.

As I was going to Oberrad one Saturday morning, I saw him from the trolley, and decided that I wouldn't change trolleys at the Schauspielhaus the next time, but would walk across the bridge with him, like we did in the old days.

The sun broke through the autumn fog on the banks of the Main, as in the old days. His familiar slender figure with stooped shoulders walked next to me. However, his expression was reserved and his eyes looked impersonally at the street. Apparently he did not notice anything of the beauty around us.

He had learned that I had been in prison and remarked that today one had to be careful of what one said.

Was this the man who taught me to hold fearlessly onto my convictions? With a cold shiver, I felt he could not wait to get rid of my troublesome presence. The bridge which we formerly had crossed all too quickly seemed endless today. Was this spineless coward who was afraid to be seen with me, actually the idol of my early youth? He parted from me with a curt nod of his head.

I stood alone on the other side of the bridge at the trolley stop. My thoughts slowly cleared like the fog rising from the water. Disappointments are like drops falling in a bowl. The fuller the bowl, the lower the tone it makes.

October 3, 1937

I.G. Farben had been interested in father's tuberculosis research for quite some time. Their interest grew when father gave a report on his work at an international congress in Bern. In any case, after long negotiations, they were willing to support him financially. Consequently, father's hospital also felt bound to help. The top floor of the hospital was converted into a tuberculosis ward with its own large laboratory, and a technician's salary was approved. Another laboratory aide and a biochemist are being salaried by I.G. Farben; father had been paying them out of his own pocket. Since father needs three laboratory technicians, hc persuaded me to give notice on October 1st and to work for him. However, I promised Dr. Münzner I would help out a few more days and train my successor.

On Monday, October 11th, I will start working for father and am very happy.

October 10, 1937

I received a short note from Sjöderbloom. He is better! The tragedy is that doctors can never be objective about themselves. However much I hope, my doubts remain. It would really be wonderful if one could cure pulmonary tuberculosis with a simple operation.

Political events follow hot on the heels of each other. While Hitler suddenly demands colonies, one large air-raid drill after another takes place. The last one in Berlin was on September 20th, with simulated enemy attacks, defense and naturally, a great victory. Manoeuvres of our great Wehrmacht were staged after this. Hitler accompanied by Mussolini, then visiting Germany, attended these exercises; and the Rome-Berlin Axis against the Bolsheviks was created.

I view the Nazis' activities with fascination. They arrange one festival after another. The people reel in a stupor from one celebration to the next, with scarcely time to think.

No professional group is overlooked, except the intellectuals. Either the Führer or a member of his entourage speaks at all of these events. The people feel important and close to their leaders.

October 28, 1937

A few days ago, when father sent me downtown to get something for the laboratory, I met Günther Rand on the street. Günther used to drive me to police headquarters on his motorcycle;

140

but I had not seen him for ages. He pounced on me with hundreds of questions. Since I was in a hurry, I promised to visit him Wednesday afternoon in his new place in the West End.

We sat in his large sunny room, and I answered all his questions and told him about my life.

"And what are you doing, Günther?"

"Still the same thing. Since not much happens any more, I also go to court once in a while. Perhaps I will specialize more in court reporting."

We exchanged memories of our colleagues who had left Germany and I inquired how things were on the *F.Z.*

Günther no longer feels at ease there and complained about the new management and a general mistrust of new colleagues and even the printers. The reduced core of old editors have to be careful when they converse with each other because the walls seem to have ears.

"And how is Karl?"

Günther's merry eyes looked at me in astonishment. "Don't you see each other any more?"

I shook my head silently, but Günther's searching look remained firm. "I was against further complicating our lives. How is he?"

Günther laughed involuntarily. "He got rather tipsy and delivered a speech to the people in Sprenger's style, from a balcony on Zeppelin Allee. You know how Karl can be. It wasn't hard for him to imitate the usually drunken Gauleiter. He concluded, 'Comrades, don't ever forget... Adolf Hitler is the man to whom you owe everything ... Adolf Hitler is your leader, and you are the ones led on!'"

I laughed as Günther continued, "Zeppelin Allee is fortunately very wide; but the balcony was almost directly opposite Sprenger's villa."

"And?" I asked a bit alarmed, "what happened?"

"Karl was debarred from practicing his profession in Hessen-Nassau." Günther got up, "Shall I play some of my new records?"

The telephone rang before I could reply. Günther handed the receiver to me, "For you."

I had left Günther's number with mother. She said, "Professor Sjöderbloom's secretary called. He is here for a few hours on his way through town and would like to see you."

141

November 7, 1937

I am happy with my new work. Although there is a lot of routine in laboratory research, I have personal reasons for not feeling bored. Moreover, the collaboration between the technicians and the interns is friendly, and the atmosphere is pleasant.

We sit in a tower with many windows which overlooks the trees of Nibelungen Allee and lots of sky. Slowly the first patients come to the ward. There are a few soldiers among them for whom the war is already over before it had even started.

What encourages me at work is the hope that I can perhaps help father succeed more quickly. Father, who checks his results and setbacks doggedly, is justifiably optimistic by observing the improvement of his patients' condition, but he is compelled to produce fast results. Last New Year's day, he received a warning notice that as of January 1, 1939, he would exceed the retirement age of sixty-five. Medical specialists are allowed to practice until seventy; but they can be forced to retire at sixty-five if notice is given them a year in advance.

Father had made the mistake of discussing his retirement with the administration chairman. Dr. deBary, a spineless individual nicknamed 'the rubber man,' told father only that he enforces his contracts. Father had not understood this diplomatic answer, with which deBary disassociated himself from the whole affair. The contract was enforced and a termination date was set. Father is extremely depressed at the thought of leaving the hospital, his patients, and nurses. He sets his hopes on solving the TB question, and is convinced that his contract would then be renewed.

It could be that in case of success deBary would forgive father his Jewish wife and politically convicted daughter; but I still believe that mother is the most important reason for father's being removed from his post as chief physician.

November 23, 1937

In our glass tower we are so engrossed in our esterases, lipases, pH values and precipitation of vitamin C that we scarcely know what is going on in the outside world. Nevertheless, a disquieting rumor reached me.

At a secret meeting on November 5th, Hitler told the foreign minister and the Army Chief of Staff that Germany's lack of space was to be resolved through force. He named Austria and Czechoslovakia as his immediate aims.

I arrived at the office of our dentist, Müllerchen, with this news. "It is nothing new that Austria has a large national socialist movement. Should Hitler annex Austria, he would be received with open arms."

Müllerchen nodded. Squatting on his swivel stool, he said disapprovingly: "The Sudeten Germans have been organized for a long time in Czechoslovakia and want to 'return home to the Reich.'"

"Would the conquest of both of those small countries alleviate Germany's lack of space? After all, people also live there. Or should the non-German elements be expelled? I'm also troubled by the question of whether a rapid and bloodless conquest will satisfy the ambition of an ex-private, who must prove to the world that he is more than nominally the supreme commander of the German army.

"That bastard Hitler — I meant that only racially! — has a Nordic-Germanic racial complex. He probably overcomes his feeling of inferiority, by appointing himself master and guardian of the Nordic-Germanic race, and jealously taking care that the precious blood of the German people will not be polluted and dishonored any further."

Müllerchen considered, "It is said that the memory of unpleasant experiences recede increasingly and only the pleasant ones remain. It is probably the same with these fools. They have forgotten the horrid picture of a ragged, soiled, defeated army, dragging itself painfully back home. Their historical memory retains only the pleasant events, the victories." He shook his head. "I, nevertheless, can't imagine that Hitler, the trench pig, will lead a war." He swung around on his stool and stood up, "This time, in any case I won't participate."

December 4, 1937

Today, Saturday afternoon, is not a working day in the laboratory. 'Fatso' invited me to the doctors' mess to give me a book.

As I approached, I heard many laughing voices. When I opened the door, I saw Fatso in a crowd of interns whose faces were flushed with laughter.

143

I looked around questioningly, "A new joke?"

Another outburst of laughter answered me.

Fatso tried to explain, "A German man . . ." Laughter. "A German . . ." She held her sides.

Finally one of the young doctors pushed a newspaper toward me. He pointed to the headline: LIBEL SUIT IN COLOGNE."

A man had said to his friend during a quarrel, "You will crawl to me on your knees one day."

In the following libel suit, which the friend had initiated, the court decided: "A German man never crawls and under no circumstances on his knees. Whoever makes such a remark to another person, expects something un-Germanic from him and thus offends his honor as a man."

January 9, 1938

The old year passed and I crossed it off the calendar of my life with a small x, like the prisoners in Preungesheim checked off every day that passed between today and freedom on the cell walls.

How many years would I still have to cross off until we can again live and breathe as free people?

Father received his final retirement notification and unless a miracle occurs, December 31st will be the end of his work in the Bürgerhospital. He has been successful with his method of treatment, but has not been able to produce a marketable drug, on which everything ultimately depends. Since such work requires time, I doubt this short year will suffice.

February 16, 1938

Political tensions have generally eased up. Austrian chancellor Schuschnigg visited Hitler at Obersalzberg, for discussions concerning the relations between their countries. Both agreed they would keep to the pact of July 1936. They resolved "implementation of measures which would ensure a closer and friendly relationship between both states, corresponding to the historical and overall interests of the German people."

I mulled over this sentence while we sat at dinner. I was probably inattentive, since mother asked me twice to pass the salt.

"Are you tired?" she asked solicitously. "Are you worried about something? Have you had some trouble?"

144

I finally replied with a sigh, "No, I was only thinking about the German-Austrian affair."

Father's large expressive eyes turned towards me. "You were thinking of the Obersalzberg meeting?" He added with relief, "The German-Austrian problem now appears to be solved."

"I cannot quite agree with you."

"Why?"

"I believe the problems are just beginning. In the Third Reich you must learn to read between the lines."

Father smiled. "You speak like the Delphic oracle. What must be read between the lines?"

"Hitler said the relationship between both countries must correspond to the overall interest of the German people. The Austrian people are not mentioned. I believe that poor Schuschnigg hasn't understood at all. He has run into a trap with his eyes open."

"In a trap?" asked mother blankly.

I explained. "He didn't listen closely, or he didn't read between the lines. Delighted about his understanding with Hitler, he has rushed home to reorganize his government, and that will probably be his last act as chancellor."

Father shook his head disapprovingly. "You see everything too one-sidedly, my child. What do you expect? What can Hitler do to Austria?"

"He can swallow it up."

Katherina, who had been silent the whole time, said reproachfully, "Really Lili!"

I looked at her with narrowed eyes. "Yes, really! We'll speak about it again in the autumn, if it takes that long."

February 27, 1938

There was an influenza epidemic in Frankfurt; father's biochemist was one of its victims.

I don't know whether I have mentioned this extremely unpleasant character. He is a very thin, graceful Ukrainian aristocrat, who walks with a cane, since he ostensibly broke his hip as a child in a riding accident on his parents' estate. He speaks with a high pitched voice and has a ludicrous sense of humor. What repelled me at my first meeting with this delicate, interesting looking man were his coarse, cruel hands which did not fit with the rest of his appearance.

Although father is professionally happy with Juretschenko, I

145

could not rid myself of a healthy distrust of the man. Father thought I imagined things when I warned him to handle Juretschenko with utmost caution.

Juretschenko had the flu a few weeks ago. He didn't want father to look after him, but asked for medicine and returned to the laboratory after the usual duration of the flu. Somehow, however, he could not recover and was conspicuously pale and coughed. Finally he yielded to father's urging and allowed himself to be examined.

Later Father spoke to me about him with a feeling of uncertainty. "Juretschenko has an inflammation at the apex of the lung. It isn't bad. With some rest and a good diet, he should be quickly cured."

"What makes you feel uneasy then?"

Father wrinkled his brow. "He only let me examine his lungs. When I wanted to see his hips, he refused firmly, and explained that they had absolutely nothing to do with it."

"Do you suspect he had tuberculosis of the hip joint?" I asked.

Father shrugged his shoulders. "I couldn't compel him to be examined completely, but something is wrong."

March 16, 1938

We did not have to wait until fall for Hitler to swallow up Austria. Chancellor Schuschnigg naively reorganized his government in accordance with the agreement, and gave the Austrian Nazis more power. The leader of the Austrian Nazis, Seyss-Inquarts was named minister of interior and security. Seyss-Inquarts immediately paid a visit to our Führer. Although the press is usually garrulous when Nazi Party interests are involved, I had the vague feeling that this time they were not completely informed about the discussions. However it happened — there were riots in Austria. The new security minister faced these so helplessly that he felt compelled on March 11th, to appeal to Hitler to send German troops.

Two days later, German troops entered Austria. The local population rejoiced in the Nazi seizure of power. "Austria is free!"

Most of the government departments and offices were seized overnight by the SA and SS. Austria entered the Reich!

Afterward, the Führer visited his new province: Austria.

146

Vienna's enthusiasm knew no limits. The prodigal son had returned home — victoriously. People shouted with joy wherever he appeared. He was feted throughout Austria, then received in Berlin by hysterically enthusiastic mobs.

I gradually realized that Hitler would have to be superhuman if he did not consider himself a superman after all of this adulation.

April 10, 1938

My birthday today fell on this eventful Sunday, when simultaneously in Germany and Austria elections were held for Greater Germany.

In contrast to my usual birthdays, something extraordinary seemed to be going on in the house. I was not allowed to leave the dining room after breakfast. There were whispers and strange steps in the hallway, until I was finally led into the music room to admire my gifts.

Spellbound I stood in the doorway. A small black ball of wool, on short uncertain legs and too large paws, came towards me. Siegrid stood with a happy smile in the corner of the room. I picked up the tiny puppy, I felt the soft baby hair against my face, while a small tongue licked my hand tenderly. We were enchanted with each other.

Looking up I saw the happy and expectant faces of my parents.

"Many thanks," I murmured. Cautiously placing the small woolly animal on the carpet, I embraced father.

For many years I had wanted a Scottish terrier but ran into iron resistance. Every morning on the way to the hospital, father and I met a man walking his two scotties. I had often called father's attention to them; and just as often he explained with utter conviction how indescribably ugly they were. He did not want this in the house. With the fulfillment of my wish, he expressed more than words could say.

This Sunday was such a happy, harmonious day that I forgot the whole political mess until father turned on the radio late in the evening to hear the results of the elections. Millions went to the polls and again gave the Nazis an occasion to prove to the world, how fully the people support them.

147

May 1, 1938

Wild activity broke out at home as a result of the decree which was published on April 27th. It requires an inventory of Jewish property, from which the non-Jewish spouse is not exempt. It requires itemizing all property, with the exception of nonmovable objects and those exclusively meant for personal use, like household effects, but not including luxury items.

Father used his free Wednesday afternoon to meet his friend Bergenhoff, the lawyer. Bergenhoff advised him to make a deed donating all valuable pieces of furniture, paintings, silver etc. to his children. So we make an inventory. Mother is getting on my nerves with her perpetual scruples, worrying whether any of us were being slighted or felt disadvantaged. My objections that it is only a formality, does not help. She apparently considers the deed as a testament and simply does not understand that it is a deception for the Nazis.

By day, I was busy in the laboratory; in the evening, we compiled the list of gifts. After a walk with my small puppy Brandy, I returned to my room and wondered. Why did the Nazis want an itemization of Jewish property? Only to satisfy their curiosity? Certainly not! Something infernal had been concocted. We would find out. Although in this case, no great imagination is required.

With these agonizing thoughts, I was not in the best frame of mind to see Sjöderbloom. But when he asks me to come, I can never refuse. The hours with him are a gift, the only gift from fate which make my life seem worth living, and I know deep in my heart that it can not last.

We had not seen each other since his return from Bühler Höhe. He was pale and his hand felt too warm. After greeting him, I looked around the familiar room, which now contains a small couch.

"Where is Bonzo?"

"Dead," he said succintly.

"Signore!"

He shrugged his shoulders and occupied himself with filling the glasses with wine.

We chatted for a while. Suddenly he stood up, paced the room restlessly, breathing irregularly with an effort, while his forehead gleamed moistly. I looked at him silently. Our eyes met.

"Signorina," he gasped, "may I open my collar?"

"Naturally!"

He pulled his tie down and opened his collar with a deep breath, which resembled a sigh. Then he sat on the couch. Fear stood in his eyes, while his breath came in irregular jerks.

"Why don't you lie down?"

He stretched out on the couch. "Signorina, I am marked. The mark on my forehead must be clearly visible."

I smoothed his dishevelled hair. "No," I said comfortingly, "No, there is no mark."

Exhausted, he fell into a brief restless sleep.

When he awoke, he looked at me brightly. "Signorina, how do I breathe when I sleep? Honestly! Tell me the truth!"

I replied, "Good. Very evenly."

His eyes slid searchingly over my face, "Is it already that far . . ."

While I lay sleeplessly in my bed, I thought, "You believe you are marked and I believe I'm damned. Each is alone in his boundless despair."

May 11, 1938

On our common path to the Bürgerhospital, father and I occasionally meet the hospital radiologist.

This screne morning, the doctor seemed to have waited for us. He was probably looking for his next victim, so as to pour out his heart about all his disappointments and the wrongs which befell him.

He is an old party member with a relatively low number. The party had requested his party membership book for registration or renewal.

"And just imagine, just think of it," said the fat, comfortable man absolutely beside himself, "When I got it back, a much higher number was in it! Think of it! They gave my low number to someone else! That surely isn't right?"

The corner of father's mouth twitched. He asked sympathetically and soothingly, "Are you sure it wasn't a mistake?"

"No, no! I immediately called the party offices. It wasn't a mistake! They spoke about a reorganization. I find this really un-

149

fair! Some new favorite has my old number."

"I'm really sorry, dear colleague. I can't imagine it. It almost amounts to a swindle."

"Yes, doesn't it? But I can't do anything about it. If I complain too loudly. . ." He was suddenly silent.

What would happen then, my dear party comrade? Are you afraid? Do you know your comrades' methods so well that you would rather tolerate an injustice than risk your neck?

Father was extremely amused that he had complained to us. I shared his gloating, but simultaneously felt a pronounced uneasiness creeping over me. If the party members already fear their own people, what can subhumans like us expect?

May 18, 1938

I.G. Farben wanted to have detailed reports about father's progress before they would give further financial support. And about the end of March, the tug-of-war between father and Juretschenko had begun. The latter ostensibly still had to write up some reports, which went surprisingly slowly, and then he had to complete some short-term serial experiments. He made one excuse after another. Father could not delay I.G. Farben any longer and was compelled to give Juretschenko an ultimatum: either he presented his part of the results before the end of the month or father would no longer be in a position to employ him. The breach came and Juretschenko no longer appeared.

Mother was horrified. "What will become of him? If you no longer pay him, he will certainly starve and his tuberculosis. . ."

Father shrugged, "Probably. That isn't my worry. He made his own decision and I have been patient long enough." He was silent and stared gloomily in front of him. "Of course, it also means the end of my work and retirement."

"But you have had such success with your patients!" mother contradicted.

"Yes, yes," father answered irritably, "but with that alone I can't convince the pharmaceutical industry. If I only had one or two more years."

June 14, 1938

Father and I probably shared the secret hope that Juretschenko would give in under the force of circumstances. However, we heard nothing from him and worked without a biochemist. The assistants, goaded on by the striking improvement of the tubercular patients, help as well as they can, while father wavers between optimism and hopelessness.

We received great encouragement from the Alt case. Mr. Alt was shot in the lungs during the World War and developed severe tuberculosis, which sporadically flared up. He was sent to father with a high fever, a large cavity in one lung, and bacilli in his saliva. Within a week the hole closed, the fever fell and the bacilli disappeared from his sputum. Now he strolls comfortably in his bathrobe and slippers in the corridors, beaming about his rapid recovery, and tells everyone who will listen, "Yes, yes — Papa Schroeder. He is quite a doctor! He made Uncle Franz healthy again."

We love this Uncle Franz, who is so unobtrusive and modest, and mentioned only casually that he is one of the very old party members. I forgave him this sin since he is the living proof that father's research is on the right track, and he is attached to father with an almost idolatrous admiration.

August 6, 1938

This afternoon I took Brandy to the veterinarian and walked home through the city. I looked at the people as they walked past me on this Saturday afternoon. Some seemed happy, others worried. They sauntered to their cafes, observed the displays in shopwindows, or like myself, were alone with their thoughts. What were these strangers thinking? Just as no one could see that I had been in prison, their serious faces did not betray their agonizing secrets.

Suddenly I felt a small dog's nose against my leg. I looked down into his inquiring eyes and had to laugh. "Are you worried that I will forget your treat?" His tail began to wag. We entered a confectionery shop on the Steinweg. Back out on the street, I opened the paper bag, and Brandy started to walk on his hind legs.

At this moment a mocking voice behind me said, "Since I know man, I love dogs." I turned around and looked into Pötz's amused face.

We went together to the Kakao Stube. Brandy vanished under my chair.

I had to give Pötz a brief report on my latest activities.

He nodded thoughtfully and suddenly asked: "And does your mother have difficulties?"

"Oh no. Her life continues exactly as it has for the last ten or twenty years."

He leaned back in his chair and assumed his characteristic pose, his thumbs hooked under his suspenders, and observed me inquiringly. "The newspapers say the Jewish question will be solved legally, step by step, and systematically."

Releasing his suspenders, he bent forward and placed his hands on the table, watching me with deep interest, and asked, "Is your mother a Christian?"

"Yes."

He turned his head slightly, "So, you were raised a Christian?" I acquiesced with a smile. "But you don't believe in anything?"

"Nothing."

He looked pensively at his dirty fingernails and seemed satisfied, "And your father?"

"My father does not believe in anything. My mother is a fanatic Christian and my sister, a converted Catholic, will someday certainly be canonized."

"A Catholic?" After a brief pause, he continued: "Are you aware that all of our leading Nazis are Catholics? Did you know that? What we are experiencing today, my dear, is a renaissance of the Inquisition. Mankind has progressed considerably and has therefore become more civilized and modern. We now have more modern methods to torment apostates and heretics, methods apparently approved by the highest authority. The former leaders of the Inquisition weren't punished by God's heavenly tribunal; on the contrary, things went splendidly for them."

I played along with his mood and asked, "And why do you assume that, in the absence of a judgment by God, these torments are approved by the highest authority?"

His face lit up with a fiendish grin, "There is an extremely cynical sentence someplace in the Bible, 'For, whom God loves, he chastises'. Since the Pope doesn't want to interfere with his boss' peculiar tokens of love, he won't actively intervene against Nazi atrocities. After all the Pope in Rome has direct contact with his superior up there." He pointed to the ceiling. "Nobody can state exactly where God lives, and nobody has ever seen him; but that isn't very important. Belief alone is important. Millions of people are led by the nose. They believe in a god, whose existence nobody can ever prove. They believe in a life in paradise or heaven, which will reward them for all sufferings in this valley of tears. The ecclesiastical authorities indoctrinate people with the fear of hell, and many pleasures are renounced to ensure life hereafter, although there is no known geographical location for hell." After a brief pause, Pötz continued, "What complicates matters is that we don't know which god is currently on duty. You look puzzled? I mean what I said, the god on duty. Consider, my dear, how many gods mankind has already had to endure. To name a few, there are Isis, Osiris, Baal, Jehovah, Wotan, Manitou — not to mention all the Greek gods. A list could probably fill a small address book, if it includes the gods worshipped by all peoples from ancient through modern times." He leaned across the table. "Many of these gods are retired; but it has always required some time before people realized that the god they so zealously worshipped was occupied with other matters, probably playing cards with his retired colleagues. I therefore ask you: Which god is actually on duty now?" He paused briefly and continued with matchless irony, "Whoever he is, I feel he is just about to retire." Suddenly he looked keenly at me, "Have I offended a remnant of your religious upbringing?"

I shook my head. "No, certainly not! I never had considered religion from this point of view."

"My friend, bear in mind that gods and tyrants are closely related. However, both have but a limited life-span; the human tyrant has a shorter one since his tyranny is bound to a particular person and dies with him. Today we hardly know anything about Baal or Wotan; similarly, those born thirty years from now will scarcely know anything about Hitler. In one hundred years, he will only be a name among many others in history books." He was silent, then he suddenly added as an afterthought: "Hitler is like many unoriginal politicians, who consider themselves great men. Some people have compared Hitler with Napoleon. Fine, Napoleon also wanted to conquer the world and came to grief, something the advocates of the Hitler-Napoleon theory cling to. But Napoleon bequeathed us a valuable legacy. What would European law be without the Napoleonic Code? But Hitler?" Pötz smiled ironically. "Hitler is an ephemeral figure in history. The only thing he will leave behind is infinite destruction."

153

For the past ten days I have been in my adopted home Hinterstein. This time I am not alone. Brandy is with me. I wish he had travelled with me from Frankfurt. Following well-meaning advice I rented a carrying case, in which he rode in the baggage car. Everything went smoothly at first, but I spent more time in the baggage car than in my own compartment. We had to change trains in Kempten and when I got off at Sondhofen, my suitcase was delivered from the baggage car, but no Brandy. I was beside myself with worry! The nice stationmaster comforted me. A freight train was due in twenty minutes and Brandy would surely be aboard it.

While pacing the rural platform I felt somebody watching me. I turned around and looked directly into the face of a smiling young SS man.

"What are you waiting for?" he asked.

"For my dog."

He tried to draw me into conversation. Although I did not like the idea of chatting with an SS man, I knew I could not treat him like a normal stranger. I could not simply turn around and leave him to cool his heels. It is doubtlessly considered an honor to be spoken to by an SS man; and to slight him would be a declaration of enmity against the National Socialist movement.

Despite my curt replies which bordered on impoliteness, he invited me to visit him. At that moment, I saw the freight train rounding the bend.

"I am staying at the Ordensburg," he explained. "You have surely heard of it?" Just then the train chugged into the station. "Will you come and visit me? I am almost always at the castle."

A dog basket was unloaded from one of the cars. "Brandy," I shouted and was answered by a high-pitched bark. I opened the basket and clasped the dog in my arms. Delighted with Brandy's return, I promised the SS man to call before visiting him. He gave me his name and rank which I forgot by the time I was on the bus to Hinterstein. Every kilometer which took me farther from the Ordensburg made the sky seem bluer. But a feeling of insecurity crept over me. Had the Nazis also spread to Hinterstein?

Brandy and I made ourselves at home in the Steinadler and my fears vanished rapidly. Almost every morning we go up to a high Alpine pasture; and in the evening, we sit with my Hinterstein friends. Heribert, with finely chiselled features, manages the tourist bureau; Philipp is the carpenter; Adalbert moves with the suppleness of a wildcat and breaks women's hearts; the fairly small Konrad, who owns the sawmill, does beautiful inlay work as a hobby; and Arnulf has dreamy brown eyes which hide the fact that he doesn't miss anything. Despite their outward differences, these men are basically very much alike. All are molded by rugged mountain life. They share a strong sense of humor; and have the gift of listening to the nonsense spoken by strangers with completely immobile, unreadable faces. All consider National Socialism a curiosity. They are too free and independent to understand coercion, fear, and lies.

I simply cannot describe what this small mountain village with its overwhelming beauty, means to me. I stand in the clear high mountain air accompanied by Brandy, looking across the border. I feel that whatever occurs in the cities is unimportant, petty, and ephemeral and I realize that the natives simply do not comprehend what a dictatorship means.

I am almost happy for a short time, untroubled and free, feelings I had almost forgotten.

September 2, 1938

Except for last minute odds and ends, my suitcases are packed. Having said good bye to my friends, I am seated in my small room on my last evening in Hinterstein and fight against a feeling of utter misery. Each trip, I have found it more difficult to leave Hinterstein. Gladly would I abandon the hustle and bustle of the city, if I could remain here. When I am in Frankfurt, I am homesick for Hinterstein, never the contrary. This time is the worst, however. I have a dread of my return. I can not explain it, but I am scared; scared of something vague from which I can not escape.

September 11, 1938

My fears seem to have been justified.

Father walks about with a gloomy face, and one can barely coax a smile from him. I.G. Farben withdrew their financial support. Father had to dismiss one laboratory technician; and we all realize that in the few remaining months, we won't be able

155

either to conclude the research or produce a marketable drug.

Mother's fears about Juretschenko likewise came true. He could not find another job and began to starve. The harmless catarrh at the apex of his lungs developed into serious tuberculosis. Juretschenko turned to an ardent Nazi physician, whom he knew to be ill-disposed toward father. To crown everything, he sued father for erroneous treatment and false diagnosis, based on the Nazi doctor's medical certificate. Father's insurance company fights the case successfully, but it is a disappointment and nervous strain!

I spent yesterday evening with Sjöderbloom. He looks much better, is more alert, and seems full of optimism and vitality. His new dog greeted me, a young Welsh terrier bitch, who stayed briefly with us. I felt that dog and master were not yet a team.

We exchanged our vacation experiences and also discussed recent political events. It seemed inevitable, that Hitler would occupy Sudeten Germany, exactly as he did Austria. The prize winning question is whether it will occur without bloodshed as in Austria, or whether the rest of Czechoslovakia and the bordering countries will fight.

"Isn't it ghastly," I exclaimed, "like sitting on top of a volcano! One doesn't know whether the next war will break out in a few weeks!"

We both fell silent and then simultaneously reached for cigarettes.

Sjöderbloom got up suddenly. "Signorina — I am fed up with loneliness. I want to have somebody around who belongs to me and lives with me."

My heart throbbed as I looked up. "Yes, Signore?" I said in a choked voice.

"Please understand me, I don't mean an affair. That would harm you."

I too stood up. "Signore, before you go on—you told me that you can't leave the country. You know about my ancestry and my criminal record. Please inquire about the consequences this will have on your life."

September 22, 1938

It is all over.

Yesterday I called Sjöderbloom as usual in the morning and he asked me to come and see him that evening. While his dog greeted me excitedly — all young dogs think people are kind — Sjöderbloom seemed insecure and a bit depressed.

"Have you already an answer?"

Avoiding my eyes, he reached for the dog's collar, which was on the desk in front of him and threw it towards the dog, which fled into the corner whimpering.

"So . . ." I nodded, "It is a refusal."

"Yes," he replied tonelessly, "a death sentence."

We stood facing each other. I was silent and tried not to lose my self-control. I had not expected anything else, but now that it was said aloud, there was no more hope.

I took a deep breath and said, "Then we won't see each other again."

"You won't come anymore, Signorina?"

I shook my head.

"Never? This will be the last time?"

Somehow I found my way home. I sat on my couch, and covered my eyes and face with my hands. A small persistent dog's nose nuzzled my hands. Brandy tried to comfort me, as my tears at last fell on his black coat. He snuggled up to me and licked my hands and the tears on my face—the only creature who felt my pain without asking questions.

October 29, 1938

Meanwhile, Uncle Franz, our famous patient, has gone to a sanatorium in the Black Forest. He seems to spend his time singing father's praises to his fellow sufferers, judging from the letters which father has received from various patients. They all want to come to the Bürgerhospital and be treated by him.

Shortly after we returned from our vacation, Reuters sent a correspondent to interview father. Although we have not seen the article, letters filled with trust and hope are beginning to arrive from England. Each letter is a stab in father's heart. He can no longer help these people, since he will be forced to retire from the hospital in two months. We learned from a reliable colleague that Dr. deBary claimed father was unacceptable at the hospital for political reasons.

Under these circumstances, father contacted a real-estate firm to sell our house and help us find an apartment.

November 14, 1938

Recent events pulled me out of the lethargy I had felt after I parted from Sjöderbloom.

On November 7, a Polish Jew named Grünspan shot five times at Ernst vom Rath, the counselor of the German embassy in Paris. Vom Rath is still alive, but his recovery is in doubt. Grünspan and his relatives were arrested in Paris, and the German press outdid itself in outrage.

Two days later, on Monday morning, an excited young doctor rushed into the laboratory as we were about to record some new results. "The synagogues are burning! All Jewish businesses are being smashed to bits!"

I sat down and placed the testtube I was holding in a stand. "What?" I asked. "How do you know?"

"I was told by patients who came from downtown. They said SA men and mobs smashed the windows of Jewish shops. They are throwing everything they find on the streets: linen, crockery, jewelry. What isn't broken is crushed underfoot."

During the afternoon, reports of other incidents trickled through to us in our glass tower. Not only were businesses destroyed; but the SA men burst into many Jewish homes to continue their destruction and looting. During lunchtime, a number of Jewish businessmen were caught at the stock exchange; they were shackled together and made to carry abusive signs and chased through Schillerstrasse and across the Zeil.

Father and I returned home to our quiet residential district in silence. During dinner, mother commented on the horrible things that had taken place in the city. She did not seem to understand that we were lucky and were obviously among the few unaffected exceptions.

Suddenly I thought of the Spiers. They live about three minutes away from us in an elegant apartment. Robert Spier is a lawyer. We had frequently waited together at the trolley-stop. One day we spoke to each other and after a while a pleasant friendship developed. His merry brown eyes always seemed to notice the humorous aspects of life. I could not ever remember seeing this pudgy man with graying hair in a gloomy mood. He spoils and idolizes his petite graceful wife Lucille. They are very much in love. I was troubled that my thoughts kept returning to the Spiers, and decided to look them up after supper.

As I stood in front of Spier's apartment door, I heard whispering inside. The door was cautiously opened, just a crack.

Lucille grasped me by the hand and pulled me into the apartment. "Lili dear! How good of you to come!"

She led me into the living room, where her brother stood in the doorway. Her sister-in-law and several friends sat in silent gloom.

I glanced around the room, "What has happened? Where is Rob?"

"Rob was arrested today with other Jews and shipped to Buchenwald," Lucille's brother replied.

I looked at the brother with the Jewish name and glanced at Lucille, impeccably dressed as always. Her black hair was carefully curled, framing her small face. How did they manage to pass as Aryans I wondered. Perhaps the family had been converted generations ago.

I remembered our last social gathering. Rob had confessed to a youthful sin, which resulted in an illegitimate daughter. The mother of his child later married an Aryan, who adopted the girl. Rob went to Berlin especially to see his daughter at a political rally, where she wore the uniform of a National Socialist Woman's Leader.

He laughed until tears came to his eyes, when he said, "I wondered what she would say if she knew she had a Jewish father seated among the spectators?"

And now this jolly soul was in the Buchenwald concentration camp.

After I returned home, I listened with my parents to the late radio news. The Reichs SS leader and chief of police forbids Jews to carry any kind of arms. In the event of violation, the guilty will be transported to a concentration camp, for a term of twenty years' "protective custody."

I slept miserably. At first, the fate of Robert Spier haunted me; then I began wondering whether any other of my friends or acquaintances were with him. Basically it is the same to me whether I know them or not: all of them are human beings who suffer and face an uncertain destiny.

I was jolted awake from a twilight sleep. The all-too-familiar sound of nailed boots floated up from the street. I sat up in bed and listened, while my heart pounded, but the footsteps grew fainter. They did not stop at our house or at the Fränkels next door.

Long before my parents were awake, I sat in the dining room and read the morning newspaper.

The paper spoke of a spontaneous "popular rage" which was vented in anti-Jewish attacks. The synagogues were "more or less" burned out. "Demonstrators broke into Jewish shops and destroyed display goods and interior decorations."

Goebbels gave a speech and stated that he understood the indignation of the German people aroused by the infamous assassination. He issued a strict order to immediately desist from all further demonstrations and any other actions against Jewish people and their property.

He stated ominously, "The final answer to the Jewish assassination attempt in Paris will be given through legislative channels, or by regulations pertaining to Jews."

I placed the newspaper on the table. How was that? I thought. "Spontaneous outrage of the people." "The peoples' soul boiled" and it reached a boiling point simultaneously in identical forms in all German cities? No. This could only have originated in Goebbels' devilish brain. He had organized this spontaneous outburst with a diabolical delight. What had Sjöderbloom said about Goebbels? . . .

Signore—it hurts me to think of you . . . but I left your life just at the right moment.

I was so absorbed in my thoughts that I did not hear the door open.

"Oh, God, Miss Lili! You frightened me," Lenchen said, "What are you doing here this early?"

Counselor vom Rath succumbed to his wounds and the Jews are being hunted down at full speed.

Goebbels delivered a big speech on November 13th to the workers of the Winter Relief. His words flowed like honey and shrouded his audience in a cloak of self-complacency. He said that through their unanimity and understanding Hitler's policy was crowned by undreamt-of success, a phenomenal proof of the people's boundless trust in their leader. Then he spoke about the murder, by a "hired Jewish youth" who wanted to wound the German people. (He referred back to the murder of the Nazi Gustlof by a young Jew in Switzerland a few years ago.) He said this second assassination ended the people's and the government's patience. Dr. Goebbels tore the web of lies apart with which the Jewish foreign press tried to disguise and excuse the crime.

The people listened as if they were hypnotized and roared with applause. The people now believe they desired everything Goebbels suggests they should desire. Isn't it wonderful how he knows what the people want and fulfills their every wish? This short clubfooted Satan must rub his hands with glee. He suggested to the people that they wanted the destruction of the Jews; and this Jewish youth, Grünspan gave him a superb pretext to destroy the livelihood, families, and perhaps even the lives of several million people.

The Jews are now excluded from German economic life and trade. Moreover, they have to raise an atonement fee of a billion marks. It is only incidental that they have to rebuild their businesses destroyed on *Reichskristaltag* ("Plate-glass Day") at their own expense. The Jews are showered everyday with new decrees from the Nazi Olympus. A "total separation between Germans and Jews" is being carried out.

I suddenly understood my dread at leaving Hinterstein. What is one individual's fate and a lost love compared to the calamity, which befalls millions of people?

November 28, 1938

This morning I awoke to the yearly birthday serenade with which the nurses honor father. The nurses have maintained their staunch loyalty and admiration for father in this time of upheaval, when old friendships cease and previously respected and esteemed persons suddenly become scum.

The usual birthday spirit did not materialize this year, although the Steinbachs and the two tall Olbricht sisters came to dinner and all tried to act as if nothing had changed.

I saw the lost look in father's eyes: his last birthday as medical chief of staff of the Bürgerhospital, his last birthday in the house he built twenty-five years ago.

Every Wednesday, a real-estate agent picks me up at the hospital, to let me screen available apartments before my parents view them. It is not an easy job. The apartment must be close to a bus stop and no higher than the second floor. The landlord has to accept a practicing physician with a Jewish wife. My head swims with all the places I see, although the agent selects them according to location and number of rooms. There is a comparatively large supply on the market because of the emigration of many Jews.

December 3, 1938

On October 1st, every German citizen could obtain a valid police identity card, with photograph and fingerprint. According to the newspapers, it is not mandatory to have such a card. Only the Jews are required to have such an identification by December 31st.

I immediately resolved not to apply for a card. The fewer photos and fingerprints of me are in circulation, the better. When my passport expires, my driver's license will serve as an identification. Mother was compelled to apply without further delay. I will spare myself from recording the endless debates and scenes which ensued. Mother, who views "these people" with unconcerned compassion, suddenly is one of them. Her identity card will contain the given names "Lili Sara."

To crown everything, she must participate in payment of the "blood-money." The first installment is due in ten days. A capital levy can be made in lieu of a cash payment. Since all Jewish-owned stocks and securities have to be deposited at an exchange bank by December 15th, the contribution would be deducted from this.

Despite father's large income, my parents repeatedly landed in financial difficulties. They were incapable of managing their financial affairs. Wolf helped them during his visit to Germany and consulted a distant relative. Fritz Bender is a lawyer, tax expert and financial adviser. Within a few months, he put my parents' finances in order, resulting in a credit position, probably for the first time in their lives. When mother received a small legacy two years ago, I advised my parents to take a nice trip or purchase a new wardrobe. They should use the money to fulfill some special wish, since we do not know what the future will bring.

Fritz Bender did not agree. Apart from three hundred marks each for Katherina and myself (with which we bought typewriters) he prevailed on my parents to invest their money in Dresden Bank stocks. My only comment was, "It is your money."

The Dresden Bank stocks have to be deposited to the account for the Jewish Atonement fine. I was beside myself and called on Bender this afternoon. He greeted me affably.

"Fritz," I started, "how could you give my parents such advice!"

"I couldn't foresee what would happen. Come and sit down."
He offered me a chair, facing him across the desk.

I stared hypnotized at the party emblem on his lapel. "You
knew what you were doing, didn't you?"

He shrugged and a sardonic grin passed over his face.

"You swine!" I stood up and left his office.

On the street, I stopped short for a moment, took a deep
breath of fresh air and shuddered.

"Come, my pet," I said to my constant small shadow. "Let's
walk along the promenades. Perhaps a walk will clear our be-
fuddled minds." Brandy trotted along obediently next to me and
looked almost pensive.

It was difficult for me to reconcile my recent experience with
the picture I had of Fritz Bender. I first met him over ten years ago
when we were both guests of mutual relatives in Mainz. The Mainz
branch of the family considers their house the ancestral home of
the Schroeder family. They cultivate this tradition by collecting
family pictures and treasures and also every distant member of the
family. I always met some cousins, uncles, or aunts whose names I
had never heard before. In this warm and affectionate atmosphere,
it was not hard to accept the jolly and amiable Fritz Bender (whom
Aunt Alice regarded highly) as a cousin.

Aunt Alice, this decidedly beautiful and proud woman,
showered me, her godchild, with love and presents. I was frequently
her guest on weekends and short vacations. She had four sons, and
I probably took the place of a daughter. I loved and idolized her,
until . . .

I still love her and nothing specific happened, but our warm
relationship became markedly cooler during the Third Reich. I still
receive her Christmas and birthday presents with a few loving lines,
which I dutifully answer, but I am no longer invited to her home.
The family relationship is limited to rare telephone conversations
between mother and Aunt Alice, with greetings to me.

Uncle Richard, father's eldest brother, explained the mystery.
He spends several months every year in Mainz and subsequently
told us that my Uncle Rudolf had become a party member. "He
couldn't avoid membership as a factory owner and a leading member of the Chamber of Commerce and Industry."

It was obvious that a true German with four fine sons and an
impeccable family tree had to join the party. We asked about my
cousins, Rudolf's sons.

"Joseph is in the family business, and Christian in the SS."

"What?"

"Yes. At first he was with the Gestapo in Munich; but he never wanted to speak about his work. He also isn't as merry as he used to be."

We had finished supper and were sitting comfortably in father's study.

"The poor boy!" I said without batting an eye. "As an SS man in the Gestapo, his conscience must have weighed heavily. Isn't he in Munich anymore?"

"No. He is in Berlin now, as Himmler's adjutant."

Father bent forward in his chair: "What?"

I jumped up and said, "How could I be related to such a creature!"

As I walked to the door, I heard Uncle Richard ask father with utter lack of understanding, "What is the matter with her?"

My thoughts went around in circles. I remembered the gay and carefree family gatherings of my generation in Mainz. What will become of us, if the Nazis can destroy even family ties? Was Pötz correct again? Will Hitler leave nothing but destruction?

For the first time, I noticed the gray and unfriendly December day: the cold wind whipped my face and broke some bare branches from the trees. I shuddered.

I will advise my parents, as gently as possible, that it would be better to dispense with Dr. Bender's services in the future.

January 1, 1939

The church bells rang in the New Year, 1939. As every year, on New Year's eve, we lit the Christmas-tree candles once again. My parents embraced. Mother wished Katherina and me God's blessings for the New Year. After recent experiences, I accepted the blessings in silence with mixed feelings. A general toast was drunk and we wished each other good night.

Now my parents are alseep. Katherina went to church to commune with her God and while Brandy snores in his basket, I try to draw a balance. So I am seated alone in front of my diary and my small desk lamp is the sole light in the otherwise dark and silent house. Only the belated explosion of a firecracker occasionally interrupts the quiet night.

Is this boundless isolation and loneliness all I can expect from the New Year? Has it come to the point where I must be thankful that I still have my freedom? Freedom? Literally, I am not behind locks and bars, but what is reality? Everything I hoped for and dreamed of is lost. I have a career that occupies but does not engross me. I am surrounded by a family who speaks a language foreign to me. I am exiled from the person who is close to me and thinks as I do.

I walked around my room for a long time, to clear my thoughts. I relived with pitiless reality many things which happened last year, but I realized it is senseless to mourn about what could no longer be changed. I do not want to slip into the same mistakes which I criticize in mother. Mother can never forget her illustrious family background. She is not ready to accept the fact that the Nazis disregard this and classify her as an inferior, whose identity card carries a large *J* and a Jewish first name on the front page. She protests constantly and views the Nueremberg Laws and its consequences as a personal injustice, which befell only her. She cannot understand that she shares her fate with millions.

And father? He is still an upright man and proud to be a German. Several days before German troops marched into the Sudetenland, he read me parts of a letter he was writing to Wolf. He stated his doubts; nobody could say what would happen if war broke out. He was prepared to believe that German objectives were as splendid as the government claimed; nevertheless, he thought the other side had superior armed forces. He wondered whether the new army could equal the imperial army with which he marched in 1914 and considered them the best army in the world. After various speculations, he concluded, "Despite everything, Germany remains Germany."

I remembered how he looked at me expectantly, and that I nodded in response and stared silently at the carpet.

His eyes gleamed with the memories of a glorious past. "You don't remember the empire, my child. It was a magnificent time!" Father never spoke much, let alone allow himself to be carried away by his emotions. He suddenly grew silent and looked at me thoughtfully. "You have no idea what it was like."

"No," I replied, "I only remember its consequences and the lost war."

Father was annoyed. "You have no comprehension of what the Hohenzollern meant to our fatherland."

"No, I don't, dad," I confirmed, "I am truly sorry, but I don't understand it. I only realize that Hitler is the logical consequence

165

of the last war and will drive us into the next war as he himself is a driven man."

"What do you mean?"

"The heavy industries, particularly the armaments industry are driving Hitler towards war. He goes willingly because he believes he is a great politician and military strategist."

Father stood up and wanted to end the conversation. "Don't you think you lack historical knowledge?"

"That is quite possible," I conceded. "But I can't ignore the fact that this German nationalist policy has loused up my whole life."

I shook my head as I recalled this conversation. Mother's Jewish identity card had not changed the family's way of thinking. Father, mother, and Katherina continued to live with their own separate illusions, whether they concern Imperial Germany, an esteemed family background, or the Catholic Church. None of them is ready to leave his pleasant dream world and soberly face reality. I am an outsider in my beloved family circle. Despite my impatience with them, I am really sorry for my parents, because to a degree, I must be a disappointment to them; and I cannot protect them against the day when they will have to face reality.

January 11, 1939

I had a toothache and went to see Müllerchen.

While he drilled my tooth, he observed, "Your father is retired now."

I gestured with my hand and he stopped for a moment. "The management requested that father remain three months longer in the Bürgerhospital. Either they haven't found a successor yet or he isn't free."

Müllerchen grunted and started to drill again, while I thought about the hospital. The research laboratory is closed, the second laboratory technician dismissed, and the instruments and apparatus are stored in our cellar.

"Have you found an apartment?" he asked and withdrew the drill.

"No. We found exactly what we wanted on Klettenbergplatz. However, when my parents told the landlord that mother is a Jewess, he regretfully refused to accept us as tenants."

Müllerchen turned his back and started to prepare the filling. "Incredible," he grunted. After he had filled the cavity, he shoved a wad of cotton in my cheek and ordered me to leave my mouth open. Then he moved his stool closer to the chair, and sat next to me. He said thoughtfully, "I don't understand what this will lead to. You know me well enough not to misunderstand me. Admittedly, there are some swindlers and cutthroats among the Jews; but because of them one can't tar all the Jews with the same brush. What does it mean that half-breeds and Aryans married to Jews are forbidden to belong to the National Socialist Veteran's Association? Didn't these men fight at the front and lie in the mud like the rest of us?" He became silent and stared at the linoleum floor.

After a while, he stood up, took the gauze pad out of my mouth and washed his hands. Brandy, who had been seated at my feet, jumped to the floor.

"Have you time for a cigarette?" Müllerchen asked. He opened the door and added, "My wife would like to see Brandy." "Ines!" he called.

A noisy greeting was heard in the hallway.

Müllerchen sat down again next to me. "Tell me. . ." He stopped abruptly and looked at the floor.

"What is it, doctor?"

"I don't know if I can ask you."

I smiled. "Didn't you just tell me that we know each other long enough to speak freely. What do you want to ask?"

"How much are you affected by what is happening? I know you can't work for the press, but what else can you do? Have you made any plans?"

"I can't get married. There is probably no profession that doesn't belong to some National Socialist organization. Even artists are members of the Reichs Cultural Chamber, the Reichs Chamber of Literature, Reichs Theatre League, etc. . . . I just realized I could not even marry a streetcleaner, since even he is organized in the National Socialist Association of Municipal Employees. And professionally, what choice do I have? Recently, one of the party bosses stated that half-castes couldn't be: civil servants, farmers, doctors, lawyers, teachers, pharmacists, etc. I have practically no choice and I can be grateful that my father needs a receptionist, who isn't required to show proof of Aryan ancestry."

January 18, 1939

Wolf was shocked and alarmed by what he read in America about *Reichskristalltag*. In addition, Katherina ·had apparently

167

written a very hysterical letter to him, which caused him to send my parents all the required emigration and sponsorship papers.

After endless family debates, the plan for emigration was rejected. Father said: "I have my old-age pension here. There I would live at my son's expense. Besides, it won't be so bad."

Last weekend I was sent to Basel especially to write a letter to Wolf. I also took two of mother's diamond brooches to friends for safekeeping.

I spent the whole day in Basel in my room. I wrote to Wolf and tried to explain that we were safe and he didn't have to worry.

Our friends were utterly astounded that I repeatedly asked their assurance that my letter would not be censored. That evening, when I wanted to call a friend in Strassbourg, I was assured that I could call him.

"Are you sure the conversation will not be monitored?"

"Telephones tapped?" They laughed and shook their heads. "That is impossible!"

They looked at me rather doubtfully. They probably thought I suffered from a mild persecution mania. This forced me to explain about life in a totalitarian state. I tried to make them understand that to telephone a Jewish friend abroad was definitely dangerous. I doubt whether I convinced them entirely.

I lay in bed, my last night of sleep in freedom. Walter Gross' voice still echoed in my ears and I remembered former times, when happiness and expectations still existed. The realization hit me that we in Germany had been transformed into mere phantoms.

I was conscious for the first time, how much we had changed in the last six years, in contrast to the Swiss. A Swiss citizen can confide everything in his letters and never doubt for a moment that only the recipient will read it. In contrast, we weigh every word before writing, since we assume that our mail is censored. A Swiss citizen says what he wants on the telephone without hesitation, whereas we express ourselves evasively and circumspectly. We are sure that a trespasser is listening to our conversations and an imprudent word could result in a horrible penalty.

That night I fought a hard battle. The temptation to remain in Switzerland and live again like a normal human being was enormous. I did not doubt that our friends would help me. What would I leave behind in Germany? My parents? Yes, my parents, who are so naive and incapable of surviving. I could not desert them. I would return to the penitentiary named Germany. With this decision, I fell asleep.

February 18, 1939

I spend my mornings in the Bürgerhospital and type father's reports. This gives me more time in the afternoon to look at apartments with the real-estate agent.

I discovered a new emotion in myself: a feeling of prejudice. In a number of flats, we meet the previous Jewish tenants, who are packing and dissolving their households. I would gladly speak to them, but the agent is always next to me. He certainly does not seem hostile towards Jews and does not wear a party emblem. However, he is an Aryan and this fact causes me subconsciously to distrust him. This attitude is contrary to the humanitarian upbringing I received at home, but I cannot overcome it.

March 2, 1939

Lenchen, who has been courted by a young man for a long time, came to my room the other evening. She seemed embarrassed as she said, "Miss Lili, I will have to marry him now."

"Lenchen!" I exclaimed in dismay.

"Yes; I should not have done it," she laughed, while tears filled her eyes.

She will be married the middle of this month. The wedding will take place here in Frankfurt, to spare her parents shame. They live in a small village, where Lenchen was always known as good and devout and presented to the other girls as a paragon of virtue.

I consider this unexpected course of nature tragic for us. Lenchen has been in our home for eight years, and this honest soul is considered a member of the family. It is a blow that she has to leave us in these bad times. When she serves meals, we never have to lower our voices or break off in the middle of a sentence. We could always leave our letters open on the desk. Lenchen has discretion and a delicate sense of tact. Who will we get in her place?

March 8, 1939

Father and I went together to look at an apartment.

We stood before a low iron fence of a small front yard located in the Hansa Allee.

"This is the number," I said. Father looked at the five-story house.

169

We rang the bell on the ground floor and a man with an emaciated face opened the door. It was obvious that his hair had been shaved, since it stood straight upon his head; it was still too short to be combed.

Crates and trunks were in every room of the apartment. Father was visibly shocked. As far as I know he had never met a Jew in this situation. With a tenderness that he normally reserves for critically ill patients, he asked the Jew to show us the apartment.

When we remarked that the rooms were very dark, the man said, "Yes, you will need a lot of electricity here."

We slowly began to converse with each other. His deadly serious eyes looked at us without expression, as if they never again could laugh or reflect joy.

Father asked, "Where are you emigrating?"

"I am going to Brazil."

Father inquired whether any difficulties were placed in the way of Jewish emigration.

"On the contrary," the man replied. "If we weren't beaten too badly and had no visible scars, we were released from the concentration camps only after we signed a statement that we would leave Germany."

He accompanied us to the small gate in the fence.

"Did you suffer hunger?" father asked.

The Jew shrugged his shoulders. "The food was so bad, we all got diarrhea. We had to muster in the yard for roll call and run in circles for hours, until we collapsed. No one was permitted to leave. We didn't even have toilet paper."

His large sad bright eyes looked at us immovably.

March 17, 1939

Shortly before supper, Siegrid called, inviting me and Brandy to come to her place later that evening. I had taken the call in the hall and as I hung up, father opened the study door and asked me, "Do you have a moment, little one?"

He took the newspaper from his desk and pointed to two paragraphs. "Have you read this story?"

Under the headline THE FUHRER ARRIVES IN PRAGUE, it reported that the Czech president Dr. Hascha and foreign minister Dr. Chvalkovsky had been received, at their request, by Hitler in Berlin. Hascha stated that they sought to safeguard peace and

170

order in this part of central Europe. To serve this goal, he wished to place the fate of the Czech people and nation in the hands of the German Führer.

"The Führer accepted this declaration and expressed his decision to place the Czech people under the protection of the German Reich, and guaranteed the autonomous development of Czechoslovakian culture."

Hitler referred to the history of the past thousand years and said, "So I decided to send German troops today." German troops marched into Bohemia and Moravia, which are now called a Protectorate.

Simultaneously the Slovak president Tiso sent a telegram to Hitler: "Because of my strong confidence in you, the Führer and Chancellor of the Greater German Empire, I place Slovakia under your protection. . . . The Slovakian State asks you to assume this custody."

The Führer replied: "I acknowledge receipt of your telegram of yesterday and hereby assume protection over the Slovakian State."

I put the paper down. "Fantastic!"

Father looked at me expectantly. "Unbelievable, isn't it?"

"Yes, it is unbelievable how these heads of state sell out their people. 'Here, Mr. Hitler, I have one more herd of sheep. Will you please accept them?' And Hitler says, 'I received your offer and accept.'" I saw father's disappointed expression; we had again completely misunderstood each other.

"But don't you see what a superb politician Hitler is?" he asked in disbelief.

I shrugged my shoulders.

Father looked at me thoughtfully and then said with an almost apologetic smile, "It is a wonderful experience for me to see Germany's resurgence to greatness and power after all these years of humiliation. I admit I have also feared several times war would break out. But now, Germany will certainly become even more powerful."

April 14, 1939

I have grown one year older. After six years, I have given up the senseless speculation of what the new year might offer me. Moreover, I realize that I can be grateful things are not worse. I no

171

longer have hopes for tomorrow, even though I know that freedom and a new life lie somewhere in the distant future.

The man who was interested in our house agreed to purchase it. The contract will be signed next week. It is almost a miracle that we also found an apartment. The location is not precisely what we dreamed of; but, after all, we can't have everything. The rooms are large, bright, and in good condition. Since the owner is Swiss, mother's origins caused no offense. A dentist's office is located on the second floor. Thus, no objections were raised against father's practice. However, we can not move in before the end of May.

April 22, 1939

The sales contract for the house is not as simple as I imagined. Because we had an hereditary tenancy, the land belongs to the city and the contract still has thirty-five years to run. We must negotiate its release with the city of Frankfurt, which will also determine the sale price. However, the price is unimportant because my parents held the house in joint ownership, and all the money which does not go to the city will be placed in a blocked account for the Jewish fine. What a mockery!

Meanwhile our Führer celebrated his fiftieth birthday. The Kaiser's birthday could not have been more grandiose. April 20th was declared a national holiday. Flags were hung throughout Germany to celebrate the event. Troops paraded in the protectorate and guests flocked in from all countries of the world. The NSDAP's birthday gift for the Führer was a collection of fifty letters by Frederick the Great, stolen from some museum. The newspapers reported that the birthday celebration made a deep impression abroad.

May 7, 1939

Siegrid telephoned yesterday, "Are you really still alive?"
"Only half alive."
"Why? Has something special happened?"
"Siegrid, have you ever moved from a large house, where you lived for twenty-five years?"
"Oh, God!"
"Yes."

"Can you come for coffee tomorrow afternoon and relax from your exertions?"

Siegrid had prepared some coffee and had placed a large bowl of whipped cream in the middle of the table.

As she handed me the bowl she said: "Here, take some more, while you still can."

"What do you mean?"

"From May 15th to September 14th, the production of all varieties of cream will be prohibited."

Siegrid placed another portion of cake on my plate. "Can I give you more whipped cream before the storm breaks?"

I laughed.

"You know," she said, "I hope for the same thing as you do. But when one sees how successful Hitler is. . . I am frequently depressed."

She bent down to give the dogs a tidbit. From halfway under the table, Siegrid said, "I wanted to tell you that if you want to give me anything for safekeeping — jewelry or such things. . ." Without finishing the sentence, she surfaced again, her face was crimson.

"Many thanks, dear, until now we really haven't been affected by the situation. The surrender of jewelry, jewels, and precious metals was requested from full Jews. Mixed marriages are still exempt from this regulation."

Siegrid looked startled when I suddenly began to laugh. "Excuse me. I just remembered that Jews are allowed to keep their dentures as long as they are in personal use. You know, Siegi, there are situations in life, where you have a choice between laughter and tears. I choose laughter."

We pack, sort out, call organizations to pick things up and are all overtired and irritable. The new owner began to press us to hurry, since he wanted to begin remodelling. But our apartment is not ready for occupancy yet. The workmen are still there. Despite utter confusion, father continues to make house calls and to examine patients covered by National Health Insurance.

Occasionally we go to Steffan's in Stiftstrasse to purchase equipment, testtubes and slides for our small laboratory. After we completed the purchases today, father and I went in different directions. I strolled towards the Hauptwache, thankful not to see any more crates or lists. Undecided where to go, I stopped at the Rossmarkt. I bent down and asked Brandy, "Where shall we go?"

173

He wagged his tail in response. I looked across the street. Pötz and Elsa stood on the curb directly opposite us. They looked at us amused, like in the old days in the Saalbau concert hall.

Instead of greeting me, Pötz said, "I knew I would see you today." A few minutes later, we were seated in the Kakao Stube.

While Elsa gave her undivided attention to Brandy, Pötz scrutinized me closely. "You look tired. Are you working very hard?"

I explained that we had sold our house and were in the midst of moving to an apartment.

"Did your parents encounter any difficulties in selling the house?"

"On the contrary," I replied ironically, "they made an excellent deal. Not only do they have to pay the moving expenses out of their own pockets, they also have to pay a thousand marks assessment to the city."

Elsa turned towards me. Her large childlike eyes stared in open astonishment, "What?"

Pötz asked: "Will you explain?"

"There isn't much to tell. Don't forget, my mother now carries the first name Sara. The branch office of the tax department acted in the 'public interest' by underestimating the value of the house by sixty thousand marks."

Pötz leaned back in his chair. He looked at me sympathetically. "I regret the financial losses your parents suffered; but in times like these I wouldn't waste a second thought on such things. If I understand you correctly, your parents will now pay substantially less rent than the house cost them? Well, all right. And your father has a pension? This loss will scarcely reduce your family to ruin. The way things are developing, your parents will be grateful someday not to own a house. What is now happening to full Jews will also happen to mixed marriages in the course of time. You look at me with disbelief? We agree that Hitler will start a war in the near future? Okay. This war will be very different from the last war. We will have a housing shortage. How do you think your parents would feel about sharing their whole house with absolute strangers, with whom they have nothing in common, except an improper family ancestry and fear? Well? Again, you don't want to believe me, but old Pötz knows what he is talking about."

He was silent for a moment while Elsa looked at him with reverent admiration. "It is amazing how he always can predict things."

Pötz continued unswervingly, as if he had not heard Elsa's remark. "We will all be afraid when the bombers come. People of Jewish blood will have to fear anonymous enemy bombs as well as the well-known Gestapo."

"How much longer will it last?" I asked breathlessly.

"How long will it be until war breaks out? Most wars start after the harvest is completed.

"For the time being, Germany's colonial demands are set aside, but Danzig is still being claimed. Goebbels made the wonderful statement, 'The Führer is a friend of peace.' Heads of state who constantly affirm their love of peace are to be viewed with extreme distrust. They speak of peace and think of war. Goebbels substantiated his demands with the argument that Germany came off the loser when the world was geographically partitioned."

"How does he know that? If it is true, why do the Nazis encourage a population increase?"

"Why? Because first of all, they need cannon fodder; secondly, because the leaders are Catholics." Pötz looked at me with a triumphant smile.

"What gives the Catholic priests the right to interfere in the marriages of the believers?" I asked.

"You provided the answer yourself, when you spoke of believers. As long as people are willing to believe and obey what an incompetent priest tells them, the priest can dictate what married couples are permitted and forbidden to do in bed. All power, my dear, is built on the infinite stupidity of the masses.

"Their gullibility is based on their obedience as believers. In marital relations, they act or abstain according to clerical advice, although the priest is not married and has no direct knowledge of what he dictates. A priest with a fixed income can't have any idea of the worries of a family man. I don't think it is really a question of how priests get their authority, it is rather a matter of how they get their deplorable presumption." He leaned across the table, smiling smugly and his eyes narrowed to slits. "The shining example is the supereunuch in Rome. He has everything he wants at his disposal, lives in unimaginable luxury, and is past the age when carnal desires affect him. He speaks of poverty, humility, and abstinence to healthy people made of flesh and blood." Pötz looked at me inquiringly.

"You are right," I said, "people of flesh and blood — but without brains."

175

I am seated at my old familiar desk in my new room. This is the first day, I can relax and be my old self again.

Moving day was absolutely chaotic. The day before we moved, the new owner began to tear down partitions in the attic. Clouds of dust floated down over the staircase and settled on all the furniture. His rebuilding activity continued when the movers came. Katherina's piano was stuck in an angle at the top of the staircase. After endless maneuvering the instrument was finally lowered one floor. Despite all the plaster dust and hammering, one of the movers played a Viennese waltz on the spur of the moment, which restored the good humor of all participants.

By late afternoon, furniture and crates were finally hauled away; nobody thought of unloading them that same day. My parents spent the night at a hotel. Katherina stayed with the Steinbachs, and Brandy and I went to Siegrid's. The next morning we arrived at the empty apartment, where we stretched our legs until the furniture van finally appeared.

We unpacked our possessions and gradually found everything that had been packed in the wrong boxes. Our household slowly resumes its normal routine.

I have a pretty room with a small balcony. The quiet of our old residential district contrasts sharply with the noise of the city streets. I must get accustomed to this racket, which I hear clearly in my ground-floor room which faces the street. Our old house overlooked a park; my present room faces the walls of a four-story apartment house.

Our three new telephones have a dial which can be turned, even when the receiver is hung in place. This means listening devices are inserted in all of them.

The apartment is large and spacious. We can even accommodate Bodo. Have I mentioned him before? Bodo has been so inconspicuous and insignificant in our life, that I probably never expected to write a line about him. When I.G. Farben was desperately looking for rooms for their foreign representatives, they contacted mother and she finally yielded. Bodo moved into our guest room more than a year ago. He is a nice young man, somewhat younger than I, with flawless manners. After a short time, he was considered more a son than a lodger. When we planned to move, he

176

pleaded like a small boy, "Dear Dr. and Mrs. Schroeder, please take me with you. I am going to Turkey on September 1st. Must I move in with strangers for these few months?" Even father was moved by this appeal. We took him along.

July 9, 1939

Dr. Bernd, who accidentally passed by while our furniture was being unloaded, called later to ask if we were completely settled and if he could visit me. He came yesterday evening. He no longer works for the radio station, but moved to a job in industry.

I remembered him as an almost boyish person. He now looks closer to his actual age; a staid man in his mid-thirties. It may be that worries concerning domestic and foreign politics produced the faint wrinkles on his forehead and at the corners of his mouth. His bright eyes and copper-colored hair are unchanged.

We spoke of the increasing number of incidents on the Polish border, allegedly Polish attacks on the Germans in Poland.

I said, "The prize question is whether the Americans will participate in this adventure. Many people believe that too much American capital is invested in Germany; others feel a war would stabilize the American economy. What is your opinion?"

"I think America will enter the war, but not immediately. America only joins when victory is assured. Moreover, the United States is in an economic crisis. Several months ago, President Roosevelt stated he wanted to bring inactive capital and unemployed labor together. Where, Miss Schroeder, could this be done better than in the armament industry? Modern warfare is only a battle of materiel. If the United States enters the war, and they assuredly will, it signifies a colossal business in armaments. Just consider what it means to manufacture a product which is destroyed shortly after it is produced, an item which must be replaced and redelivered immediately. This industry is the only genuine example of perpetual motion in the economy: every shot of ammunition and every bomb, once fired, is irretrievably lost. War, Miss Schroeder, offers the best business industry can wish for."

"Do you think Germany stands any chance under these circumstances?"

"No, not the slightest chance," he replied with conviction. "You only need to sit down and calculate what Germany can produce under the most favorable conditions and compare it with the

177

production of other countries with American support. Only a madman like Hitler would embark on such a venture. He is convinced of his lucky star or his superhuman abilities. I don't know if anyone still has the courage to contradict him. He apparently goes into incredible fits of rage, if someone disagrees with him."

I refilled Bernd's glass and noticed that he glanced at my bookcases. "Take your time and look at the books if they interest you."

He stood up and looked at the titles. After a while, he remarked, "You have a considerable collection about Napoleon."

"He is a fascinating personality! That reminds me of a question: What do you think of the Maginot line?"

"I don't have a high opinion of the military, and I fear the Maginot line will bear me out. Some French generals, victorious in the last war, want to conduct the next one along the same lines that attained their previous successes. Other generals have already foundered because of such mental stagnation."

While he stared silently in front of him, I asked, "Are you, therefore, convinced Hitler will again attack France?"

"Yes. He will unleash the next world war and. . . Oh my God!" He clutched his forehead. "The French worry about how to beautify the Maginot line. They want to cultivate roses there! Roses!"

"Well, at least they will have flowers to decorate their veterans' graves."

August 22, 1939

In two days I leave for my vacation. Today, I went to the cellar to get my suitcases. A thick iron door leaned against the wall in the hallway. The superintendent was supervising two workmen, who were placing support beams against the ceiling of the room. He saw my astonished expression and explained, "We are installing an air-raid shelter."

Dr. Bernd came this evening. Apparently he has discovered me again; neither my family tree nor my previous arrest deterred him from taking me out twice. Today, he wanted quickly to say good-bye, as he was also leaving Frankfurt.

To reach my room, one has to cross a living room where we take our meals and where my parents spend their evenings with a book, a bottle of wine, and father's solitaire cards.

Since his days at the radio station, Dr. Bernd has been terrified of father. He wanted to escape quickly after a rapid bow.

Father said with a friendly nod, "Good evening, doctor. Won't you sit with us for a while?"

The poor fellow could hardly refuse, and politely complied with father's request.

Without beating about the bush, father asked, "What are your views on the situation?"

"Things look very black," Bernd answered cautiously.

Father nodded silently and then said meditatively, "War seems unavoidable, doesn't it?"

"As an economist and historian, I am uneasy about these military preparations."

Suddenly father's patriotic optimism gained the upper hand, "I don't know. According to everything one sees and hears, we have an excellent military establishment in addition to Göring's air force. I also believe that other countries initiated their armament programs somewhat belatedly. It is to be hoped that we will be victorious if things come to a head. Please don't misunderstand me. I too would like to be rid of the Nazis for understandable reasons, but I am and remain a German above all. A second lost war—no. After this resurgence, it would be intolerable!"

Bernd and I went into my room and sat facing each other.

"There you have it," I said.

He shook his head and looked at me perplexed, "Tell me, how can you take it?"

"Badly, but he is my father and never directly did me any harm." When Bernd wanted to contradict me, I gestured defensively: "I know, Doctor. I deliberately said 'directly.' I am completely conscious that I owe the kind of life I now lead to my father and his generation. I have racked my brains, whether one can reproach a person for what nature denies him. One doesn't rebuke a color-blind individual for his inability to distinguish red from green. Perhaps, one even feels sorry for him, because his handicap prevents him from finding wild strawberries. Am I justified in reproaching my father for the way he thinks? Although he is very intelligent, he simply can't disregard Germany and assess life from a more elevated point of view. Apparently nature allowed one of his organs to atrophy."

"Miss Schroeder, I admire your attitude; but tell me, do you have the same excuse for Hitler?"

"No. I think there is an enormous difference between Hitler

179

and my father, and the millions in every country who are like him. My father served as a doctor at the front. I doubt if father would have been capable of shooting another human being, merely because he belongs to a different nation. Hitler, however, is a murderer, and relentlessly exterminates everything that doesn't suit his plans, even an old and proven friend. To reduce it to a common denominator: If you contradict my father politically, he won't want to see you again as a guest in his house. This attitude may offend you, but it does not threaten your life. If you oppose Hitler's system, I can safely say it would endanger your life."

Bernd stood up, placed his hands behind his back and stared absentmindedly at a Dürer etching which hangs above one of the bookcases. He then turned towards me and asked incredulously, "You mean to tell me, your father would be incapable of shooting an individual, but sanctions the killing of hundreds of thousands?"

"Yes, I mean it. One individual, who faces him, is a human being. Hundreds of thousands are, however, an anonymous mass. They can be placed under a collective concept of the French or the Russians. Therefore, my friend, I mentioned the atrophied organ."

Bernd sunk into a chair. Half laughing, he said: "I concede defeat. Something is wrong with your argument; but I can't put my finger on it. I must think it over, and we will talk about it again."

August 30, 1939

The sound of many small waterfalls cascading from mountain to valley interspersed by the melody of cowbells lulls me to sleep. I stretch out comfortably in bed. As always, I am very relaxed and happy as I can only be in Hinterstein.

I broke my trip in Stuttgart, and was the first guest in the hotel breakfast room, as I had to catch an early train. After serving me coffee and rolls, the waiter disappeared. Several minutes later, he approached my table in great excitement with a newspaper in his hand:

"Have you already seen the morning headlines?"

"No."

"I don't know what to make of it. Look here!"

It read GERMAN–RUSSIAN ECONOMIC AGREEMENT.

"After the way our government cursed the Russians, how could they reach an agreement with them? To sit together as if they were friends? I don't understand it!" The man was completely baffled. Shaking his head he repeated the headline several times. Finally he asked in desperation: "What do you think of it?"

"I think Hitler will invade Russia, just like he attacked all the other countries with which he made an agreement or treaty."

The elderly waiter stared at me: "Invade Russia? But we can't attack Russia!"

"No, actually we can not, but we will." I looked at my watch and asked for the bill.

In Hinterstein, I thought, Hitler and his politics can go to hell! Hitler can't move my Hinterstein mountains.

To some extent I was wrong. Hitler could certainly not move mountains, but his murderous policy cast its deathly shadow even on this peaceful patch of earth.

While Brandy and I approached our paradise by train, the first newspapers informed the people that: "through decree as of today in the interest of economical and with that also of the Reich's political freedom, a number of essential commodities will be rationed."

The next day, the Rhine frontier between France and Germany was closed, after the last train had crossed the bridge at Kehl. Two days later, air traffic between both countries was suspended. In Poland several villages were evacuated, and Polish tanks appeared near Danzig. Paris is partially blacked out. The population was urged to go to the provinces as long as trains were still available. The art treasures of the Louvre and the books in the National Library were transferred to the vaults of the Bank of France; similar actions were taken with valuable church windows and other objects. Some British cities were evacuated. German ships were not allowed to enter British harbors and British ships were not allowed to exit. Stranded Americans waited desperately for Scandinavian ships to take them home. Holland mobilized.

I sat in the hotel lobby and read the newspapers. In addition to all the other calamities, the weather is bad. The outlines of the mountains are hidden behind masses of thick clouds. Brandy and I cannot go hiking.

All Europe echoes with war cries and the sound of armaments. The German army celebrates the twenty-fifth anniversary of the Battle of Tannenberg as they have celebrated for the past several weeks the twenty-fifth anniversary of the outbreak of the World War. Instead of proclaiming an international day of mourning for the millions who were senselessly murdered in Europe, the

181

Germans rattle their sabres like Kaiser Wilhelm and deem themselves very heroic and manly. They cannot wait to slaughter a new generation.

September 2, 1939

Yesterday evening Arnulf, Adalbert, and I played several rounds of table tennis at the Cafe von Ehr. None of us had our heart in the game so we stopped and went to the Steinadler for drinks.

We were lost in thought, until Brandy got up and put his front paws on the bench.

"Come up here, pet." He sprang on the bench and pressed close to me. "I'm afraid we won't go mountain climbing, but will have to pack our bags."

"It won't be so bad," Adalbert said, showing his even white teeth, trying to appear unconcerned.

"Poland is already mobilizing," I warned.

Adalbert stood up and stretched: "I am going home."

"I do understand how you feel," Arnulf, who kept me company, said. "During the last two summers, we also thought war would break out any moment, and nothing happened."

I nodded: "Yes—but this time?"

We were both silent again, until I asked: "What will happen to you, Arnulf?"

"Me? They won't induct me that quickly. You know what? I'll come and have breakfast with you tomorrow morning and we'll see how things are."

We arranged a time and parted — for the last time. When I came to breakfast the next morning, Arnulf was not at the table. After a while, I asked about him.

"Arnulf? Oh, he and the others were picked up at 5 A.M. straight out of their beds."

With a few of the postseason guests who are in Hinterstein, I listened to the radio. It was claimed that Polish troops started shooting for the first time. This afternoon, the Germans return fire.

A few days ago, the British government volunteered to act as mediator between Poland and Germany. The Germans maintain now that they waited two whole days in vain for a Polish negotiator and that the Polish state rejected the proposed peaceful solution.

182

Hitler then declared: "To end this insane activity, I have no choice from now on, but to oppose force with force."

Later I stood at the window of my room in the Steinadler and looked out at the clear night sky, where the stars seemed so much brighter than in the city. For the last time, my eyes gazed lovingly over the black silhouette of the silent mountains.

"Force against force!" I said shaking my head and closed the window against the cold Alpine air.

My eye fell on the letter I had cut out from the newspaper. A few days ago, French Minister-President Daladier sent Hitler a last request for a peaceful settlement with Poland.

Daladier indicated France had commitments to other countries, such as Poland, for example, and ended, "If French and German blood will flow anew, as it did twenty-five years ago, each country will fight confident of its own victory in a still longer and more murderous war. The only victor will be destruction and barbarism."

3.   War

September 5, 1939

I am in Frankfurt again, after a return trip which seemed like a bad dream.

The small Sonthofener train station swarmed with people who came from nearby vacation places. Somehow everyone was crammed into the train, but there was barely enough room to stand. We had to change trains in Kempten. The station personnel were mobbed by hundreds of travellers, who wanted to know when and where they could get connections. But, since timetables were no longer valid, we could not learn much. However, a train to Stuttgart was expected.

I sat on my suitcase, thankful that Brandy obeyed me implicitly and was no additional problem. We looked at the general confusion. Some people were excited, some were depressed and silent. Small children screamed, mothers lost their patience, baggage was sought, and a dog sniffed around for his owner. An endless stream of travellers went to the water faucet with all sorts of containers; several people squatted on the floor and rummaged in their suitcases for diapers and other necessities. Finally the train to Stuttgart was announced and a crowd of people rushed to the platform.

Brandy and I stood in the vestibule of a car crowded with people and luggage. I tried to protect his paws as well as I could, but he whimpered when we rounded a curve. The people around us tried to look down and a young woman exclaimed, "Look, there's a puppy!" They moved closer together to give him more room, despite the narrow space. The crowd became more friendly and cooperative, the longer we were squashed together. A sort of grim

185

humor spread around; laughter and children's cries mingled. I was astonished to hear no political remarks. Everyone seemed to be in shock and unable to speak about the war.

After many hours, we reached a station. Outside we heard the cry: "Buchlohe. Everybody out! This train does not continue!"

After the initial sigh of relief at being able to stretch our legs, general confusion broke out. The scenes at Kempten were repeated. Many people were tired and the children had become irritable. We saw the first troop transports pass; they had priority over other trains. Finally the train for Stuttgart arrived, where we had to get off again.

An unimaginable confusion reigned in the Stuttgart station. Soldiers, officers, stranded vacation travellers—I became dizzy from looking—until I found an empty bench spread with newspapers. I gave Brandy a dog biscuit, procured some water for him, then turned my attention to the old newspapers and learned that the Führer had ordered the Wehrmacht to assume active defense of the German Reich.

German troops were massed for counter attack on the German-Polish border. Air force squadrons started to attack military targets in Poland. The navy sailed to protect the Baltic Sea; Gdynia harbor was bombed by the air force.

More bored than interested, I leafed through the newspaper until I was absorbed by the patriotic and impressive Wehrmacht orders of the day.

General von Brauchitsch called: "Soldiers! The hour of trial has arrived. . . . We believe in the Führer!"

Grand Admiral Raeder proclaimed, "Mindful of our glorious tradition; we will fight with unshakable trust in our Führer, and in the firm belief of the greatness of our people and Reich!"

The last quote was by Field Marshall Göring: "Soldiers of the air force! — Our beloved Führer stands in front of you and the whole German nation united in National Socialism stands behind you."

Late that night, Brandy and I arrived in a totally darkened Frankfurt. As I entered the apartment door, I heard my parents' bedroom door open. Mother became emotional and threw her arms around my neck; father appeared in his camel-hair housecoat and said: "I'm glad you're back, little one."

Dr. Bernd was amazed that I had brought Brandy as well as my luggage back with me. He had to leave his suitcase behind and was thankful to have found a place for himself.

"I missed some of the news. Could you tell me what, exactly, caused war to break out?" I asked.

"It was a variation of the Reichstag fire. Apparently, the Poles attacked the Gleiwitz radio station, and this unleashed the catastrophe. It is rumored that concentration camp prisoners and SA men were dressed up as Poles."

"The official cause is probably rather inconsequential now," I reflected aloud. "In any case, the outbreak of war reminds me somehow of the spontaneous outburst on *Reichskristalltag*."

"That's right," agreed Bernd. "The fact that food ration cards were handed out four days *before* the surprise attack on the Gleiwitz station confirms the similarity."

I nodded. "Basically, the Nazis are very stupid. They also boasted how prepared they were."

"Miss Schroeder, even the cleverest criminal sometimes commits an error, over which he stumbles."

I lifted my glass. "Let us drink to the errors of criminals!"

We clicked glasses, but the tinkle died away as we put them to our lips, and our relaxed mood likewise evaporated.

"I foresee a long war. The war machinery of Germany's enemies will get underway slowly; but once it is in full swing, it will be unbeatable. Sure—the German air force is superior at present. But for how long?"

I shrugged, "Somehow I know that Hitler will lose, but it is nerve-racking to hear only about German victories, the Polish evacuation of Upper Silesia, and the incredible number of captured prisoners compared to negligible German losses."

"Miss Schroeder! If it were really only a victorious campaign without losses, as the Nazis would have us believe, why the strict prohibition against listening to foreign broadcasts? The Nazis claim that foreign radio stations try to influence our people with their lies and wear down their spiritual resiliency. This would be impossible if the victories had occurred! Why are we punished, if we listen to foreign broadcasts? Obviously, something isn't as rosy as is being claimed."

187

"Yes," I said with a slight sigh of relief. "You are right. A government with nothing to hide doesn't forbid its citizens to listen to foreign radio programs."

September 20, 1939

War — war — war! One reads, sees, hears nothing else. Everything which we experience is related in some way to the war.

More and more victuals are now on allocation only. Therefore, the ration cards become bigger and bigger. Gasoline is only available on submission of a gas ration card. This ration card is only given to holders of valid drivers' licenses. Tires are confiscated from all unused cars.

If one goes out after dark, a person finds himself in a ghost town. Black and deserted houses surround the empty streets. Since several French and British airplanes have already been shot down over German territory, the population realizes the necessity of the blackout, and the block wardens watch with Argus-eyed vigilance that their area gives no cause for complaint.

Father who had originally counted on a small and comfortable practice, instead, has his hands full. Apart from his devoted patients of long standing, he feels the loss of his Jewish colleagues and the induction of many Aryan doctors into the army. Now that father is so busy, I also do not have much free time. I therefore welcomed my parents' decision to spend the last weekend in Niedernhausen; they could have a brief rest from all the telephone and house calls. Dr. Strüder would care for father's patients during this period.

Etta invited me for coffee on Saturday afternoon. Both of her sons now wear the Führer's uniform. She is besides herself with fear.

My comforting words fell on deaf ears.

"I know what is going on! We are at the beginning of a second world war. Don't think I'm selfish, Lili. I know all mothers are worried about their sons at the front. But . . .since they were born, I have been afraid that this would happen. I simply know . . ." She burst into tears.

Changing the subject gradually we turned to less captious topics as for instance her husband's charge of the former Bürgerhospital, now converted into a military hospital.

Etta went to a large antique cabinet to fetch some brandy. While looking for the bottle, she said: "Did you hear that Sjöderbloom will marry again?" My heart skipped a beat. "They are supposed to honeymoon in Davos for several months."

Brandy and I returned home, like two shadows, through the dark streets. I was relieved and thankful that neither searching looks nor questions awaited me in the empty apartment.

October 1, 1939

This afternoon Dr. Strüder came and requested that father take over his practice, because he was obliged to serve as a country doctor in a remote part of East Prussia. An emigrating Jewish doctor had turned over his practice to Strüder and probably felt that his Jewish patients were in good hands with this politically persecuted man. This had not escaped the Nazis' attention. Dr. Strüder left us his car along with his practice, since he cannot use it in a countryside which is either swampy or icy. Tomorrow he begins his forced move; and that is what it really is.

Father was somewhat confused by Strüder's farewell and his introductions to several Jewish households.

I spoke about this with Dr. Bernd who visited me again this evening, and added that father had two souls conflicting in his breast.

"Your father still does not see what is going on?" Bernd asked in disbelief.

Searching for an explanation, I replied, "Somehow Germany is his brightest idol; and it is still *Deutschland über Alles!* Somehow he is so proud of Germany's victories. However, it vexes him that the newspapers make comparisons between the armies in the First World War and the present one, and that the Imperial Army required a year and a half to achieve what Hitler's soldiers accomplished in a few weeks. He explains that the Germans then faced an excellently trained and armed Russian army in contrast to the present small, badly organized Polish army. He can really get worked up by these things."

When I fell silent, Bernd asked, "That is one soul. You spoke of two. What is the other?"

"His other soul is outraged that a colleague, whom he respects and personally esteems, is sent to live in exile. Today, he was bewildered by his experience with his Jewish patients. He learned that about a week ago, in a surprise move, the Gestapo seized all Jewish radio sets for more suitable use by Germans.

"This is where the fight between his two souls begins. He

189

thinks the military victories are splendid and is delighted that Germany is again a great power. On the other hand, he is outraged and mortified by the methods employed to deal with political opponents. He never loved the Jews, but he repudiates what is happening today."

Bernd smoked thoughtfully and asked me, after a while, "What does your father say about the food shortage?"

"But, my dear doctor, there is no shortage," I replied ironically. "Misuse is only being curbed. He finds this very sensible and gladly complies with these measures in the interest of the whole nation. But the way things are developing, the bread basket will slowly be emptier and shortages will become more noticeable. One day, even my parents will also realize this."

Dr. Bernd reached into his breast pocket and took out a small newspaper clipping, which he placed on the table in front of me. It was a black-bordered obituary with a military cross in the lower center of the box.

He saw my questioning look. "No, it is nobody I know. It was but the first notice I saw. It appeared on September 23rd; and I find it very characteristic."

I read: "On September 8th, in Poland, the young life of our only beloved, son and brother was given for the Führer and Fatherland."

I returned the piece of paper to him. "It is fantastic — for the Führer and Fatherland — for the Kaiser. When will these imbeciles awake? He gave his life for the Führer?"

"Yes, for this comic Austrian ham! There will be hundreds of thousands of men who will sacrifice their lives on the altar of the fatherland."

October 11, 1939

It is very useful that I have a driver's license because I became father's chauffeur after he took over Dr. Strüder's practice and car.

A routine slowly developed. At nine o'clock, the first National Insurance patient arrives. I take down his medical history, so father can remain at breakfast a few minutes longer. After these patients have been examined, we make house calls. During the afternoons, except Wednesdays and Saturdays, we keep office hours. When necessary, I drive father afterwards to house calls. His consultation hours grow as do the telephone calls requesting his visits.

Brandy turned out to be an enthusiastic car passenger. He accompanies us daily and provides me with company, while father makes his various rounds.

We arrived late for lunch today and I excused myself to feed Brandy. I took his bowl into my room, and left the door to the hallway open. My parents were already at the table.

I heard mother ask: "What happened today?"

I did not understand father's reply until I heard the name Sjöderbloom and pricked up my ears.

"How horrible!" said mother in a subdued voice. "How long were they married?"

"Exactly eight days," father replied. "It was an ordinary influenza. She was a thoroughly healthy woman."

"The poor man!"

The conversation stopped when I entered the dining room. I picked at my food and it required an effort to get more than a few bites past the lump in my throat.

Getting up from the table I asked father: "Do you still need me?"

"No, you can put the car in the garage."

Before I left the house I telephoned Pötz and we agreed to meet in the Kakao Stube.

Pötz already sat at the table we usually occupied; he held a book in front of him, in which a folded newspaper was stuck.

A pleased smile appeared on his face as I entered the tea room. He got up and greeted me in a formal manner. "And what provides me with this unexpected pleasure, and why did you finally decide to make use of my telephone number?"

"My completely selfish wish to converse with an intelligent person and have an exchange of thoughts and ideas."

He looked at me attentively, "Are things that bad?"

I nodded silently and tried to hold back my tears.

"Whatever it is, my dear, one can overcome everything, as long as one doesn't feel sorry for oneself. Self-pity is debilitating. You are too brave and strong, to let it get you down. You surely know it is your fate to carry the burden of others on your shoulders." He looked at me with a reassuring smile. "You also know that you will meet the situation. Your shoulders are young and strong."

191

He opened the book and removed the newspaper to end this very personal discussion. "Three days ago, a thanksgiving service was held in the Berlin cathedral for the victorious conclusion of the Polish campaign and in memory of the dead. In the Berlin cathedral . . ." the corners of his mouth pulled downwards. "Isn't it edifying that we cannot do anything without God? First, we ask him to bless the weapons which we use to destroy the life he gave and then we ask him to accept the souls of the murdered murderers."

"The nation of poets and thinkers will enthusiastically obey Göring's call for a while. 'The Führer commands and we obey.' And the Führer will invoke God's help on every suitable occasion." He laughed soundlessly. "'A god who created iron did not want slaves.' I have a suspicion this god was a German. It seems to be entirely acceptable that Czechs, Poles and possibly French and English are slaves. Only the Germans are the master race. Truly, a strange god. A god, who creates human beings and lets them be bestially destroyed. No artist, who created a work, would take a knife and destroy his canvas, or smash a finished sculpture with a hammer. Only God in his impenetrable wisdom. . ."

Pötz looked at me searchingly: "This is a perverse creation of fantasy, this imaginary Christian God."

"Yes, but people seem to need to believe in something. If it isn't in this fantasy, then it is in Hitler.

"That is, my dear, until Hitler, the Superman, plunges from his height like Icarus and reveals himself as a fallible human being. The hatred of the disappointed will be terrible, and none of his believers will want to admit they followed him."

Pötz leaned back. He looked at me through half-closed eyes and added with irony: "I believe the Christian god is much better off. No one has ever seen him, since he lives beyond the clouds; consequently he can not plunge down and disappoint his followers."

December 3, 1939

Bodo had to return from Turkey because of the war. He visited us briefly, before he moved to Berlin, and asked my parents to house a colleague of his. This man is also an I.G. Farben representative from South America, who was overtaken by the war during his European vacation. After an endless debate, my parents finally agreed, since Bodo assured them, it was only for a short time.

Gunter Siegurd Kunz is the absolute opposite of Bodo. Bodo has black curly hair, large dark eyes and is vivacious and full of good humor. Kunz has reddish-blond hair, smoothly parted, and blue eyes. He is a well-tempered, cool, Northern German, who smells of Old English lavender. For the time being, he works in the I.G. Farben building and waits to see whether he can travel back to South America or will become a soldier.

Occasionally, he drinks a glass of wine with my parents. He is very polite, but by my standards, he is an unbelievable bore. He tells about the German Colony in South America and all the society gossip: who married whom, what the women's maiden names were and who was divorced and why. Whenever Dr. Bernd appears during these breathtaking conversations, Kunz looks at him disdainfully, and I see how my mother's matchmaking instincts awaken.

December 13, 1939

To walk in town does not appeal to me anymore, not only because of the bad weather. There are other reasons, which spoil a stroll through the city. I thus prefer to spend my free afternoons at home.

The early twilight cast shadows in the room. I had not turned the light on. Bernd, seated with his back against the balcony door, appeared as a massive black figure, his face a lighter spot of color, although his features could not be clearly distinguished.

He asked in a pleasant voice, "There must be a very good reason, why you hate to go to town?"

I was silent and thought, his left eyebrow is now raised in gentle amusement. His large shadow laughed softly. "I had grown accustomed to seeing you hurry through the streets at such a pace that I always worried you would fall down."

"You're right," I replied, "I now have something against the city. Everytime, when the Germans have won a victory. . ."

When I stopped short, he continued with understanding, "then there is the sound of music."

"That's it," I exclaimed. "I am not a born admirer of Liszt — but this! One already hears the victory fanfares from the Schillerstrasse. Around the Hauptwache, the Steinweg, Biebergasse, they

193

are inescapable. Everywhere loudspeakers blare out that melody. It simply makes me sick!"

The match, with which Bernd lit his cigarette, momentarily illuminated a suppressed smile on his face. While I turned on the small desk lamp, he said:

"There are different interpretations for the Nazi's partiality to Liszt's 'Les Preludes'. One is that these fanfares announced the victory over Napoleon. One would almost assume a jokester chose precisely this theme from all musical literature." After a pause for effect, he added: "From this point of view, the motif may be somewhat more tolerable to you."

Bernd finally convinced me to go into the city with him yesterday, a Saturday afternoon, to do some Christmas shopping.

In the *Frankfurter Bücherstube*, I selected a small music dictionary for my former music teacher.

After I made my selection, Bernd said, "Not so fast! Can I have a look?"

I gave him the dictionary.

He looked at the index, opened the book to the corresponding pages; pointed to the entry for Mendelssohn and read aloud: "' A decadent Jewish hot-house flower!' Nowadays one must check for this when one buys books."

December 26, 1939

I have survived Christmas again. At least, I got a heavy wool blanket, which can be buttoned around the waist like a skirt. As an old customer, mother got it for a price and some kind words, but without a ration card. She worries about my health, since I sit for hours in the cold car.

Yesterday afternoon, Siegrid came to hear my new records. She met a couple and their daughter in the doorway and wanted to know if we knew them.

"It was probably the Schindlers, who live in the apartment above us. We know them, just like all the other tenants."

"Are the other tenants bearable?"

"They are partly a source of purest joy, like the Schindlers. He is a deaf mute, and she is Jewish. Since he can't hear what she says, he can't correct her." I began to laugh. "We dubbed her the 'Ebinent,' her version of *eminent*. Mr. Schindler is a dentist. Now they are worried because he converted to Judaism as 'equimament,' as she puts it, for her marrying a deaf mute. Recently she warned me: 'Now, Miss Lili, please don't do anything which could cause you ovations!' (She meant complications.)"

After we laughed ourselves silly, I continued, "The Colliers live on the floor above the Schindlers. He does something at I.G. Farben. Anyway, he seems to travel abroad frequently. Collier's wife sings. Mother likes her very much; they bake cakes for each other and are like one heart and one soul. One of her two sons has already been drafted."

"Isn't there still a floor above the Colliers?"

"Yes. Half of it is built into garrets for the servants, the other half is an apartment. The Rodenhauers live there with their daughter. She is a widow, who operates a fur shop. The mother is a simple middle-class business woman; the daughter is a hussy."

"An interesting collection of people," Siegrid observed. "What is Schindler's daughter like?"

"A nice thing. She is preparing to leave the country. It is all so idiotic! Racially she is only half-Jewish, but since she was raised as a Jewess, she is considered a full Jew."

January 1, 1940

We had the usual New Year's celebration with the members of our intimate family circle. Except for Katherina, none of us could fully concentrate on the old social games.

Mother suddenly pressed father's hand. When he looked at her in surprise, she said, "I am so thankful, I have you here. I just remembered the last war, when I was all alone with the children. Ach, and poor Etta!"

This comment seemed to be the cue for the conversation to turn to the war. I listened with half an ear. I had heard all the pros and cons of German warfare, the glorious successes of a Germany, which arose from the ashes like a phoenix to become Greater Germany.

Suddenly Katherina asked, "You are so silent, my dear. What are you thinking of?"

I looked at her thoughtfully. Did her question and affectionate expression hide the anticipated pleasure of a quarrel?

When my parents also looked at me, I shrugged. "I thought of my Jewish friends who fled abroad and wondered where they would celebrate their New Year and how they were. I also thought about our Jewish patients, who could send their children away, but probably can't get out themselves. And I thought of the Nazi slogan 'Germany awake!' My God, will that be an awakening!"

"What do you mean?" asked father. "You certainly aren't alleging that Germany can be defeated again?"

"Yes, father."

"And how do you come to this conclusion?"

"I have heard from two men, whom I consider well-informed and intelligent, that modern warfare has nothing much to do with bravery, but is a battle of materiel. Since Hitler has already collected and ground the garden fences into scrap metal, we don't seem to be all too richly endowed with material resources."

"You again take a negative point of view," father replied. "We will get not only additional manpower, but also industrial capacity from all the conquered territories."

"Shoes and textiles are only available with ration cards because military requirements precede civilian needs. This doesn't exactly sound like a surplus."

"But my dear, it takes a while until things run smoothly in the conquered countries."

I was silent. Katherina said sweetly: "Lili seems to have a different opinion."

"Yes," I confirmed. "The occupied territories don't have only manpower and agricultural products for us."

"What else?" asked father ironically.

"They have a population, who hate the Germans from the depth of their hearts and they also have snipers, partisans, and guerrillas, or whatever they may be called. Furthermore, since the Nazis have clearly stated, that they will begin war with England and since the battle against France is already halfway launched, the front will be dangerously strung out. The population of occupied territories, who makes it possible for us to have special quotas of food, will not only have to starve, but are already treated as subhumans. The military will therefore be compelled to hold these people by force on a long-term basis."

"I simply can't imagine that Hitler will also fight against England," mother objected.

"But he wants to attack England," I retorted. "Goebbels said in his Christmas speech that, today, Germany is conducting a total war. He furthermore said; 'In this war, we fight for our naked existence!'" I laughed. "I fear it will be more naked than existence."

"But dearest," mother said, "let us forget the war tonight."

Together with father, she lighted the Christmas-tree candles one more time.

I looked doubtfully at this symbol of Christian love, from which the pine needles already fell, as though Christianity disintegrated before my eyes: small particles, falling piece by piece, until only a naked skeleton remains, to be thrown away on a refuse-heap, like Pötz's concept of sending another god to his well-deserved retirement.

My rather unfriendly thoughts were interrupted by twelve high-pitched but gentle tones from father's pocket watch. He stood in front of the Christmas tree, looked at his gold watch, which he held in the palm of his hand, and seriously proposed a toast to the New Year. Father made a slight effort to smile. The sounds of church bells reached us from outside. Fireworks were prohibited because of the war.

January 6, 1940

Immediately after the new year began Hedwig had to leave. She moved into the municipal hospital, where unmarried mothers work for their keep doing light household jobs, dishwashing and the like.

Hedwig was the victim of our move. We don't know whether the culprit was the electrician, the locksmith or the carpenter, who all had access to her room. Mother let her remain in the house as long as possible, took the necessary steps to place her elsewhere, and concerned herself with the spiritual welfare of this bewildered expectant mother. Since Hedwig did not want to return to us after the birth of her child, mother looked around for another maid.

Yesterday, another gem appeared, a plump, smart person in her late thirties. Mother, instead of telling her that she was Jewish during the negotiations about wages, free time, etc., waited for an opening this afternoon, after the woman was already settled in and preparing supper.

The reaction to mother's revelations was prompt: the maid was pale with horror, ran to her quarters in the attic as if chased by Furies, and packed her things again. A loud bang of the apartment door announced her departure.

197

January 17, 1940

I forgot to mention that our famous patient Uncle Franz returned from the Black Forest. Sometime in October, he suddenly appeared in front of me during office hours.

"Uncle Franz!"

"Aunt Lili!"

We simultaneously extended both hands and his good-natured suntanned face beamed at me. He now comes regularly and I wonder how he feels, being surrounded by so many Jewish patients in father's waiting room. He acts as if it doesn't disturb him and he is invariably friendly and in high spirits.

February 28, 1940.

Pötz telephoned day before yesterday, to ask why I never came down town?

"I am off on Wednesday afternoons," I replied.

So we met today as usual in the Kakaostube.

His familiar observant glance rested on my face. Only this time, his look lingered so long that I finally raised my eyebrows and asked: "What is the matter?"

He smiled in a friendly way: "It is interesting to note the transformation of a person. When I first saw you, you were still half a child with round cheeks and dreamy eyes. The round cheeks disappeared, the lips became a shade narrower and the eyes. . . they can still dream, but they can also see the world realistically." He nodded with satisfaction. "It is nice, if one can see things clearly, and despite this, not lose the gift of dreaming occasionally."

I was rather embarrassed because his last words carried a sense of having lost something.

The next moment, he sat up straight as an arrow and a smug expression appeared on his face. "Hitler will try to drive our last dreams away. By the way, have you heard his speech?"

"No, I leave that to my mother."

"What? Your mother listens?"

"Yes. Everytime she expects him to say something new."

He shook his head in disbelief, "Your mother, a Jewess?"

"Mr. Pötz, my mother is Christian and German, and no one

198

can take her Germandom away from her."

"Hmmm." His head was tilted so far back that his small goatee stood almost horizontally. Looking down at me he said ironically: "As a Christian, she certainly must enjoy the Führer's speeches." He then reached into his back pocket and removed a folded piece of newspaper. "I also can't listen to Hitler, but I glance at what he says in the newspaper. His speech on Monday at the celebration of the founding of the party is interesting and decidedly revealing. Somehow, Hitler is afraid and struggles with his god. Just as he spellbound the German people, he now tries to influence God and implores providence. Here," he pointed to several underlined lines and read, "I believe in one thing: there is a god!' After this observation he declared: 'we Germans have behaved badly, but then the resurgence of our people began through hard work. Throughout this entire period providence has again blessed our work. The braver we were, the more we received the blessings of providence.'" Pötz glanced at me diabolically: "Now comes the doubt and the promise: 'Heaven has blessed our struggle until now'; 'could fate have let this occur if it were her intention, to suddenly let this fight turn against us? It can't be otherwise: we must win and therefore, we will win!'" Pötz lifted his head and looked at me triumphantly: "How does this sound from a man, who said a few months ago, at the start of the war: 'I have never learned the word *capitulation*. Therefore I would now like to assure the whole world: November 1918 will never again be repeated in German history.' At that time, he neither spoke about providence, nor sought God's help."

Pötz carefully folded the Hitler speech and it disappeared in the pocket of his jacket. He then bent towards me, "Remember, my dear: always distrust people, who constantly mention God. The more pious someone appears to be, the greater the likelihood that he is hiding more wickedness than other people. Take a look around you; think of the God-fearing Irish, who detonate bombs in England to the delight of the Nazis. They want to help a few English people into the hereafter, motivated by pure Christian charity."

I had to laugh and Pötz looked at me amused, then asked: "I would like to know, when did you begin to have doubts about Christianity, although your mother certainly tried to indoctrinate you?"

199

"When I was about thirteen years old, I was reluctant to say my prayers before going to sleep. But occasionally something like fear crept over me."

"What sort of fear?"

"Fear that perhaps this man with a long beard was watching me from above the clouds and would punish me for my disobedience."

Pötz nodded. "After that, when something in your life didn't go according to plan, let us say, your jail sentence or career prohibition — did your doubts ever return?" His eyes were wide open, as he looked at me searchingly.

"No," I shook my head decisively. "What happened to me is really nothing unusual. Thousands of people experience the same thing, in one form or another. Certainly, many are good Christians, which makes no difference to their god. They at least have the consolation that God is concerned, since he subjects them to these trials."

When Pötz looked at me with satisfaction, I asked: "What will Hitler do, if his god doesn't play along?"

"It would be better to ask, what will become of us. I believe I am not deceiving myself, if I give you the assurance that Hitler's god will not play his game and that providence has the horrors of the apocalypse in store for us. In the short or the long run, America will actively participate in this war; America will conjure up an almost inexhaustible arsenal and thereby set its sinking economic ship afloat again." His left hand moved through his gray hair, where it stayed for a moment. "Hitler hasn't decided whether he should emulate Frederick the Great or Napoleon. If it should be Napoleon, Russia will be Hitler's death trap."

March 31, 1940

Today, Sunday afternoon, we for once had tea all together.

Mother disappeared for a moment and returned very proudly with a cake: "What do you say to this?"

"Splendid!" father replied.

"Cake!" cried Katherina enthusiastically.

"Is something wrong?" mother asked me, because I was silent.

"No, no," I said and tried to smile.

200

"But, my dear," mother persisted, "something must be wrong."

"Okay," I answered. "A lot of things are wrong. Have you ever reflected, how insane it is that we consider it special to obtain a piece of cake for Sunday? There is enough in the world to feed everyone. But no! We must sacrifice for a few fools."

The three of them looked at me completely baffled.

Father pulled himself together first, "But there is a war going on."

"Exactly," I said, "that is precisely what I meant. I remember how someone gave me a present of some chocolate wrapped in tin-foil at the end of the last war and I didn't even know what it was. Neither did I know normal bread, milk without a blue watery rim, butter, eggs, and other similar things. That experience was probably child's play compared to what awaits us now. I only hear of sacrifices. One Dish Sunday, to help the unemployed, may have been a very good idea. But now we don't have any unemployed, and One Dish Sunday has been transformed into Sacrifice Sunday. For whom? For what?"

"But, it is for our people," mother said astonished.

"First of all, they are not our people, since they fortunately don't accept either you or me as a member; and secondly, it is certainly not for the 'people'."

"But, for whom else?" asked father visibly irritated.

"It is for a few power-hungry, ambitious men; for an emperor, president, chancellor, or whatever the head of state is called; a handful of generals and several industrial magnates."

Father clearly fought for his self-control and asked, "Don't you think you have oversimplified matters?"

I shook my head. "What have the people ever received from these wars, but cripples, fatherless children, widows, and debts?"

The doorbell rang. I opened the door because our maid had the afternoon off. Dr. Bernd stood in front of me.

"You arrived just in time! I need your help" I said to him, while leading him to the living room. "I hope I brought an ally with me."

Everyone laughed and this eased the situation somewhat.

"Why do you need an ally?" Bernd asked.

I reported briefly what the quarrel was about and we looked at him expectantly.

201

He explained without hesitation, his eyes on father: "I fear, I must choose your daughter's side."

"Why, doctor?" inquired father amenably. "What is your opinion as an historian?"

Bernd thought for a moment, while he looked at all of us attentively. He turned to father: "May I first inquire what time it is?"

Father pulled out his heavy gold watch obligingly.

"Didn't a gold chain once belong to that handsome watch?" Bernd inquired. I had spoken to him about the watch chain, a long time ago.

Father replied: "Yes, it was a sacrifice for the war."

Bernd nodded. "'I gave gold for iron,' isn't that the correct phrase? That is what your daughter wanted to express, among other things. Dr. Schroeder, as a normal citizen, you were permitted to retain the iron, while your emperor fled across the border with your gold."

While father searched for a reply, I interjected: "Today the metal collection is a sacrifice of the German people so that they may survive the struggle for their lives. Once again a sacrifice. And who forced the people into this so-called fight for existence, if not Hitler and the armaments industry?"

Father did not react to my words, but turned directly to Bernd: "Our *lebensraum* was overcrowded. Since we couldn't get our colonies back, we must at least recover the old German provinces on the European continent."

Bernd shrugged his shoulders. "I can't agree with you. We must remember Germany lost the war. I grant you, without further comment, that the reparations demands were unreasonable. In addition, Germany had to cut its coat according to its cloth. In my opinion, the Czechs, Poles and Lithuanians have the same claim for living space as the Germans . To return to the initial point of your discussion, it is like your daughter said, the people must always carry the burdens. The fat party bosses, who stuff their homes with valuable carpets, paintings and furniture taken from the Jews, don't lack anything; they have coffee, butter, cream and all the foods which have grown rather scarce for us."

When Bernd and I were alone in my room, he said: "Your father is a phenomenon. It's been a long time since I've dealt with people of his mentality. I had forgotten they still existed."

"This kind of thinking still goes on, doctor. It is typical among wide circles of the upper middle class."

I was silent and stared in front of me, until Bernd asked: "What are you thinking about?"

Involuntarily, my hand ran over my forehead: "I was just thinking whether my father — if he weren't married to a Jewess and didn't have a daughter with a criminal political record . . ." I could not say the rest of the sentence.

But Bernd completed it, "whether he wouldn't have joined the Nazi party? Probably."

"Miss Schroeder, for every person — man or woman — who has a definite patriotic feeling, and for whom the word *fatherland* represents a very special and personally elevating ideal, a Hitler or a Mussolini or whatever the popular hero may be called, is the personification of a national dream. Though this dream is tied to murder and bloodshed, this is considered a necessary evil, since the end justifies the means and no sacrifice is too great — especially when others make it."

May 5, 1940

Somehow it has almost become a rule that when Bernd visits me, we usually stop and briefly discuss recent political events with my parents.

The fighting between the Germans and English at Narvik and Trondheim has increased. All four Norwegian railroad lines to Sweden have fallen into German hands, and all English landing attempts in Norway have been repulsed. Three days ago, the Norwegian troops capitulated.

Despite all these victories, father began to have doubts. "Everything is going too well and too smoothly," he said to Bernd. "We also experienced this in the First World War."

Bernd nodded. "I'm sorry to have to say it, but Hitler's victories are slowly making me sick. On the other hand, I believe that this can't continue. How can he hold this gigantic front? It is only a question of time, until France will become restive. The numerical advantage of masses of people lies on the other side."

May 10, 1940

Events follow in rapid succession. Yesterday, the German government sent a memorandum to the Belgians and the Dutch. It is evident that Belgium and Holland are not neutral, since they support England and France and have built up their fortifications only on the German border. Therefore, German troops will march in.

Today, the Führer's headquarters reported that at dawn the German army attacked the western border on a broad front, because of the impending enemy threat to extend the war to Belgian and Dutch territory and the related danger to the Ruhr region. The air force with army ground support successfully attacked enemy airfields. Numerous German units landed on Belgian and Dutch airfields. Holland declared war and since the Belgian government allegedly called English and French troops into their country for support, the Germans attacked and destroyed military targets in France, Belgium and Holland.

While I am entering these facts, my parents are listening to Hitler's speech in the next room. "Soldiers of the western front! The hour of the decisive battle for the future of the German nation has arrived."

I jumped up and knocked on the connecting door, "Can't you turn down the volume on that fellow?"

"The battle which began today," his voice from next door rang out, "will decide the fate of the German nation for the next one thousand years."

I took the dog's leash. "Come here, Brandy dear. We'll take a walk."

When I returned, I asked my parents, "Anything special?"

"They occupied Luxemburg."

May 18, 1940

Katherina moved to Munich on May 15th. She lost her job here and could not find another one, but hopes to have better prospects in Munich. A few days before leaving, she invited me to her room one evening. She explained that she wanted to be alone with me which made me decidedly uncomfortable.

After several questions about my current work, she said that I would never have been able to pursue my career in journalism and was now better off than she was professionally.

While looking at her attentively, I wondered whether by this she wanted to ease her conscience. I asked, "Do you mean that the verdict of the Special Court which prevented me from following my career isn't important?"

She hesitated and avoided giving a direct answer, "Aren't you satisfied now?"

"Satisfied?" I echoed. "I am simply ecstatic about working in a profession which I would never have chosen under normal circumstances; and I am happy to have lost the man I loved, because of the added burden of a political conviction."

She looked at me aghast: "Because of the sentence?"

"Yes. And I don't even know how I will find out when he dies . . ."

"If he —? But why?"

I bit my lips and left her room.

The day after Katherina's departure, I went to the pharmacy with father. We met one of his colleagues in front of the store.

After we had greeted each other and made a few remarks about the war, the other man asked: "Have you heard about Sjöderbloom?"

"No," father replied. "What?"

"He apparently had a hemorrhage during an airplane trip and died."

Father was stunned. "When did this happen?"

"Two days ago."

I am alone in my room. For the first time in my life, I understand why people bash their heads against a wall. Senseless questions torment me with the refrain: "Too late."

June 5, 1940

Frankfurt night life is gradually acquiring a character of its own. We had a few enemy overflights, although no bombs were dropped. After people had to seek shelter from metal fragments, the result of flak, stricter regulations were issued for blackouts and alarms. Even night watches were organized, after the surprise attack on Belgium and Holland.

To avoid collisions in the completely darkened streets, people wear luminous patches on their clothing and jackets. Staircases and house entrances are coated with luminous paint. Passageways to neighbouring houses and emergency exits are built in cellars, and cellar windows are reinforced. Searchlights sweep soundlessly across the night skies, like ghostly fingers.

Yesterday bombs fell on Frankfurt causing the first deaths.

When Bernd came this evening, mother pounced on him with the words: "Listen, doctor, isn't this horrible? People are being killed by the bombing!"

He shrugged his shoulders: *"C'est la guerre,* dear lady. I'm afraid, Mr. Meier has promised more than he can keep."

"Mr. Meier?" asked father.

Without trying to hide from father his malicious joy at Göring's misfortune, Bernd replied immediately: "Göring once stated that if a single enemy airplane should appear over Germany, he wanted to be renamed Meier."

We were silent and all of us probably thought about the latest events. German troops were in the Hague and Amsterdam. The surrender of the Dutch army was signed. A breakthrough took place at Sedan and the Maas River was crossed on a wide front. While the Belgian government fled to Oostende, German troops marched into Brussels. Ten days later, the Belgians capitulated unconditionally. Eupen and Malmédy returned "home to the Reich."

"The German successes are simply incredible," father observed with a mixture of doubt and admiration.

"Our Führer also thinks so," I confirmed. "He is so enthusiastic about the current victories, that he ordered the flags to be put out for eight days and the bells to ring for three days. The fighting will then be resumed!"

June 26, 1940

Bernd came rather early today, my free afternoon.

He was deeply depressed. Not only has Strassburg been captured and Paris fallen into German hands, but yesterday, an armistice with France was declared, after the total military collapse of the French front between the Aermel canal and the Maginot line. As a result. Hitler issued a proclamation:

German People!
Your soldiers have ended the war in the West within barely six weeks, after a heroic fight against a brave opponent.

Their deeds will be recorded in history as the most glorious victory of all times. With humility we thank the Lord for his blessings.

I order the flag to be raised throughout the Reich for ten days, and the bells to ring for eight.

"Whatever Hitler starts is crowned with success!" Bernd observed in despair.

"But my dear friend!" I exclaimed. "You told me long ago that the Maginot line was worthless. You were correct. Why are you now depressed about something you knew in advance? Someone, who knows the French as well as you do, must also know how they can hate. All of these subjugated countries will pursue the Germans with hatred. How long do you believe, Hitler can hold all of them in check? Apart from this, he has now declared that war against England will continue."

"He will win again!"

"No, he won't win. The Americans will see to that."

He sat with his head in his hands, as if bent over in pain.

"Dr. Franz Bernd!"

He pulled himself together and looked at me.

"I will tell you something. These victories don't give me any pleasure; but I also know that Germany will lose the war."

"How do you know that?"

"I simply know it. If I didn't have this conviction. . . Dr. Bernd, what do you think a person in my situation can expect, if Hitler wins? If I weren't convinced of his ultimate defeat, I would have capitulated long ago."

"Capitulated? What do you mean?"

"Put an end to it all. Do you seriously believe, I would wait for the Nazis to murder me?"

A small gleam of hope appeared in his eyes. "You are really, absolutely convinced?"

"Yes, positively. Moreover, much has happened during the air attacks that we don't know about. Haven't you heard that advances up to three thousand marks are paid for air-raid damages, on condition that the things can be obtained or repaired? If such ordnances have already been issued, all kinds of things must have taken place."

He stood up somewhat comforted and took a few steps through the room.

"Come along," I said. "We'll take a short walk with Brandy."

July 21, 1940

Apparently, one even grows accustomed to war. Punctually at 12:30 every night, the sirens sound off and we go to the cellar. Brandy is always the first. Long before the sirens howl, he lifts his head, listens, and goes to the door. It isn't that he is afraid, but there are biscuits in the air-raid cellar.

Frankfurt was hit by several bombs, and one house was totally destroyed resulting in seven deaths: a gentle foretaste of things to come. Despite this, movies and restaurants are well frequented, since there is more money than things to purchase. Although food is rationed, we don't suffer actual hunger. After each new country is occupied, special allotments are distributed.

Gunter Siegurd Kunz left and went to his father in Hamburg. As we learned in the course of time, his parents are divorced. His father lives in Hamburg, while his mother is in Bonn. She remarried a well-known physicist, who lost his position as professor at the University because he is Jewish. Kunz speaks of his Jewish step-father with great respect; nevertheless, I can't shake off a decided mistrust.

Now that Kunz is out of the way, I made his room, which has running water, into a darkroom. Bernd helped me build an enlarger from an old camera, and I spend many evenings enlarging old photos from Hinterstein, since I want to avoid having too much free time for thought.

August 11, 1940

My pleasure with the darkroom was of short duration. During one of the first heavy raids in Bremen, Uncle Fritz was totally bombed out. House and furniture are gone; so he and Aunt Lotte came to stay with us until they are assigned another place. Where else could they have gone? Uncle Fritz, with his Jewish identity card, could not find accommodations in another house in Bremen, as other air-raid sufferers could. He was not even able to move to a hotel. The logical place of refuge was the house of his favorite sister.

It was a tearful reunion, because Uncle Fritz is like mother, composed primarily of emotions. Aunt Lotte, a tiny, level-headed person, is attached to him with unbelievable love. His excessive emotion seems to warm her, while her coolness holds him down to reality.

August 31, 1940

Pötz and Elsa sat opposite me in the Kakao stube.
Elsa asked, "Where is your dog today?"
"Brandy is sick."

Pötz raised his eyebrows: "So sick that he can't accompany you?"

I explained to him that Brandy suffers from a skin disease, which causes an unbearable itch. He had scratched his skin until it bled. After all other cures failed, the veterinarian prevailed on me to entrust Brandy to a couple who cares for animals, since the required treatment with ointment could not possibly be carried out at home. Thus, we were separated for three weeks.

"Do you miss him very much?" Elsa asked.

With gentle self-mockery, I smiled and replied, "As if he were a part of me."

Pötz curled his lips: "That song "I had a comrade," is becoming Germany's theme song."

"Remember the mass murderer Haman? Yes? All of Germany and a large part of many foreign countries were horrified because this Haman murdered several hundred people. He was handed over to justice and executed. But what will happen to mass murderers who are heads of state?" He laughed silently and ironically, "My dearest, one admires and cheers them. However, we are the helpless witnesses of the rise of one of the greatest mass murderers of our time." Pötz sat up so rigidly that he seemed to grow. He firmly held onto his somewhat threadbare suspenders. The corners of his mouth turned downwards. "Unfortunately, I have the horrible feeling Hitler is only the first of a series of prominent mass murderers who will bring this century to a bloody end. Every new war will be more merciless than the last one, as Spengler foresaw in the eighties."

We fell silent, until I asked: "The war has gone very successfully so far, right?"

"Yes," Pötz confirmed, "too successfully to lead to victory in the long run. But what are you driving at?"

"Under the circumstances, I don't understand why it is necessary to give so many explanations. I am thinking about the secret documents of the French General Staff on the outbreak of the war. They were allegedly captured a few months ago, and are now published in the form of a "white paper." I thought they were probably forged documents to justify the war. But, why?"

Pötz let go of his suspenders, bent forward and placed his hands on the table. "Why? My dear Miss Schroeder, the clever man is only taking precautions for the future. Despite Hitler's alliance with providence, he seems occasionally to have doubts about his lucky star. Thus, while fortune still smiles on him, he must now prove that he was forced into the war by others. With this explanation, he can influence the people to view the fighting as justified and also prepare them for sacrifices, should failures occur. The whole thing is pure psychological preparation."

I nodded.

Pötz's face suddenly turned into a fiendish grinning mask. "We just spoke about psychology. Consciously or not, Hitler repeats the Delphic Oracle." He took his billfold out and removed a small, printed piece of paper. He then continued: "Hitler's last Reichstag speech reproached the enemy heads of state and protested that he had no intention of waging war, but wanted to build a new social state of the highest cultural level. He complained that every year of war is depriving him of this achievement. As victor, he again offered England peace and predicted to Churchill that otherwise 'A great empire will be destroyed; an empire I never intended to destroy or harm.'" He lovingly placed the small piece of paper back in his wallet. "I wonder whether Hitler is aware that he speaks of the destruction of his own reich?"

September 22, 1940

Churchill answered Hitler's peace offer with a definite No.

Germany is now waging a bitter air war against England, whose airplanes likewise visit us at night. We, who receive these blessings from above, don't know how things are in other cities, since the newspapers print the same stereotyped report: "Individual enemy airplanes flew over Northern France, Belgium, Holland, and Western Germany. No military targets were hit; but some civilians were wounded and buildings damaged."

When occasionally, a heavy attack is made on Berlin, Hamburg, or Bremen, the danger exists that wide circles of the population will be informed by travellers. Indignant reports then appear about the beastly "raids, which are always directed at residential districts and never hit military targets. Once in a while, it is conceded that a number of civilians were killed or wounded, but we never learn the exact number of deaths or casualties. However, our Führer foams with rage and threatens, "We will eradicate their cities!"

I said to Bernd, "It is a mystery to me, how the English can continue to wage a war. Once 1500 airplanes were shot down; then 500 planes were again lost in just one week; the next time, the figure is 133. Simultaneously, hundreds of thousands of gross registered tons are sunk within three days. Furthermore, they daily fly these enormously successful retaliatory air attacks and nothing seems to happen to the Germans."

Bernd said, "Yes, isn't it astonishing? If we had kept a record, we would probably come to the conclusion that England can't have a single airplane or ship left, that no buildings are standing in London, and that the population is exterminated. Nevertheless, the English are a tough people and Roosevelt's war budget was approved. I presume, he has already delivered them some airplanes."

"Tell me," I asked, "why are the Germans so terribly upset by these 'cowardly British night flights?' Don't they also fly nighttime attacks?"

Bernd began to laugh: "Yes; after they could no longer achieve anything during the daytime." He lowered his voice instinctively. "An acquaintance of mine heard the Basel radio. According to their broadcast, the Germans suffered heavy losses in a bitter daytime aerial battle over London on the 15th. Since then, they fly hardly anything except night raids. They are enraged that the English also fly at night, since they probably recognized long before the Germans that this is less dangerous. The Swiss radio maintained that German anti-aircraft fire is poor."

October 13, 1940

Uncle Fritz and Aunt Lotte are packing. They will leave us tomorrow and move to the Bohemian Forest.

Yesterday evening, I had a brief chat with Uncle Fritz, while Aunt Lotte was ironing.

"At least, you will be spared air raids and the scenery is very pretty."

Uncle Fritz nodded, while he thoughtfully smoked his cigar. "I have never been there. It must be very remote and lonely," he said rather plaintively.

"But your wife will be with you." I tried to cheer him up. "Who knows, Uncle Fritz, perhaps things being as they are, you might be safer in every respect in the Bohemian Forest than in Bremen."

He sighed, "These bastards!"

211

We both stared into space, until he suddenly exclaimed, "They can say what they want, but they can't make me a Jew. Whenever I am very depressed, I look at this ring." He tapped the ring on his left hand with his forefinger. I strained to look at the coat of arms engraved on the dark stone, but I could not recognize it. He continued in a choked voice, "My grandfather's ring. It always restores my self-confidence. They can't take away from me the fact that I am a grandson of General von Kusserow."

His brown eyes shone moistly behind his thick glasses; the eyes were those in the picture of his Jewish grandfather, Simon.

November 23, 1940

Until recently, war was more or less something one read about in the newspaper. Now, however, it is reality in the raw. The sirens go off at a set time almost every night. If there is an occasional delay, people ask with grim humor: "Let us hope nothing has happened to them?" Since the sleepless nights are not offset by a more nutritious diet, many people lose weight and look pale and are nervous. Butter and meat products are already cut back to a minimum of what was normally consumed.

More and more frequently, sons, husbands, and brothers of friends and acquaintances are known to be at the front. Etta's two sons fought in France and the older one was wounded. Waldemar Hensel died in France. My friend from Hinterstein, Arnulf Tannheimer, writes me letters from the front, which are a headache to answer, since I can not forget for a moment that my mail is probably censored.

Large headlines appear daily on the first page of the papers announcing that the Germans bombed London for many hours. In contrast to the English, who ostensibly always hit only residential districts — this is reported in the back section of the newspaper — the Germans bomb only essential military targets. We daily destroy an immense number of British aircrafts, and sink thousands of tons of shipping and English submarines. The Führer hands out Iron Crosses wholesale; efficient workers on the home front are given Distinguished Service Crosses in addition to promotions. Göring, already a field marshal, was named Reichs Marshal of the Greater German Reich.

What we are not told is that the English not only destroy the harvest with incendiary devices, but also drop metal foil which jams the radar stations, and reduces the accuracy of the flak.

212

Siegrid lives diagonally across from the Adlerflycht School, which has an anti-aircraft position on the roof. She explained, "As soon as one hears the most distant drone of an airplane, they begin shooting. They certainly haven't hit a plane to date; but every time, I have to sweep up broken windowpanes in our house."

On the evening of November 8, our Führer spoke in the Löwenbräu in Munich; he assured us that he has learned a lesson from the past and taken it to heart. "I have tried not to let the German people face similar dangerous situations as they encountered in the past."

December 14, 1940

Bernd left me a few minutes ago. Although both of us are night-owls, one does not any longer dare to be out very late because of air-raid alarms. Until now, nothing much has happened in the inner city; the bombs mostly fell on the periphery. This danger does not worry us; but the regulation that during an air-raid alarm one must go to the nearest shelter did disturb us. Both Bernd and I felt uneasy about the possibility of being forced to sit for several hours in a shelter with Nazis, and thus compelled to listen to their patriotic speeches.

"The Nazis are absolutely convinced of victory. You only need to read all their plans for after the war! Blueprints are already being prepared for new housing."

He paused when I began to laugh. "Why do you find that so funny?"

"If the war continues like this — in my opinion it is just the beginning — we will urgently need a new housing program." I restrained my impulse to grab Bernd by the shoulders and shake him. "I no longer have much time to read the newspapers; whenever I look at them it is always the same. German planes have bombed London, Liverpool, Manchester and occasionally Malta for many hours; and they conclude with 'no enemy activity', or 'no enemy raids'."

I continued, "If this were all true, why do the Nazis bluster about the evacuation of children from Hamburg and Berlin to the so-called recovery districts in the countryside? By the end of October, almost 300,000 children had been evacuated. How many children have been sent by now? and how long will you believe that this is a voluntary evacuation? It deals with Germany's most precious possession, her children."

213

He smiled a bit embarrassed: "You are right, of course, only. . ."

"Only what?" I asked patiently. "Nazi successes depress you?"

"Yes, they depress me terribly. As an individual, one is utterly helpless facing this brutality."

"But what about your mathematical calculations? Don't they still hold true?"

"Yes, certainly they do. But it takes so long."

"My friend, to whom are you saying this? After all, you are a first-class German, while I belong to the subhuman category. Thus, almost nothing can happen to you, if you don't say something bad in the wrong company, or if you don't listen to foreign broadcasts too loudly; whereas I — and practically my whole family — are in a really precarious situation."

He looked at me alarmed: "Has something happened?"

"No," I reassured him. "I only remember what Mr. Pötz predicted a long time ago. With the increasing difficulties caused by the war, mixed marriages and half-breeds will more or less fall under the same laws and decrees which affect full-blooded Jews today. Waiting is therefore more difficult for me than it is for you. You understand why Seckl couldn't be with us? It is shortly after nine o'clock; Jews must be home by 8 P.M."

"What?" Bernd exclaimed, clutching his forehead. "What did you say? I never comprehended why Seckl made excuses when I invited him to visit me during the evening."

Bernd stared in front of him: "So that's why he always nervously looked at his watch at dusk. But why didn't he tell me?"

"Why?" I had to shake my head. "Can't you imagine what it means to a proud man like Seckl to submit to the humiliations which the Jews must suffer? It is probably asking too much to have him recount those details."

After a while, he said: "I never read anything about these curfew hours. How do you know about it?"

"From our Jewish patients. You will scarcely find anything about it in the press."

"My God, it's even much worse than I thought."

January 12, 1941

Christmas and New Year's passed as usual. Fewer gifts were displayed on the table. Fruitcake, Christmas goose, and turkey were omitted from the menu. Königsberg marzipan is a distant memory, and the few Christmas pastries and cookies lack shortening and are hard. Despite this, I can't complain. Mother gave Mrs. Rodenhauer an old East-Prussian lambskin foot-muff to make into boots with the fur turned inside. I also possess a pair of fur-lined leather mittens. Now I drive the car clothed for a Polar expedition. The more our Jewish patients are forced to live closer together the less frequently I can go inside to warm up during father's house calls.

Father becomes thinner and grows more serious. This afternoon, he sat in the living room with the Sunday edition of the *F.Z.* open on the table in front of him. I was in my room, when I suddenly heard his loud laughter, an unfamiliar sound.

It took some time for him to calm down. "They have set up a center to collect mother's milk!"

"They what?"

He began to laugh again, "A mother's milk collection point. Since milk is so scarce and mother's milk so nourishing, women who have an excess are urged to sell it to this center, for young mothers unable to breast feed. They are paid two and a half marks per liter." His body shook with laughter: "Now we not only have the maternity cross for broodmares, but we also have human milk cows!"

February 5, 1941

One of our Aryan patients told father about a business friend who committed the deadly sin of offering some cigarettes to a prisoner of war on the street. He was arrested for this forbidden contact. The result was seven days arrest and a 70-mark fine.

Any contact with prisoners of war borders on high treason. A rather naive man, who allowed POW's to listen to foreign broadcasts in his office, was sentenced to six years hard labor.

Mother could not get over these and similar stories. By accident, she met Uncle Franz yesterday in the lobby.

Busy in the consulting room, I missed the beginning of the conversation but I came in just as mother exclaimed: "But that's horrible, dear Uncle Franz! Prisoners of war are also human beings."

Uncle Franz's friendly brown eyes became serious and wrinkles appeared on his forehead. He nodded and shook his finger like a schoolmaster: "You're right Mrs. Schroeder. Our Führer does not know this; our Führer does not want this."

215

How frequently during the last months have we heard this vindication from Uncle Franz? So often that this statement slowly became a household word.

March 8, 1941

Active building started at different places in the city. Thick concrete bunkers are built in Sachsenhausen, Bockenheim, Glauburgstrasse, the main train station, and many other places. They are allegedly more secure against air-raid attacks than the air-raid cellars. Rescue stations and first-aid posts are set up in schools and other public buildings. Sand for fire fighting was unloaded in all open places, and the population is urged to keep sand-filled containers ready in their houses. Water hydrants for the fire department are thickly wrapped in straw, and encased in wood to protect them from freezing.

Pötz and I talked about these small accompaniments of war.

Pötz said sarcastically: "To quote the words of our esteemed Führer: 'I now look to the future with fanatical confidence.' It isn't quite clear where he gets his confidence; his fanaticism was never in doubt."

I was silent and waited to hear whether this clever man would have an encouraging word to raise my sinking spirits.

"There are certain laws of nature, my dear, which even a Hitler can't defy. For example, there is no eternal rain. Every rain ends sometime and the sun shines again. There is no dictatorship, which doesn't end — some time. Only conservatism doesn't want to face the truth. If there were a way to stop time — ah!— we would all be slaves of the Roman Empire. Until now, no man has been able to ruse as much of the world as Hitler has in mind. As soon as the leader of a nation — whether he is an emperor, a general, or a combination of both — engages in a war of many fronts, he has already lost. You look skeptical, my young friend? Why? Can you furnish historical proof to the contrary? No?"

"I am thinking," I replied, "of the Berlin-Rome axis, the alliance between Germany, Italy and Japan, which Rumania recently joined. It means more support for Hitler."

Pötz's hand made a disparaging gesture in the air. "Forget Japan, my dear. It doesn't count at all because it has been engaged for many years in a war with China. Since Japan and Germany distrust each other, they made a precautionary alliance which assures each that it can wage war undisturbed in its part of the world, without interference from the other. That the Italians and Rumanians are allied to Germany is theoretically disturbing; practically, it is only a matter of inflated rhetoric by their heads of state. How long do you think the Italian and Rumanian people will pull Germany's chestnuts out of the fire? I will tell you: only as long as the sacrifices aren't too great. When the trouble exceeds certain limits, the average soldier will come to his senses. He will ask why he should be slaughtered for Germany and why his family at home should starve. This, my dear, will be the end of the grand alliance, which the Germans believe promises them so much and in which they place their highest hopes. Although the war has lasted one and a half years, it really hasn't started yet. Everywhere Hitler has met comparatively little resistance." Pötz's left hand released his suspenders for a moment, and rubbed his forehead. He continued. "If we try to forget our human way of thinking and the fate of individuals and juggle statistics with greater objectivity, we then must admit that German losses were comparatively small in relation to those of all the nations which were conquered or occupied without a fight. This will change. A new factor will become important; this time, the civilian population will experience the war directly. One month ago in Düsseldorf, despite a defense barrage, English bombers hit the city center and killed thirty-five people. This illustrates what I mean." His face drooped as if he mourned the senseloss loss of these thirty-five human lives.

When he looked at me again, his expression showed a mixture of sorrow and despairing scorn. "Mr. Hitler assured us at the start of the Polish campaign that he wanted to attack only military targets, not women and children. From the beginning of the war with England, he has daily told the German people that he had hit only military targets across the channel. But suddenly he dropped his mask. Now the government boasts that from September, 1940, until January, 1941, over 23,000 English civilians were victims of German air raids. Even if the figure is exaggerated, these losses are substantial." He supported his elbows on the table and rested his forehead in his hands, while he murmured to himself: "We are dealing with a madman." After a while, he spoke again: "One of our highest civil servants, paid by our taxes, has gone crazy. He runs amok and kills everything that stands in his way, even if it costs the lives of his own people."

We were silent for a while, until I asked: "Will America help the English?"

Pötz replied, "Certainly, they will help the English." He

217

suddenly began to laugh in his soundless way. "If it weren't so utterly tragic, it would be comical to observe how those smart Americans can't change their nature, even in this crisis. Everything is business for them. They are economically up to their necks in trouble, but they know England is fighting for its naked existence, and out of this fact, with a slight tactical delay, they will make a business deal."

May 14, 1941

Two days ago, the Nazis had to admit that Rudolf Hess, the Führer's deputy, secretly took an airplane and flew to England. He sought to achieve an understanding by personal negotiations with old acquaintances. The Nazis maintain he suffers from delusions; and our Führer declared that war against England would be continued "until the English rulers are either overthrown or ready for peace."

June 11, 1941

We leased Katherina's room. To guard against all contingencies, we sought a tenant to our own tastes. Miss Wurm is a young violinist, approximately my age. The "Wurmchen" — as mother has dubbed her — is nice, unobtrusive and fits smoothly into our household, whether in the kitchen or the air-raid cellar.

"Little Levie" is another person who is beginning to play a strange role in my life. Levie barely reaches to my shoulder, and is a modest, quiet, serious man, who although over sixty still has dark hair and thus appears much younger than he is. I no longer remember why he came to the laboratory, or why I offered him a chair. The next time he came during office hours he asked me shyly whether he could come visit me again. Since then, he has come daily. He sits for a while and we discuss current political events; occasionally, he tells me about himself.

June 24, 1941

Large headlines in the newspaper greeted us at the breakfast table with BATTLEFRONT AGAINST BOLSHEVISM. Underneath, we read in smaller typeface: "Europe's security against Soviet threats.

Moscow breaks German-Russian agreement. German counter-attack with Finland and Rumania from the Arctic to the Baltic Sea."

Father hit the table with his fist, "Has the fellow gone mad?"

I was silent and suddenly remembered the waiter in the Stuttgart Hotel who commented: "But we surely can't attack Russia?"

The Führer gave yet another endless speech; this time he even referred back to 1914. The poor man is happy that he finally could speak frankly after being condemned to months of silence; and he prayed to God to help all of us in this fight.

Dr. Bernd came that evening. He was upset and depressed at the same time. "This Hitler is successful everywhere!"

I nodded silently in order not to interrupt his litany.

"He occupied Yugoslavia and Greece, chased the English out of Crete, and concluded a German-Turkish friendship treaty. Italy supports him everywhere and is now also at war with Russia!"

I waited to see whether he would enumerate any more items. Then I asked, "Is that all?"

He looked at me, taken aback.

"Dear Doctor Bernd, you were the one who spoke of a mathematical calculation. You have now itemized all the negative things. May I draw up a counter list of items you apparently overlooked? Roosevelt was given approval for ten billion dollars for rearmament; and the eight-hour day is suspended in the American armament industry. The Germans and Italians closed American consulates in their countries. Such steps are usually the last acts before a declaration of war. If Hitler conducts war against both Russia and America, then he will really need all the help his god can give him!"

Bernd looked at me a bit skeptically, "But until now, only his successes were evident."

"What do we really know? According to military communiqués England should be totally destroyed and helpless. Despite this, a month ago the German battleship *Bismark* sank in the Atlantic, because of English supremacy there. How is that possible? I will tell you, doctor: because we are told incredible lies. If that weren't the case, we could listen freely to foreign radio stations. Newspapers repeatedly publish lists of 'radio criminals' and their heavy prison sentences. These punishments are probably intended to serve as an intimidating example."

219

July 28, 1941

I have already spent a week at Gaschurn in Montafon, where grandfather and many other members of the Schroeder family used to spend their summer vacations. As usual, I took a room in the Rössle. Bernd has the room next to mine.

A few weeks ago, during an evening walk through Holzhausen Park with Brandy, Bernd and I had an intimate conversation, and discovered that both of us were trying to forget someone. We decided to go on vacation together, and keep each other company. I now wish I had never gotten myself involved. We had barely arrived in Gaschurn when the weather turned cold and unfriendly, and snow came down from the mountains into the valley.

Hitler's constant, and until now uncontested, victories in Russia are announced daily, usually at lunch time. Liszt's victory fanfares boom loudly up through the stairwell, and trigger Bernd's hysterical outbursts. After I went through this several times, I suggested that we go to the dining room and eat with the late-comers. We thus avoided the loudest victory fanfares.

I had not travelled to Gaschurn to comfort a person on the brink of despair, I needed comfort myself. Finally, I had reached the point of packing my bags and leaving.

After Bernd had taken his afternoon nap, he called at my room and was surprised to see me in front of my open suitcase. "Are you looking for something?"

"No. I just can't make up my mind whether I should unpack everything or repack."

"Why?"

"To be honest, I came here to rest and relax and to gather new strength, which I probably will urgently need."

Somewhat ill at ease he looked down at the floor before shifting to the offense: "I don't understand how you can calmly accept all these German victories!"

"I don't accept them — either calmly or otherwise. They don't interest me. These early victories will not change my mind. I daily see in the newspapers an increasing number of obituaries with small iron crosses; obituaries which announce that a beloved husband, brother or son died a heroic death in the East; or an occasional laconic notice about a nineteen or twenty year old, who fell in the East with a comment: 'He was our only son'. I read about the systematic continuation of operations in the East and that the potato shortage is caused not by war, but by inclement weather. I read about the great gains achieved in the East and that a national collection of textile fibers will be held from today through August 23rd — a community sacrifice, where every contribution serves to attain a victorious conclusion of the war. And it occurs to me that I can not find any mention of enemy overflights into the Reich, nor that day or night enemy airplanes were active over Germany, but I see that the children's evacuation program will be expanded."

Bernd was silent, stepped to the window and looked at the now again sunny scenery. He suddenly turned around and said: "And you really believe—?"

"No, my friend, I don't believe — I know. This knowledge gives me the strength to live from one day to the next. I can't afford to let my hard-earned composure be destroyed."

He nodded, extended his hand and said, "I'm sorry, maybe I let myself go. Have a bit more patience with me."

I agreed and closed the suitcase.

August 10, 1941

Bernd and I took a long walk and sat down on a bench overlooking the whole valley. It was similar to the view at Hinterstein.

I had just made an unfriendly comment about God, on whose help Hitler heavily relies, a god who is nothing but a crutch.

The Catholic in Bernd was aroused. "Don't you believe in God or in Christ?" He looked at me rather shocked, as I silently shook my head. Bernd folded his hands behind his back and paced the small path in front of the bench, deeply sunk in his thoughts. Suddenly he stopped in front of me. "But you do love Bach's *St. Matthew's Passion?*"

"Yes."

"You can't love this work, where music and text go hand in hand, and simultaneously reject religion. It is illogical."

"Is it really, my dear? Let us refrain from dealing with historical questions: whether Jesus of Nazareth lived at all, and if he did, what is truth and what is fiction in the history of his life written five hundred years after his death. *St. Matthew's Passion* is indescribably beautiful music about an ancient human tragedy which we are experiencing again today.

"I don't understand you."

221

"Let us forget that the Church claims Jesus was the son of God. If you remove that part, all you have is the story of a man who fought against the traditional system and tried to change it. This brought him hatred and persecution by righteous citizens and betrayal by his two closest friends. His friend Judas sold him for thirty pieces of silver; Peter repeatedly denied knowing him. How often are similar tragedies repeated today in the Third Reich? They involve every Aryan who gets a divorce when he discovers the evil of having a Jewish spouse; or my friend Reiss, who landed me in prison. How many Aryan Judases are running around Germany today sending people to concentration camps for money or self-advancement? Or, if you permit the simile, they deliver them to the cross.

"*St. Matthew's Passion* represents for me our times with all its human variations; including the helpless judge, who washes his hands of the blood of this just man, but doesn't have the power to free the alleged traitor.

"The Nazis are also susceptible to the *Passion* and — excuse me — superstitious as Catholics. They have deleted one sentence from current performances: 'He who takes the sword, will perish by the sword.' This, of course, won't alter the facts."

"So, that is how you see it."

"That is how I see it. One of the most moving passages for me is when Peter starts to swear, 'I don't know this man,' and the cock immediately crows. Peter remembers Jesus' words, 'Ere the cock croweth, even thou shalt deny me thrice'; Peter then leaves and weeps bitterly.

"It will be some time before the German people begin to weep bitterly; unfortunately, tears will not return the innocent back to life. Reality is not a fairy tale, where the dead rise again."

August 24, 1941

The first thing which greeted father after we returned from our vacation was a letter from the director of the State Medical Association for Hessen-Nassau, in reference to an increased food quota.

We hereby inform you that your application for additional food allotments for overburdened physicians cannot be granted. We conclude that you do not appear to be over-

222

burdened, since it is evident that you still have time to treat Jewish patients.

Heil Hitler!

Father's only comment was, "The swine!"

The demands on doctors are enormous. During the day the waitingroom is overcrowded and the telephone rings for housecalls. At night we assemble with the other tenants in the air-raid cellar. The alarms last often until dawn. All of us are overtired, hungry and despondent.

September 27, 1941

On September 19th, a police regulation was put into effect which requires all Jews above the age of sixteen to wear a six-pointed yellow star, four inches in diameter, with the word *JEW* stamped on it in black.

Yesterday, father came to the lab while Little Levie was visiting me and greeted him affectionately. His face darkened when he saw Levie's Jewish star; and he shook his head disapprovingly.

Little Levie, however, stood stiff and erect. His eyes became hard as he said, "Yesterday, a Gestapo man stopped me on the street. 'Why don't you wear your star in the right place?' he bellowed. I replied, 'I have it exactly where I wore my Iron Cross, first class.' With a mixture of dignity and disdain, he added, "Then, he left me alone!"

For us, the star means an additional burden since we have to keep separate office hours; the morning for our stars, the afternoon for Aryans and sandwiched in between, we make house calls. In the evening we are exhausted and to all this strain, food becomes scarcer and the nights shorter.

October 12, 1941

At the beginning of October, the Führer gave another speech in the Berlin Sportpalast. He spoke about Germany's peaceful intentions, Great Britain's wish for war, Moscow's treachery, and the greatest conflict in world history.

The first death sentences for 'radio criminals' were recently carried out. Why? And why does the *F.Z.* print excerpts from articles written by a Colonel Scherff in the *Völkischen Beobachter?*

The colonel writes about the Russian winter, and draws comparisons between the current war and Napoleon and 1914-1918. The colonel assures his readers that things today are much better than in those days. Moreover, he reassures us, we are not fighting a two-front war. I had to laugh as I tried in vain to count all the fronts. It is possible that the editorial stated the truth when it claimed that the die has been cast.

October 22, 1941

On Sunday morning, Bernd called me in great agitation. "The Gestapo is rounding up the Jews in the West End in preparation for deportation. I was at the Seckls. Risa, (Seckl's sister), was crying hysterically." Bernd asked me to be ready if I were needed.

He called me again in the early afternoon and said he would expect me at the Hauptwache. As far as he could discover, the Jews were allowed to take some baggage with them, especially blankets and sturdy shoes. They were being kept under surveillance by SA men, while they packed their belongings. Afterwards, once the houses were sealed up, they were marched to the Grossmarkthalle under SA supervision.

We took the next trolley to the Grossmarkthalle.

Divided in groups, the Jews stood with their scanty baggage on the cold concrete floor of the drafty market hall. While we searched for the Seckls among the more than a thousand people gathered there, hands reached out to me. Others called out in alarm, "Miss Schroeder! Get away from here!"

I saw old Mr. Neuhaus, whom father suspected was suffering from leukemia. The deaf-mute Jacob sisters cowered there; one of them, married to a deaf-mute, was in the last stages of abdominal cancer. Mrs. Bing stood there; her every breath scattering a drizzle of tuberculosis bacilli. We finally found the Seckls. Risa had regained her composure and stared disinterestedly into the closely packed crowd; while Seckl looked at us with old tired eyes, a tortured, almost apologetic smile on his lips.

"Franz," I whispered to Bernd, "Come. Perhaps my father can save a few of them."

We drove back home. Father was besides himself, when I gave him the names of the patients we had seen. He immediately sat down at his desk to write medical certificates, with which we returned to the Grossmarkthalle.

224

Meanwhile it was evening. The Jews were still crammed together like cattle, although animals are treated better. These poor people, whom the SA rounded up at 7 A.M., had had nothing to eat or drink. They stood so thickly packed that only a few at a time could sit on their suitcases.

Bernd and I made our way through the crowd seeking the chief officer of the convoy. Finally we stood before a tall, unmistakably German SS man. He politely bowed to us from a raised platform.

I no longer remember the exact words of the conversation which followed. At any rate, I told him that he had several seriously ill people and I handed him the medical certificates. With great interest, he inquired about my connections to the Jews, about Bernd's relationship to them, and about Bernd and myself. After we answered him, he climbed down, and standing next to us, he asked for our names and addresses, which he wrote down. I was fully aware of the consequences of these questions and the hidden threat; but my worry and concern for our friends and patients by far overshadowed any personal fear.

We stood together with the Seckls to say good-bye. Seckl's eyes followed my glance, which repeatedly strayed to the remarkable face of an old Jew. A pair of dark eyes burned from his finely chiselled features framed by white hair and a white beard.

Seckl said in an undertone, "That's Dr. Ascher of public health."

On impulse, I walked over to the enclosure where this well-known city doctor stood with the calm dignity of a patriarch.

"Dr. Ascher?" I asked shyly.

His dark eyes stared at me.

I introduced myself. "I am Dr. Schroeder's daughter. Is there anything I can do for you?"

He shook his head gravely. "No, there is probably nothing that can be done."

"Doctor, do you have any medicines or injections?" He nodded, "And morphine?"

"Yes, some morphine, but not much."

"Some of my father's patients are here."

His dark eyes softened. "I will help as much as I can."

We silently shook hands.

I returned to the Seckls. Risa and Fritz stood behind the rope, Bernd and I outside. This ludicrous piece of hemp, which separated us, seemed the dividing line between life and death. So many words remained unspoken. It was like a farewell at a train station, when one desperately searches for what could still be said before the train pulls out. We could not even wish them a pleasant journey.

"Our thoughts are with you" was all we could say before we tore ourselves away.

As I left, I glanced one more time at the sea of faces and directed a parting word at an acquaintance here and there.

I stood dazed for a moment in front of the market hall.

Bernd's hand gently supported my elbow. "I'll take you home."

"Oh Franz, we are going home; we can move freely. We could pass them by and leave. It gives me an indescribable sense of guilt."

"It was a long day. You are overtired. Tomorrow you will understand why you left. There are still so many others there who need your help."

The next day, after office hours for our 'stars,' we drove to the homes of the patients for whom father had written medical certificates. The doors were sealed. Our last hope that perhaps they could be found in the Jewish Hospital in Gagernstrasse likewise came to nought.

Uncle Franz came the same day. He had been in father's study for a while, when father called me in.

When I walked into the office, father just said: "All of them were terminal cases. Last stages of cancer with intestinal obstruction, consumption, serious paralysis."

Uncle Franz shook his head, "Dr. Schroeder, be assured that our Führer does not know this; our Führer does not want this!"

"Exactly!" father said. "That's just what I think. That is why I sent my daughter and her friend with medical certificates to the market hall."

Uncle Franz turned to me, "Do you know the officer's name?"

"No."

"What did he look like?"

"Tall, slim, in his thirties, SS uniform, blond, blue eyes. A really handsome man, without a trace of feeling."

"The description fits Lieutenant Colonel Meurer. Yes, yes. You'll hear from me again, doctor." Uncle Franz said good-bye and accompanied me to the lobby. He looked at me with his kindly eyes and said with a comforting smile, "Don't be so worried. Uncle Franz will see what he can do."

In all my tearless despair about the transports, Uncle Franz' good and friendly face appears before me again and again. I envy him. How happy would I be, if I once again had this childlike trust in somebody or something as he has in his Führer, the mass murderer Hitler.

October 27, 1941

Uncle Franz came with glad tidings. The matter was settled: we need no longer worry. He spoke with Lieutenant Colonel Meurer. Everything was all right.

This removed a load from father's heart; mother was overjoyed; and I expressed my thanks and tried to feign relief.

Numbed by the preceding events, I felt neither fear nor happiness. Uncle Franz beamed; for once he could do something for his beloved doctor.

At the door, however, he looked at me seriously: "Be more cautious in the future, Aunt Lili."

As I looked at the floor with a frozen smile, he said, "I do understand you. But please believe me; our Führer does not know this, our Führer does not want this! His subordinates, the little Hitlers. . . ."

November 16, 1941

Another transport left at the beginning of the week. Only this time, the victims were given written notice three days in advance. Ever since the Jews were forced to wear stars, they were no longer allowed to leave their community without written permission from the local police; thus they could no longer escape their fate.

Those of father's patients who received these notices came and requested our help. Father wrote medical certificates for the seriously ill, and explained exactly why they were not transportable. In a few isolated instances, the departure of these sick people was postponed. It caused father a difficult inner battle to refuse this help to others. He explained with a tormented expression, "If I issue a certificate which I can't justify, I impair the valid ones."

Little Levie came the day after the transport left. The Hoffmann couple, from whom he rented a room, were taken away; the

227

house was sealed and all his linen and possessions were inside. Until a solution could be found, we had to provide him with socks, collars and underwear. This was not a simple matter, since father's clothes were too large for him. We finally managed to gather the required outfit. Levie is now lodged with other Jews, and spends more and more time in my laboratory corner.

He sat there withdrawn. "I had an uncle." He fell silent.

I looked up from the microscope, "I am listening Mr. Levic."

"This uncle was a moneylender, and he could never get enough money. I knew he did evil things and cheated many honest people of everything. Perhaps I was still too young and dumb to properly appeal to his conscience, since he only laughed at me when I said anything. It was his way of paying back the Goyim for what they did to the Jews, as he expressed it. I ask myself sometimes whether we are now being repaid for these outrages? Must we do penance for the harm those Uncle Schmuls caused?"

Between laboratory tests, telephone calls, and the door bell we had a long conversation. Consoled, he left the house with the last patient, holding himself somewhat more erect. A smile on his lips, he turned once more towards me, who followed with my eyes the small figure, limping down the few steps.

November 30, 1941

Levie came on the morning of November 19th. His expression was unchanged, but he was white as a sheet.

I asked in alarm, "Mr. Levie, what happened?"

"My name is on the list. The transport goes on the twenty-second."

I took him into the laboratory corner and telephoned father's study. "Mr. Levie is on this Saturday's transport list."

Father came immediately. Of course, he would give Levie a medical certificate.

"If I could only get my things!" Levie moaned. "The house is still sealed."

Indirectly, through our Jewish connections, we appealed to the Gestapo officer who serves as liaison in the Jewish Welfare Office, and Levie was finally able to get into his room.

He brought two suitcases and asked that we look after them in case he should return. I received a silver liqueur set and other small personal gifts, which he had obviously selected with love.

Mrs. Bamberger came to ask me if I would help her. I promised to go to her house, which was located close-by, after office hours. As it turned out, Mrs. Bamberger did not need any help. She pointed to innumerable crates which stood in her room, filled with exquisite porcelain.

"Take what pleases you, Schroeder dear! Take it! And the carpets."

I refused with thanks. It was really impossible for me, in view of what lay ahead for these people, to act like the other vultures and pounce on their possessions. I wanted nothing; I have what I need. I only wanted to keep these people here!

Mrs. Bamberger, elegant and full of vitality even in this situation, rushed back and forth on the well-cared-for parquet floor. She clasped her hands together, when I didn't make the slightest move to help myself.

"Please take what you want! What you won't take will only go to the Gestapo!"

When I still didn't budge, she grabbed at random and gave me some hand-painted Rosenthal coffee cups, several plates, and a crystal candy box. She stuffed a cushion in my arms: "Here, place them in between."

The afternoon before the transport left, Little Levie came once more. He was appointed supervisor.

Father grumbled later, "Just think of it, as supervisor, Little Levie with his hip ailment. What a mockery!"

Our good-bye was heartbreaking.

The trunks our Jewish patients gave us in safekeeping accumulate in our cellar.

Supper that day and breakfast the next morning proceeded in total silence. Later, when we left for house calls, father suddenly said with great admiration; "What self-possession these people have! Not a word of complaint, no tears. Just imagine what wails and cries would be heard if something like this happened to the Aryans!"

Several days later, a woman came during office hours, with greetings from Mrs. Bamberger. She delivered a small pigskin suitcase, which contained stationery, a small Meissen duck, and an open bottle of perfume.

"Mrs. Bamberger asked me to tell you she is having a burgundy-red silk dress made for her at her dressmakers at number 5 Kroeger Street. It is already paid for and you should have it fitted to your size."

I repeated the address and thanked the woman, who somehow infused a vague feeling of distrust in me.

When I showed mother the small suitcase and told her about the dress, she asked. "Why didn't Mrs. Bamberger tell you about the dress herself?"

"I also wonder about that. Apart from the fact that I could never wear the dress, I have the feeling I am being lured into a trap."

After careful thought, mother said: "I can understand you wouldn't wear the dress." Her eyes filled with tears. "But aren't you a bit too suspicious?"

I shrugged my shoulders: "It could be."

Several letters came from Lodz, now renamed Litzmannstadt, where the first transport went. Bernd also received greetings from Seckl. We at least know that our friends are there. There was a report some time ago about this gigantic ghetto, where Jews are separated from the Aryans; they live and work under their own administration — but under German police supervision.

A rumor slowly leaked out, which froze our hearts. The last two transports were apparently gassed in a tunnel near Minsk.

I looked into the microscope and tried to imagine that Little Levie sat next to me. I looked up. The place where I always left a chair for him was empty. "Karl Levie . . . no, they couldn't have done it."

The telephone rang. I removed the receiver and answered: "Dr. Schroeder's office."

"Good day, my young friend." I heard the sound of Pötz's voice.

"Oh, good day."

"Is everything all right?" he asked.

"Yes," I replied. "Things are going splendidly for us," and my voice faltered.

There was a moment of silence on the other end of the line. "Do you have this afternoon off?"

"Yes, I'm free."

"Good, let's meet around 3 p.m. as usual."

Pötz's glance was fixed on the door as I entered the Kakaostube. He stood up and walked towards me, looking at me with concern.

"Have you had a bad time?" I nodded silently. He continued, "I just learned yesterday about the deportation."

"About one?"

"Were there more?"

"Yes, three." I began to tell him what happened.

He listened in silence until I finished. After a while he said, "These deportations are not only deeds of madmen, but also acts of despair committed by the defeated! You surely know that rats attack only when they are cornered? At the beginning of the war, Hitler was the aggressor and victor. Now the tide has turned; he is cornered and in his vicious despair lashes out all around him. To begin with he exterminates the helpless. With Russia, the *Danse macabre* has begun."

"Mr. Pötz," I spoke in an undertone because other guests sat close to us, "I must admit that the reasons for these exterminations don't interest me. I only know that human beings who were close to us during the last two years are now being murdered; or, if they are still alive, probably vegetate under extremely degrading conditions."

Pötz stared at the table in front of him, and then looked at me. The next moment, he said, "But don't you have the same sympathy for all the young men who are now losing their lives in Russia?"

"No." I could not help laughing. "These young people belong to the 'master race,' and can defend themselves with weapons. If the Russians shoot faster, that's just bad luck. No one ever gave the Jews a chance to defend themselves."

After a while, he said: "I understand. If you had the chance to avenge your Jewish friends, would you do it?" I nodded. "An eye for an eye, a tooth for a tooth"?

"Yes!" I said with conviction.

He looked at me genuinely grieved.

"Do you know what hatred is? Hatred is a spiritual ghetto! A ghetto is a small, well defined area, whose inhabitants have almost forgotten there is another world. If you join this society of haters, you no longer basically differ from the Nazis, who have lost all humaneness in their blind hatred." He curled up his lips and looked at me challengingly. "You don't want to listen to this, do you? My dear, a person like yourself, who can be understanding and generous in many ways and derides every form of orthodoxy, should realize that hatred and orthodoxy have the same parents: intolerance

231

and narrow-mindedness. Orthodox believers, Catholics, Jews, or Nazis, have not eaten from the tree of knowledge.

"I prefer to believe that you are confusing your legitimate pain with hatred. Hatred, orthodoxy and religion are unproductive and not worth the waste of time." His searching look gave way to an understanding smile.

"The ancient Jews weren't all revengeful, but had several wise teachers. It is written in the Talmud: 'Always be among the persecuted, never with the persecutors.' It would be well if the Jews carved this sentence in stone and displayed it before the gates of Palestine; if they ever forget this, they will perish."

"My dear, hatred has never built anything yet, it has only led to destruction."

January 1, 1942

By the end of November, the Russians finally began to repulse the Germans at Rostov and the Donets basin. From this date on, one repeatedly reads of hard fighting in which the enemy suffered heavy losses. How things look on the German side is tactfully concealed. The newspapers are slowly being filled with obituary notices.

Although I wish the Germans everything bad, I am still occasionally upset when I read the names of the sons and grandchildren of our patients, names of my childhood playmates as well as the brothers of my school friends; all these young people condemned by their parents to sacrifice their lives.

We entered a new year of war. No bells rang on New Year's eve and there wasn't any punch. With tearful eyes, mother announced that Etta's son was now in Russia. As soon as I could decently leave, I withdrew to my room.

In contrast to former New Year's eves, the streets are totally silent. In this stillness I am surrounded by the spirits of all who were close to me. But my thoughts find no response, since the dead are silent. The hour seems unreal and ghostly. Only the deep and even breathing of my small sleeping dog reassures me that there is still a living creature in the world besides myself.

January 11, 1942

Several days ago, I received a letter through the army postal service from Gunter Siegurd Kunz.

Mother had seen the letter; she came to my room with a thin excuse. While she spoke to me, her eyes wandered to my desk, where I had thrown the pages of his letter. She finally could restrain herself no longer: "What has Siegurd Kunz written?"

"He wrote that his mother divorced her Jewish husband."

"No; really?" mother exclaimed nonplussed.

"Yes. This man was only appreciated by them as long as he was a professor at Bonn University, a respected member of society. Now he is only a Jew, who must wear a yellow star. Gunther Siegurd feels a divorce is the best solution for all participants."

She stared speechlessly and asked after a long silence: "How will you answer his letter?"

"Answer? If I were to write what I think of him and his mother, and the letter went through censorship — what do you think would happen to all of us?" I tore his letter up and threw the scraps in my wastepaper basket. "I hope he'll be blown to bits in Russia!"

February 18, 1942

Yesterday, on my afternoon off, I went downtown with Brandy. The closer we came to the Eschersheimer Turm, the more soldiers we saw. Many moved forward on one leg with the help of crutches; some had arms in splints, some hobbled wrapped in bandages. We were near the Adult Education Center, which had meanwhile become an auxiliary military hospital as had the Elizabeth School.

A plump middle-class woman walked slightly ahead of me; she suddenly slowed her steps and turned towards me. "Isn't that a shame?" she said indignantly. "All these young men are so crippled. Where will this lead?" My silence was interpreted as agreement. She continued, "One is constantly hungry. You wouldn't believe what a hard time I have to get enough food for my teen-age boys! They are growing like weeds, but there is no fat on them." Suddenly she stopped talking and glanced at me mistrustfully.

I gave her a friendly smile. "I understand how you feel as a mother; the war will certainly come to an end sometime."

March 18, 1942

There is not much to report. Or is it news that almost daily reports are published about heavy fighting on the Donets front, tough battles in the Crimea, and bitter fighting in the East? The enormous Russian losses are cited in endless repetition with small variations. I frequently devote my time to reading the revealing obituaries. Some young men went to war with enthusiasm to die a hero's death for the Führer and Fatherland. Others fell only in fulfillment of their duty. It was said of one man that he lost his life in the East at the age of twenty.

"No word of Führer or Fatherland" I remarked to Bernd. "The poor parents lost a son, forced into uniform to die for — nothing."

"And for what were six hundred people killed during an English bombing raid on Paris?" countered Bernd. "They weren't even combatants. My God! Beautiful Paris! These barbarians!"

"*C'est la guerre.* Isn't that what you told my mother when the first bombs fell here? And how do you think London looks? I was never there but I heard it is a very beautiful city — or was."

He nodded. "Certainly Hitler can no longer win this war, but this ghastly destruction until he loses . . . ."

"Why are you again convinced that he will lose?"

"My arithmetical example," he replied triumphantly. "All raw materials are running short. It is necessary to bring a suitcase along when purchasing clothing, in order to save wrapping paper. And just look at the housewives, when they go to the food stores! One could believe they were on their way to a picnic, carrying baskets, glasses, bottles and all sorts of containers with them. Even the copper pennies are being withdrawn from circulation."

"Food rations are increasingly smaller," I added.

"This seems rather ironical. Hitler once criticized Brüning and von Papen when they demanded that the Germans tighten their belts. He promised the people work and bread, a slogan he stole from the Socialists."

"And?" I asked, "hasn't he kept his word? They have work to the point of exhaustion. There is also bread, although only four pounds a week, made from the chaff of rye and wheat; and less than half a pound of fat is distributed per week. After all, he never promised any spread with the bread."

March 28, 1942

A happy excitement suddenly prevailed among Frankfurt's Jewish community. According to rumor, they would be granted another chance to leave Germany. At a specified time, a number of them went with their baggage to Hamburg, where they were to board a ship and travel to America.

Dr. Goldschmidt, the former economics editor of the *F.Z.* was one of these select few. He lived near us with his two nieces and was one of father's patients. We were happy for the old man, who would now be reunited with his daughter Lotte in America.

A few days after his departure, one of his nieces called and requested father to come quickly because Dr. Goldschmidt had heart trouble.

"Isn't he in Hamburg?"

"No; the trip came to nothing. None of them could leave Germany; he had to return to Frankfurt."

The disappointment was almost too much for his old heart, but Dr. Goldschmidt seemed to be recovering.

We made our daily house calls at the Goldschmidts. One day as we stood in the doorway ready to leave, one of the nieces called us back. "I forgot this." She handed father two pounds of butter.

Father looked speechlessly at the butter. "No, no. Many thanks! Please keep it for yourselves."

"We don't need it, Dr. Schroeder! We really don't need it!"

In the street, father remarked that Goldschmidt must certainly have good connections on the black market.

When we came again the next day, other tenants in the house stopped us on the stairs, "Are you Dr. Schroeder?"

When father affirmed this, a woman said: "You don't have to go upstairs. The Goldschmidts committed suicide last night."

March 31, 1942

On March 28th, the official military report stated that British bombers attacked several places along the north-German coast, especially Lübeck. The population suffered "some losses."

On the 29th the newspapers reported that primarily residential areas in Lübeck were bombed; the civilian population had "heavy casualties."

On the 30th, a full article was devoted to Lübeck. It was filled with outrage and reported senseless destruction.

Slowly, the populace begins to wonder, why is this terrible news being served to them in homoeopathic doses; and what else is being withheld? Uncertainty, bordering on distrust, is eating into many people, like an insidious disease. Didn't Göring promise that no enemy airplane would cross the border? And how does the great security of the Siegfried line help against Russia? Why must our husbands and sons fight and freeze in the unmerciful Russian weather?

When we make house calls, we occasionally stop at our butcher. Her husband is in the East. She always gives us a bit more than is allotted by our ration coupons.

Recently she looked at us angrily. "One can't believe anything anymore! I only know how things are with respect to the food supply. But what is going on in Russia? My husband can't write the truth. This constant fear! This house-to-house and hand-to-hand fighting near Kharkov. I don't even know where he is. I have only an A.P.O. mailing address. You should listen to what the people say sometimes. They certainly didn't elect Hitler for this, to drive us all into such war and misery!" Filled with resentment, she added an extra piece of sausage to our meager ration. "I'm sorry I can't give you more. One works like a horse, and then there isn't even enough to eat! It is a disgrace!."

April 12, 1942

At present, a resettlement is taking place in Frankfurt. Jews are removed from their homes in the West End and placed in the East End, where they live in a kind of ghetto. Married couples have one room; and occupants of a floor must share the kitchen and bathroom. The Jews who live near us don't know whether they will also be resettled or whether they will suddenly be included in another deportation transport.

A few days ago after office hours, Father Siegel came by. A very affectionate relationship exists between the Siegels and us. I often felt that Siegel transferred some of his fatherly love to me, since his own children live abroad for many years.

"Miss Lili," Father Siegel said, "I want to ask a great favor." He reached into his coat pocket and removed a small case. "Would you please keep this meerschaum pipe for me, and give it to my son Willi after the war? He often saw me smoke it."

I agreed, and promised to carry it with me in my air-raid luggage.

After he left, I stared at the place where he had stood. What had father said about the self-possession and composure of these people? The elderly Mr. Siegel had voiced no complaint. With an al-

236

most completely paralyzed wife, he soberly faces a situation which he cannot escape; and he prepared himself for the final departure. To keep things in order, he also asked that I retrieve my typewriter which I had lent to his wife; she laboriously typed letters, with one finger, to each of her children.

But there is not much to write about. Since Germany declared war on America, communication with American relatives is maintained through the Red Cross; these Red Cross letters are limited to twenty-five words. But even if we were permitted to write one hundred, what could we say that the censors would allow to pass? Could we write about the constant distress, in which we live? About the endless disturbed nights, when we bring our air-raid luggage into the cellar and then run back to save equipment important to our profession: Father's microscope, Mrs. Rodenhauer's machine for sewing fur, and other similar items? Can we write about what happened to certain individuals?

On a Saturday afternoon, the doorbell rang. A pale care-worn young girl stood before me; she looked half starved. "You surely know me; I'm Lotte Lyon."

I tried to find a resemblance between this ghost and the lively young human being with rosy cheeks and flashing eyes, whom I met at the Rodenhauers' about a year ago.

Lotte told us how she travelled with her mother by train to Aachen, where they wanted to cross the border. They had given Persian carpets, silver, and money to a Jew, who provided them with the necessary papers and tickets; but at the same time betrayed them to the Gestapo. They were arrested in the train, brought back here to prison; from which they were finally released after she went on a hunger strike.

May 10, 1942

The day before yesterday another Jewish transport left.

We learned how these transports are made up. In the spring of 1941, the Gestapo required the administration of the Jewish congregation to make a card index in triplicate of all members of the Israelite congregation. After the completion of the index, the Gestapo handed back a list with twelve hundred names, which made up the first transport. From then on, the congregation had to keep ready a list of twelve hundred members who would receive written notices three days before departure.

237

On Monday evening, the 4th of May, we received the first telephone calls from ostensibly sick people, who requested house calls. In reality, it was a matter of completely healthy people who learned before official notification that their names were on the transport list. Whoever was in the hospital before notification could gain a delay. Unfortunately, the medical superintendent of the Internal Medicine Division of Gagern Hospital is also seriously ill; and father quietly is taking charge of the whole ward.

While he went from bed to bed and gave the necessary instructions, I slipped into the basement, where Wolf's friend and former schoolmate, Dr. Ernst Stamm is in charge of the ear, nose, and throat division. He also lives in the hospital.

After a brief council of war, we came to the following conclusion: I could call him at any time during the day or night. I would ask "Ernst, can I see you?" and if he replied yes, it meant a bed was free and whomever we brought would be received at the gate. Everything would be done to make a healthy person ill, which usually meant injections to induce fever.

What else can I write about this, except that the source of my tears seems to dry up? There were many heartbreaking situations, when patients with helpless expressions held out the cards which ordered them to report for their journey to death on May 8th; and we said good-bye. A few went with a small senseless hope that perhaps they could survive; others were conscious that it meant the end of their lives. A very small number decided they would rather take their own lives, instead of letting the Nazis do it.

Father said, "And people speak of God being good."

The second transport this year left on May 24th. The number of calls increased. We were on the move from dusk to dawn; climbing up and down stairs; looking for telephone booths in the darkness in unfamiliar neighborhoods; and hiding in the shadows when a figure suddenly appeared. We suspected every man on the street at that hour to be a Gestapo agent.

Every time we arrived at Gagern Hospital, Ernst Stamm received us exhausted with fatigue. He wordlessly took charge of the patient, made him ill and thereby gave him a week, perhaps a month of life, as was the case with the little Miss Goldblatt. She was a willowy slender young girl whose tiny face seemed to consist of only two large dark eyes. She wasn't sick and didn't want to die before she even had started living.

I once asked Ernst while I was in his consultation room why he had not left long ago.

He had once been on his way; but fell ill in Paris. His friends found him unconscious and a major sinus operation saved his life. Meanwhile his exit permit expired, his money ran out, and he returned to hell. "A few hours in the cold and I am finished. I am fully aware of it—" He made a resigned gesture with his shoulders.

There are patients who became our friends, like the Mays. Willy May, with a badge for combat and medal for wounds, had a kidney filled with stones. But he stood slim and erect, with an ironic smile in his gray eyes, and an encouraging word for his despairing wife, whose careworn features failed to hide her charm. They sent their son Rolf abroad in the nick of time; but Günther, who is not sixteen yet lives with them. He is a tall and lanky youngster, with astonished childlike eyes. Occasionally, father visits them in the evening for a game of skat.

Suddenly, the ominous card arrived; Günther was to hold himself ready for the transport on June 11th.

"No!" Mrs. May protested; her emaciated hands pressed against her dark hair. "No! I know very well we will all have to go. But at least, I want us to stay together."

We agreed that Günther was sick; he ostensibly had typhus. A temperature chart was set up and hung over his bed. At midnight before the impending date, father would give the boy an injection.

We made our usual day and night rounds before the departure of the transport, as well as our regular house calls. Father was nervous on the 11th. He asked me to drive him to the Mays' residence; I went inside with him.

Mrs. Mary, who was beside herself, pounced on him. "He hasn't any fever! We only claimed he is sick, and we expect the Gestapo physician any moment."

Father gave Günther a second injection, and we departed.

Later, Mr. May reported that Günther had severe chills when the Gestapo doctor came and was temporarily struck off the transport list.

July 18, 1942

In hell one loses all sense of time. It must have happened ages ago. Shortly after the last transport, the Gestapo telephoned and politely invited father to come for an interview. We learned from Dr. Strüder, that he was to be there half an hour before father.

I drove father to the Lindenstrasse and entered the Gestapo

building with him, a huge mansion in a fancy neighborhood. As the door closed, I talked a little louder to distract him from the lock's click. The porter would never push the button to open the door for us, if not ordered to do so by his superior.

While we waited in the corridor, speaking in a low voice, Dr. Strüder came out of an adjacent room, accompanied by two Gestapo officials. His face was pale; passing us he whispered, petrified: "I am arrested."

The next moment, Baab the feared Gestapo official, called father, but did not allow me to accompany him.

For a few minutes only I stood alone in the hallway when the door to another office opened, "Miss Schroeder?"

I looked up.

"Please come in."

And thus began a prolonged interrogation. I sat at the head of a long table; a Gestapo official was seated on both my right and left.

"Tell me, Miss Schroeder, what do you actually do?"

"I am my father's office assistant, secretary, laboratory technician and chauffeur."

"Is that so. What do you do with these Jews?"

"Give them medical care," I replied icily.

"And what do you receive for this?"

"They pay their bills like all other patients."

"Hmmm. Do you also go to their homes?"

"My father usually goes in alone, while I wait in the car."

"For what kind of case do you go inside?"

"When it is very cold; and if the patients in question have another room where I can wait."

"And in addition to this? Do you also associate on a friendly personal basis with these Jewish patients?"

"Excuse me?" I asked incredulously.

It was a warm spring day. The sun shone through the large open windows; I sat facing the bright light. Despite this, I froze. I held my trembling hands under the table, clasped between my knees, to conceal every sign of fear or alarm.

The second official, who until then seemed to be taking notes, elaborated. "For example, does your father occasionally play cards during the evening with his Jewish patients?"

Was this merely a trap, or did the Gestapo already know about father's evening visits at the Mays?

240

"After a strenuous day, my father prefers to spend his evenings at home."

The first Gestapo man asked: "Have the Jews, who were deported, given you things for safekeeping?"

"No."

The thought ran through my head, what would become of mother, if both of us were arrested?

The second man helped his partner out: "But they gave you gifts, didn't they?"

I was silent.

"No? Are you sure? Miss Schroeder, think it over carefully."

Fear seized my heart. What was happening two doors away? What was father being asked? Would he heed my warning? The last thing I whispered to him in the corridor was: "Lie! You must deny everything!"

In an almost kind-hearted manner, the first Gestapo official continued, "You probably know that your father is arrested?"

"No," I replied rigidly.

"Well? Then, I'm telling you. You must certainly want to return home."

I nodded.

The second man asked, "All right: what kind of gifts did you receive?"

"I didn't receive any gifts."

I got caught in the cross-fire.

"No?"

Gloating, he continued, "For example, wasn't the leather bag a present?"

"The leather bag?" I repeated, genuinely surprised.

"Yes. Or was it a suitcase?"

"Ah," I said, "correct. I completely forgot."

"So, you forgot?"

"Yes. It was a very old-fashioned suitcase with a handle in the middle; something nowadays not in fashion. I put it in the cellar and forgot about it."

I remembered the strange woman, who brought me the case on behalf of Mrs. Bamberger, together with her farewell greetings. So I hadn't been duped after all.

"And what else did you receive?"

I knew exactly what the pigskin case contained, but I acted as if I was giving it careful thought.

241

"What else?" pressed the first official.

"Stationery!" I exclaimed with relief.

"What kind of stationery?"

"An open package of writing-paper with envelopes."

"Did you also put it in the cellar?"

"No; I used it."

"Do you remember anything else? Perhaps some perfume?"

"Right. Perfume."

"Do you still have it?"

"No; I used it long ago."

During the last question, a door opened and a man in shirt-sleeves, black trousers and shiny jackboots entered the room. He spoke softly to the official who was interrogating me, while the second Gestapo man continued: "Do you want to tell us anything more, Miss Schroeder?"

As my name was mentioned, the third Gestapo man glanced at my face casually. I had seen this man somewhere.

"By the way, how did you get here?" the second inquisitor persevered.

"By car."

"Should we inspect it?"

I probably did not completely succeed in suppressing a mocking smile, as I threw the car keys on the table. "Only my dog is in the car;" and he will bite you, I hoped.

Without looking up, I felt the third man glance at me; then I saw out of the corner of my eye that he scribbled something on a scrap of paper and pushed it towards the first official, before he left the room.

"Has anything else occurred to you?" asked the first official, while he crumpled the piece of paper

"Yes," I replied. "I received as a gift a small Meissen duck."

"So? Look around at home and see whether you find anything else. You will deliver the bag and the duck here tomorrow morning." After a moment's reflection, he said: "Perhaps, it would be better if we came and checked the house, to see if there is anything else. You can go now. Heil Hitler!"

I walked downstairs on shaky legs and crossed the street to our car. I though about the frequent warnings, which all of us — Bernd, Etta, and I — had given to father and his almost indignant rebuff: "They wouldn't dare touch me, a former medical officer with the rank of colonel in the First World War and former

242

medical superintendent of the Bürgerhospital."

They had dared.

Brandy probably felt the danger I had been in; and he greeted me excitedly. I hugged him to me. "My little pet, they dared! They arrested a good patriotic German, who paved the way for National Socialism."

I drove the two blocks to Bernd's house. His mother opened the door and showed me to his room.

The smile of welcome froze on his face, when he looked at me.

I said: "They arrested father." Then, I broke down and sobbed.

When I arrived back home, I went to the cellar immediately, to examine the trunks our Jewish patients gave us for safekeeping. Bernd and I wanted to get them out of the house that same evening. The trunks contained more fur coats, suits, bed linen and other items than we could ever own personally. If the Gestapo should really make a house search. . . I could barely wait until it was dark, and we could get rid of these incriminating trunks.

"I thought it over," Bernd said, "we'll get these things to Reinhardt tonight. Nobody will look for them there. He can take part of them to his weekend house in Kahl. I'll take the rest with me to Bavaria, the next time I go."

We dragged four trunks to the street and hid them in a dark corner and I went to a telephone booth and asked for a taxi. I used a false name, and gave the address of the house opposite me.

"One moment please," the man at the taxi station replied. I hung up.

"I don't trust him," I explained to Bernd. "Why 'just a moment'? Must he first look through a list or check back with the Gestapo?"

We started carrying all four trunks down Lehrbachstrasse, crossed the Opernplatz, and dragged them over the Taunusanlage to Taunusstrasse. We had to put the heavy trunks down more and more frequently. Our fingers could scarcely hold the handles anymore; and we felt as if our arms would burst out of our shoulder sockets. As soon as someone approached, we tried to hasten our steps, as if we were on the way to the station. It was after midnight, when we arrived at the Reinhardts. Despite the cool air, we were bathed in sweat.

243

Reinhardt, a pure Aryan, an old socialist and embittered enemy of the Nazis, was already asleep. He was genuinely astonished to see us. We briefly explained what had happened, and asked him to help us. He agreed to store the things for us. He was very upset at the news of father's arrest.

He led us into the kitchen, so we could rest for a moment. He asked me: "Have you anything else at home? If the Gestapo really comes and finds something there . . ."

"Yes; we still have a whole suitcase full of photos and letters from a patient. But we couldn't carry it over here. Moreover, those things have no value."

"Whether they have any value or not, Miss Schroeder, please burn them. Or is the patient still alive?"

"No. They gassed little Levie in a tunnel near Minsk."

He stared at me, shook his head, and then stood up. Taking three glasses from the kitchen cabinet, he said, "I think all of us can use a drink." His hand moved through his sleep-tousled hair, and he looked at us pensively. "Where will all this end? Almost every day, I hear about a friend or an acquaintance who is arrested. Not only Jews are exterminated. There are also Communists, Socialists, Jehovah's Witnesses, Fundamentalists, and anyone who opens his mouth to criticize the Nazis. Let's not fool ourselves. I don't know which is worse, to be killed rapidly or to die a slow death in a penitentiary or concentration camp. We already don't have enough to eat; political prisoners get even less."

Bernd said, "These subhumans are of no importance. The death sentence is meted out for the theft of clothing coupons, for the theft of woolen goods, and for illicit butchering. In addition, the SS is arbitrarily shooting these convicts claiming they 'resisted' or were 'trying to escape.' "

"My friends," said Reinhard, "the Nazis will regret they murdered these 'enemies of the state', when they can no longer find enough manpower to be blown to bits on their battlefields!"

I returned home, exhausted, in the final darkness before dawn. I unlocked the door and there on the bench in the foyer I found mother and Miss Wurm huddled together in their bathrobes.

Mother looked like a ghost. Her frightened eyes gazed out of deep hollows from her deathly pale face; "Lili dear! Oh, Lili! I thought they also arrested you. My child. . ."

I held my trembling tiny mother in my arms; she barely

244

reaches up to my chin. I was again amazed how she kept her self-control in an emergency.

Suddenly she said, "I don't know what I would have done without the good 'Würmchen'."

The good 'Würmchen' stretched and smiled with relief. "We were really terribly frightened because of you!"

The next day, I delivered Mrs. Bamberger's case and porcelain duck to the Gestapo. With a courage born of despair, I went to Baab's office to inquire what father was charged with.

This creature, Baab, sat behind his desk; his face was pale and somewhat bloated. I thought I detected a slight satisfaction in his expressionless features. Wasn't it wonderful for this nobody to suddenly have the power to watch 'fine people' whimper for mercy?

Baab told me father's medical certificates were invalid, since they were written out of complaisance and only served to sabotage the Gestapo's work.

"And if I can prove to you that the medical certificates are legitimate?"

His cold fisheyes looked at me indifferently; "That could help."

I received permission to bring a pillow, a blanket and some linen for my father in the jail. I wrapped them in my car blanket, and hoped he would recognize this as a sign I was still free.

Friends negotiated with the foreman of a well-known photographic lab. He came with his Leica camera and reproduced case histories from father's books, for hours at a time, of those patients for whom father had written medical certificates.

I was completely exhausted when I went up to the third floor to see Mrs. Rodenhauer. She told me, via her daughter, that she wanted to speak to me. This usually cool woman embraced me with moist eyes and asked me about the interrogation.

"Do you remember," she inquired, "that a man came in during your interrogation?"

"Yes."

"That was our friend, Hildebrandt. He had once seen you on the staircase, and told me he didn't want anyone from our house to be arrested. You owe your release to his intervention."

About three days after father's arrest, I was called to the telephone. District Court Judge Schmidt wanted to speak to me.

245

After he greeted me, he asked: "Is what I heard about your father true?"

"Yes."

"And you didn't call me?"

I was silent.

"When can I see you?"

I became acquainted with Waldemar Schmidt when I was a journalist. He is a widower with two daughters who are slightly younger than I. We got along well, and I enjoyed talking with this extremely intelligent man, who also has an excellent sense of humor. We met at various times in wine taverns during the afternoons, and spent several merry hours together. As with so many other personal relationships, I broke this one off after my conviction by the Special Court.

Now, however, I sat in his office in the district court, and told him the story of father's arrest.

His lively dark eyes set in a sharply featured face looked searchingly at me. "Precisely what is your father accused of?"

"I don't know. At first, it was for writing invalid medical certificates, which sabotaged the Gestapo's work. When I refuted this with photographic copies of father's medical records, the Gestapo official Baab wasn't at all interested. He maintained that father was not even permitted to treat Jewish patients. When I replied that father had explicitly inquired about this at the Medical Association and received assurance that this injunction applied solely to party members, Baab again spoke about sabotage. In general terms, they simply want to deprive the Jews of the last good doctors and punish the physicians who adhere to the Hippocratic oath."

Schmidt nodded meditatively, "Give me some time. There must be a way to get your father out of prison."

Once I was permitted to visit father briefly, to fetch his instructions for his Aryan patients. I somehow had the feeling that he did not take his arrest seriously and expected to be released at any moment.

But time passed and he remained in prison.

Our Jewish patients seemed to have disappeared from the surface of the earth. We told our Aryan patients that father was sick. Those, who learned that father is in prison, came from time to time and asked whether we had heard anything. They brought flowers, wine, tea, and other things, which we kept for his return. They had

246

certainly all heard about such arrests; but their own doctor? One scarecely dared to say anything anymore.

Waldemar Schmidt finally telephoned and asked to see me.

"Your father will be released in a few days."

As a judge, Schmidt had dealt for some time with a high Nazi official concerning a real-estate case. Recently, this Nazi came to see him. Schmidt said: "You know that I suffer from asthma as a result of gas poisoning in the last war? I wanted to see my doctor last week and learned he is in prison." He regretted that the real-estate affair would be needlessly delayed, since he did not feel well and was not about to locate another doctor.

The Nazi took some notes and returned a few days later to inform Schmidt that they had planned to send father and Dr. Strüder to a camp in Poland for educational purposes.

The same afternoon I went to the prison with fresh linen for father. The gate sergeant, an older man, knew about father and was honestly incensed. "But," he said confidentially, "I heard that he and the other doctor would be released soon."

I nodded silently, and then asked, "But does my father also know this?"

"Certainly not," the sergeant replied. After a brief reflection, he continued, "I have an idea, Miss. Please wait here for a while. In about a quarter of an hour, he should come downstairs. If you are standing here at the door, he can see you and you can give him a sign."

For the next fifteen or twenty minutes I sat with the sergeant. Shaking his head, he said, "I could never have dreamed about the kind of prisoners we now have in custody. Formerly, oh well, you know what I mean, we had real criminals here, or men who were suspected of a crime. But now? If I were permitted to speak, Miss Schroeder . . . your father and the other doctor aren't the only gentlemen here!"

Suddenly he said, "Quick, stand over there. They'll be here shortly!"

I looked at all the feet which walked down the concrete steps. And then father came. I recognized his shoes, the color of his trouser legs, the hands which held his pants in place. Belts and suspenders were taken away from prisoners, to prevent them from hanging themselves.

Father stared grimly in front of him until I made a movement

247

which caught his attention. I looked at him with a triumphant expression, and believed I saw a hopeful response in his questioning eyes.

He is back home now.

After three weeks of solitary confinement and hunger, he had to sign a statement that he would no longer issue medical certificates for Jews.

I picked him up at the prison and our trolley trip home will probably haunt me for the rest of my life. My well-groomed father sat next to me in the streetcar, with an almost wild expression, staring in front of him; he was in a wrinkled, stained suit; his sunken face was covered with thick white stubble, while his lips formed silent words.

We do not know how the news spread so quickly. Patients came, flowers and greetings of welcome; cakes, bread, fruit, and even some real coffee beans.

Father slowly loses his hunted look, and even begins, occasionally, to speak about his imprisonment. "At first, I recited the *Odyssey* by Homer and the like, then came Schiller's and Goethe's turn. After a while, I began to invent stories — but they all ended in a gigantic feast. The hungrier I became the larger the platters of food seemed to be; all the food which one can imagine. Finally, I thought of nothing else but eating." He grew silent with memories. "Just as I was about to give up all hope, Lili stood downstairs on the prison steps. At that moment I knew I would regain my freedom."

August 19, 1942

I am spending my vacation with Brandy in Murnau, while my parents are at a Carinthian estate belonging to old friends. Although every fibre of my heart drew me to Hinterstein, I chose Murnau, because it is a place where no one knows me. I rented a room in a private house, which lodges summer visitors.

There are many reasons for my flight into seclusion. I not only want to rest and sleep again undisturbed by air-raid sirens, but I also want to detach myself from people who are close to me. I want to give them the choice, when I return, either to resume contact with me or to silently and unobtrusively disappear from my life.

An unanswered letter from Arnulf lies in front of me. I re-

248

ceived it a few days before father's arrest. With a certain nostalgia, I see Arnulf's thin face and dark eyes before me. I can never write him how glad I was to receive his letters; nor can I ever explain that any association with me is dangerous. It seems as if I were infected with a deadly disease, which poisons others who come in contact with me. It is difficult to imagine this son of the mountains in the lowlands of a foreign country. My thoughts are with him, and I very much hope he will return to our mountains healthy in body and soul.

My thoughts returned to the deportations, and to our friends and patients. I suddenly realized that it makes practically no difference whether a person is Jewish or Aryan; only high party membership makes a difference. The Jews know where their journey ends and can calculate how many days are left to them. Similar feelings gradually take hold among the civilian population in the cities whenever the sirens sound. Air-raids on specifically named cities are mentioned more frequently; we concluded from this that the population must have suffered considerable losses.

I also thought about many soldiers, who are fighting reluctantly. Whoever has scruples, whether from religious or humanitarian motives, must decide for himself to either wear the Führer's uniform or be executed. I remembered our conversation with Reinhardt that night. Strictly speaking, no Germans are exempted, whatever their race or religion, except for the favoured party bosses.

Unfortunately, it does not even give me satisfaction that the man who promised the German people bread and work and therefore received their overwhelming support, gives them less and less bread, and generously distributes misery and death.

August 31, 1942

My vacation has come to an end. Tomorrow, I will meet my parents in Munich where we will spend a day with Katherina before returning home.

Father wrote that Uncle Rudolf's factory was destroyed and the tradition-laden family house was burnt to its foundations, during a heavy air raid on Mainz on August 12th. The first bomb destroyed the newly installed sprinkler system.

Initially I was overcome by sentimental feelings when I read the news. Once again, I recalled the large well-cared-for rooms with family pictures, old furniture and my handsome, jolly cousins. Then I remembered the newest childrens' game, which Uncle Rudolf put on the market as — When We Sail against England.

I felt compelled to laugh. Our entire tradition had disintegrated into ashes! Our ancestors on the Aryan side of the family were free, upright people, who despised any coercion. They were men who fought for their ideas in the Paulskirche, and would certainly have opposed Nazi oppression. However, tradition is not only upheld by the preservation of inherited objects. Dear Uncle Rudolf, who knows — perhaps one of our common ancestors came out of his grave to burn the clever games with which you tried to poison childrens' minds? With those games, you wanted to lay the basis for hatred in innocent childrens' hearts, so that as adults they would, without hesitation, take up arms to murder and wage war. But now the English are playing "when we sail against Germany."

September 4, 1942

During the last week of our vacation, we did not have our mail forwarded; so father sat at his desk looking at what had accumulated.

He came into my room with a letter in his hand. "The National Health Insurance Association has dismissed me as its senior consultant." He handed me the letter.

We discussed all the possible ramifications of this new blow, but father was still not ready to reconcile himself to his fate. He didn't realize that he was an outsider and could no longer consider himself a full-fledged member of the German people. Mother's indignant remarks did not make things easier.

Father racked his brains to find a way out. "A political blunder!" he repeated angrily. "One should discuss the matter with them personally. But, I can't do it myself."

Silence followed.

After a while, mother exclaimed enthusiastically, "Couldn't Lili go to Berlin?"

Father looked at me inquiringly.

"Do you really expect something will come of it?" I asked.

"We must at least try it," mother insisted.

"My dear, if you don't want to go," father said in rather a disappointed tone of voice.

"Of course I am willing," I replied. "I am ready to go. Only I

250

don't want to raise your expectations too high as you will be disappointed if I fail."

"Of course, I understand," father said.

Mother tried to arouse my enthusiasm for the project, "The director will certainly be willing to listen, when he learns the truth."

My parents would only learn by experience, if at all. They can't be convinced by words. I will go to Berlin next week, although I know it will be a senseless waste of time and energy.

September 23, 1942

Meanwhile, I have arrived in Berlin. The German trains, once renowned for their punctuality and cleanliness, no longer live up to their reputation.

As I expected, the train was overcrowded with soldiers in transit and civilians, many on their way to funerals or leaving bombed-out homes. After a while, I grew accustomed to the tired and hungry faces. When one got out, another took his place with the same weary and hungry expression. If ever a brief conversation between travellers took place, the subject which preyed most on everyone's mind was avoided.

During a stop at a railway station, my thoughts began to wander. An elderly gentleman, standing on the platform in a gray gabardine coat, reminded me of Father Siegel, who pursues me like a ghost in my dreams. The train moved forward again and I saw the pale, drawn face of a very young soldier. He looked as though he were on casualty leave. The military communiqués now often report attacks repulsed after indeterminate fighting, or counterattacks which were repulsed or halted. What had the disillusioned eyes of this boy in uniform seen? Did he know how we were lied to at home, after his direct confrontation with the horrors of war?

My last conversation with Bernd came to mind. He spoke about the doubts of ordinary people, based on scraps of conversations he overheard at trolley stops or standing in line for special rations of herring or cottage cheese. The common people feel uneasy that Hitler who had always been glad to give long speeches, appealed in writing to the 1942-3 Winter Relief organization. They ask, "Why doesn't he talk to us now when we need an encouraging word? Why doesn't he make a personal appearance? Is he afraid to appear in public, because I lost my son, father, or fiancé? or because our house is a rubble heap?" The common man frequently has a very sensitive ear, and feels a tone of powerless rage in Hitler's appeal for unity to defeat the "gold hyenas" of international finance and the bolshevik beasts. These words sound shallow to them and contain no solace.

I looked once again at my wretched fellow travellers and wondered whether people will ever learn to distrust politicians? With very few exceptions, when politicians make promises the sky is the limit — until they are in power. Promises are then forgotten and only power itself counts; power which is ruthlessly misused; and the people are the ones who pay for this . . .

The director of the National Health Insurance Association received me with extreme reserve. I lied that I was in Berlin to visit relatives and wanted to use the occasion to clarify a misunderstanding about my father.

Director von Gimborn, a tall, elderly gentleman, raised his eyebrows as I began, "Your letter spoke about a 'political blunder.' The sin my father committed was to remain true to the Hippocratic oath; that is, to grant his medical help to all patients without exception."

"So, he also treated Jews." von Gimborn said with a cool impersonal voice.

"Yes, after he inquired at the Medical Association and was informed that non-party members were allowed to give medical care to Jews."

"Does this authorization still continue in force?"

"No," I replied, "eight days after my father and his colleague were released from detention, the Medical Association felt compelled to issue circulars which informed Aryan physicians that they were forbidden to treat Jewish patients."

Director von Gimborn looked at me thoughtfully and cleared his throat.

Since his silence continued, I concluded by saying: "Unfortunately, I cannot see it as a political blunder, if a doctor adheres to his highest professional vows."

"But it is necessary to make a distinction here," he explained with sudden animation. "When I was at the front in the First World War, I treated wounded French soldiers. However, I only performed my duty and did what was necessary as a doctor. I behaved differently and personally looked after our German soldiers.

One must make a distinction in professional attention and personal treatment!"

"Of course," I agreed with him. "We have also treated Jews very differently from Aryans." I thought about our Jewish patients who had no means of transportation and whom we drove in our car to Gagern Hospital; about the medicines we got for them at the pharmacy and delivered to their homes. We had never done these things for our Aryan patients.

Dr. von Gimborn crossed his legs, cleared his throat and sat up very straight. "I'm sorry, Miss Schroeder. We have valued your father's work very much! But as things stand, I cannot and will not rescind our decision."

We got up at the same time. When I entered his office, I forced myself to use the Nazi greeting, so as not to spoil anything. I said "Good-bye, doctor," in response to his Heil Hitler.

I took the next train home. It did not make me feel proud that my fears had come true. I was depressed and brooded on how I would gently break this rebuff to my parents. Perhaps, it would be best to tell them the truth bluntly, and hope they would finally face reality.

My parents were terribly disappointed, in spite of my forewarning. They expected the impossible with unalterable optimism.

October 3, 1942

The Führer spoke in the Berlin Sportpalast two days ago and reported on developments.

I skimmed over his speech in the newspaper, but stumbled over a passage where Hitler spoke about heroic deeds on the home front. He spoke about a single conspiratorial unity, "who knows whether we will survive this war victoriously or are destined to be exterminated together."

Are we destined to be destroyed: We? These were new words in the Führer's mouth! Hadn't he claimed until now that Germany was the strongest nation in the world, victorious and unbeatable? And what is this about extermination? Didn't Spengler state over forty years ago that war would become increasingly brutal because of progressive mechanization, and lead to total destruction of all enemy people, troops as well as hostile civilians? Had Hitler started the process of extermination, which would be deservedly and successfully continued by a successor nation? The Turks scarcely treated the Armenians worse than Hitler the Jews. But Hitler is not satisfied with a small group of people. He now speaks in one breath of Jews, Poles, and Gypsies. England is bombed mercilessly and Russia — ah — if only he had the power and technical means to destroy the Bolsheviks!

He miscalculated and believed that if he marched into Russia, the population would hail him as a liberator. He had not understood that the Bolsheviks liberated the people from Tsarist oppression and that the Russian people were never as well off as they are now. And because they did not receive Hitler with jubilant acclamation, they must be destroyed. Had he overreached himself? He pointed to his triumph over General Winter in 1941-2. In a few weeks he would face a second General Winter. Would he conquer him too?

October 31, 1942

"Why did you disappear for such a long time, my dear:" Pötz inquired.

"I was on vacation for four weeks, and before that — my father was arrested by the Gestapo. I didn't know whether we would ever see him again."

For the first time since I knew Pötz, he lost his superior attitude. He leaned forward and asked anxiously: "Your father was arrested?"

"Yes, because he upheld the Hippocratic oath. . ."

"Oh," he added thoughtfully. He then folded his hands over his slightly shrunken paunch. After a long silence, he inquired: "How was he affected by his imprisonment?"

"His hair is completely white. He returned from prison with a wild expression in his eyes, but that has given way to a look of uncertainty. As a good German, he somehow considered himself invulnerable. It didn't occur to him that the Nazis would dare touch him."

"And the nimbus that was Siegfried's collapsed?"

"Yes, it did."

His thumbs slipt under his suspenders. He asked with a mixture of curiosity and kindhearted patience, "Am I right that you love your father, this good, patriotic German, although you owe a great deal of your present misery to him?"

"Yes."

Pötz raised his eyebrows and smiled tauntingly: "My dear,

why do you have so much understanding for this man, except for the fact he is your father? I know you well enough to be certain that you oppose with all your youthful energy, the ideals and thoughts your father holds sacred. Why are you suddenly so tolerant? Only because a whim of fate made this man your biological father?" He inclined his head towards his right shoulder and looked at me challengingly through half closed eyes. "Well?"

I took a deep breath. "Mr. Pötz, I was the cuckoo's egg fate left in his nest. You and I have no patriotic feelings; we don't die in awe before an emperor, a president, or a führer, unless a personality who compels our respect stands behind the title. With our independence of thought, it is easy to laugh at the beliefs of people who place others on a pedestal, decorate them with flags and honor them. My father will be seventy years old this year. He devoted the greater part of his life to patriotism. It requires great personal courage for such a man to turn around 180 degrees and consciously violate governmental orders. He risked his freedom, and perhaps his life, for his newly held convictions. Although he is basically an anti-Semite, he risked his neck for a Jewish boy; he gave him a fever-inducing injection, although he knew the Gestapo was expected at the house any moment. Yes, Mr. Pötz, I love and respect him, since he possibly represents the best qualities of the German people."

Pötz stared silently at the table in front of him. Then he nodded. "So he has changed under the impact of the Nazis? Yes — that does require personal courage. How many people are awakened to a harsh reality, but don't have the courage to behave consistently with their convictions. In the last analysis, the success of a dictatorship is built on lack of principle and fear. All power is based on fear. There are complementary feelings like complementary colors. Like red and green, power and fear supplement each other." He suddenly laughed soundlessly. "What a bubble would burst, if people lost their fear!"

January 27, 1943

Horror of the incredible events is beginning to grip the unbelieving population, especially those who have a husband or a son in Russia. They do not know, whether he is still alive, crippled by frostbite, half-starved, wounded or sick. People follow the news and crave a word to give them certainty.

Naturally, I want the Germans to be defeated like Napoleon's army was. But then I think of the people, who are not Nazis and who are slaughtered senselessly on this field of dishonor. My cousin Joseph, Uncle Rudolf's eldest son, who never wanted to have anything to do with the Nazis, died in the East in August. I see the rapidly aging, despairing Etta, whose youngest son is missing in France, and whose oldest son is fighting in Russia — if he is still alive. Even her husband was sent to a military field hospital in Russia.

March 16, 1943

Several days ago, Jewish spouses of mixed marriages were summoned to the office of the so-called Jewish Congregation where for years a Gestapo agent gave orders. They had to produce their identity cards and answer all kinds of questions.

The evening before being summoned, I asked mother whether she had her identity card. She replied hesitantly.

"Do you have it?" I asked again sharply.

"Yes, yes."

The next morning, like other Aryan spouses, father accompanied mother to the Jewish Community office. When they returned, silent and haggard, I met them at the door.

Finally I asked, "Did something happen?"

"Mother did a terribly stupid thing," father replied. "She wrote something on her identity card."

Next to the big *J*, which is printed below the words Identity Card, she wrote "of a Christian;" on the next page, under remarks, she added: "My grandfather was the pure Aryan Lieutenant General von Kusserow."

Gestapo official Holland swore at her; completely aghast at her insolence, he telephoned the Gestapo in Lindenstrasse.

There she sat, my tiny mother huddled on the enormous blue sofa. "Oh, God, what have I done! I have plunged all of you into disaster!"

An indescribable fury, softened only by a vague sympathy, possessed me. Mother had always persisted in her conviction that she was a Christian, a German and had this damned general as her grandfather. Now she even tried to prove it to the Nazis... As usual, she acted first and thought afterwards.

"It would have been smarter, if you had told me this yesterday," I said. "We would have destroyed the card and said it had been lost. But it is futile to talk about that. We had better think what we can do next."

Father and I racked our brains. I have no idea what mother was thinking. She was probably silently praying to God for forgiveness.

The next morning I called the office of Mr. Eissner, a lawyer, highly recommended by several people in our situation. Mr. Eissner was away for several days. We were asked to speak with his representative, Assessor Brandt. I hesitated, but the secretary who had no idea of the issue involved, persuaded me to see him.

Several hours later, father and I met with this young man.

"I am married to a Jewess." Father began.

"Aah, the young fellow interrupted us, beaming, "and you want a divorce!"

Father looked at him aghast, while I began to laugh. Father tried to explain the situation, but met with complete lack of understanding.

Finally I got up. "Come father, I believe we are in the wrong place."

Once we were on the street again, father asked: "What do we do now?"

"We must speak directly with Mr. Eissner."

It would be senseless to record all the people we contacted and everything we considered. Even Uncle Franz could not help this time. When he learned the facts, his smile disappeared for the first time.

It seems to me that all our thoughts are concentrated on one thing. It is as if we sit with our heads bent down, awaiting the blows, which would inevitably rain down on us.

March 23, 1943

The Gestapo summons came and my parents lost their nerve. They spoke of suicide and wanted to leave me behind. I went with father to the pharmacy where he bought eighty barbiturate tablets.

I implored my parents: "You can't expect me to sit quietly in my room, while you are killing yourselves. You can't tell me about your plans and leave me behind!"

"We will sleep on it for one more night," father finally declared.

That was on Saturday. Bernd visited me the same evening and saw my misery. I couldn't help it: tears continuously streamed down my face. Bernd, who knew that mother was summoned for Monday, kept me company in silence and we listened to phonograph records.

I could not bring myself to tell him what worried me. I found myself in a hopeless situation. As long as a spark of hope existed, we should not commit suicide. But, considering the situation mother was facing, I didn't believe I could persuade my parents to wait and see what would happen.

On Sunday morning, they came to breakfast as if there had never been a crisis, as if they never had to decide between life and death.

Yesterday, I went to the Gestapo with my parents. Father waited downstairs in the street, while I entered the building with mother.

Once again, it was Gestapo official Baab who called her into his office and forbade me to go with her. After some time, Baab opened the door — perhaps it was only minutes, but it seemed like hours to me. "You can come in now and say good-bye. Your mother will stay here."

She sat on an ordinary office chair and looked chalk white in contrast to her black coat and black hat. Only her eyes were alive; the rest of her features were rigid.

I gently stroked mother's cheek with my right hand: "Be strong!" While I bent over to give her a farewell kiss, I whispered almost inaudibly, "We won't abandon you!"

Baab's light-brown eyes in his bloated face seemed disappointed, when I turned and left his office without tears and with the merest hint of a bow.

Father, who had been pacing back and forth, came to an abrupt stop and stared at me in disbelief. He could not believe that mother had been arrested. We went home in silence. I thought father's demeanor gave new evidence that he still did not understand the whole situation. He really had believed it would be settled with an interrogation.

That evening I went to visit our neighbors across the street, the Fischers. The Fischers are nice, helpful people, who occasionally invited me to listen to foreign radio broadcasts. I called Uncle

Rudolf in Mainz from their place. He was in deep mourning, I knew, because two days before mother's arrest, we had read about Joachim's death in the East on February 6th. Joachim was closer to me than most of my numerous cousins. He utterly rejected the Nazis and was forced to sacrifice his life senselessly. My pain over his loss was eclipsed only by my concern for mother.

Uncle Rudolf answered the telephone.

"We want to ask for your help," I said. "Perhaps you can use your influence. Mother is arrested and we are afraid for her."

After a brief pause, he replied cautiously and gently: "I'm very sorry, but I can't do anything. As you probably know, I just lost my second son; and I must be especially careful."

After a slight hesitation, since his logic bewildered me, I said in a resigned tone of voice: "I understand," and hung up.

Mrs. Fischer placed her arm around my shoulder. "Don't be too depressed. If there is anything I can do for you, please come over here."

Father faced me expectantly when I entered the room. I gave him a verbatim account of Uncle Rudolf's answer.

He stared at his golden wedding band, which he turned absentmindedly around his finger. "What is the saying? Blood is thicker than water." He laughed dryly.

April 3, 1943

I finally reached Mr. Eissner personally. We at once had rapport. He is intelligent, warm-hearted, and has a sense of humor. I learned from him that he deliberately chose as his legal partner an SS man with good connections in the Gestapo. This man secured the Nazi-legal assistant as his vacation substitute.

"Let's not fool ourselves, Miss Schroeder," he said politely. "The situation doesn't look good; and you know that as an attorney, I can't do anything officially. I will however prevail upon my associate to look at the Gestapo records. Rest assured, I will do absolutely everything in my power."

He called me on Monday, the 29th. "Take the next train to Berlin. The file is being sent there for the final decision. Be there before the documents arrive. See what you can do; and call me when you have returned."

After I called the station, I explained to father that I was leaving for Berlin in two hours. He should urge Katherina to come from Munich and take charge of the household, since we had no maid at that time. Perhaps Sister Ruth could substitute for me during office hours.

Throwing a few things into my suitcase, I raced to the station. I was lucky and found a seat.

The train became fuller at every stop. People sat on their suitcases in the aisles. They dozed off exhausted until new travellers boarded at the next station and tried to squeeze their way through into the next car, which was just as full.

Overtired and depressed, I arrived in Berlin, left my suitcase at the luggage checkroom and went immediately to the Gestapo in the Prinz Albrecht Strasse. I explained my mission to two exceptionally polite SS men, who informed me that I had to go to Lützow Platz.

Having sat in the train all night, my feet and legs were swollen; and my usually comfortable shoes felt too tight. Every step was torture.

Finally I stood in front of an enormous building — a palace. Wide marble steps with elegant wrought-iron banisters led to the next floor, to which I was directed. And then I stood opposite the mighty. The huge room was covered with valuable carpets and behind a large carved desk sat a bull-necked party boss in brown uniform.

My heart missed a beat. Two worlds collided. All the splendor, with which he surrounded himself, could not obscure his crudeness.

Modestly I explained why I was there.

"And she has written that on her identity card?"

"Yes," I replied, "It was certainly a mistake."

"A Christian?" he asked.

"Yes. Her parents were already baptized and racially — she is not one hundred percent Jewish."

"And how about the General? How did she dare to —!"

It was not only his outrage at mother's impudence in writing something unauthorized on an official document. His rage was provoked by this dirty Jewess' claim that her grandfather was a General. He, this brutal depraved mercenary, could not tolerate this.

I knew I had lost and stated courageously: "After all, it is the truth."

He turned red, jumped up and roared: "The truth! The truth! Get out of here! The truth —!"

I walked slowly down the marble steps which were covered with a runner.

The truth—I thought—that is the last thing these pigs can accept.

Meanwhile, Katherina had arrived and put the household slowly and creakily in motion. We alternate with each other, in bringing fresh linen and fetching the dirty laundry from the prison. Friends and acquaintances are supplying us with addresses of influential people in Berlin.

A friend of Katherina's knows the head of the Frankfurt Security Service. I went to his office and looked with disbelief at the face of a cultured educated man. What was this type of man doing in the Security Service?

Helplessly he explained that he could not interfere in Gestapo affairs; but he wanted me to meet his assistant, who could perhaps find a way out. He got up and led me into another room, where several desks stood.

He stopped before a sympathetic young man. "Mr. Lamm, could you please see if you could help Miss Schroeder?" He turned towards me with a troubled expression, and said: "You can trust Mr. Lamm."

I was bewildered. There I was inside the office of a leading Nazi agency, and it was occupied by educated, apparently warm-hearted people. Nevertheless, I didn't lose my old distrust and I merely gave him a short factual report.

Mr. Lamm listened attentively, said he would think the matter over, made several suggestions and requested that I return on Monday with specific documents.

I brought the required papers and Mr. Lamm promised to do everything he could.

He looked at me openly laughed resignedly: "What do you think, Miss Schroeder? If the situation is ever reversed, people like myself will be hanging from the lampposts down there on the street."

Outside again in the radiant spring sunshine, I stared at the next lamppost and tried in vain to imagine Mr. Lamm hanging from it. I shook my head and walked on.

April 10, 1943

Mr. Eissner enjoined me to try every means, and not be discouraged by failures. "Miss Schroeder, I will not claim your

261

mother's life lies in your hands; but so far as I know your father and your sister, you are the one who carries the burden."

He induced father to turn to his old friend and colleague, the famous internist Professor von Bergmann, whom I wanted to approach with a letter from father.

So once again I sat in the night train to Berlin. My thoughts wandered back and forth between Frankfurt and Berlin. How was mother? Did she suffer from hunger? Did she know what awaited her, and was she afraid? I had to think of something else, otherwise I would go crazy. My thoughts raced ahead of the train to Karl. Would I see Karl again? All I could learn about him was that he works in a news agency. Could I locate him? Would he welcome me? I would see Karl again! With this hope, I slipped into a restless sleep.

My cousin Ruth met me at the station at eight in the morning. From the first telephone booth, I called a news agency, uncertain it was the right one. I was in luck. Karl was expected at nine o'clock.

During a quick breakfast with Ruth, I told her the most important facts. Then she drove home with my suitcase while I went to Karl's office.

When I walked through the door, he was behind his desk telephoning — a small pretext to win time. He nodded in greeting and pointed to a chair.

We looked at each other and the old magic enveloped us. The years of separation were forgotten. His eyes caressed me and burdens fell from my shoulders. I had come home again, after endless wanderings.

The telephone conversation ended. We went up to each other and embraced.

I told him why I was in Berlin. Karl had to cover the story of the state funeral for Reichs Sport Führer von Tschammer und Osten, and we agreed to meet in the city in the late afternoon. Meanwhile, I went to Aunt Luise's where I was to stay and made several telephone calls.

Karl met me in a wine tavern, where because he was a good customer he could not only order wine but also something to eat.

As many years ago in my own case, I had to tell Karl all the details and what we had undertaken so far. While he would make inquiries among his many connections, I was to call on my list of contacts. He also advised me to find more centrally located lodgings, where I could come and go as the situation required.

We were parting at the subway entrance at Potsdamer Platz, when the sirens started to blow.

"Now you can't leave," Karl said with satisfaction. He grabbed me by the hand and pulled me across the square to Columbia-House, where his office is located.

At first we sat in his pitch black room. Karl had raised the Venetian blinds, so we could see what was going on. We heard the airplanes and the first bombs strike in the distance.

Karl, who had restlessly paced back and forth, asked: "Do you want to go upstairs? From there we can have a better view."

We climbed to the top floor of the house which is encircled by a narrow, partly roofed balcony.

Just in our range of vision we saw fires on the other side of the city and heard the bombs drop, which after a brief rain of sparks triggered new fires. The ghostly white fingers of the flak became fewer in number until they disappeared.

Karl, whose hand rested on my shoulder, said triumphantly: "When Göring bragged so proudly about his defense, he never thought that his search lights would make such wonderful targets." He began to laugh. "The little boys, who help man the anti aircraft guns, do the only sensible thing in such a situation: They leave their posts and go for shelter."

"Do you have many attacks in Berlin?" I asked.

"Yes," he replied, "and alarms every night."

We stared in fascination at the lethal fireworks. An especially heavy bomb must have fallen; we already saw the explosion before we felt the pressure wave which reached us simultaneously with the noise.

"Here," said Karl, "you have a practical demonstration of the difference between East and West. The Chinese, who first invented gun-powder, used it for pleasure. They produced harmless fireworks. Westerners however misuse it to kill just as they generally contrive to develop ever more horrible means of destruction. The explosions we are watching over there—how much death and destruction do they bring? If it would only eradicate the Nazis . . . It is the innocent however who are hit."

The next day I could not arrange any appointments. So I went from one hotel to the next between the Potsdamer and Anhalter stations. In one of the smaller hotels, a youthful desk clerk finally said that perhaps he would have a free room in a couple of hours. He said it rather hesitantly and looked at me searchingly, while I wondered what a young, apparently well-bred person was doing as a hotel porter. I had to call back several times, until I finally got my room.

Professor von Bergmann was honestly shocked by mother's arrest. He had followed the results of father's research, considered them very promising and could affirm that in a good conscience. I was to return on Monday when he would give me a letter to that effect and perhaps mobilize still other assistance.

Nobody could be reached on Saturday and Sunday. So I went to the post office where my mail is sent in care of general delivery. Today is my birthday but there was not even a greeting from father.

In the afternoon, Karl came for a while and we discussed our strategy, and groped hesitantly into our personal lives. We knew that we belonged together. But what had happened in the seven years we were out of touch?

Karl is still not divorced. His wife is not prepared to set him free, although she did not accompany him to Berlin.

"Karl, why is a divorce so important?"

He was embarrassed.

"So, you have another woman. What is her name?"

"Diana."

"Are you living with her?"

"My dearest, how could I know . . ."

I laughed a bit. "No. I couldn't know either."

He raised his eyebrows and looked at me inquiringly. "Franz Bernd," I explained, "is not what you would call the greatest love of my life, but he is a habit and a convenience."

"He loves you?"

"He wants to marry me."

Karl stood up and paced the room for a while. Suddenly, he stopped in front of me. "You know, my dear, that wouldn't be such a bad idea in this situation. An Aryan husband would be a great protection for you under the prevailing circumstances."

I am alone in a strange hotel room. My diary is the only familiar object — a silent comrade, who only listens but does not answer.

How long has it been, since I spent my birthday in such loneliness? Even in prison, I still received a letter from my parents. Now mother is behind bars. It is absolutely nerve wracking that I have to sit here and wait until Monday, without being able to do anything. My imprisonment was a vacation compared with what mother has to endure. At least, I knew the maximum limits of my sentence. But mother? I don't want to think about the rumors which circulate, especially not those about the "cold way" of liquidating mixed marriages.

From the butts of already smoked cigarettes, I rolled a new one with the little machine Bernd gave me. The thing stinks, but it smokes.

What a birthday! I should share the man I love with a strange woman and marry another man? Would that save mother's life? No! But it could endanger Bernd's, who has a Jewish ancestor somewhat farther back in time. And now that I have found Karl again, the marriage would be utterly intolerable.

I went through the deserted hotel hallways to the clerk, with the pretext of asking for a newspaper. I could no longer endure my lonely room.

He handed me a paper and said semiapologetically: "It isn't the latest one." I had just turned to go, when he called my name.

"Yes?"

He looked at me attentively. "Can I do anything for you?"

"Why?" I asked in astonishment.

"I have the feeling you have worries. Excuse me, are you Jewish?"

"Only half."

He came from behind his desk and introduced himself with a bow. "I am Wolfgang Borger, also half Jewish."

His Jewish father is in prison. We sat together until midnight, exchanged experiences and considered ways of freeing our parents.

April 20, 1943

Professor von Bergmann gave me an excellent letter, in which he wrote about father's pioneering research and expressed his conviction that everything should be done to follow up these results.

"You must go to the university hospital. Professor Sauerbruch also has a letter for your father."

I had to wait there several minutes, because Professor Sauerbruch wanted to give me his certification personally.

The world famous surgeon stood in front of me. "Here, my dear Miss Schroeder." He handed me an envelope. "I am not held in the greatest esteem at present — I am rather a black sheep. But perhaps, this will help anyway. I wish you success!" After a firm handshake, he disappeared behind a door which closed noiselessly.

Karl came in the evening to dictate a memorandum based on the documents we had, for submission to the Reichs Medical Chamber. I was to take the brief to Mr. Eissner for corrections, type it, and bring it back to Berlin. I would then submit it personally to the proper authorities.

When I returned from Eissner's office, Katherina was unpacking a bag of laundry on the kitchen table, which she had picked up at prison. I looked in the empty bag and pulled out a small scrap of white paper, which I saw at the bottom.

We stared at mother's handwriting. "Send me some sandwiches along with the linen. We are starving! With love, Mother."

Katherina's face turned red: "Oh God! How awful! She's starving!"

I looked at her silently and swallowed a comment.

Until midnight, I sat at the typewriter. The next morning, father and I went to our butcher to plead for some sausage for mother. I helped Katherina make the sandwiches and packed them between pieces of laundry, said good-bye to Brandy and arranged with Bernd to take me to the Berlin night train.

The next morning in Berlin, I went to the Reichs Medical Chamber. I had to tell my story many times, until I finally reached a higher official, who brought two other gentlemen to our meeting, as they were in charge of the care of tubercular patients. Even these Nazis, impressed by the brief and medical pamphlets, understood that a scientist can be incapable of concentrating because of worry about his wife. They promised to help.

I reported this to Karl, who waited for me impatiently in his office. "The reception was good and the people visibly impressed by von Bergmann's and Sauerbruch's statements. They promised to do everything to help father continue his research." I uttered a sigh of relief.

Karl smiled at me sympathetically. "You can't place all your hopes on this one promise. It sounds good; but in case they inquire in Frankfurt—and I fear they will—they might become less enthusiastic. If you haven't called on all the names you were given, you should pursue all the other routes."

266

For supper we met in the wine tavern. Karl inquired about my eating habits in this strange city.

I reassured him. "Apart from the fact that Bernd gave me some travel coupons, I receive breakfast without ration coupons."

"From your desk clerk?"

"Yes. He also functions as breakfast waiter and told me about an organization which has grown up here."

"What kind of organization?"

"There is a whole group of similar-minded people, who work in hotels, food stores, and even in ration-card distribution offices. They steal food cards to supply their Jewish or politically persecuted friends, who have gone underground. Borger thought I qualified for breakfast at least."

"Where do these people live?"

"They move from friend to friend. They present themselves as brothers, cousins, nieces, nephews — depending on their age and sex. They seek refuge in public air-raid shelters, churches, warehouses and other places in Berlin. Borger told me some of them have done this for years; and until now, none has been caught."

April 26, 1943

Tomorrow I am returning home. My chief activity here consisted of waiting, waiting until I could reach someone by telephone, until the time arrived for an appointment, until someone called back. I spent hours in my hotel room waiting. I knew every petal of the flowers on my wallpaper, every small crack in the ceiling and every scratch on the black telephone, which stared at me without pity.

I thought of mother starving and racked my brains as to what else I could attempt. I repeated and repeated her story as if I were playing a record, but all the appointments I made, all actions I took, were in vain. One person after another sent me to a new address, which again proved to be a dead end, whereupon I turned around and tried another path. I met with sympathy, cooperation and — helplessness.

When the day was finally over and Karl had to work late, I again sat in my hotel room and waited, waited until he came, so I could report my failures. We contrived new plans and for a short time I could find comfort and forgetfulness in his arms.

Finally I had called on all the addresses which were given to me, and we decided I would return to Frankfurt and wait there.

Perhaps the Reichs Medical Chamber would do something after all?

Karl said thoughtfully: "I still have one iron in the fire, but I will only use it when all other efforts have failed. It would be in last resort . . ." After a long pause he added: "You must get a message to your mother. I learned that the Gestapo have a form to be signed by the prisoners, according to which the prisoner is willing to let himself be transported to a retraining camp. What kind of camp that is I don't have to explain to you. Your mother must on no account sign; listen: on no account! Once she signs, we can save ourselves all further trouble."

May 8, 1943

I am back again at my Hotel 'Westend,' although in a different room.

At home I did not have the time to write my diary. I will catch up now, even at the risk that everything is confused — exactly like my life, which appears to me like an endless journey; back and forth; Frankfurt - Berlin; Berlin - Frankfurt; hope - despair; new optimism - deepest depression. Conversations, appointments, new faces, briefs, office hours. Father's grim helplessness, Katherina's emotional tearful outbursts. I stand in the midst of this whirlpool, outwardly so unmoved, that Katherina once shouted hysterically at me: "Don't you have any feelings at all? It breaks my heart; and you —?"

"I what?" I asked with icy irony. "It breaks your heart? And what else do you do? You scream and behave hysterically."

She apologized with a new outburst of tears.

There were the nights when bombs fell somewhere in the city. After the 'all-clear' signal we rushed as if driven by the Furies to the prison. We looked at this unscathed building of horrors with a relief that made our knees feel weak.

I live in an unending nightmare. From the available dates I determined that prisoners are deported exactly three months after their arrest. Mother's date would be June 22nd. On June 22nd, my mother will be loaded on a freight car, to die within the next weeks. Between June 22nd and July 14th my mother will be murdered. In one of her laundry bag letters she informed us that she was called out of her cell to sign the form. She is apparently the only one who refused, to Baab's complete dismay. How much longer can she refuse before force will be used?

I learned to sleep standing up with my back resting against a side of the train. When I awoke I heard the rhythmical rattle of the wheels on the rails, calling to me: "Mother will be murdered - mother will be murdered . . ."

Confused, I looked around for an escape. All I saw were other miserable figures, sleeping while standing in the train corridor or squatting on their suitcases. In the pale blue light of the little bulbs, which barely lit the darkened train, they all looked already dead. Exhausted, overtired, hungry and desperate, we formed a silent community of misery.

Now back to the latest events in Frankfurt.

After my return home, one of my first questions of Katherina was: "When does the next laundry package go to prison?"

"On Tuesday; why?"

"I have to tell mother something."

"Oh Lili . . ." Katherina began to cry. "Mother complained on the last slip of paper that we did not put spread on the bread."

"What!?" I looked at her aghast. "What a miserable rabble! So the prison personnel even steal from helpless inmates."

Since there is a severe shortage of paper bags and packing material, it would hardly be noticed that the sides of the bag were held together with tape. I had however cut the bag open and had written on the lower inside half something which would not be discovered by looking into the bag from the top. I wrote that I had been in Berlin, that Karl is helping and that she should not lose her courage. "Whatever happens," I emphasized, "under no circumstances place your signature on anything." At the bottom of the bag I placed a pencil stub and more tape. Then we packed the bag and I drove to the prison.

Mother's first official letter had arrived during my absence. What could she write under the circumstances, realizing that every word she wrote was read by the Gestapo? Apart from the lies about her health, she asked for some laundry and her Bible.

"We need the approval of the Gestapo to send her Bible to prison," father said.

"All right," I replied. "I will go."

The thought of having to face Gestapo official Baab again gave me stomach cramps.

The next morning I entered the office of this hated individual, but was directed through a door on the right, leading to a second room.

269

I could not believe my eyes: "Mr. Gabbusch!"

"Heil Hitler!" he said.

"Mr. Gabbusch —!"

"Well now - sit down, nenenene."

My reaction touched him and he behaved like a human being. With a side glance at the open door, he did not protest when I stood up cautiously and quietly closed the door.

"Miss Schroeder," he contemplated, "what kind of trouble are you always getting yourself into?"

My attempt to discuss mother's case met with silence.

"Why did you come today?" he wanted to know.

"My mother asked for her Bible, for which we need your permission."

"Bible?" he asked in disbelief. "Well, if it makes her happy, she may have it."

"Mr. Gabbusch—" I looked at his cyanotic face, his trembling hands, the typical symptoms of an alcoholic, "what is the matter?" With all the warmth and concern I could muster, I continued: "Don't you feel well? You are so nervous."

"I was in Poland. It was terrible — simply dreadful — that would make a person nervous, wouldn't it, nenene? But it will be better here. Perhaps I could give your father a visitor's permit for two persons, okay?"

I went home with this happy news and the visitor's permit. A discussion followed as to whether Katherina or I would accompany father. I saw tears well up in her eyes and feared a hysterical outburst.

"You go," I decided firmly. "The next time it will be my turn."

She was pleased and accepted my offer, while I wondered whether there would be a next time?

After the visit I sat in Katherina's room. "How is she?"

"She lost weight and her hair is completely gray; it looks as if powdered; she has prison pallor. Oh, it is . . ."

I interrupted her: "Now look here! I let you go and I expect a sensible report. How is her morale? Do you believe your visit helped her spiritually?"

"Oh yes." Katherina looked at the ceiling of her room transfixed, and said with emotion, "She was like a drowning person, whom one hands a glass of water."

I beat a hasty retreat from her room.

One of father's patients, a Mr. Bartel, had a Jewish wife who was arrested many weeks before mother. She had been sent to Birkenau, which we learned is the name of the railroad station for Auschwitz.

One afternoon when I was on duty in the office, Mr. Bartel came in. Instead of a greeting, he pulled a postcard from his breast pocket. "I received this today."

The printed form informed him that his wife Sara died of angina on a particular date. He was to advise them whether he wanted the urn with her ashes.

"How horrible, Mr. Bartel!" I was honestly shocked. The words of condolence stuck in my throat. When Mr. Bartel made a move towards the waiting-room, I implored him, "Please Mr. Bartel, don't show that to my father! I beg you!"

Tears ran from under his glasses over his emaciated cheeks. He turned around and left without a word.

Our car began to break down: it would not start and had all kinds of problems. I went to our mechanic.

Mr. Landmann is a careful workman of the old school. His Jewish wife is in prison with mother. He worked on the machine unsuccessfully. As he bent over the open hood, his glasses slipped down over his nose, and the old man's sad eyes peered at me. "So, Mrs. Schroeder is now with my wife in prison. What a mess! Now, Miss Schroeder, I will tell you something. A person can't even trust his own behind anymore — it slips away."

After a detailed examination of our car, he gave me the address of a repair shop in the Grossen Friedberger Landstrasse, which specializes in generators.

I drove through the archway of a tall building: the repair shop is in the courtyard surrounded by small houses at the back of the premises.

While I stood waiting in the yard, a woman came through the archway and went to one of these little houses in the back. I remembered her. Her self-confidence and friendly face impressed me when I saw her at the prison.

I asked one of the mechanics: "Do people live in private residences here?"

"Yes, certainly."

271

"Really?" And I inquired further, feigning astonishment, "What kind of people? For example, the woman who just went in?"

"That is Mrs. Marten. She is the superintendent in the women's prison."

Before I drove off I directed Katherina to the backyard after I gave an exact description of Mrs. Marten.

Katherina flared up, "Why don't you go?"

"Because she would recognize me. We observed each other closely in prison. However, she didn't see me in the courtyard and she doesn't know you at all."

Katherina told me what happened. She appeared suddenly out of the afternoon shadows of the archway and stood next to the woman who was returning home. "Mrs. Marten?"

She turned to Katherina.

"Mrs. Marten, we would like to ask your help. My mother, Mrs. Schroeder, is in your prison."

The supervisor turned white. "How do you know where I live?"

"I just know it," Katherina replied. "Please don't let my mother starve! The spread on the bread . . ."

"I have never seen or spoken to you," uttered the superintendent in horror. "Do you understand?" During these last words she unlocked her door with trembling fingers.

"Yes. I understand," Katherina said, "but please help us!"

Then she stood in front of the closed door.

When I told Bernd about this meeting, he was aghast. "Good God!" he exclaimed. "Are you all crazy? Don't you know the rules?"

"What rules?"

"Even in normal times, relatives of prisoners were not allowed, under any circumstances, to contact prison personnel; and their addresses were kept secret. These regulations are naturally intensified under the Third Reich. The superintendent is practically obligated to go to her superiors and report the incident, which can have very negative consequences for her as well as for you."

"Why?"

"Why? My God, you are naive! She will have to face endless interrogations about how you knew her address. You'll get into difficulties and your mother . . ."

272

"My mother will either starve or be murdered. Moreover, Mrs. Marten won't go to her superiors."

"Why are you so sure of this?"

"Because she will get herself into difficulties and perhaps ruin her career. She will probably wait several days to see if the families of other prisoners come to her home, or if we are the only ones who know where she lives. This woman, who until recently has dealt only with criminals, realizes that now her prisoners' only crime is to be Jewish."

He shook his head, "Nevertheless . . ."

"I know. You're not in my shoes. Your mother is at home and can at least eat her allotted rations. What else could I do? One must risk something in such a desperate situation."

On my last trip to Berlin I took the morning train. The train was not too full in Frankfurt. I found a seat in a compartment with a married couple and their four lively children; the youngest was still almost an infant. I looked at the family with extreme distrust and leaned back in my seat. People who produce so many children in these times can only be Nazis.

The couple probably felt my negative attitude and tried to keep their children from running back and forth between the window and the compartment door, brushing against me. Once I stretched out my hand to save one of the children from falling. The parents made several remarks, hesitantly and with extreme caution, which I answered curtly. I examined them more closely. The freckled redhaired man had a round face and close-cropped hair. He was dressed in an ordinary woolen jacket and could have been a laborer. His somewhat tired looking wife wore a simple dress and completed the picture of a petty-bourgeois family.

He must have observed me staring at the lapel of his jacket, which hung on the wall behind him. An understanding grin covered his face. "We're not members," he added reassuringly. This loosened our tongues.

They are communists and own a restaurant in a working-class district of Berlin.

"It isn't so simple," the man explained, "but if you are not conspicuous, you can manage to get along. Almost all of my customers are Communists or Socialists, and we know the Nazis who come in. They can't trap us." He was silent for a while and then slapped his hand against his thigh. "Yes, the Social Democrats now are together with us and view us as fellow-sufferers. But back in 1933, when it counted, they wouldn't have anything to do with us. Instead of an alliance with us to prevent Hitler's rise to power, they had to preserve their independence. So, like they voted in 1914 with the Emperor for war, they voted in 1933 with Hitler for the Enabling Act. They rubbed their hands and waited for rewards." He laughed. "The reward was that they were promptly fired from all their pretty positions and there were no Social Democrats anymore — finished, through, wiped out. This is no loss for the people. After the war of 1914-18, there was hunger and unemployment. And what will follow after this war? Where will the leading Social Democrats be? I'll tell you. They will do everything to please the government in power, to keep their well-paid jobs—these *schrebergarten* capitalists. Their attitude is: To hell with the people! In the end, every party boss considers himself first. Isn't that so?"

After a while I asked, "How is morale in your district?"

"Excellent!" he laughed. "We know the war is lost. There will surely be some bad times until it is over: everyone hopes to keep his home; but you know, Miss, we are waiting for the Russians."

"For the Russians?" I looked at him in astonishment.

"The Russians will come to us. Perhaps I won't own my restaurant then, but will only be employed as an innkeeper. However, what am I really now? What are we all? Slaves to a pack of madmen, who only think of exterminating or exploiting other peoples."

His wife interjected, "None of the big Nazis has a son at the front. Either they have no children at all, or they are still too young."

The man said, "Right, but we make the sacrifices. There were convinced National Socialists in our neighborhood. They were men who suddenly found a job again after years of starvation; but their enthusiasm has fizzled. Whole groups of houses have been smashed by bombs; husbands and sons are crippled at the front; and with the money they earn, they can't even buy anything substantial to eat. In the end, they are worse off than before Hitler came to power. They still had hope then, but now . . ."

They unwrapped some food and offered me a pickled cutlet. "Take it, Miss. It doesn't mean less for us. There is always enough since there are things even the Nazis can't control." We ate in silence.

274

I looked at the life of these simple people from a new perspective: a life where one avoided the regime of terror, helped one another, and received each new decree with mockery and scorn. It was considered a duty to sabotage the state as much as one could, since every small failure hastened the end.

May 14, 1943

It was after midnight and I shared the hotel lobby with the other guests during the air-raid alarm. We placed our suitcases ready to be grabbed, next to our chairs and waited for the signal which would decide whether we could return to bed or run to the nearest bunker.

In the silence, maintained by the tired hotel guests, my thoughts had free play. I remembered a Swedish journalist saying: "the fortress of Europe has no roof."

Karl, whom I had to myself for a whole week—Diana had to take a trainload of children to Silesia—introduced me as a guest at the International Press Club. This was a world whose existence I had long forgotten. Conversation and laughter sounded in the large, high ceilinged, brightly lit rooms. We sat at a table elegantly set with a white tablecloth and starched cloth napkins. The menu contained dishes which the average citizen no longer ate. After the meal, which was served with wine, there was coffee and liqueurs or cognac.

With a happy smile I tried to converse with the people who sat with us after dinner, as if I had no problems in the world. I had come to Berlin for pleasure, to visit relatives. In reality, I carefully listened to the scraps of conversation which buzzed around me.

I heard the sounds of various German dialects as well as Swedish, Swiss, Italian, and Japanese accents; the accents of the press representatives of the countries with whom Germany was not at war.

Suddenly I felt strange and lost among these people: the privileged few who are allowed to know what is going on in the world. All at once I felt the iron clamp which the Nazis had placed on our minds and which paralyzed our ability to think. I learned, however, that not only the German people are stupefied and lied to. According to some members of the foreign press, the American citizen is not treated much better. Pearl Harbor was repeatedly mentioned in connection with names like Hearst, Pulitzer and Mexico. The American people believe the lies of their government, exactly like the Germans, and are forced into a similar restive mood.

That evening opened my eyes and I began to understand what politics really are. There is no German, French, American or other national politics. There are merely different categories of men who obtain the confidence of the masses by false pretenses; then once in power, they pursue their own selfish ends. The objectives may be different — one person wants to go down in history, others only want to fill their pockets — but whatever it is, it is achieved at the expense of the people since they prefer illusion to the truth. The business of a politician is anchored in this self-deception.

These correspondents can see behind the scenes. The foreigners exchange knowledge with German colleagues they trust; in return, the Germans tell them secrets from the propaganda ministry. They learn from each other things the government so diligently seeks to suppress.

When I returned to the hotel with Karl, he asked: "You are so silent. Didn't you enjoy yourself tonight?"

"Of course, Karl. Only suddenly I realized how isolated we are in the provinces. It was as if I had come from a different planet."

"You share that with almost all the other citizens of this noble nation. The only difference is that the others are not conscious of it, while you had a chance to look through a crack in the curtain. But it won't be much longer until the curtain is raised. Then everyone can see — if they want to."

"Why wouldn't they want to?"

"Because the picture which will be shown them is not very pretty."

The sirens sounded an 'all clear' and brought me back to the present. Everyone grabbed his luggage with relief and returned to his room.

May 18, 1943

If nothing exceptional happens, I will return home tomorrow night — back to an orderly bourgeois life, as long as the war does not disturb it.

Everything I do seems like a dream. The only realities are my indescribable fear about mother and the love which binds Karl and me. I still pursue, daily, every tiny trail which could lead to success.

On one of my excursions I met Christian, Uncle Rudolf's SS son, on Prinz Albrecht Strasse next to the Gestapo. We met on the broad empty sidewalk. He greeted me with delight, "Hello, Lili dear! What are you doing here?"

"I'm here because of mother." I stopped short.

He looked at me in astonishment.

"She is in prison." I explained.

A mask fell over his face. "It serves her right! She probably deserved it!"

I stared at him speechlessly, then I turned and left. My own cousin!

I go by bus, local railway, subway, and trolley to the most remote areas to speak with either high clergymen, retired ministerial counselors, radio people, and others. I travel with Berlin citizens who look increasingly thinner, more haggard and anemic, and listen to their biting remarks. If I have to wait at a bus stop, it is not long before a complete stranger speaks to me and tells me all his worries.

Electricity is curtailed; and the reduction in meat rations will be balanced by more miserable bread.

When the new reduction of house coal was announced — only seventy-five percent of last year's quantity would be distributed — I overheard two men talking on the elevated railroad, "Wasn't it already damned cold last year?"

His companion replied, "You lack the proper attitude. Just think of the straightening of the front and how we successfully disengaged from the enemy. Then you will feel much warmer."

Both men laughed.

The Americans, who are occasionally mentioned in military dispatches, are now unloading 'blockbusters' over Germany and the population is ordered to protect the outside of their air-raid shelters with sandbags. The Berliners however make bitter jokes about their city's bombed-out areas: "Didn't our Führer state 'Give me four years' time and you will not recognize your cities any more'?" And they remove the debris and try to keep the streets open for traffic.

Most evenings I go with Karl to the International Press Club. I am well-groomed, well-dressed and wear nail polish. I smoke the

277

cigarettes offered me and accept the empty compliments with amusement. I am politically interested but not affected.

Karl told me: "There is only one person we can not deceive about your ancestry." Stadler, a German journalist with an English wife, had remarked to Karl: "A charming woman, Mr. X. Nevertheless, I admire your courage."

Occasionally I join Karl at noon in the Badische Weinstube, where his regular circle of friends meets in the back room. What holds this colorful group together is their common hatred of Nazi oppression.

Gathered together were a press photographer, Donner; businessman Schimmel; a physician, Dr. Markgraf; Captain Göller, whose stomach seems about to burst the buttons of his uniform and his beautiful young wife, who is a writer. A number of other men came and went sporadically.

Schimmel began, "Yesterday I had a visit from a business friend who has an enterprise in Poland. . ."

Someone laughed, "You have fine friends!"

"All jokes apart, the man told me something about officers' brothels in Poland, which I found unbelievable. Do you know anything about it?"

"Yes," Karl replied. "When I was in Warsaw to get information about the care of troops, I asked the responsible authorities for permission to visit a whorehouse, not accessible to civilians. Permission was granted. My choice was an intelligent, cultured Polish woman. When we were alone in a small elegant room with a large bed, she explained that she was a doctor and had been rounded up with other Polish academicians and aristocrats by the Nazis for their officers' brothel. Does that answer your question?"

"I didn't want to believe it," replied Schimmel aghast.

"Why not?," said an ironic voice from the door. It was Mr. Enten, a lawyer I had known in Frankfurt and who was now hiding out in Berlin. "The best is just good enough for the German master race."

May 26, 1943

Upon my return home I was overcome by a feeling of alienation. All warmth is missing. Father and Katherina, never very close to each other, seem to lead separate lives, incapable of speaking to each other; each sunk in his personal concern for mother.

278

The household was relatively disorganized. Father and Katherina decided not to look around for a new housekeeper. Katherina, unfamiliar with running a household, tried her best to keep the apartment clean—though unable to buy the necessary utensils. She tried to put edible food on the table despite shortages and sometimes questionable supplies. Everything either of them could save from their own portions or beg was placed in mother's laundry bag. Mother wrote with great delight that the spread now remained on her bread.

Occasionally Etta comes to help. Sister Ruth, who took over my office hours, lends a hand as far as time allows.

In the evening, Katherina frequently has her pious girl friends for a visit; father calls them "old petticoats." He often goes up to the Schindlers, with whom he plays skat and who touchingly care for him.

June 1, 1943

I am alone again. After spending every free minute together, I accompanied Karl to the Berlin night train an hour ago.

He was indescribably happy to be in his beloved Frankfurt again. "I must look at everything carefully, while it still stands," he explained with a depressed smile.

The first evening, we went to the Schwarze Stern, where unrationed mussel salad is served.

A muted sadness, a vague farewell mood overlay Karl's joy.

"What depresses you?" I asked.

He answered with a deep sigh. "Everything. The whole situation is so hopeless... The destruction, hunger, murder — and how long can I continue to evade military service?"

"The army?"

"Yes, my child. I am still in the age group that should wear the Führer's uniform with pride; and unfortunately I am not in a professionally "exempt" occupation."

"How have you avoided the draft until now?"

"By changing my residence. I moved from Berlin to Breslau. It took time until my papers were sent from Military Command Berlin to Breslau. Before they could reach me, I moved back to Berlin. Then I moved from East to West Berlin. Officially, I can't stop long anyplace."

He turned his head towards the window. His glance wandered

over Justicia, who stood with the scales in her hand in the fountain and over the dark silhouette of the Römer. His lower lip pushed forward; he thought a moment and then observed ironically: "Now we are seated opposite this historical building, where once emperors were crowned, who were not all bad; some of them were even outstanding personalities. But this corporal has taken over everything, to destroy us."

"How many wars must we — I mean you and I — still endure?"

"I am afraid that this is not our last one," Karl said thoughtfully. "With ever-increasing technology, wars will follow each other in ever-shorter intervals. The armament industry can not let their most modern instruments of murder be outstripped by newer ones, before they are used. The generals are only too ready to give the industry a helping hand." He uttered a short painful laugh. "Later on new generations will read of the enthusiasm and patriotism, with which heroic sacrifices were made in wars initiated by those in power. Looked at closely, this fairy tale of heroic sacrifices is nothing more than historical exploitation of cadavers, produced by school teachers."

My fingers walked through the small forest of hair on Karl's chest until he caught my hand and kissed each fingertip.

We lay on the bed in his room in the Frankfurter Hof.

I said thoughtfully, "Sometimes I think I am absolutely perverse."

"Perverse?" He lifted himself on his elbows and turned towards me. Uncomprehendingly, he pulled my head to his shoulder. "What's the matter?"

"I am so indescribably happy. Then I think about my mother in prison."

His hand awkwardly stroked my face. "My heart, to love deeply is never perverse. If we would not dare to love because of the atrocities committed on this earth, what a desolate place this world would be!"

My lips pressed against his body and felt his strong regular heartbeat. "But you understand what I mean?"

"Yes, I understand, my dearest. You feel obliged to have a guilty conscience because you are happy. Would it change anything in your mother's situation if you were unhappy? No. But perhaps our love will give you more strength?"

280

"Yes, as long as we are together."

He leaned over me and said firmly, "This time we will remain together. I will not let you go again."

"And Diana?"

His face assumed a somewhat tortured expression. "Diana — I know I must end that now. For some time she has felt that something isn't quite right and I must tell her. I simply cannot lose you again."

We agreed before his departure that I would go to Gabbusch once more. If I did not get any encouraging information, I should come to Berlin at the end of the week, where Karl would play his last card.

June 8, 1943

I arrived in Berlin on Friday evening. Karl was waiting at the station.

"From your call, I gathered that Gabbusch wasn't very helpful," he said.

I sank exhausted on the sofa in my hotel room. "Karl — it was a catastrophe, caused by my father. Gabbusch, who somehow is still fond of his former friends at the press, received me relatively politely but with extreme reserve. He waited to see what I wanted. I asked if he could give me any hint as to mother's release? Instead of an answer, he turned his head towards the window and drummed his fingers on his chin. Then he took a deep breath, opened a desk drawer and asked: 'Tell me, Miss Schroeder, what is the matter with your father?' He placed a letter from my father on the desk. 'Has he gone mad? He writes your mother that he hopes to visit her again. Lili will achieve this through her connections.' Gabbusch began to shout, 'The idiot! What was he thinking of?'" I shrugged my shoulders.

Karl paced the room. "It is really unbelievable!"

"Karl," I was close to tears, "that the swine called my father an idiot was like a slap in my face. Nobody has ever dared speak that way about my father. But at the bottom of my heart, I have to agree with him. I must admit I am at the end of my strength and wisdom."

"Do you have any friends well out of harm's way?"

"Yes, in Carinthia."

"Then send your father to Carinthia. The farther away he is,

281

the better for your mother." He shook his head. "Unbelievable, it is incredible!"

He stopped pacing the room, looked at me attentively, and took my face in his hands. "You don't look well, my little one. Are you only upset or don't you feel well?"

My glance left his eyes and strayed to the floor.

"Look at me. What is it?"

"I - we — we are going to have a child."

He beamed for a moment and then said under his breath, "Just now —." His face expressed a whole range of emotions which went through his heart and mind — joy, hope, worry, happiness. "A few days ago I went to the National Association of the German Press to see one of the big bosses who is favorably disposed to me. I said I was inquiring for a colleague who loves a girl with close Jewish relatives. He told me there is not a chance for approval of such a marriage; and if the colleague should marry her, he would lose his membership. The man looked at me sharply. 'I warn you, Mr. X.'" He paced the room. "What will become of us?" He stopped in front of me: "Do you have something to smoke?"

I rummaged in my handbag and found several bad cigarettes; the smell made me mildly nauseous. Karl took one and sat down. "First, we must get your mother out of prison; and then we will straighten out our personal affairs, okay?"

I am waiting in my hotel room once again. I seem to wait and wait. From time to time, Karl telephones, "I haven't reached him yet. Have patience! I'll get him."

I do not know who "he" is; whom Karl is trying to reach and if this person is ready to do what Karl hopes he will. I must be prepared if the great unknown wants to see me. I only leave the hotel for lunch. Otherwise I am trapped in my room, which I have gradually begun to hate. It has become a symbol of my despair and helplessness.

June 10, 1943

The waiting continues. I look at the calendar with horror. Only twelve days are left until mother's three months of imprisonment are up. In the past, all prisoners have been transported the day after a three-month period. She must have realized this by now.

282

Does she still believe in my promise to rescue her?

My nerves are strained to the breaking point. I walk around the hotel room, as I formerly paced my jail cell, waiting until the telephone finally rings. I lift the receiver with eager hands and hear Karl's depressed voice, "Nothing yet. I still haven't reached him."

I leaf through the mass of newspapers which Karl left me to pass the time. The only things of interest were the speeches Speer and Goebbels gave three days ago in the Berlin Sportpalast. They boasted about everything we have: weapons production, improved weapons, and German inventiveness. Retaliation is spoken of more and more frequently. Rumors circulate among the people about a new weapon, rumors nourished by such talk.

This evening with Karl, I asked, "Is there really a new weapon?"

"They claim there is. As far as we can learn, there is feverish work on something to do with rockets at Penemünde; but with the raw material shortage and time pressures, I doubt they will produce it. How did you hear of it?"

"Katherina sent me to a Nazi who could perhaps be helpful in mother's case."

"What type of Nazi?"

"A colonel in the SA."

"What does your sister have to do with such people?"

"He is a very kind, believing, practicing Catholic, who lives with his elderly mother, whom he cares for so lovingly that he has to be absolutely reliable according to my sister."

Karl nodded and asked: "A double agent?"

"No; just convinced and stupid."

"You went to see him?"

"Yes. Of course he could not do anything for mother but he talked about the war, the evil enemy and retaliation. He spoke of the new wonder-weapon and I quote: 'When in New York the sky-scrapers totter and the brains of Americans spill out of their heads —' "

Karl started to laugh: "What did you say to this?"

I made admiring, astonished eyes: "Fantastic," I said breathlessly. "Really?!"

"Yes," he replied, "that will be something we will live to see."

"They are working on something" Karl repeated, "but not every SA-chieftain would be informed about it. These lovely dreams keep up the morale of the little Nazi who is prepared to accept still more sacrifice if he is assured that the hour of retaliation is near."

"Hmm" I muttered, "and he, who is a true Christian is delighted with the idea that other people's brains are spilling out of their heads."

Karl nodded thoughtfully: "I don't know why Christians in general and Catholics in particular always claim hell is someplace beneath the earth. They have created it here in this world with their kind of mentality and prayers." He added ironically: "During air-raid alarms not even purgatory is missing."

June 19, 1973

On Tuesday, exactly one week before mother's deadline, Karl reached the mysterious person. He did not call me but rushed into my hotel room. "I finally spoke to him."

"And?"

"He promised to do his utmost."

I hung on Karl's neck, laughing and sobbing, utterly beside myself.

"My dearest," he repeated only "My dearest."

I finally wiped the tears from my face and asked with a voice still choked with emotion: "Now tell me who he is and how you accomplished it?"

"He is Heydrich's brother. You surely know Reinhard Heydrich, the feared head of the Security Service and a general in the police force, who was murdered in Prague. Our agency was the first to learn this news and I called his sister-in-law to inform her of the tragedy. Since then Willi Heydrich feels somehow indebted to me. We occasionally meet professionally; he works for the *Berliner Illustrierte*. But I have never asked him for a favor.

"When I approached him and mentioned 'Jewish,' he repulsed me immediately. He didn't want to have anything to do with it. I explained that it is not a matter of any vagabond Jew; but your grandfather, a cavalry captain, married the daughter of an Aryan general." Karl began to laugh. "You have absolutely no idea what a family your mother comes from! Anyway, I did convince him that this was an unusual case and he promised to intervene. Although he is not very bright, the name Heydrich will certainly open doors to him."

Subdued and completely exhausted after the incredible tension, I asked, "What now?"

"Change your clothes. We'll go to the club. I have a surprise for you there. We'll have dinner to celebrate. Then you must go home tomorrow — send your father away so that at that last moment he doesn't pursue some wild notion, and wait for your mother."

At the International Press Club, Karl led me past our usual table into another room to a round table in a corner. As we studied the menu, a large figure in gray uniform approached. A familiar voice said, "Good evening, ladies and gentlemen."

I looked up and saw Gerhard Straube. Our fat friend from the *General Anzeiger* was home on leave from Denmark. One familiar face followed another, all old colleagues; some were in uniform on leave, others living here in exile. For the first time in months, I was thoroughly delighted and enjoyed this evening with our friends.

Karl took me to the train. He will come to Frankfurt in July. Meanwhile, we can only hope that Heydrich keeps his promise.

Karl said, "Enten will be in Frankfurt from the 19th to the 22nd. Whatever you want to communicate about your mother, tell him. He is more reliable than the post office, and I have already instructed him to contact you."

We parted with heavy hearts.

When I arrived home, I made Katherina my ally. Together, with a great deal of persuasion, we finally convinced father that it would be better for him to go to Carinthia for a while.

As Katherina and I waved after the departing train, she turned to me, "Now tell me why you wanted to get rid of father?"

"Käthe, if it works out, mother will return home next week. I didn't want to take any chance of father destroying everything with more of his folly. Until now, he has not really comprehended what is going on. If. . ." I was silent.

Katherina's eyes turned towards me and her voice became shrill, "If. . . Say it!"

"If she does not return? What then? Then father will be better off with his friends. I really don't know what he would do here."

285

June 22, 1943

Enten called daily and always received the same stereotype answer. "We still don't know anything." We finally agreed that I would meet him at the train before he returns to Berlin.

It was early afternoon, a few hours before my rendezvous with Enten; I walked down Lehrbachstrasse to do some shopping.

A ghost approached me. I ran up to mother breathlessly. She dragged herself towards me with difficulty, deathly pale in her black woolen dress.

"Mutti," I called out, "Oh, Mutti."

She stared at me with big weary eyes — entirely expressionless. Her face reflected no joy, no relief — nothing.

I took her little suitcase, supported her under the arm and led her slowly home.

"We didn't know that they would release you today," I explained apologetically. "Did you walk all the way from the jail?"

"No, I come from the Gestapo. That dog wanted to kill me!" She grew paler and more agitated, while her eyes darkened. "He wanted to kill me!"

"Baab?"

"Yes! That monster - that murderer!"

"My dearest," I said soothingly, "how you have suffered! But now you are with us again."

We finally reached home. I pressed the bell several times, while I pushed the heavy staircase door open. We just reached the last step, when Katherina opened the apartment door.

"Mother dear! Dearest mother!" Tears streamed down her face.

Mother's glance strayed searchingly across the foyer and down the open hallway. "Father is in Carinthia. We will call him."

We led mother into the music room. She sat on a chair, her dirty hands folded in her lap. Her stockings hung crookedly; they slipped in circles around her thin legs. The skirt of her formerly elegant dress was stained and worn through just above the knees. The masklike rigidity remained on her face, while she sightlessly brooded, reliving some endured horror again.

Katherina rushed into the kitchen to prepare tea and bread. We didn't speak. When Katherina placed the tea in front of mother, I left the room to call Enten.

When I returned to the music room, I found the scene unchanged.

We finally persuaded mother to drink some tea.

"You were with Baab at the Gestapo?" Mother's dull eyes turned to me. "What did he want?" I inquired pitilessly.

"My signature," she replied with hatred. "He wanted to compel me to sign a form saying that I would go to the concentration camp of my own free will."

"And you refused?"

The little bit of color which the tea brought to her cheeks, disappeared again. "'No, I won't sign that,' I said firmly. He began to curse me. I still refused to sign. As he was about to hit me, I ran out of his office down the stairs, just as Gabbusch came up. I cried out, 'Mr. Gabbusch! Mr. Gabbusch, this man wants to kill me! Help me!'" She fell silent, her face reflecting a deathly fear.

"What did Gabbusch do?"

"He said, 'Now, now, Mrs. Schroeder, calm down. He won't do anything to you,' and he brought me back to Baab's office. However, Gabbusch stayed with me."

I pressed for more information. "And Baab didn't dare try anything in the presence of his superior?" She nodded. "Baab had to release you."

She exhaled a deep sigh. "He probably was to have released me anyway; but, if I had signed . . ."

Suddenly she broke down and a flood of tears followed. Mother's unnatural rigidity dissolved.

July 7, 1943

Slowly our household returns to normal. Father, overjoyed and relieved, hurried home, and Katherina left for Munich again.

Every new day since mother's release helps the terrors fade gradually; and mother slowly returns to her old self. She spoke of her fellow sufferers with deep emotion; many of them have since been murdered. She describes the small iron cages where they were imprisoned, how two people had to sleep on one mattress because of overcrowding. She told us about hunger, fear, and the very young girls—really just children—who were imprisoned with them. Mother's strength was her Bible and her faith. She prayed with the other women and tried to give them comfort and cheer.

I returned to my room shaking my head. Had Jesus not said

to a sick girl, "Arise my daughter, thy faith has made thee whole"? That was what mother clung to without realizing that her belief would not have saved her without Karl's and Heydrich's help. Our good Father in heaven looks on with a gracious smile, while Jew after Jew is bestially hastened to his grave. He would also not have listened to the prayers of Lili Sara Schroeder.

Young Mrs. Germann, nee Geier, whom mother taught to pray, enters my thoughts. Shortly after mother's release, I met the Aryan Mr. Germann on the street. He asked me how we had rescued mother, and I explained that I spent more time in Berlin than in Frankfurt and left no stone unturned.

Mr. Germann sighed, "Yes, yes, perhaps I should also try something."

Although his wife learned to pray from mother, she was gassed in Auschwitz with the others.

September 7, 1943

During his visit in July Karl and I decided that if nothing better suggested itself, I would move to his place when my condition could no longer be concealed. Somehow, we would both survive the Thousand Year Reich. When we were not together, we maintained contact through letters and telephone calls.

He called me in late August. Instead of a greeting, he said tonelessly, "I have been drafted."

After a moment of dazed silence, I declared, "I'm coming."

As so many times in previous months, I threw some things into my suitcase and took the night train to Berlin.

Borger, who still works in the Hotel Westend, had been told about mother's release. He was surprised to see me. "What has happened?"

"X has been drafted."

"That's the last straw!"

"What happened to your father?"

"Still in prison," was the laconic reply.

Karl was more depressed than I had ever seen him. We looked at each other helplessly: what now?

I could not remain in Berlin alone; but in a city like Frankfurt I would have the Gestapo immediately at my heels. If I revealed the name of the child's father, Karl and I would be tried for "racial disgrace." If I kept his name secret, they would presume the father to be Jewish, and I would land in a concentration camp.

"I must leave the final decision up to you," Karl said depressed and stared at a corner of the room. "Perhaps Ella will have an idea," he added hopefully.

Ella, Karl's stepmother, was to arrive the next day.

Ella is a warm-hearted woman, and we understood each other perfectly. Her complete rejection of Diana eased my situation.

"Has Karl really made up his mind?" I asked her, still uncertain.

"He told me that he no longer has any doubts; that it can only be Lili." She smiled at me encouragingly. "It will work out, Lili-child."

These were hectic days. We had endless discussions with Ella; and Karl and I spent hours together with despair and bliss intermingled.

After a farewell dinner at the Adlon, Ella returned home. Soon after Karl and I spent our last hours together before he had to leave. I remained behind in the loneliness of night with the burden of making a decision.

I lay wide-awake in bed with endless agonizing thoughts. I knew Karl's heart was set on my having our child. I recalled an early day in June. Mother was home again; and as I went to the post office, I walked past Holzhausen Park and the multicolored gardens. The sun shone from a perfectly clear sky; everything was green and bloomed exuberantly, since nature knows nothing of war. For a brief space of time, I also forgot the war, Nazis, and persecution. I could sing and rejoice because I carried the child of the man I loved. I was happy — and foolish.

I thought how gladly we would have this child. Then I saw Pötz before me, explaining that parents are egotists who fulfill their own wishes without asking whether the child would want to come into this world. What could we offer our child? Karl is not even divorced. The office of his lawyer in Berlin suffered a direct hit, killing the attorney and destroying all his records which were buried under a mountain of rubble. I could not even give my child the essential food. We would be on the run from the Nazis and the bombs, while Karl fought someplace in the East.

That night I made my decision and fell asleep exhausted.

The next morning, I went to see Dr. Markgraf, a regular at Karl's lunch table. He explained that he could not help me. Apart from the fact that he is an internist, he would not do anything like that. He was sorry, but he was also unable to suggest any colleagues who might.

This time I was running hither and yon for myself. I turned, directly and indirectly, to people I knew but met a regretful shrug of the shoulders everywhere. Either they knew nobody or the doctor who would have helped was at the front.

As a last resort, I turned to Borger. "Mr. Borger, I need a doctor. Do you know somebody?"

In answer, he whistled through his teeth. Then he shook his head. "No, I don't know anyone, but I'll ask my sister and let you know tomorrow morning."

The next day he told me the doctor who had helped his sister was at the front. "But tonight is my night off. If it is all right with you, we will visit a friend of mine."

We entered a large elegant apartment with lots of books. Borger introduced me to his friend Wolfgang Haarich. His name was familiar, since his father had visited my grandparents' house in Königsberg. His father died many years ago, and his mother was out of town for the moment.

The two young men cooked a risotto. After this ritual, we sat around the table; all political aspects of my problem were discussed in detail.

Wolfgang Haarich suddenly said, "I don't know of a doctor, but I would like to make another suggestion. We could enter into a marriage of convenience. I'll marry you and recognize the child as mine."

At my incredulous expression, he explained, "It would only be for appearances. We could get a divorce immediately after the war."

Both of them urged me to accept the offer. I looked at the eager face of this young man who was willing to make such a sacrifice to help me out.

Of course, that would be the solution. I would take advantage of him, this inexperienced youth, a good six years my junior, who offered me his helping hand. Through my ancestry I would tarnish his immaculate family tree. He would encounter difficulties, the extent of which he could not imagine.

After a prolonged silence, I finally spoke. "Thank you, you don't realize how much your offer means to me, but I can not accept it."

"Why? It is meant seriously. We can get a divorce immediately after the war!"

I declined. Both young men could not understand — it would be, just as they said, only a fictitious marriage.

This afternoon, as I forlornly sat in my hotel room, mother called. "When are you coming home?"

"I don't know yet."

"Hasn't Karl already left?"

"Yes."

"Why don't you come home then?"

"I can't."

"Lili! Are you . . .?"

"Yes."

"Good God, child! Come home at once."

I will leave tomorrow morning.

September 10, 1932

I set out for Frankfurt with mixed feelings. I was happy to be able to return to my parents and my work — but I dreaded the reunion with father.

Mother received me tearfully. She had that particular expression that always gets on my nerves: a mixture of indignation and heroism, a hidden reproach for my misdeeds paired with a promise to protect her daughter as a lioness would her cubs.

She opened the hall door and I saw the familiar picture: the large round table cleared after dinner, father playing solitaire. Only the bottle of wine and the glasses were missing. The lamp, which hung exactly over the center of the table, shone not only on the polished tabletop but on father's bald pate.

Father looked up and his glance took me in. I became conscious that my skirt just reached my knees in front, while the back still covered half of my calf.

Instead of a greeting, I heard the reproachful words; "This is indeed a very sad reunion, my daughter."

291

"Yes. I think so, too!" He ignored my answer, which probably sounded like a challenge.

He rebuked me for being unstable and said that a "decent girl" simply did not have that kind of relations with a man. He was shocked and bitterly disappointed. He forgot that he no longer had his little girl before him, but a full-grown woman.

I could not stand quietly in front of him, so I walked back and forth.

When he had finished, I burst forth; "Did it ever occur to you that at my present age your wife already had two children in school? Have you ever thought what kind of life I must lead? Under normal circumstances, I would probably have already married. Is it my fault that I am half-Jewish and the Nazis are in power? I was, unfortunately, not born to be a nun like my sister, whose life is not to your taste either. I am a normal woman who loves a man, and he loves me. However, we can't marry. Do you want to rebuke me for this? Was I to return home only to hear your reproaches?"

When I now look back on this scene, I truly feel sorry for father. I had been too desperate to consider what the situation meant to him. He held so firmly to his old moral principles. While I was returning to Frankfurt, he had doubtessly thought things over and prepared a speech, which he believed his patriarchal duty required. He had not expected my outburst. It confused him; and for the first time, he was helpless against me and did not know how he should act. In the end, he seemed willing to help me.

September 18, 1943

It is all over. A very deep sadness and emptiness holds me in a spell. I laugh and chat as though everything were the same, but I can't wipe out the memory of my small son. He was so perfect—a tiny, complete person. He did not know life and was still happy in his ignorance, and I could love him only the short time he grew within me. I think of all the sacrifices, offered with pain and grief on the fatherland's altar by grown up people, who can not determine either when the bell tolls for them.

To console myself I recalled Pötz's words: "It is better that the unborn remain unborn." Reasonable words which do not alleviate the pain of my loss.

292

September 26, 1943

Today is Karl's birthday which we once thought to celebrate together. He is still in training near Berlin. We spoke twice on the telephone; but I don't know exactly where he is at this moment.

Thus I join the gigantic army of lonely women who wait for a sign of life with fear in their hearts. Until now, I felt sympathy for them and admired their strength in this war of nerves. But what a difference there is in sympathizing with other people's worries and feeling them personally.

September 30, 1943

This seems to be a year of major farewells for me.

My small black companion has left me forever.

His skin disease grew constantly worse. Even his stay at the Giessen Veterinary Clinic brought only temporary improvement. His back was a large sore and he suffered. The veterinarian tried to convince me that I must end his misery. I hesitated until it was obvious that my procrastination was selfish and cruel.

Dr. Dietz reexamined Brandy thoroughly and shook his head sadly. "It makes no sense to wait any longer. It will only get worse."

While he took the injection from his leather case, he asked, "Are you sure you want to stay here?"

"I certainly don't want to leave him now!"

Dr. Dietz filled the syringe, while I held Brandy on my arms.

"Now, place him on the ground," and he injected the cyanide.

Brandy stood up on his hind legs as if he wanted me to take him in my arms, and then collapsed lifeless.

I stared in shock at my small dead friend. The veterinarian, well known for his rudeness, pulled my head on his shoulder. "Cry, my child. I know how you feel."

October 3, 1943

Yesterday I met Pötz again after a long interval.

"My dear young friend," he greeted me, "what happened?

You look as if you have been in purgatory."

"I have been through my own personal purgatory, in all its variations. You know — I have discovered that Hell really does exist. I'm not even sure whether I have definitely left it."

He nodded and told me he had called once during the summer. A strange voice answered the telephone and, after he assured her he was a personal friend, told him that I was in Berlin.

I reported to him about mother's arrest, my trips, and her last-minute rescue.

"What happens to the other prisoners?" he asked.

"The Aryan spouses receive a postcard after a few weeks, with the news that their Jewish husband or wife died from angina, appendicitis, influenza, or something else. The survivor is to notify them whether he wants the ashes."

Pötz looked at me wearily. Nightly air raids, hunger, and nervous strain had left their mark on him too. He was an unhealthy gray color and he had lost weight.

He observed bitterly: "No animal ever tortures another member of its own species as cruelly as humans do. Of course, the Nazis deserve special distinction!"

His right hand moved through his gray hair, and he grasped his suspenders firmly. "It isn't enough for them to sacrifice the lives of youth and men in their prime, and to exterminate whole races. No, they destroy everything in their own country which does not correspond to their racial or political ideas. Only the noble German master race has the right to live. My dear, we are now experiencing the decline of the western world, which began in grand style in 1914. The incompatibility of Christians, the fight for hegemony among members of the caucasian race, must lead to the decline of the West, while the Eastern and yellow non-Christian worlds perfect themselves."

He paused briefly while the shadow of an ironic smile flitted over his face. "Isn't it interesting that the Christian world, which according to its tenets should not kill, rushes from one war to the next and kills, kills, kills. Until now it was exclusively a male virtue to kill another male. Now, women and children are included in the Christian orgy of slaughter. To return to our original theme, I am convinced that one or two generations after this civilized Western debacle, there will be a dreadful conflict between East and West. After that, the Caucasians, or whatever is

294

left of them, will no longer be the master race, and those subjugated for so long will take over."

"But there is still the United States with its huge population resources."

He smiled at me condescendingly. "America, my dear, is merely a geographical concept because the Americans are not a nation. They call themselves a melting pot. However, in reality, they are not blended together at all. This so-called nation disintegrates into innumerable ethnic groups, who look down on each other." He suddenly laughed soundlessly. "The British look down on the Irish, the Irish on the Italians, the Italians on the Poles, and the white on the colored. Unfortunately, a large percentage of Germans emigrated there; and this German blood will bequeath a heritage of warfare to America. When Europe has bled itself to death and stagnates in exhaustion, America will take up the war cry. When there is no longer anything to fight in Europe, America will turn its interest to the East. And this will happen well after the present war with Japan." He looked at me partly amused, partly skeptical. "You don't agree, and would like to object?"

"Yes, I would like to say that there are not only Germans in America, but hundreds of other nationalities, who are not so predisposed towards war. Since the United States has a democratic form of government, the peaceful element should predominate."

"My dear young friend, although you have been through hell, you are still ready to believe in fairy tales. You say America has a democratic form of government? Do you know what democracy really is? Democracy is *not* the rule of the people; it is the art of ruling the people. It was clearly the case with the ancient Greeks and will also be true in the land of milk and honey."

Both of us were silent. After a while, I asked him doubtfully, "But why should America fight against the peoples of the East?"

"Because the leopard cannot change his spots. Don't forget, America is built on the eradication of the Indian. A state whose existence is based on something so brutal, callous, and inhuman will not suddenly change its character. My dear, don't misunderstand me. This is my own very personal speculation, which could be wrong; but in my opinion, the next logical war zone for America is in the East with its rich natural resources, a soil which contains all the treasures America does not possess. This war will seal the supremacy of the white race."

I stared at the tabletop meditatively, while my fingers unconsciously drew circles on the smooth marble. "Isn't America superior to the Asiatics because of her technology and immense power?"

Pötz looked at me challengingly. "You have picked the correct word: power. How did Rome's power help her against Christianity? Did the power of the British Empire help in its fight against Gandhi? Ideas won't be eradicated with weapons. Ideas are always stronger than cannon."

October 10, 1943

Frankfurt finally had its "terror attack," as the government now labels them. I had worried that maybe we had been forgotten. Last Monday, our liberators came not once but three times.

What a grotesque situation! We heard the "enemy airplanes" approach with their distinct humming sound, very different from the noise of our planes. The long wait was finally over. We heard the impact of bombs, closer than ever before; and suddenly dust was loosened in the air-raid shelter and the heavy house gently swayed.

A moan of fear came from Mrs. Rodenhauer's large bosom. She clung to her small daughter Ingrid and groaned. Ingrid handed her mother a glass of water with Hoffmann's Drops, a remedy once thought to prevent fainting.

After a brief moment, the whole shelter smelled of valerian. I said to father, "They have opened the bar."

Mother had no understanding of such jokes. Her hands were clutched so tightly together that her knuckles turned white. She moved her lips silently after each heavy bomb.

I scrutinized the tenants gathered there. Mrs. Collier was paler than usual; and her right eyebrow was a bit higher than normal on her asymmetrical face. Her stout husband, who reminds me of a Buddha, sat next to her with an impenetrable expression.

The deaf-mute Mr. Schindler, who only felt the vibrations of the house and the pressure of the blast, uttered inarticulate sounds to ask his wife, "What is happening?" She explained, gesticulating with her hands, that a bomb had fallen nearby.

The light flickered and dimmed; and I noticed a triumphant smile on father's face.

296

Another valerian cocktail was mixed while the light regained its former intensity. I wondered about father's expression. Did my patriotic father also hope the enemy would free us? Did this convinced German want his fatherland to be again the loser?

There was a pause in the bombardment. I left the air-raid shelter, and went into the hallway where I smoked a smelly cigarette made from butts of butts. I asked myself whether it were possible that the right seducer of a nation could succeed at letting his most ardent patriots hope for an enemy victory? I remembered the time after the First World War, when father almost broke down with the realization that his fatherland, his Germany, had lost the war. He suffered as if his most beloved friend writhed in agony. Now when we heard bombs fall, father beamed at me with relief.

Suddenly young Rodenhauer came into the hall. "Damn, I'm tired!" She yawned loudly and inhaled the smoke of my cigarette with a wrinkled nose. "It's time the Americans came. Then we will smoke Lucky Strikes."

Suddenly the whole house shook and we ran back to the shelter. Ferdinand Collier, home on furlough for several days, had crawled into the farthest corner. This youth in uniform tried in vain to appear manly. This morning around 11 A.M. when bombs fell somewhere in the city after the first alarm, we were on the staircase trying to save Mrs. Rodenhauer's machine. Ferdinand wore his steel helmet; he almost dropped the sewing machine as he unheroically ran to the air-raid shelter. Was this only a child's fear or the premonition of someone marked for death?

After the all clear sounded, I was the first to reach the telephone. It still worked. "Siegrid," I called, "Is everything all right?"

"All the windowpanes are broken again, but the house is still standing."

The next afternoon Nurse Ruth came. "What I'm wearing" she said, "is all I have left."

The house near the zoo, where she and her Jewish husband lived, was completely destroyed along with several neighboring houses. The inhabitants crawled through several cellar wall openings unable to take any luggage with them. They had just saved their lives, and that has little value in the Third Reich.

We collected some clothing and kitchenware, while Ruth

went to the Schindlers to ask for help. She returned with a large shopping bag and a strange smile.

"Well?" mother asked, looking curiously at the bag. "Did you get something?"

Ruth began to laugh while her eyes were moist with tears. "She collected a dozen silk stockings, so ragged I can't mend them, and two patched blouses."

"My dearest Ruth!" Mother embraced this proud woman, who bravely tried to swallow her bitterness.

Afterwards, I could not concentrate on counting red and white corpuscles. I thought about the ragged stockings, the "Ebinent" so generously donated. How was it possible for a person not to be able to part with material possessions, when standing in the cross-fire between bombs and the Gestapo? Is it human or only Jewish to cling to material things? I can not understand it.

November 14, 1943

We have partly rearranged the apartment, because we have received new lodgers — in order not to call it billeting. I moved into the smaller room opposite the lab, where Gunther Siegurd Kunz and Uncle Fritz once stayed and where a young Dutch couple had temporarily slept. He had been drafted in a job at the post office and she had worked in our house. But the employment office transferred them to a pure Aryan household, since mother's influence would probably be deleterious. Now I live there. It is somewhat narrow, but I made it as comfortable as possible.

The Würmchen had to move out. Her room and mine now house the Seligmann couple and their daughter. The Seligmanns are little people. Mrs. Seligman is Aryan and he resembles a damaged garden dwarf. His head, with a protruding lower jaw, rests on a leather padded metal brace. He loves to shuffle through the hall during office hours in his slippers and gray woolen jacket, to go to the toilet at the other end of the apartment. Frequently, standing in the open doorway, he gives his wife instructions in a clear nasal voice, to attract the attention of the waiting patients.

Mother is both angry and annoyed: "If he were at least decently dressed! Haven't these people any sense at all about such things?"

"No mother," I replied and began to laugh while visualizing tiny Mr. Seligman in his wool jacket, the head with the curly gray hair protected by the heavy brace from disappearing between his shoulders, as he shuffles importantly past the Aryan patients. "Office hours," I explained, "are the high point of his day. He can keep track of how many patients come and what sort of people they are. He probably would give a lot for permission to talk to them."

Mother looked at me stonily: "I don't find that funny at all . . . I will talk to Mrs. Seligman about it."

"Really?" I asked, "And tell her that her husband can't go to the bathroom and take a pee during office hours?"

"How can you use that kind of language?" asked mother irritably. "I only want to tell her that he should at least wear shoes."

"You had better not," I commented.

Mother spoke to Mrs. Seligman and met with complete lack of understanding. "We do live here now, Mrs. Schroeder," the woman had replied, "here we are at home now and I can't demand from my husband that he not be comfortable at home, only because it does not suit you."

Mother left the conversation with a crimson face and red spots on her neck. "Why couldn't we get people like the Stäubchens?"

"Because the Gestapo, in its inscrutable wisdom, selects the worst partner for everyone."

The Stäubchens moved in with the Schindlers and live directly above me. He is a journalist and writer. His wife is Jewish; and they own a dachshund bitch called Sabine, who howls in high-pitched soprano during the evening meal if she is not fed tidbits.

This mixed society meets almost nightly in the air-raid shelter.

December 2, 1943

At the end of November, we had a daylight air attack during which bombs were dropped all over the city. The victims of the air raids are now called "fallen ones." We don't know how many people have been killed, but it must be a considerable number. Future casualties are estimated to be even higher.

An employee in the City Construction Administration told father during office hours that, according to new instructions, not more than a thousand corpses should be transported in closed coffins to the cemetery. "If there are more than one thousand corpses," father reported, "they are to be transported in open coffins and the lids set in place at the cemetery so as to use the vehicles more efficiently. If there are two thousand or more corpses, each receives only half a coffin."

"And what if there are more than three thousand bodies?" I asked.

"If there are more than six thousand 'fallen,' they are wrapped in paper covers. The paper and suitable ropes are made available."

"How horrible!" exclaimed mother.

I was astonished: "I did not know that we still have so much paper and rope. Nice prospects, indeed!"

December 24, 1943

"Silent night - holy night -"

Silent it is and lousy cold. The furnace was already turned off several hours ago. I am at my desk, on which a carbide lamp burns, a present from a patient who made father happy with two such treasures. I am wearing my fur boots, winter coat and have a blanket draped over shoulders and back; my stomach grumbles.

Four days ago, on the 20th, we had a massive air-raid in the afternoon, which lasted into the evening. Amongst other things our irreplaceable bed sheets burned in the laundry. We don't have gas, because in Leerbachstrasse yawns a big hole, in which the main gas line for the whole neighborhood was buried. But then—there is almost nothing to cook anyway.

The Christmas tree is a midget compared to what once was my parents' pride; no red apples decorate it as in former times and only some candle stumps were lighted, the leftovers of last year.

Katherina could not come for Christmas. So we spent a brief, dismal Christmas eve. My parents, overtired, cold and hungry, turned in early.

Something of this night's sentimental mood, which normally is spent in close family circles, has rubbed off on me, and my thoughts are searching for Karl. My heart is crying for him, but it is as if this call is choked in a fog which neither carries the sound nor returns an answer. We wrote to each other; letters of love and confidence, letters in which, between the lines sadness and despair alternated. The letters reveal a despair perhaps only a man can feel who struggles against an ocean of desolation and who is not permitted to have tears in his eyes.

In vain I try to imagine Karl celebrating Christmas somewhere in Russia. I can not find him in any Russian peasant house or in any barracks with other soldiers. Fear holds my heart in its black hand. I know that nothing has happened to him, because I don't doubt that we both will come out alive from this inferno. Despite all his assurances and promises which I never demanded, I can not completely shake off the fearful uncertainty with regard to him. Perhaps I just lost the ability in this life, in which nothing is certain anymore, to believe in a future in which I will have inner and outer peace. Peace . . .

I catch myself saying this word aloud, this word which encloses so much happiness and which people never appreciate, as long as they have it. My first childhood memories are those of war and war seems to accompany me through my whole life. War and death. Death, which some deranged heads of state offer their subjects as a gift, bedecked with medals and badges of honor, accompanied with heroic songs of sacrifice and enthusiasm for their homeland. In front of me glides the dance of my dead cousins and friends: Joseph and Joachim, Etta's sons Karl and Paul, who are missing in Russia and France and never will return. Waldemar Hensel and young Ferdinand Collier, whose death was reported last week. My gentle, tender colleague Jo Dirks, whose name with the iron cross was printed in the newspaper on the same day with Joachim's. Erich Kohlhöfer, the "sub-human," whom they had placed in a suicide commando. They all were made into reluctant heroes for the glory of an insane mass murderer.

I will never understand patriots. Fathers who went through the carnage of the First World War raised their sons to repeat these horrors. Mothers whose men remained on the "field of honor" in the last war spurred their sons to copy their fathers' example and commit suicide. Are they all deranged or is something wrong with us?

February 13, 1944

Now we are also frontline fighters. On Sunday, January 29th, our district had its first really heavy attack. Large areas of the city

301

were destroyed. The house next to us no longer has a roof, and is covered with a tarpaulin. Diagonally across the street where Major Schneider lived, only the frame of the house is standing; and the empty charred windows stare at us.

That night we heard airplanes droning directly overhead for the first time. We felt bombs fall in the neighborhood. They seemed to lift our house off the ground and return it roughly to its place. The air-raid cellar was filled with plaster dust, which made us all cough.

The Rodenhauers usually climb on their bikes as soon as the warning signal sounds, and pedal to the Gestapo bunker in Lindenstrasse. They were not with us this time, so there were no valerian drops. Most of the tenants were composed and silent. Mother kneeled on the floor of the shelter and said her prayer like a phonograph record stuck in its groove, "Our Father who art in heaven, our Father who art in heaven . . ." Only Gerold Stäubchen joined her. The dachshund Sabine was squeezed under his stomach as he crouched half kneeling, half lying on the ground.

After the 'all clear', we hauled water to extinguish the fire next door and to protect our roof. After that we took up fire-watch positions in hourly shifts in the water-soaked attic next door. The Rodenhauer girl and I had duty from 5 to 6 A.M. Shortly before our relief, we saw flames burst out again at the Schneiders. Only the lower two stories of the house still stood, and were deserted, since our neighbours left after the fire was extinguished, and found overnight lodgings with friends.

Help arrived in no time, but we could not put out the fire. So we emptied the Schneiders' residence, dragging whatever we could from the burning house and piling it in the street.

Morning dawned. A drowsy sun tried to send its rays through a curtain of smoke and dust. We had done everything we could and stood exhausted amongst what was left of the Schneider's possessions. The sudden inactivity made us notice the cold. We shivered; we were overtired, hungry and unbelievably dirty. We looked at each other with smoke-reddened eyes, when we heard the sound of hobnailed boots.

Three officials — referred to as "gold pheasants" because of their gold braid — emerged from the haze. They looked neither to the right nor left, but marched in the middle of the street with their eyes straight ahead. They wore immaculately clean, pressed uniforms; their shining gold epaulets glittered on their shoulders.

We stared, momentarily speechless, at these apparitions from another world.

Then a member of our group shouted a sharp, hate-filled "Heil Hitler!"

"Those swine!" raged another voice.

"Those guys should help and dirty their hands."

"Rap rap rap," marched the shining hobnailed boots as if their wearers were deaf.

After I helped my parents sweep up our broken window-panes, I tried to wash with the small piece of brown clay issued on our soap ration; then I stretched out on my bed.

I must have just sunk into a deep sleep, when fists began relentlessly hammering at my door.

"What is the matter?" I called drowsily.

"Our roof is on fire! Please come!" Miss Rodenhauer stood in front of me.

We now have a charred beam in the roof, but everything else is standing. I sat on this beam with a Gestapo man and we extinguished the fire together.

He had come to visit the Rodenhauers. As all the doors were open, he followed the voices and finally vaulted opposite me on the burning beam in his shirt-sleeves, black breeches and jackboots of his SS uniform. Who ever would have thought I would sit opposite a Gestapo man on the joists of our roof.

Five days later, the angels of death flew again. This time they brought something new: chain bombs, four bombs chained together. Scarcely a stone remains standing after these bombs are dropped. The next morning, they carpeted the periphery of the city with bombs, and returned again several days later. Since they seem to be especially partial to the Heddernheimer Copper Works, and our house lies on their flight pattern, we usually have lively hours in our shelter.

The splendid Nazi defenses seem to falter. Fire extinguishers no longer function, and the fire brigade finds many streets impassable because of rubble and bomb craters. The carefully constructed water troughs are often empty, damaged by bombs. The hoses and pumps are defective and inferior in quality. It is impossible to direct the fire brigades to the most urgent locations, since the telephone lines are often destroyed in the target areas.

Auxiliary trains are sent with provisions for several city districts. These are small gestures, a short-term satisfaction for hungry mouths. This will neither rebuild bombed houses nor bring the dead back to life.

The population becomes rebellious. Enthusiasm and fanaticism give way to depression and doubts. The news, coming in from different fronts is crushing. Slowly it dawns even on the blockheads, that probably no hour of retaliation will come and no wonder weapon will materialize.

Father, whom I drive as usual to his patients (we now receive only 35 liters of gas a month), asks me occasionally to drive slowly so as to be able to view leisurely the changing city silhouette. At many intersections, signs have been placed which read "escape route." They point in the direction of parks and open places where one can escape to during major fires. In front of giant rubble heaps, which once were proud houses, are plaques and posters fastened to wooden poles. We repeatedly got out of the car to read the same message: "We are still alive! Moved to the Meiers. Family XYZ." "We all have been rescued. Live with the Müllers." and then the name of a village in the Taunus, Odenwald or Spessart follows.

Returning home, mother placed a hot watery broth on the table. Something floated in the tureen. Each of us got two slices of bread made from turnips and probably — as malicious scoffers suspect — some sawdust. Within 24 hours it turns mouldy from the inside, cultivating thick white-green threads. A small square of margarine completed the menu.

Furtively I observed the movement of father's jaws, over which his skin stretched tightly. His collar must have grown at least two, if not three, sizes too large, and his eyes appeared enormous below the arched forehead with its sunken temples. The sight of him caused my heart to contract.

February 26, 1944

It was late evening. Karl's last letter, written before the great bombardment of Frankfurt started, lay in front of me. Someone knocked cautiously on my door. At my invitation, father came in.

Slowly he came closer until his hand rested fleetingly on my shoulder. "I saw that you received a letter today. You have looked dejected since then." He hesitated. "I will not press the point, my

304

dear. But if you want to confide, consider me your best friend."

I was deeply moved. Never before had my shy and reserved father spoken to me in this manner.

"Karl wrote me a farewell letter."

Father looked at me in disbelief.

"He wrote that he spent Christmas in Berlin with the woman he left because of me. Conditions in Berlin must be worse than here, and the poor woman is so helpless. He simply cannot abandon her."

To a man like father, faithful to the same woman for over forty years, Karl's action was simply incomprehensible. Shaking his head, he could only say, "Unbelievable."

After a while I said, "Karl is not a strong man. . . . If he can help when somebody is in trouble, he becomes strong and grows. He rushed to my assistance when I first had difficulties with the National Association of the German Press, when your assistant denounced you, when I appeared before the Special Court, and when he saw my despair because of mother's arrest. But he knows I am now comparatively secure in the lap of my family. I don't even have a helpless baby who needs his protection. He probably believes that I can exist without him. But he practically pulled Diana up from the gutter and made her a journalist. She is his creation, like Pygmalion. That is the power she has over him. I, however, have forgotten how to write letters of distress and how to cry for help."

Father looked thoughtfully into space. "So, he is a weakling," he observed bitterly.

I shrugged. "Perhaps that is stated too harshly. Whatever he is. . ." I stopped.

And father asked: "You still love him?"

"Yes, I still love him. . ."

After a long pause he asked hesitantly, "Are you sure he won't return to you?"

"I don't know, father. We have broken up several times. But this time? She is in her weaknesses probably stronger than I am."

February 27, 1944

Pötz telephoned. "Since no bombs have fallen for over two weeks, would you risk going out?" When I agreed he asked, "Where can we go? The Kakaostube is destroyed."

305

I proposed we meet at Opernplatz. "There is a small restaurant in Kettenhofweg, whose owner I have known for many years."

We walked up four stone steps and entered a dusky restaurant.

"We have still survived, my dear," Pötz said. "I don't think these air raids were the last ones. Hitler promised the English to eradicate their cities; and the English now show him that they can do the same in this country.

"After one of the night raids, Elsa and I walked around our neighborhood, to see what had happened. Our local party leader stood before the ruins of his house. He was so absorbed in his sorrow that he didn't observe what was going on around him. I gently touched his back and said, 'For that you fought fourteen years.' Before he turned around, we had disappeared in the darkness and smoke." Pötz laughed noiselessly.

I nodded, looked up and saw the face of the innkeeper Hubert Stumpf. He greeted me, "Schroederchen! How good to see you again!"

We invited him to sit down with us.

Stumpf, in his slow awkward manner, first shook his head a few times, and then said, "Pardon me, Miss Schroeder, but this is a lot of nonsense. The corrupt brown gang just wants to silence us with their idiotic wonder weapons."

Pötz had again anchored his thumbs under his suspenders and leaned towards Stumpf, who stared at him eagerly with slightly open lips. "When the first cannon shot its cannon-ball, it was a wonder weapon. When the first shell exploded in enemy lines, it was a wonder weapon. Today's wonder weapon will be the most employed one tomorrow. The bombers of the First World War were such a weapon. And in this war an anonymous enemy destroys anonymous masses, not being restricted to able-bodied men, but killing women, children and old people. And now we dream of a new wonder weapon.

"Although I don't believe Germany can make its new instrument of murder in time, I don't doubt that it will be developed. It will merely kill more people at one time than bombs do now. And, one day a weapon will be created which can erase whole peoples by pressing a button." He looked searchingly at Stumpf and me. "You don't believe me? But isn't that the logical development if one can

306

learn from history and believe in evolution?" He laughed ironically.

Stumpf leaned across the table; his work-worn hand pointed at Pötz in anger. "That isn't a solution! The masses must come into their rights."

"That is a good idea," confirmed Pötz. "To insure that the masses get their rights, you will need a supervisory authority, a government. Mr. Stumpf, socialism is only a system, just like communism and capitalism. All systems are, sooner or later, saturated by corruption or misused by the power hungry; the man who has sipped from the cup of power without becoming intoxicated is a rarity. Even if the present systems collapsed in all nations, a new power structure would probably develop in a short time, which would be scarcely better than the old one. In the end, your system — socialism — also depends on a doctrine. The masses will always be misused if they must submit to a doctrine."

Hubert Stumpf shook his head energetically. "No," he said. "No, that can't be so—not after this hellish war. No—this war will force people to think. . . . They will have had enough."

"Is this the war to end all wars, Mr. Stumpf" Pötz said almost sympathetically, "How often have we heard that already, only to experience the next bestial war? And mankind won't learn anything this time either." He was silent and suddenly asked me: "Do you doubt that?"

"I am convinced there will be no such hero worship in the future. After this experience, women will make their voices heard, to end such insanity!"

"Women?" Pötz raised his eyebrows and said with matchless irony: "You women did not even deserve the right to vote. You women are the only supply organization, which delivers the raw material, man, with which generals fill up veterans' cemeteries. No my dear, as long as women are ready to unscrupulously produce cannon fodder, I don't expect them to change the course of history."

"And yet —" Stumpf pondered, "And yet — after this war, when the Nazis have lost . . . when we Socialists again will have something to say . . ."

"What then, Mr. Stumpf?" Pötz placed his hands flat on the table and bent forward: "I will tell you what will happen, since you can actually condense history in one sentence: The oppressed of today will be the oppressors of tomorrow."

307

March 31, 1944

Frankfurt is no more. Our beautiful old city was turned into a fiery mass grave. Occasionally a solitary Madonna stands on a small pedestal, looking with a sweet smile at her folded hands, unaffected by the stench, filth, and ashes. In the Römerberg fountain, Justicia still stands with blindfolded eyes, her scales elevated above a background of ruins. The inner city is a rubble heap; even in the outskirts, every street has at least one damaged house.

I will try to record as well as I can the confusing experiences of the last two weeks.

On Saturday, March 18th, I called Siegrid around 9 P.M. to tell her I would come over for a short visit. While I was on the telephone, the early warning sirens sounded, actually an evening routine.

Mother appeared in the hallway, completely beside herself. "Under no circumstances can you go now." She had a large enamel pot in her hand, which she wanted to fill with water.

So I told Siegrid, "I'll come after the 'all clear'."

As mother filled the bathtub with water, she called out, "Bring our emergency luggage to the cellar!"

The first bombs fell almost simultaneously with the renewed wail of the sirens; and then all hell broke loose. We spent over two hours in the cellar, heard the bombs fall around us, and felt the heavy blasts. We did not know if our roof or our apartment was hit. It was impossible to leave the shelter during this rain of bombs.

The Rodenhauers had not left the house in time, and remained with us. The odor of Baldrian mingled with plaster dust, which the bombs shook loose from the cellar joints. When the noise of the explosions subsided, we heard a chorus of sighs floating up from the cold concrete floor, a leitmotif, humbly imploring God's help: "Our Father, who art in heaven. . ." The light flickered a few times and finally went out.

When at last we heard a single siren in the distance, we rushed out of the cellar. Our stairwell was ablaze. A phosphor canister had penetrated the roof and two floors; it stuck on the landing between the Schindlers' and our apartment. While some of the tenants used the back stairs to get through the Schindler's apartment and remove the canister and the burning floor boards, the rest of us handed up sand and water from below. After a while, we left the smoldering hole and discovered that the Colliers' kitchen was burning. The Colliers were out of town. A phosphor canister had fallen into the broom closet. The furniture was on fire, but the tile-panelled kitchen and the stone floor had withstood the flames.

We were hampered in our efforts to extinguish the fire by a lack of light. All we had were a few miserable candles, whose small flames flickered in the wind blowing in through the empty window frames. We stepped on broken glass and looked for shovels and sand buckets, while father made the rounds with a bowl of lye to keep the phosphorus burns to a minimum.

A gasoline can had exploded on the roof in front of Rodenhauer's window, but luckily their cactuses stopped the flaming fragments.

After the fires were brought under control, we removed small incendiary bombs from some of the balconies and window ledges where they had stuck. I tried to call Siegrid. The telephone was dead. Saying good-bye to my parents, I went out to see what had happened to her.

Before I left the house, I dipped a towel in the bathtub; we all put this protection in front of our nose and mouth, after the government-issued gas masks proved to be entirely ineffective.

Skirting the burning houses in the wide Wolfgangstrasse was not hard. But I froze with horror when I decided to take the shorter route through the narrow Sömmeringstrasse. A small path in the middle of the street led between two walls of fire. I buckled my leather auto cap tightly over my hair, tied the damp towel over my nose and mouth, put on my goggles and raced through the fire storm, hoping that a burning beam would not fall on me. A rain of sparks whirled around me but could not penetrate my strange attire. At the end of the street I saw only more fire and flames. The whole city seemed to be burning.

Finally I reached Siegrid's house, the roof and upper floors were on fire. The tenants packed what they could save in a small pick-up truck which stood on the street.

Siegrid had taken a large laundry basket to her room. We opened closets and drawers, filled the basket, dragged it to the car, and ran back into the apartment, surrounded by smoke, while burning debris whizzed past us. We glanced overhead to estimate how long the staircase and the roof would hold. Everything was deposited with a neighbor in a side street, whose house was not hit;

309

and we returned to reload the van. The moment came when we could no longer enter the apartment. We stood on the street, with our arms filled, surrounded by trunks and household effects, as the roof fell in with a gigantic crash sending a cone of fire into the sky. At that moment, Siegrid nudged me and pointed to an elderly woman who occupied the top floor. She put the only things she had saved into the car; three umbrellas and a chamber pot.

Once my parents emerged from the smoke and fog, worried because I had been away so long. When they found us alive, they fought their way back. The two bent figures disappeared like ghosts in the glare of the fire.

On one of the countless trips between Siegrid's house and the neighbor's, Siegrid suddenly disappeared. We had taken turns, alternately carrying a suitcase, while the other stood guard, and from one of these trips she had not returned. I ran back and forth, searched the streets in the fiery glow, called out her name, but she seemed to have vanished from the face of the earth.

At dawn I returned home and found all the tenants in the shelter, the only place which was not drafty.

"Lili dear!" exclaimed mother with relief, and embraced me. "Where is Siegrid?"

"I don't know."

"Why?" father asked. "You were together."

I felt faint for a moment. Tears ran down my dirty face and I sobbed, "I couldn't find her. . ."

Siegrid had fainted in the street from smoke inhalation. A stranger had picked her up and carried her into a house. Several hours later she appeared in our shelter entrance. We offered to house her; but by evening she and her father were assigned temporary accommodations elsewhere.

Towards noon, father persuaded me to drive him to the ghetto, now located behind the zoo. The houses were partly burned out. Nobody was killed. But our Jewish friends looked pitiful. The little water that had been saved was reserved for drinking. They were dirty, with swollen inflamed eyes; some were hoarse and coughed from the smoke and dust. Some had mild burns or other wounds. Father promised to bring them medicines. We drove on but discovered that none of the pharmacies were open. So a little later, I drove to the neighboring town of Hanau with a handful of prescriptions.

The farther I got from Frankfurt, the more normal everything looked. When I reached Hanau, I felt as if I had landed on another planet. I drove through this intact and entirely undamaged small city, where all the houses had windowpanes, and clean people strolled through the streets in their Sunday best. I had forgotten it was Sunday.

As I stopped and asked directions to the pharmacy, the people stared at me in disbelief and answered hesitantly. When I got there, several pedestrians turned and stared at me. My dark blue winter coat was covered with ashes and stearin spots which had dropped from the candles. The legs of my slacks, visible under my coat, were dirty and singed. Under the leather cap, my face was sooty. Nobody asked any questions. Even the pharmacist handed me eye drops, cough syrup, ointment, and bandages silently, and he took the money from my dirty hand without expression.

Slowly I drove out of Hanau towards the highway, conscious of the well-dressed and contented pedestrians. I was bewildered. These people lived only a few kilometers away from us, and behaved as if our fate could never overtake them.

Can most people only have sympathy when they were personally affected? Must a bomb destroy their own house to awaken their imagination? Must a close relative be at the front to make them conscious of the war? Must one have a Communist or a Jew in the family to know about concentration camps? Are the masses in every country so obtuse, or is this complete lack of perception the privilege of the unaffected few?

My unfriendly thoughts were distracted by a figure on the highway who waved to me. I stopped and picked up an ordinary woman in her fifties. She was loaded down with bags and packages and wanted to visit her daughter who lived on the outskirts of Frankfurt. She could not reach her by telephone, and had heard something about an attack on the city.

"Are all the telephone lines destroyed?"

"Yes; also the electricity, water, gas, and streetcars."

"That's terrible!"

When I let her off at her destination, she rummaged in her bag and gave me some brown bread. "Here," she said, "Perhaps this will help a little. I still have enough for my daughter."

The next morning, Monday, the first trucks came from Giessen, Bad Vilbel, and elsewhere with large kettles of noodle soup, which even had pieces of meat in it. Sandwiches with butter

311

and sausages were also doled out at strategic points in the city. Our distribution center is the I.G. Farben building.

Meanwhile, I went in search of water and discovered a small dripping faucet on the outer wall of Diakonissen Hospital, located one block above the ruined water main. We removed everything that was not bolted to the car, filled it with cans, buckets, and pots. Then I drove off. When I came back with a rather damp automobile, the other tenants greeted me with cleaning rags and scrubbers. Although I drive as if I were moving over eggs, a certain amount of water always spills. It usually takes three trips for the day's needs; and the operation runs smoothly.

Then a new drama unfolded. According to a new decree, owners of registered cars were obliged to drive bombed-out victims to the suburbs or the nearest train station. Suddenly our small car was surrounded by people asking to be driven out of Frankfurt. Where they got the gasoline was a mystery to me. They brought it in old rusty cans and jam tins. Without asking questions, I filled the tank and drove them to the Taunus, Offenbach, Wiesbaden, or wherever they wanted to go. Five-member families were squeezed into our four-seater; with usually a pile of things on everybody's lap. Trunks and bedding were tied to the fenders with straps and twine. On the return trip I collected lonely travellers who were headed towards the destroyed city, worried about their families.

When I returned home at night, my parents met me at the door with a kerosene lamp, eager to learn what I had experienced. Often I had a gift for them since my passengers usually gave me a small token as we parted: some butter, bread, a candle, two apples, or an egg — something which helped us out. My head swam with family stories of people whom I had never seen before, and would probably never meet again.

Meanwhile, in the city center, the indomitable inhabitants began to work their way out of the rubble. Business people started nailing planks over their store windows, and tried to get their business going again. Happiness, however, was short-lived.

On Wednesday, March 22nd, the early warning signal sounded about 10 P.M., and that was the last time we heard a siren. We learned later that the German defense was misled by a feigned attack on Kassel.

The raid was brief but it was unbelievably intense and destroyed almost everything which was still intact. Miraculously, almost nothing happened to us. The house next door was levelled a bit more. The ground floor is still standing, and the tenants dragged furniture and bedding from the upper stories onto the street.

A house on the other side of us also burned. The flames threw their ghostly shadows and red light over the street; black figures scurried silently back and forth in the crackling blaze, carrying possessions to the street — where they often caught fire from the rain of sparks — or were stolen.

Confusion, misery, destruction, and fear grew. We can not keep office hours without water and light. The pharmacies are closed and the telephone lines are destroyed. It is depressing to live in a windowless apartment and commune with one's grumbling stomach. So I continued to transport neighbors out of Frankfurt, if they could bring the required gasoline.

Late one afternoon as I began my return trip from the Hanau station, I was stopped by a military patrolman in Fechenheim, which did not make me feel better.

"Where are you going?"

"Frankfurt."

He motioned to a person hidden from my view and said in a commanding voice, "You must take this officer along."

I was relieved.

The officer saluted me and placed a small suitcase on the back seat. He wore a dark blue uniform with gold stripes on his sleeves and a dark blue cap with an anchor on its bill. He was young and as far as I could see at a glance, looked nice. However, he seemed to be a career officer, which caused me to stare at the road in front of me in icy silence.

After a while, he cautiously asked, "Were the air raids very bad?"

"I should say so."

After a long pause, "You are driving a doctor's car?" [A medical insignia with the word Doctor is on the windshield.]

"It is my father's car."

"Please excuse my curiosity. Why did you come here?"

"I brought bombed-out neighbors to Hanau."

"Is the Frankfurt station completely destroyed?"

"Yes, entirely."

After a silence he said, "I am stationed in France and re-

313

ceived a telegram from my parents that they were bombed out. In such instances, one receives a short bomb furlough."

As we approached Frankfurt, the twilight was deepened by smoke still rising from the city. The mutilated skyline of the old city, once so characteristic with its cathedral, spires and gables, appeared across the Main River.

"Is that Frankfurt?" he asked bewildered.

"No. That was Frankfurt."

Smarting smoke drifted into the car carrying the smell of burned wood, singed material and charred bodies. I heard my companion shudder and breathe deeply. From time to time a delayed-action bomb exploded with a dull thud.

"Where do your parents live?" I asked.

"On Sachsenhäuser Berg."

"I'll drive you there."

He gave directions until we reached a rubble heap that had been his parents' home. It was obviously destroyed by an aerial mine, since I did not see any charred beams.

"Oh my God!" he groaned. He turned away, placed his hands on my right shoulder and buried his face.

Suddenly he seemed so very human that I forgot the uniform. Stroking his tousled hair I said reassuringly, "Your parents are still alive, otherwise they couldn't have telegraphed."

He sat up, gave a deep sigh, got out of the car, and walked towards the ruins. On the remnants of a gatepost was a note indicating that his parents were in Oberursel.

"Well?" I asked. "What now?"

"I must go to Oberursel."

"I'm sorry; but it's too late to drive to Oberursel now."

"I hadn't expected you to." He stood irresolutely before the open car door. "But what should I do?"

"Get in," I said, and started the engine.

It was completely dark by now. We were in an unfamiliar area and the car crept slowly forward. I continually watched for bomb craters, which were very difficult to spot in the dim light that fell from the slits of the covered headlights.

After I considered the situation, I said, "You can stay overnight with us. It is neither elegant nor luxurious, but at least we have a roof over our heads."

My parents received Naval Lieutenant Hans Helm amiably

314

and we shared our meagre meal with him. After my parents withdrew, Helm and I sat and talked in my room, wrapped in our coats.

The evening seemed unreal. The flickering light from the candle stump picked up the gold of his buttons and braid. We were surrounded by a deathly silence except for occasional bomb explosions. The young officer facing me was a stranger whom I had encountered through bizarre circumstances. He told me about his fiancée, the daughter of his staff physician, and described his minesweeper and crew. I realized with amazement that apparently someone was wearing his uniform with pride; he apparently knew nothing but his life at the harbor and on his ship.

In the quiet of my dark little room, we both felt as if we were the only people in the world. In this intimate atmosphere, the reserve between strangers fell away. Our subdued conversation became more personal. Initially I evaded his questions about our life, but I finally explained our situation to him. Until then, I never believed there were people in Germany who still knew nothing about death camps and the crimes perpetrated by the Nazis against Jews, Poles, and Gypsies. However, from Helm's incredulous reaction, I recognized that such people did exist. He could scarcely believe what he heard and he kept on asking questions. It was beyond his comprehension that all of us—my parents and I—had been in prison. Why were we arrested? What had we done? We were not criminals!

He paced the room restlessly. The dying light of the candle stub threw its flickering shadows against the wall. When he sat down again, the wick fell and drowned in the wax.

Out of the pitch darkness I heard him ask, "How is morale here otherwise?"

"Bad." I reported the increasing hatred of the population for uniformed Nazis; those well-fed bosses who try to keep the hungry, fatigued and overworked population in check. "Our Führer promised to fight until five minutes past twelve. The people here realize the war is lost, but they must continue to struggle because the Nazis lash them into obedience."

"Do you also believe the war is lost?", he asked uncertainly.

"That was probably decided at Stalingrad. Mr. Helm, take a look outside of your naval base at Brest; and then ask yourself for whom are you fighting this war? Did somebody invade Germany?

No?—because a madman claims the fatherland is in danger, you reach for arms, compel other people who don't want to fight to defend themselves, and set the whole world in flames."

The next morning, father and I were in the hall with Helm, who stood on a ladder and tried to seal off our windows. We were waiting for some of the tenants, including Mrs. Stäubchen, who had gone to the I.G. Farben building to fetch breakfast.

Five antiaircraft shots sounded, the alarm signal since the sirens had died. It was only nine in the morning, and we did not take the warning too seriously. Nevertheless, we picked up our air-raid luggage and I prevailed on Helm to take his coat and suitcase along.

We were in the cellar for nearly two hours; bombs fell all around us and the house shook. After an especially heavy strike in our immediate neighborhood, Stäubchen lifted his head, which he had buried in his hands. "My wife!" He groaned aloud. "She knows how upset I get!" His dachshund Sabine licked his hands comfortingly.

The valerian bar was in business, mother prayed out loud, and I felt the remaining tenants were in a state of disintegration. We were all overtired, hungry, and cold; and we were fed up with spending half our lives in an air-raid shelter and the other half in a damaged and filthy apartment. Everything seemed so hopeless. The cardboards which Helm had just fastened to the windows, had certainly long since been blown away by the pressure and blasts.

Later I thought how strange it is that it never occurred to me that our lives could likewise be snuffed out. I merely saw an endless chain of days ahead of me which would be strung together into weeks and months, a time we temporarily filled our stomachs and ceaselessly fought against dirt and destruction. I was too tired to reflect on what would happen if no bombs fell, and the Gestapo could rage unhindered.

Fleetingly I considered whether I would ever be clean again and wear a pretty dress; a real dress with a skirt and light elegant shoes. I looked at my work-worn hands with black under the broken fingernails and bluish-red fingers swollen from chillblains. No, I could not imagine ever being clean and well groomed again.

The rain of bombs subsided and after a while we heard the antiaircraft shots which announced the 'all clear'.

316

Our house was not hit, but only a few scraps of cardboard remained on the window frames. The rest lay on the hall floor.

Helm asked father if I could take him for a drive. We would be back soon.

On the street we looked at the new devastation. Part of the furniture, which had been saved but not yet hauled off, had caught fire. The feathers from a burst pillow whirled through the air; no one had water to extinguish the fire.

We went the few steps to our garage in the basement of a five-story house, which was no longer there. The garage doors were hanging in a tree on the opposite side of the street. The house and two others had been hit from the rear by an aerial mine. What remained standing was the garage and one room above it.

Just when we were about to go to the car a party official stopped us with a flow of abusive words. He owned the remaining room of the house, and maintained that our car could explode and destroy his last possessions. He forbade us to park our car in the garage.

"Are you the landlord?" Helm asked.

"No, but that has absolutely nothing to do with it. I forbid you."

The Lieutenant, already angered, answered, "Sir, get out of here and leave us alone."

"I won't stand for this!" screamed the uniformed 'gold pheasant.' "Who do you think you are?"

"Shut up!" Helm shouted. "You miserable creature! You know you can't give orders to a military officer."

Nevertheless the official was about to start a fight when Helm reached under his coat for his service pistol. I grabbed him by the coat sleeve. "Please! The guy is half mad."

Helm dropped his arm and faced the functionary once again. "Listen, the car is going to stay in this garage. And if I hear the slightest complaint, you will be sorry!"

The car did not even have a scratch, and the engine started immediately. Helm was terribly upset by the incident with the Nazi.

"What just happened illustrates what I told you last night, Hans. If a Nazi behaves like that towards a Naval officer, how do you think he acts with a civilian? By the way, where do you want to go?"

317

"To Opernplatz," he said thoughtfully. "Last night, I thought you were exaggerating, which is understandable in your position. But now —. We naval people on our ships don't know what is happening at home. Everything I represent is a lie. If things are really like this, I ought to take off my uniform."

I thought to myself whatever the uniform is, most uniforms are worn to show externally one's power, a power which oppresses. Nurses and forestry officials are exceptions; but all the others?

We arrived at Opernplatz. The Opera House was burned out, and the storage wing across the square had collapsed. The few remaining trees raised their burned and mutilated boughs to heaven like accusing arms.

"Where do we go now?"

"To Kettenhofweg to see whether the building is still standing."

The small pub hidden in the bend of Kettenhofweg was completely untouched. We got out and Helm took a key chain from his pocket. He opened the fence and the door. Seeing my astonished expression, he said, "This belongs to my parents and me."

We groped our way through the dark house to a large kitchen, where some daylight seeped in from the backyard.

"There must be something to eat," he said, opening the pantry cupboards. We found jars of preserved meat, soup and fat. He gave me several containers and loaded as much as he could carry in his arms.

Back home, he presented mother with his treasures, and then helped repair the windows and doors again. I asked him when he wanted to drive to his parents. "Tomorrow," he answered.

That evening I had a full stomach for the first time in months. A large candle which Helm had brought, burned on the table.

"I watched you this morning in the air-raid shelter and admired your courage," he said. "You don't seem to know what fear is. Why?"

"You are mistaken, Hans. Apart from the fact that lack of fear is not necessarily a sign of courage, I have lived through too many other fears to worry about the bombs. If that weren't the case, perhaps I would be scared to death during every air raid."

"I don't understand."

"You can't understand, since we live in two different worlds. I will tell you something. When I take a letter from the Gestapo

318

out of my mailbox, which can only be a summons, I get weak in the knees and have a primitive, horrible, trembling fear."

The next morning I drove Helm to Oberursel and delivered him to his parents, simple, care-worn people whom he had outgrown long ago and with whom he had little in common except his name and a small restaurant.

Now that he was gone I began to clean my laboratory corner. A thick layer of plaster dust lay over everything. Mother was busy in the kitchen, and we talked through the open door. I was just about to go to my room when I heard the crash and splintering of an object on the stone kitchen floor.

"Shit!" mother exclaimed.

I stopped short as if rooted to the ground. "Mother?"

"Ach, but it is true," she said half laughing, half crying.

The war of nerves was greater than her good upbringing, and mother's ladylike restraint had finally broken down.

April 5, 1944

On Sunday morning I stole away for a few hours to search for my past.

The streets were deserted; I encountered nobody. I passed the giant crater at the intersection of Eschersheimerlandstrasse and Grüneburgweg, which had been filled up so often, but after every air-raid gaped at one anew with its toothless mouth. The Eschersheimer Turm appeared taller because of the levelled devastation surrounding it. I climbed over all the rubble and the large stones in Eschenheimer Gasse to cast one last glance at the ruins of the Frankfurter Zeitung, lingering a moment to recall the curved stairs which Karl and I so frequently had walked down together. Then I looked around. Diagonally across the street, where the Völkermuseum once stood, only an archway was left, in front of which lay two large sandstone heads, torn off their bodies. Rubble heaps — wherever the eye could see.

Part of the steeple of Katharinen Kirche swayed next to the shattered roof. I looked for the familiar path to the Reformed Church, where Schrader had so often played the organ for me, but I could not find my way. There were no longer any streets. All the buildings had collapsed and only charred beams rose towards the sky.

I stared at this complete devastation in which the wind stirred

319

up the dust, and walked cautiously over a small beaten path, which others during the week had probably crossed.

Suddenly I saw a bent figure coming towards me through this fog of mortar dust and ashes.

"Mr. Pötz —!"

"Oh — my young friend" he said with the hint of a smile.

The wind played through his gray hair, blowing it over his forehead and tousling it upward again. His cheeks were sunken and his small paunch had disappeared. Only the suspenders held up the much too big trousers.

He looked at me with deathly tired eyes: "Did you find it?"

"Find what?"

"What you were looking for?"

"No," I replied. "Everything that was connected with pleasant memories seems to have vanished in the ruins."

"Yes, my dear. Didn't I once promise you that Hitler's legacy would only be destruction?"

I nodded.

We sat down on a huge stone which once formed part of the wall of the Reformed Church; now it stuck out from the rubble, warmed by the sun.

"Is your house still standing?"

"Yes," I answered, "slightly damaged but it still stands." My gaze fell on his shoes, whose uppers were broken. "And yours?"

"Oh, I am lodged in a house."

"Bombed out?"

"Yes."

My eyes were caught by his frayed shirt collar: "And Elsa?"

His face contorted into a grimace and he shook his head.

I angled a miserable crushed cigarette out of my pants pocket and lit it. Pötz, who never had smoked, looked voraciously at my hand, which guided the cigarette to my lips. Almost embarassed I gave it to him and he greedily inhaled the smoke.

"I was away only a short time — to fetch some bread at the soup kitchen. It was the morning they came back once more. When I went home —" He fell silent. "—the house was gone. Then we dug, dug, a whole day. . . Her foot was there, her foot with the little black and gold slipper, but it was already so stiff. . . So I walked away. . . ."

I stroked his hand lightly and comfortingly; this small gesture of human sympathy seemed to reawaken the old Pötz.

With his voice now full of energy and superiority he said:

320

"You know, my dear, the Americans should build a monument to Hitler. Hitler delivered them from their economic crisis and eliminated their unemployment. War is always the salvage for a sinking economy. Hitler has saved Mr. Roosevelt." An ironic smile played over his lips. "They should place the monument next to the statue of Liberty. You know this lady." He jumped up. There he stood, this small emaciated, shabby Faun, in the midst of dirt and ruins, in the posture of Liberty, the hand in which the torch was supposed to be, raised "This lady" he repeated, "who so grandly receives foreigners, until they have entered the land in which the streets are paved with gold. Then she turns her back on them." He burst into bleating laughter. "When you are in America, my dear, Liberty turns her back on you. Next to her the Americans should erect a monument to Hitler." His voice trailed off and the upraised hand fell to his side. "A monument," he sniggered, "a monument for Hitler in America!"

April 26, 1944

We — and I mean all the inhabitants of Frankfurt — try to pursue our daily lives and give the appearance of normalcy. Cellars, schools and bunkers were outfitted with air-raid beds, to offer mass shelter to thousands of homeless people. Old men and women of all ages, alone or with small children, regularly sit in front of the public bunkers and go inside at the first air-raid alarm. They let their households deteriorate and live only for the alarms.

After the first attacks last autumn part of the civilian population left the city to sleep in the suburbs, or even camp outdoors. They were labelled worthless cowards because the *Oberreichsleiter* announced at that time, "We all have to stay in the places where we live and work, and defend that place to the last man." Such a flight was prevented now. The Kreisleiter issued the following proclamation: "Whoever abandons the city without suffering bomb damage will have their shop or home made available to bomb victims."

Announcements other than the addresses of the departed can be seen painted on the stones of the ruins. "Red Front lives" is smeared in thick red block letters on the remains of many walls. "Hitler is a criminal," and similar slogans catch one's eye more often. Even the death sentence for such treasonous graffiti does not seem to frighten their authors.

Our telephones work again. Doctors are given preferential

service. Electricity has likewise been restored in our quarter of the city. Thus we are able to hold office hours again.

Moreover I moved back to my old room. The officials of the so-called Jewish Congregation ordered Miss Seligmann to share the same room with her parents, so that space would be available for another racially mixed couple in our apartment. Since the room where I had been living has running water, we gave it to Mr. and Mrs. Reuter. Mrs. Reuter is Jewish.

May 14, 1944

For many years father has been the physician for the Schüssler family, who although ardent Nazis, are very devoted to father. Over a year ago, Mr. Schüssler underwent major surgery and died on the operating table. It was father who broke the tragic news gently to Mrs. Schüssler; and afterwards he even advised her and her daughter in personal matters. When the Schüsslers were bombed out, they left Frankfurt.

Every month I sent a bill for the last consultation in September. Instead of a check, we now received a letter. Mrs. Schüssler wrote that she had reported her last conversation with father to her son, home on leave from the eastern front. She had hesitated a long time as to what she should do. Her son had advised her to denounce father for his defeatist attitude and she had decided to do so, since father represents principles contrary to what her son is fighting for.

Terrified, I asked father, "What did you tell her?!"

He had a sheepish expression when he admitted that he dissuaded Mrs. Schüssler from sending her daughter to a training camp for leaders of the German Girls' League, since he saw no future in this career after a defeat.

Would father never learn to keep his opinions to himself? What a glorious idea, to tell a fanatical Nazi that the war was lost! A denunciation for defeatism would seal the fate of our family. I must try to dissuade this creature from writing to the Gestapo.

So I used my free afternoon to take the train to Schlüchtern and pay a visit on Mrs. Schüssler.

Whatever sins I have committed, I atoned for on this unbelievably slow journey. The train crawled over the tracks and each stop at the smallest station seemed endless. I tried to imagine how I should greet Mrs. Schüssler, and every turn of the conversation. I rejected one approach and thought of a new one. I saw nothing of the springtime landscape which glided past the window; nor did I notice my fellow passengers but racked my brain how I could convince this dangerous woman not to pronounce our death warrant.

Finally, at the Schlüchtern station, I said to myself; "Take a deep breath. Don't show any fear; no fear, no fear."

I knocked on the door of the neat little house in a quiet street. Mrs. Schüssler opened the door; she is tall and pale with gray-blond hair and light-colored eyes, the ideal German woman. I believe I saw a fleeting touch of surprise on her face when I suddenly stood before her. She led me to a modestly furnishd sitting room; sun flooded through the windows.

While my heart was in my throat, I looked around nochalantly and said, "How pretty it is here, Mrs. Schüssler! So bright and friendly, quite a contrast to Frankfurt."

She sat opposite me without expression; only by folding and unfolding her hands did she betray her nervousness.

"Mrs. Schüssler, you probably can guess that I came because of your letter."

"It is still incomprehensible that your father could have made such defeatist statements! I have thought a long time whether it wasn't my duty to denounce him to the authorities. My son was incensed and reinforced my decision. He agreed that I should do it."

I shook my head uncomprehendingly. "Honestly, the whole thing is inconceivable. My father is a nationalist through and through. He attaches great importance to Germany's fate. There must be a horrible misunderstanding."

"No," she stated firmly. "He expressed himself very clearly about the war being lost. It was unmistakable!"

"Mrs. Schüssler, you know how much interest my father takes in you and your daughter, far more than a purely professional interest as a doctor."

"That's just it. I have always appreciated that; but these defeatist statements . . ."

"My father is only human. Occasionally he too succumbs to moods. He had great personal worries last year, was depressed and saw everything in a gloomy light. This could have been reflected in what he said."

She looked at me searchingly. "Do you really believe this? But how could he . . .?"

I interrupted her. "That doesn't fit his convictions. A man

who returned from World War I with the Iron Cross, first and second class, and other decorations — could he have changed so much? Never!"

"But he may have said similar things to other people."

"He certainly did not. He scarcely holds such personal conversations with his other patients."

Mrs. Schüssler's expression brightened and a heavy load fell off my heart. Fortunately, she had not heard about father's or mother's arrests.

We parted as friends with her assurance that she would "once more refrain" from denouncing father.

June 6, 1944

Father received an invitation for all of us from Mr. Bub to take a vacation on his farm in Dietershahn in the Röhn. Bub had been father's orderly during the last World War, and they had maintained a rather remote relationship through all these years.

The invitation was very tempting. It would not be far to travel, and we would be away from the nightly air-raid alarms and able to eat our fill for a short time. The only obstacle was that mother, as a Jewess, was not permitted to leave the city.

Father sent me to see Dr. Stauffer, who had not been drafted because of his age and who is on friendly terms with father. Dr. Stauffer immediately understood the situation and wrote a certificate which stated that father was in poor health and should leave the city for a rest under care of his wife. I went to the Gestapo with this certificate.

Neither Baab nor Gabbusch was there. Instead, a young blond man with a vulgar expression received me. He kept grinning at me in a rather familiar way and agreed, all too willingly, to issue mother a travel permit.

When the conversation ended, he followed me into the corridor where I noted he wore black SS trousers and shining jackboots.

He stood in front of me with legs apart and swaying hips, while his somewhat slanting eyes inspected me from head to toe. The provocative grin on his face grew broader. He said in a very uneducated Frankfurt accent, "And if you ever need a certificate again, come to me. I am now the official in charge. My name is Schmitt — Heini Schmitt.

"And when will you come back?"

I hedged. "I don't know exactly, probably towards the end of June."

The memory of my conversation with this repulsive creature almost sours my vacation, which is otherwise peaceful and relaxing. I feel like an insect, wriggling helplessly in a spider's web. Someday the spider will appear and will attend to me. . .

June 21, 1944

We must return home day after tomorrow. The quiet and the food here have done all of us good. Both of my parents have better color. Father gained a little weight, but he needs many more pounds before his collars will fit again.

During these weeks we were surrounded by people who tried to pamper us, surrounded by blue sky, green valleys and hills. Occasionally we took walks together or I sat alone at the edge of a field and let my thoughts float with the white summer clouds.

I recalled the destroyed city of Frankfurt, which seemed so far away from here that it was almost unreal. But the dead underneath the ruins are very real. I remembered the little Rodenhauer searching for one of her mother's employees who lived in the old city. She went to the cemetery several times and saw horribly charred and mutilated bodies. She told me, "You know, some of them are shrivelled up so small," her hands indicated the size of a little child.

The authorities speak of "the fallen" when they mention bomb victims. Fallen? They are charred, roasted, and killed; and there is nothing heroic about it. The small children who could not flee with their parents and slowly suffocated or were burned to death by phosphorus, certainly did not want to be heroic sacrifices, but wanted to live.

Mothers of all countries unite and protect the embryo; don't sin by not creating life, otherwise what else could you later offer to emperors, chancellors or presidents?

June 25, 1944

Last night I passed my trial by fire, from which I did not emerge purified but horribly soiled.

When we came home day before yesterday, Friday afternoon,

325

our maid told me that a man had called several times to inquire when we would return. He did not leave his name.

We had just sat down to supper when the telephone rang. The dirty old witch who is now our maid winked at me. "It's him again."

I answered the phone.

"Good evening, Miss Schroeder. Did you have a nice vacation?" He laughed. "This is Heini Schmitt speaking."

My heart sank when he suggested I go out with him tomorrow night.

As agreed, I met Schmitt at Opernplatz, opposite the Esplanade. In high spirits, he told me we were going to the Schumann Theater where we would meet another couple. Relieved by this disclosure, I tried to appear happy and lighthearted.

The restaurant on the upper floor of the theater was poorly attended. We found a table on the balcony overlooking the damaged Bahnhofsplatz.

A few minutes later, an SS man with a young blonde girl appeared at the balcony door. Schmitt stood up and beckoned to the couple.

I looked at Schmitt with a frozen smile on my face. He had combed his carefully parted blond hair with water, so it was smooth and neat. His profile with a slightly curved nose, sculptured lips, and hard chin reminded me of an advertising poster for the Waffen SS, on which a steel helmet caps a martial profile. Only the forehead is a little too short and the blue eyes cut too obliquely. Looking at Bahnhofsplatz down below, I wished I could disappear among the busy people rushing back and forth there, instead of sitting here at a table with a Gestapo and an SS man.

As it became dark, an elderly waiter asked us to go inside. They had to close the balcony doors because of the blackout.

"How much longer are you open?" Schmitt asked in his dreadful Frankfurt accent with a somewhat too sonorous voice.

"We close in half an hour."

Schmitt conferred with his friend; and they decided to go to Schmitt's place. At this point I learned that he is married and has two children. The family is evacuated to the Taunus region.

Shortly afterwards in Schmitt's spacious living room, we drank wine and had an empty conversation.

Unobtrusively I let my eyes wander over the large, wretchedly furnished room. The Gestapo had probably assigned this former Jewish apartment to Schmitt, who had the furniture as well as his wife and children moved away from this bomb endangered city. There remained a couch, a shabby arm chair, two wicker chairs from the balcony, a table and a shaky floor lamp. The room appeared cold and empty.

It was after midnight when the SS man and his girl left. I also stood up.

"No," ordered Schmitt. "You stay."

The couple had barely left the apartment when he sat on the arm rest of my chair, putting his left arm around my shoulder: "I really like you . . ."

I did not move.

When his right hand slipped into the neck of my dress and reached for my breast, I made a rejecting movement.

"Just as you wish" he said with the hint of a laugh, while a metallic sharpness crept into his voice. "I mean — you are familiar with the situation your mother is in, and I am the one who puts the transport lists together. You understand: — *I* —"

He got up from the armrest of my chair.

For a moment I was petrified. Then I stood up silently. Without looking at him I undressed and let my dress and underwear drop to the floor. Then I stood motionless.

Now he stared at me without a word. His eyes wandered slowly and appraisingly over my body. With a gloating sneer, he walked around me and kept silent — silent — silent.

I heard him light a cigarette behind me; there was also the sound of a wineglass being replaced on the table.

Then he stood in front of me again, a cigarette between his lips, and stared provocatively at my thighs. It was clear that he wanted to break my silence; but I stood motionless with my lips pressed together, although the heavy silence strained my nerves.

Suddenly he threw the half-smoked cigarette into the ashtray and pointed commandingly to the couch.

As I lay down, he ordered, "Raise your knees and spread your legs."

Without taking his eyes off me, he slowly unbuttoned his shirt and trousers and placed his things on the wicker chair.

Later, when I started to get dressed, he said, "Just a moment. I got your file today. I must say! Any other German with such a record would have been hanged long ago.

327

"Your father has a file all to himself. To crown matters, he landed in prison for falsifying medical certificates.

"Your mother altered legal documents. Everyone knows he must not change an official document. It is a mystery to me that she was released. And you are previously convicted as an enemy of the state.

"I will keep my eyes on you, and what I see depends on you. Well, you can finish dressing now." While he returned to the table and his bottle of wine, he said incidentally, "What did the English broadcasting station say yesterday?"

I closed the last hook of my dress and replied without haste, "We haven't had a radio for many years."

With the wineglass in his hand, he turned towards me. "I never claimed you had a radio, only that you listen to English radio broadcasts."

He lit the stairs for me with a flashlight and as I pushed past him to go out, he said tersely, "Tomorrow at the same time."

The first dawn of the new day appeared afar on the horizon as I dragged myself home. Sleep, I thought, nothing but sleep and no more thinking. A mixture of shame, revenge, humiliation and hatred, hatred, hatred seethed in me. Tomorrow the same thing would be repeated — and the day after tomorrow and the day after . . .

As noiselessly as possible I unlocked the apartment door.

At the same moment mother rushed at me: "Lili dear! Oh God, child! Where have you been so long? We were terribly worried about you!"

She drew me through the open door into my parents' bedroom, where father sat, fully dressed, at the edge of his bed with a book in his hand. He looked at me absentmindedly, his thoughts still with his reading.

"What's the matter?" I asked irritably.

"We were so worried," mother repeated, still almost insane with fright. "I must confess — I went to the Rodenhauers after midnight to ask if they knew him. They did not know anything about him, but Mrs. Rodenhauer thought I had better not call the police."

I stared at her aghast. "The police? And you told the Rodenhauers who I was with? Have you gone completely mad? You . . ."

I turned on my heels and without another word, went to my room.

July 9, 1944

One no longer sees laughing faces on the street. The people look miserable and exhausted, and crawl like ghosts in worn-out, patched clothing through the destroyed city. Father faces his patients during office hours, depressed and helpless. With few exceptions they all show the consequences of many years of malnutrition.

Yesterday evening when I returned from my visit with Schmitt, father opened the door for me. He looked at me lovingly. Then he stared at my thick swollen legs; the ankles had disappeared. He automatically felt my pulse, which beat regularly, and then reached for a leg. Deep marks remained where his fingers had pressed. "Hunger edema," he said with relief. Why should I not have edema from malnutrition? Most women become bloated by inadequate diets, while the men are walking skeletons in too big suits.

The jokes become more malicious, and morale increasingly desperate. Fear of the knout grows proportionally with the use of it. The more hopeless the situation becomes, the harder the punishments are against so-called alarmists and grumblers. Because so many soldiers fall at the front and thousands of civilians are killed at home by bombs, one is no longer petty in regard to human life and the death sentence is generously meted out for defeatists and those who listen to foreign radio broadcasts.

When, oh when, will it be five minutes past twelve?

August 2, 1944

At least four times a week I put on a summer dress and leave the house in the evening. To mother's fearful question, where could I be reached in an emergency, I said, "Nowhere."

"But if there should be an attack?"

"Then I will be home again."

"You surely can tell me where you are going?" she persisted.

"I have learned the hard way that I can't, and would appreciate it if we could avoid these unpleasant debates."

Every time I go the short distance to Schmitt's apartment, I hesitate before I take the last steps. How often have I sworn not to go and somehow to free myself from this affair. Countless times I did not turn into his street but went further around the block, then finally gave in. Mother's life or death depends on whether Schmitt is satisfied with me, a cheap substitute in his wife's absence. He, Heini Schmitt, the son of the lowest post office worker, revels in being so powerful that he can have the daughter of a well-known physician as his mistress — and she does whatever he demands of her.

Meanwhile I have become acquainted with the glitter in his eyes and the metallic sound, which creeps into his voice — the warning signals I am afraid of.

I walked around the block once more and contemplated whether a woman can feign love for an individual she loathes, without being punished? But why should I rack my brain? If I do not want mother to be murdered, I have to pay the purchase price. And I am that price.

A bit out of breath I arrived at Schmitt's. "Excuse my lateness. I had to drive my father to see a patient."

Schmitt accepted this frequently used excuse with a silent nod. He did not ask, as usual, where the patient lived and what was wrong with him, and he gave a distracted impression.

Finally I asked, "What is the matter with you, Heini? Is something wrong?"

"I don't know. One Jew didn't come today. Of all people, just the one with whom we always had our fun."

I stiffened inwardly. With great effort, I smiled and asked, "What kind of fun?"

"Oh, we had him recite poetry."

"Poetry?"

"Yes, he used to be an actor before he had the movie theater; and he could recite so nicely."

"Movie theater" rang a bell. I pictured the fine, slender gentleman who always greeted me with an almost old-fashioned courtesy at the Saalburg Cinema. Impeccably dressed with gray spats over his black shoes, he stood in the lobby of his small empire and surveyed his guests; while his Aryan wife sat in the office and occasionally looked up from her desk through the open door.

"How often did you have him come?"

"I don't know; five or six times."

"Why?"

"Oh, we had all the Jews come for a while."

We had heard about it. A number of elderly Jewish men were forced to come to the Gestapo every morning. Usually they were kept standing in the corridors for many hours, and were then ordered to return the next day.

Heini Schmitt was obviously uncomfortable. If such a criminal has a conscience at all, it made him uneasy today.

I nodded. "You are speaking about Mr. Landes?"

It gave him a shock when I spoke the name.

"And today he didn't come?" I persisted.

"No. Also he didn't return home. We checked with his wife. She said he left punctually as always." He grinned embarrased. "He will come again."

"No," I said somewhat more sharply than I had intended. "Heini, from what I know of Mr. Landes, he won't come again. In his quiet manner, he left home and went straight into the Main River."

"Do you really believe that?"

I looked at him. This young fellow with a dumb, primitive face, who held life-and-death power over hundreds of people. He and his companions would never understand to what humiliations they exposed this man. Through what hell had Landes been chased, before he decided he would rather go into the Main River than to the Gestapo? Now his sufferings are over. What an irony that a gentle, quiet Jew caused this Gestapo man remorse.

The next evening one of my first questions was "Did you learn anything about Mr. Landes?"

"No. Besides, I don't give a shit! Do you hear me? I don't give a shit!"

His voice sounded metallic and his half-closed eyes glittered mean. He forgave neither himself nor me that I had seen him in a moment of weakness bordering on humanity. I had to pay for it.

"In your place I wouldn't worry so much about this dirty Jew. I looked at your file again today. What a fine family — you and your parents! In your place I wouldn't talk so big! Or do you believe you are safe now? Do you believe that?" he screamed. "Answer me!"

"No, Heini," I whispered meekly.

"Then get undressed!" he commanded, and abused me brutally.

331

Today during office hours we learned that Mr. Landes' body was pulled from the Main River early this morning.

August 26, 1944

At first I did not want to admit it; it is so incredibly horrible. But there is no longer any doubt. I am pregnant. I can't think clearly any more and am close to madness.

September 16, 1944

Last Tuesday we again had a bad air attack. Darmstadt was heavily bombed the night before, so Frankfurt send help there, which was now lacking here.

Shortly after the 'all clear' we heard the rumor that the Westend and Bockenheim were heavily hit.

We were in father's room; the cool autumn wind carried the familiar burnt smell through the broken window. Father rubbed his cold hands. His eyes seemed huge in the weak light of the kerosene lamp, whose glass chimney was broken. He said thoughtfully: "We should go and check on Etta."

We set out, passed old bomb craters, detoured around rubble heaps, and headed towards the fire glowing in the west. In passing I noticed that Bernd's house still stood and the Gestapo was untouched.

Flames shot up from the upper stories of the house where the Steinbachs occupied the second floor. We ran to Etta and began to carry all movable objects down the stone back stairs. I deliberately chose heavy objects which I could drag only with extreme effort. Mother finally cried, "Lili! Be careful, child, and don't get a rupture!"

Hysterical laughter tickled my throat. A hernia, I thought, and looked around for something heavy. But all my exertions caused was pain in my arm muscles.

Later we took Etta to our apartment, and sat in the music room, wrapped in our coats. No tears, no word of complaint came from the lips of this admirable woman whose two sons are missing, who does not know whether her husband in Russia is alive, and who now had also lost her home.

The next day she reported her damages and received quarters

332

in emergency housing in Miltenberg am Main. I took her to the Hanau train station with several suitcases.

Apart from the usual destruction, a bunker was hit this time. As far as I can remember, the bunker in Mühlgasse in Bockenheim was the first one built here. Its designers still lacked experience concerning concrete and foundation resilience; it had not withstood a two-ton aerial mine. The direct hit cost 172 lives; ninety seriously injured people were saved. In addition, our winged angels of death achieved a spontaneous explosion of popular sentiment. The people's soul seethed — though this time without the help of Goebbels or other wire-pullers. That a bunker which was considered absolutely safe became a mass grave unchained an indescribable fury and indignation. Fear that other bunkers could cave in under the bombs unleashed a mild hysteria, which made people forget to watch their words. Pent-up hatred vented itself. Neither the police nor the Nazis intervened. Were they afraid, or had they deliberately opened a valve? After all, they could not lock up the whole population.

Things can't be all that rosy amongst the troops either. Himmler announced several days ago that in the future all relatives of deserters would be shot. If such measures had to be taken, the number of deserters must already be considerable.

October 1, 1944

Schmitt's hand was on my bosom when the sirens sounded, and he didn't want to take me with him into the air-raid shelter. Since I would rather die on the street than beside this Gestapo swine in the cellar, I ran for home.

Individual searchlights scanned the night sky. I heard the buzzing of airplanes and saw the signal flares fall as I reached our house. I opened the apartment door as the first bombs fell. The next strike was so violent that I threw myself flat on the hall floor. Then I ran into the cellar where I was received with relief. Explosions raged around us without interruption. Something rumbled above us in our apartment. During this hellish spectacle, we heard the shrill, incessant ring of our telephone.

When after three and a half hours, we were finally able to leave the protective cellar, we determined with relief that our house still stood. The windows, which had been approved and installed in physician's offices, lay in thousands of fragments in the apartment. The telephone receiver had been blown from its cradle, and the ringing stopped when we replaced it. Our heavy grandfather clock was pushed into the middle of the foyer. The shutters in my room hung crookedly and half into the room, since they were not pulled up before the raid.

There was no electricity again, so we had to wait until morning to begin cleaning up. We were surrounded by a sea of fire. Even the old ruins were hit again and collapsed totally.

Barely forty-eight hours after this heavy attack, I was in the study talking to father, my arms resting on the back of a Gobelin armchair, when an uncanny roar sounded above us. Father involuntarily drew his head in, while I sank to my knees. The evil roaring buzz grew more distant and I emerged from behind the chair. We looked at each other perplexed and said simultaneously, "What was that?" A powerful strike sounded in the distance.

It was a glider bomb, a new British weapon. It had landed in Bornheim where it levelled eight houses, damaged ten heavily, fifteen moderately, and fifty slightly.

"Where is the retaliation?!" screamed the outraged people. "Why doesn't the Führer do anything?" They comprehend it now, the poor fools, that they were lied to from the beginning, but are now forced to hold out until final victory. Over and over again the people gather the bitter experience of being enticed by a politician with fantastic promises and elect him. Constantly and willingly they listen to these siren songs, which assure them a better future. When they finally understand the big lie, it is too late. Half sunk in mire, they will believe that the next charlatan will pull them out. Politicians profit by the stupidity and gullibility of the people, generation after generation.

In addition to the misery caused by the bombs, the food situation becomes increasingly precarious. Instead of fat we receive lean pork; and I suspect the pigs died of malnutrition since we are now eating its fodder. Flour, allotted by ration cards, is simply not available. The peasants refuse to bring potatoes to the cities because they are afraid for their horses. In reality they would be foolish to deliver their produce for worthless money, though they can get anything they demand for something edible. Gossip has it that on the farms even the cow sheds are covered with Persian car-

334

pets. I suspect this is true, since one piece from my hopechest after another lands with Mrs. Fischer, whose house still stands opposite ours. She has some peasant connections and exchanges my bed and table linen for sausage and bacon. Mother has no notion of my transactions. She is constantly speechless when in our direst need something suddenly appears on the table again. At the moment, even mother has given up hopes for my early marriage. For some time she has not showed me the treasures she accumulated for my future connubial bliss; else she would have found out that not much is left.

November 11, 1944

Today, when I look back on the months when there was no doubt that I was pregnant, they seem like an endless nightmare from which I could not awaken. In a trance I did my familiar work automatically, without forgetting for even a second what was taking place inside me. My last thought before falling asleep and my first when I awoke dealt with the monster who grew in me, procreated by a loathsome ruffian, a cold-blooded murderer. The myth of motherly love appearing with pregnancy is a lie, like so many other fairy tales. I hated the new life developing within me against my wishes, and I shuddered with disgust at myself. I was possessed by the idea of tearing it out of my body, but the tightly stretched skin over my swelling stomach seemed to mock me.

I swung between hopeful optimism and depression — where suicide appeared to be the only solution.

I secretly injected myself with high doses of hormone preparations, which was effective for many women, but not for me. I swallowed quinine until I became dizzy, but this was the only effect the tablets produced.

Exhausted, overtired, and hungry, I frequently caught myself dozing at the microscope. When my forehead touched the cold metal, I started to curse anew this hated thing within me.

Finally I plucked up the courage to turn trustfully to Dr. Fonrobert, whose care I was under for a food-related skin irritation. Dr. Fonrobert is unpolitical, and I knew he would not denounce me. But I was not prepared for the conversation which ensued. Although I tried to make it clear that a Gestapo man had forced the relationship on me, he simply would not believe me. He could not be dissuaded from the idea that I must love this man,

335

"otherwise a woman simply wouldn't do such a thing." I should bring my child into this world.

Thoughts on how to find a solution raced through my head. All the doctors we knew well were at the front, and father under no circumstances should learn about my condition. Whenever I thought of father in this connection, I remembered the large pistol he kept in his bedside table.

In the middle of my thoughts, mother said, "You no longer look well in slacks. You have grown too heavy."

In final desperation I staked everything on one card and went to Dr. Stauffer.

The kind-hearted eyes of the elderly doctor looked at me questioningly from beneath his handsome forehead and thick, white hair.

"Do you remember I was here last summer for a certificate for my father?" I began.

He nodded. "It served its purpose?"

"Yes. My mother was permitted to travel with my father." I hesitated and then took the most direct route. "The Gestapo official who issued the permit forced me to have an affair with him. I am pregnant."

"The pig!" he flared up. "That swine! Hopefully he is not ill and didn't infect you in addition to this."

While he examined me, he said reproachfully, "Why didn't you come to me sooner?"

"I didn't know . . ."

"At any rate we can't wait any longer. On Wednesday I have no office hours. Be here at two o'clock."

Awaking I felt myself being lifted up. Dr. Stauffer placed me cautiously on a sofa in his treatment room. "I must make a house call and I'll drive you home afterwards." He added emphatically, "Lie here until then, and please don't leave the room for any reason!"

I dozed until he returned.

"How do you feel?"

"Good," I said, still slightly dazed. I swung my legs over the sofa and sat up. Suddenly I realized what had happened. With a deep sigh of relief I said, "Dear doctor, you have no idea of how grateful I am!"

He sat at his desk. The dim light of the rainy afternoon fell

336

through a window, delineating the profile of his carved head.

"What do I owe you?" I asked.

His head turned towards me. "My dear child, it was so horrible, I don't ever want to hear of it again."

November 23, 1944

It seems to me as if I had returned from Hades to the living and my interest in my surroundings is reawakened.

The Heine quotation, which I heard from Karl's lips nine hundred and ninety-nine years ago in a less burdensome life when the Thousand Year Reich just began, comes frequently to my mind.

"The morning after, yet, you feel amazed.

The multitudes, who, yesterday, were drunk with zeal

And followed jubilant their rulers' cue,

Now sank into a deep and awful gloom

Caused by a hangover of a furious force."

Truly, the people are low spirited. Most of them scarcely remember the times of intoxication, when swollen with pride, they experienced the rise of the Greater German Empire; how they stood packed in the streets to listen to their Führer's words and later to military reports, roaring from the loud speakers, announced by Liszt's victory fanfares, which in his time rejoiced in the fall of the great Commander-in-chief, Napoleon.

Now the next dawn has arrived. The Greater German Reich becomes smaller and smaller; but nobody looks at the map to see that which was once briefly and gloriously conquered and is now lost again. The Führer once so understanding a father to his people, who thoughtlessly shed his children's blood, this Führer one barely hears speaking any more. The master race looks like a crowd of tramps, ragged and hollow cheeked. The victory fanfares have ceased since there are no longer victories to be announced. The tall houses from which they rang are no longer standing. They have collapsed into rubble and ashes, hiding the bones of those killed by bombs in their cellars.

The people are no longer interested in what happens at the front. They are seized by a deadly apathy, born from exhaustion and the length of the war. With the beginning of the sixth year of war, two months ago, one becomes tired of hearing about the sacrifices of battles which always lead to defeat. One merely wishes to

337

know whether a husband, son or brother is alive at the front and still has all his limbs. Military communiqués are irrelevant.

Everyone is so overcome by his own personal worries that he no longer cares about the fate of Germany. It is far more important that one gets something to eat, that shoes will last a little longer, and above all whether there will be an air raid. Will we have a roof over our heads tomorrow, or even be alive?

Only a small group of fanatics now speak, as before, about a final victory. Shrugging their shoulders, the people lethargically accept the fact that the Allies have landed in Normandy, the eastern regions are lost, that not one place is left to the Germans for which they fought so bitterly under the pitiless African sun. While the fanatics assume the Führer has only decoyed the Allies: an ingenious chess move. Afterwards he will drive them all into the sea. At the last moment, when the enemy is lulled into false security, Hitler will strike back with a powerful blow and lead us to a final victory.

These diehards still believe in the wonder weapon which will shoot all the way to America and destroy the skyscrapers. Their eyes glow; they cannot admit or bear the thought of a defeat, and speak with autosuggestive enthusiasm about the great things which will occur before a final victory. They remind me of the man who whistles loudly in the graveyard to drown out his fears.

December 1, 1944

The end is approaching with giant steps. In October, the "Volksturm" was called up with no upper age limit; they are men with physical defects, who were not suitable for combat service, but could still carry a gun and serve if needed. Simultaneously, those born in 1928 and 1929 took physical examinations. These small fifteen- and sixteen-year-old pictures of misery would receive four-week, then six-week training in premilitary camps. Will Hitler really use these children as cannon fodder?

In the middle of November, the "Volksturm" was placed under oath. Hitler called the people, to the last man, for the final victory! Children and old men will be sacrificed. Then he promised to fight until five minutes past twelve.

If only I knew what time it is now! I am desperately waiting for a final Allied victory. Above all, I am concerned for my parents.

During one of the last nights, I heard an unusual noise that awakened me. I started up, and thought I had been dreaming. Then it became clear that the doorbell was ringing. I threw a coat on and ran from the room just in time to see the plump figure of Dr. Dorfmann disappear into my parents' bedroom. As Chief of Surgery, Dr. Dorfmann had worked with father for twenty-seven years in the Bürgerhospital.

Shivering and fearful I sat on the bench in the foyer until Dr. Dorfmann reappeared.

The kindly eyes embedded in masses of fat looked at me anxiously. "Your father's hernia has strangulated again. I have reduced it with great difficulty. This can't be allowed to happen again. You must use your influence on him. He can't delay the operation any longer."

Father's hernia belongs to the symptoms which are as common today as starvation edema. Because of enormous emaciation, the abdominal wall loses its normal cushion of fat. Especially in elderly people the muscles no longer join closely and an intestinal loop squeezes through the gap.

Naturally I spoke with father, who understands his situation very clearly. But "an operation is out of the question. If anything happens to me, what will become of mother? Her Aryan husband is her only protection."

Again, I have a hearing at the Gestapo. It began last week with a summons.

Two unfamiliar officials sat opposite me at their desks, which were pushed together. The one who questioned me took down my personal data first, and then asked about Wolf. Astonished, I told him I didn't know much more about my brother than we learned through the Red Cross letters we receive about twice a year.

"But you know he works in the White House?"

"In the White House?" I repeated, and almost laughed. "I hardly believe they employ emigrants there. As far as I know he does social work."

"Aha — welfare. You don't have a high opinion of our money, what?"

"I beg your pardon?"

"You —"

Someone stuck his head in the door and called my tormentor out.

He had barely left the room when the other man looked up. He was an older, quiet man, without a uniform. During the interrogation he had stared at a file without even turning a page. "Are you Dr. Bernhard Schroeder's daughter?"

I nodded.

An almost radiant expression covered his face. "I was once a patient in his ward."

His eyes returned to the folder when his colleague returned. "Where were we now? Oh yes. What do you think of our money? You obviously believe it isn't worth anything anymore?"

"I don't understand what you mean. One still needs money to purchase food and pay rent."

"Miss Schroeder, you ought not give such flippant answers. Or do you think you can take such liberties because you have special connections here?"

I was silent and completely confused. Someone had denounced me. But who? And for what?

"What do you have to say to that?"

"I don't know what you are insinuating," I replied perplexed.

"Then go home now and think it over. You will hear from us again."

Saturday afternoon Erwin Süss arrived. He is an old acquaintance whose Jewish father and Aryan mother live in the ghetto. Süss is conscripted to work out of town during the week in a machine factory. Since the Gestapo preferably appear in the ghetto early Sunday morning to fetch male half-breeds to unload coal, shovel snow and perform other such labors, Süss came to us. For the past several weeks he sleeps Saturday night in our apartment and visits his parents late Sunday morning.

He listened to my story and then questioned me closely and systematically. With whom had I talked during the last weeks? What had I said? Who knows I have a brother in America? He repeatedly said, "Think carefully, with whom have you talked? Who knows you fairly well?" Who — when — what?

My head spun.

After a long time he said, "I know who it was — your neighbor Buchholz."

"Impossible!" I rejected the suspicion.

Buchholz, whose family evacuated to Spessart, had taken his photographic equipment. He had asked me whether he could use

340

my equipment to make some enlargements. He came several times and we made prints together.

"Nothing is impossible," Süss said firmly.

"Why should he denounce me? What does he gain by it?"

"We will find out later. If it wasn't Buchholz, who then?"

Süss tightened the net around Buchholz. Buchholz knows I have a brother in Washington. He saw a picture of Heini Schmitt in SS uniform, when he appeared unexpectedly one evening. Since he is an engineer, I asked his advice about purchasing a radio, which I could get and which would represent more stable value than money.

Ernst Süss said with satisfaction, "Now we know who it is. Go to your lawyer. Perhaps he can help you."

The next afternoon I saw Buchholz on the street and beckoned to him. He inquired how I was.

"Fine, so far as one can claim when involved with the Gestapo."

He looked at me without surprise or dread.

"Someone denounced me."

"Denounced?" Not a muscle moved in his face when he asked, "Who would do such a thing?"

"I have also asked myself this, Mr. Heinz Buchholz. It must be a very base character."

January 3, 1945

I noticed with astonishment that over a month has passed since my last diary entry. Exhaustion and the energy required to sustain the will to live are so great, one loses all sense of time. One air raid follows on the heels of the last, food grows scarcer, and one staggers like a sleepwalker through the daily routine. One lies down in bed partly dressed, conscious that the night's sleep will be interrupted by sirens or bombs; and even this sequence is out of balance. Occasionally bombs fall first, followed by the warning sirens.

Christmas and New Years passed without songs and without sounds.

During the last days of the old year, there was a heavy air attack at noon. A munitions train exploded at the main freight yard; a hospital train with seriously wounded and disabled

341

soldiers stood next to it. Numbed by their own misery, the people shrug their shoulders unemotionally and return to salvage work.

The high point of the season should have been Hitler's speech. Our Führer had been so invisible and silent that the wildest rumors circulated about his death. Therefore, because of the pressures of circumstance, he gave a New Year's speech. He stated that "my belief in the future of our people is unshakable. On whom Providence has imposed such severe tests it has called to the highest tasks." These words sounded hollow to the people who only vegetate. Secretly in a corner of their hearts they waited for a positive comforting word. However, the wonder weapon was not mentioned, and the speech sounded lame. That our Führer thanked God for his help in this hopeless situation does not improve matters. I suspect word has spread, meanwhile, that God fights with the Allies, since he is always on the side of those who own the best arsenal.

January 20, 1945

Meanwhile I saw Mr. Eissner because of my denunciation. I went to his private residence; at the place where his office used to be is a gigantic crater.

The attorney listened attentively. "You don't have much to use to defend yourself, since it is simply statement against statement. Even if the man is not a party member, he is probably politically irreproachable." He reflected, "There is only one possibility. We have to try to make him appear untrustworthy. I have a detective on hand, with whom I work frequently. I will set him on Buchholz's trail immediately."

The detective brought astonishing results. In the firm where Buchholz works, another employee had a diamond ring stolen which turned up in Buchholz's desk drawer. Nobody could prove anything directly, but he is a prime suspect.

Eissner was elated. He beamed at me. "Now you have a trump card you can play at a suitable moment." He became silent and asked after a pause, "Could he be after your photographic equipment?"

The next day I had to report to the Gestapo, but came early to call on Gabbusch before the interrogation.

He received me with an expressionless face.

I came directly to the point. "Mr. Gabbusch, I need your

help. I have been denounced." I didn't get any further.

Gabbusch's cyanotic face turned bluish. "And you saw fit to brag about your acquaintance with me, nenene?"

I stared at him with my mouth open and then fought against a fit of laughter. I was so embroiled in the Schmitt affair that Gabbusch had not even entered my mind.

He became more enraged. "You boasted about your good relations at the Gestapo. That can only refer to me!"

On edge and under great stress, the humor of this grotesque situation struck me anew; however, I pulled myself together. "Mr. Gabbusch, do you think I am so idiotic? Now, please listen to me for a moment."

"To drag even me into this whole thing!"

It then occurred to me that behind his apparent anger he was hiding a trembling, deadly fear.

"Mr. Gabbusch, I assure you that the whole denunciation is based on purest fantasy."

He looked at me directly for the first time.

"Just as my brother isn't employed in the White House, so I don't have any connections in the Gestapo. This is all pure fabrication and has absolutely nothing to do with you."

"I mean," he began again, "I will not tolerate that my name appears there, nenene."

"Was your name stated? No. That is scarcely possible. Please believe me. This whole denunciation rests on a single lie."

"Why did you come to me again?" he scolded.

"Because I wanted to ask you to see to it that I am not kept here today."

"So that you can boast again afterwards about your connections?"

He became angry again, and I lost my patience. The rumor that the eastern border regions were already evacuated gave me a feeling of security and peace. "Mr. Gabbusch," I said sharply, "it is probably clear to you that the war has been completely lost."

The deadly fear was obvious in his eyes.

"You help me now," I said firmly, "and I will think about you later, when you need my help."

The whole man trembled as he stared at his desk and nodded silently.

"The morning after . . ." I thought as I knocked on the door of the officer who summoned me.

343

The questioning which followed was practically a repetition of the last one. I was reproached that I wanted to buy an expensive radio on the grounds that money no longer had any value and that one could not buy anything with it. I pointed to the obvious lack of logic in this accusation, and dared to raise doubts about the credibility of the denouncer, whose name was finally stated. I proposed that they inquire about the character of this man at his office.

Officials came into the office during the interrogation, rushed out again, and placed notes in front of the interrogator. Finally I was released with the comment that they would question Buchholz on the basis of my testimony.

I breathed the air of freedom with relief. Slowly strolling home through the cold winter day I reflected that it was now a matter of a race with death for me.

Although the Nazis are in a desperate situation, they still try to catch and destroy as many of their enemies as possible. The old "stab-in-the-back" legend was resurrected in a somewhat changed form. The Gestapo's justified fears are paired with powerless rage and feelings of revenge.

I thought of the small Browning father had given me last summer, familiarizing me with its use and of the potassium cyanide with which he had provided himself, mother and me. He wanted to prevent our ever being helplessly at the mercy of the Gestapo or the SS like so many others in our situation had been.

I knew the war could not last years; it was a matter of months, perhaps only weeks. Would it not be ironical if I had to take cyanide so close to the end?

February 8, 1945

I could not find out if Heini Schmitt knows anything about my proceedings at the Gestapo. Neither he nor I ever mentioned it. Moreover, I see him less frequently, since he discovered there are other half-breeds whose love he can barter for the life of their Jewish parent. Even he probably has doubts about the victorious conclusion of the war and takes whatever he can get, enjoying life according to his primitive tastes.

Nurse Ruth lives in the ghetto and is relatively well informed about what goes on. She told me a while ago that she knows three half-Jewesses who visit Schmitt regularly and have orgies in his apartment.

344

I am grateful that under the new arrangement I have to go to him only once, occasionally twice a week. These evenings I am humble and obedient, and try not to annoy him, lest I destroy at the last moment what I have built up with months of humiliation and bitter sacrifices. The closer we come to the end, the more my fears for mother increase.

February 11, 1945

Today two people were beheaded. Both offenders committed the crime of listening to foreign radio broadcasts and were denounced. The newspaper carried a laconic headline: TWO TRAITORS LESS.

Fear, terror, and oppression assume more lurid forms daily. The shadows of violence spread a cover over us, under which we are suffocating.

The last months of the Thousand Year Reich will be the most horrible ones. The intoxication of power must be fully enjoyed once more and a senseless orgy of violence celebrated again — the last satanic triumph of those who are doomed and know it. They can rage unchecked one last time, with all the cruelties only man can devise. For us only horror remains.

Father bent over the table and stared rigidly at the article: "Axed to death?"

But was it not always this way? How many people were condemned to death by the Emperor during the last weeks of World War I, when the ground already shook under his feet? With iron discipline, he indulged in his divine rights the last few weeks to decree the death penalty.

"What did you say?"

I must have thought aloud and did not know whether father had understood my words. He stared at the paper; his hand rested on the article as if he wanted to stop the words. But it was too late. The men are no longer alive; they were — beheaded. The orgy of horrors has begun — Hitler's last stake in a lost game.

Father's hand slowly released the newspaper, and said as he left the room, "You can't compare the Emperor with Hitler. The Kaiser wanted to save Germany; Hitler will destroy it."

The words no longer sounded convincing, and were spoken in the voice of one whose imperial dreams sank into the same ruins in which the Third Reich will end.

Hitler's barbarity has been concealed until now behind penitentiary walls and concentration camp barbed wire; now it openly assaults the whole country.

The party members, brown-shirted, half petty bourgeois, half beasts, want to anesthetize their impotence against the hopeless end with the intoxication of their still-present omnipotence. Their erstwhile great goals lay buried in the ruins of the cities. The stage thunder of the master race dies away, their players remove their makeup, and reveal themselves as a group of miserable lackeys who gather for their last great appearance and outdo themselves in vulgarity and brutality. The base instincts, unleashed, rule the day, a day which may be the last one for this system of governmental terror.

But fear also sits in their throats and they don't want to quit. Since human life has no value, the Nazis murder every suspect, kill small boys for cowardice, and hang soldiers from the trees as deserters. This way they hope to gain one more day. One day of life for them — a day of hell for us.

February 20, 1945

Fear — fear — fear; will it ever leave me?

A persistent rumor circulates that the last Jews would be transported, now — at five minutes before twelve.

Schmitt had not called me, and I knew he usually disappeared over the weekend to an "alternative office" in Kronberg. So I mustered up my courage, went to his apartment Saturday morning, and timidly rang the doorbell. The next moment he stood in front of me.

"Well!" he said unpleasantly. "What do you want here?"

"I hadn't heard anything from you and happened to be in the neighborhood." I followed him into the kitchen.

An open suitcase, filled to the brim with files, lay on the floor. He was packing objects spread out on the kitchen table in a large briefcase which stood on a chair, the flap supported by the chair back. These preparations seemed to be planned for more than a weekend.

Schmitt reached for the thick leather case which held his revolver and weighed it in his hand while he bit his lower lip thoughtfully. Suddenly he stared at me. "Do you remember old Landes, the actor who jumped into the Main?"

His hand with the heavy revolver case moved up and down,

346

and I froze with fear. "Many will follow Landes now." He laughed. "They will drown like rats in the Main."

The revolver disappeared in his briefcase with the other things he threw in absentmindedly. Then he turned around and walked to the kitchen window, which looked at the back wall of the house next door.

I didn't dare move. The quiet was sinister and oppressive; it paralyzed my muscles and thoughts. I waited for something.

Suddenly he turned with a diabolical grin on his dumb face. The cruel glint returned to his eyes, and he looked at me contemptuously. "Turn around." He spoke slowly and without emphasis.

I stood with my back to him, heard him walk back and forth, move objects around. Seconds crawled like hours. Then something fell from the table and rolled past my feet.

"Pick it up !" he commanded.

I bent over.

He said in a calm and ice-cold voice, "Stoop properly. Legs apart, the upper part of your body bent forwards."

I just extended my hand for the roll of film, when he lifted my skirt and hit me between the legs with the edge of his palm. I lost my balance and my face struck the gas stove.

"Direct hit!" he roared.

For a moment everything went black. Then I picked up the film and placed it on the table without a word.

A smug grin spread over his face. He pointed to the case on the floor. "Those are the transport lists. I struck your mother's name from all of them. The others received their cards today." He shut the lid with his foot.

I left the apartment, stumbled down the stairs, and ran around the corner away from the house.

Trembling, I leaned against a wall until I calmed down. Then I inched toward home with weak knees.

Mother opened the door before I could unlock it. "Lili!" she pounced on me. "Mrs. Stäubchen, the Ebinent, and Mrs. Reuter received postcards for the transport."

I leaned against the door.

"I always warned them not to sign anything!" mother said knowingly.

"Who said they signed anything?"

"But they must have—" She stopped short. "What happened to you?"

"I stumbled and fell in the rubble."

"But how did it happen?"

I went to my room and lay down on the couch. She ran after me. "Don't you feel well?"

"Yes, I feel fine and am happy that you didn't sign anything," I answered irritated. "And now leave me alone for a few minutes."

Offended, she left the room.

February 26, 1945

Everything is in a state of total disintegration. Refugees from East Prussia and Silesia fleeing the Russians stream deeper into the country to be greeted by American and British bombs. I have no idea where these miserable people are lodged and how they are provisioned. Uncle Franz, who fled Frankfurt with his wife long ago, comes to mind fleetingly. What would he say now? That our Führer did not want this, that our Führer did not know this? Our Führer, who promised his people the skies and gave them hell.

People's faces take on a dull, almost animal expression. They can not satisfy even the most basic needs of life; they live for the present, without room for hope or future. Nothing remains of their dreams, however modest they were. They live in bunkers, or like rats in sooty, filthy cellar holes under a ruin.

The air space over Germany belongs to the Allies, whose bombers search freely for their targets. In the countryside, the peasants are strafed at their work in the fields.

Old men in civilian suits are identified by armlets as members of the Volksturm; children are drilled in the art of fighting and murder.

I am too weak and tired to continue writing.

March 20, 1945

We are in the Taunus. Several undisturbed nights and some rest have worked wonders.

A wild time lies behind us. I will try to record it chronologically, since at home I did not seem to have the strength to keep my diary up to date.

During the last weeks we had air raids day and night, and spent the better part of our lives in the cellar. When no bombs fell for once, I ran to the Fischers under the protection of darkness, to listen to English broadcasts. The news was prefaced by four muffled drumbeats from Beethoven's Fifth Symphony. We were too battered to cheer, but found an unspeakable relief in the rapid Allied advance.

On the night of March 16th, General Eisenhower via English radio appealed to the population to leave Frankfurt, as there would be heavy artillery bombardment and he wanted to avoid further bloodshed among the civilian population. Every small suburb on the periphery of Frankfurt was specified by name to disclose the limits of the danger zone.

The Fischers said spontaneously, "We are going! What will you do?"

"That depends on my parents' condition."

When I returned to the air raid cellar, I considered what I should do. I watched my parents secretly and decided that both of them would be unable to endure this air raid shelter existence much longer without risking serious harm.

After the all clear, I informed them about Eisenhower's appeal, and stated categorically that we would leave Frankfurt.

They agreed, but asked, "Where should we go?"

"Pack your things while I go to the Dorfmanns. After that we will see."

I climbed on the bicycle the Rodenhauers had given me.

The Dorfmanns always stay up until the early morning hours, and were not even surprised when I appeared at their place after midnight. They had not heard the broadcast, and decided to pack immediately and leave Frankfurt with their daughters. I asked Dr. Dorfmann, then Chief of Surgery at the Bad Homburg hospital, if he would admit father who had contracted a bad cold in the drafty cellar.

"Of course" was the answer.

Father was relieved by the news, but asked with worry, "Where will you stay?"

"With Mama [Karl's stepmother]," I said with conviction.

We set out towards dawn. Since we did not dare use the car, our air-raid luggage was strapped to my bicycle, which I pushed.

We walked along Eckenheimerlandstrasse, through Preungesheim, past the prison and farther and farther away. The sun appeared in a clear cloudless sky. Walking became increasingly harder; the rest stops grew longer. With every sound, father turned around wistfully and hoped a car would pass and take us along. I tried not to let my parents notice that I had difficulty balancing the heavily laden bicycle and I spurred them on with the promise that we would find a train for Bad Homburg at the next place. We marched courageously to the next place, and to the one after that; and finally, there really was a train!

I gave my parents their knapsacks, but kept their blankets in which shoes, underwear, linen, jewelry and other things were rolled. They would wait for me at the terminal in Bad Homburg.

I went on, not paying any attention to where I was. Staring at the dusty highway, I pushed the loaded bicycle in the almost summery warmth. Lost in thought, I didn't notice a strange noise overhead. Suddenly I looked up and saw a low-flying plane. Instinctively I turned off the road and crouched against a single standing wall. The plane flew in a circle and withdrew temporarily. I stood up and saw I had found protection at the edge of a cemetery. The plane came again. What an ending, I thought, to be shot near a cemetery wall at the last moment. But it was not the end. The plane flew away and I straightened the bicycle and went on, while perspiration streamed down my face and every muscle in my body ached.

Finally I met my parents and father was admitted to the hospital.

Then mother and I went to Karl's mother's house. She looked embarrassed when she answered the doorbell. "I can't take you in, Lili child. Diana is here. Karl simply sent her here." Tears stood in her eyes. "It isn't my fault. I didn't want her."

She gave us the address of an acquaintance who accepted us willingly. This lady even provided us with a modest supper. The next noon, however, she appeared completely hysterical, and explained that we must move immediately. She had not known that mother was Jewish. We could not remain in her home under any circumstances.

After several detours, we landed with a painter's family in Obereschbach, and share a bed so small that mother's feet lay at my head and mine at hers. The husband is clearly prejudiced against us, although he has no idea whom he is sheltering. However, the moment he leaves the house, his wife cooks or bakes something for us.

Except for a few travel coupons and hard sausages which I

procured in January, we have nothing. I consider it dangerous for us to apply for new food ration cards under the prevailing circumstances.

So we are waiting for the Americans to come. For the first time in months I have time again to think about world history, so often formed by power-hungry fools whose deeds inflict all this tragedy upon mankind. Death, misery and terrifying suffering of human beings lies in their path to history. It is incredible that even in our time insanity can again celebrate such a triumph. Although it is five minutes past twelve, the fighting goes on. As Hitler once said: there is one word he never had heard of — to capitulate. Thus the devastation continues and the dead pile up. From the East the Russians push forward, from the West the Americans and large areas of Germany are already occupied. In the face of reality, the Nazis demanded nine days ago in their speeches for Memorial Day, to honor the dead by committing ourselves to the utmost exertion until victory is ours.

March 27, 1945

Yesterday morning I pedalled once more on my bicycle to Frankfurt to fetch the last canned goods from our apartment.

We had learned that the Gauleiter had meanwhile urged the population of Frankfurt to evacuate the city. Therefore I expected to meet the fleeing inhabitants; but the picture presented to me exceeded my imagination by far.

Towards me came the defeated army of believers, the remainder of the victorious proud master race. Their last belongings loaded on garden carts, wagons, wheelbarrows and baby carriages, they dragged themselves half starved, on ragged shoes, along Eschersheimerlandstrasse in the direction of the Taunus. They no longer marched in unison in orderly rows, but stumbled singly and in small groups towards a goal where food and lodging were promised them.

Slowly I passed this train of despair, which I encountered on this radiant spring day. At Dornbusch, in the middle of the long abandoned streetcar tracks, stood a bust of Hitler, his face turned towards the ravaged city. Someone had disgustedly rid himself of his idol's image, which probably had once occupied a place of honor in his home.

In our neighborhood, some of the stalwarts were inde-

351

fatigably at work. They dragged heavy stones and charred beams from the ruins into the street and erected barricades.

Near our home I met the old communist gardener, with whom I had often talked.

"What are the fools doing there?" I asked as I jumped down from my bicycle.

"Building antitank traps."

"What a joke," we exclaimed.

"In half an hour," he continued, "the Main bridges will be blown up."

As I returned to Obereschbach, I heard the muffled detonations behind me.

I can't ever remember such a warm radiant spring; however the nights are still bitterly cold.

I looked out of the kitchen window at the large meadow which begins at the opposite side of the street and fills the hollow of the valley until it reaches the woods far beyond.

The whole pasture was in motion. Thousands of Frankfurt citizens spent the cold night there. There was neither food nor lodgings for them, not even blankets or tents. One last time they had believed the promises. Now they run back and forth complaining and lost. These people, trained to obey orders, suddenly had no one to tell them what to do. Left to themselves, they were totally helpless.

I realized that one can guide people to good as well as to evil. It lies in the hands of every head of state to convert his obedient, civilized citizens into a band of criminals who murderously invade a foreign country, to which the patriots at home give their encouraging applause.

Casting one last look at these people running about in confusion like a startled flock of hens, I turned away somehow depressed. A vague question formed: is this really the end or will another nation assume the Nazi inheritance?

March 29, 1945

I am home again. A small, round bullet hole in my balcony door is the only evidence in our house of the battle for Frankfurt.

Yesterday I had a last hour to myself in the room which the Obereschbach couple had left to us. Mother had not returned yet from her visit with father, and I sat in front of the small table which we had pushed to the window, and tried to think about the

352

future. I looked out into the garden.

The trees and shrubs seemed to lose their colors and slowly turned into silhouettes, growing out of the mist, which rose from the meadow towards the dusky, silky spring sky. In a nearby bush a lonely blackbird sang a wistful song in the seemingly peaceful evening. From the distance the wind softly carried the rumble of artillery fire.

Darkness swallowed the landscape, and my eyes followed the soft light and shadows of a candle, to remain on my hands. I spread my fingers and looked at my dirty hands, disfigured by chillblains and roughened from hard work. Then I stared into space.

It had now come to pass. The day for which I yearned and waited all these years, which gave me the courage to hope and hold out against all reason, this day had come. The Americans had probably already entered Frankfurt at this hour, and the Nazis had vanished like evil spirits.

I was overcome by a feeling of infinite weariness. I felt very old and extinguished. The goal which I had fought for all these years was achieved: my parents had survived the Third Reich alive. For that I had lived. And now? What was my purpose now?

The man I love I have lost. In my old profession I have no interest at all. I can not imagine myself adjusting again to a normal middle class life.

The Nazis are gone and have taken my youth with them, have stolen twelve years of my life, ruined my health, and made a very different person of me than what I originally was supposed to have become.

I personally won the war but lost the peace, since I can not imagine a future any more and don't know what I should look forward to. I have no goal and am burned out.

As previously agreed upon, I bicycled this morning to Frankfurt with Marina, one of the Dorfmann daughters, to see if our homes were still inhabitable, and to arrange for gasoline to perhaps bring our parents back tomorrow.

We pedalled again through a warm sunny day, but the highway was deserted. From all the houses we passed hung white cloths, tablecloths, bed linen, and towels of all sizes.

As we rode through the suburbs of Frankfurt, we suddenly had the sensation of being in the center of a marching army. The long Eschersheimerlandstrasse was populated only with Americans. They stood together in small groups, sat on large trucks and in jeeps; tanks were rattling over the cobblestones and heavy planes roared overhead. The civilian population seemed to have disappeared from the earth's surface; only the white sheets streaming from houses and windowless ruins gave evidence that people were living there.

In this chaos my eyes were caught by a solitary figure sitting alone on the remnant of a little wall which had been robbed of its fence. Something about his wild gray hair and beard seemed familiar to me.

I called Marina to wait for me and dismounted from my bicycle. "Mr. Pötz!"

He did not react.

I leaned my bike against a tree and looked at the thoroughly exhausted man who did not seem to notice what was going on around him.

Placing my hand gently on his shoulder, I said cautiously: "Mr. Pötz?"

He lifted his head and looked at me but I had the feeling that his thoughts were far away because no sign of recognition appeared on his face.

My hand still rested on his shoulder as I asked softly: "Dear friend, is there anything I can do for you?"

He frowned and listened strainiously to the sound of my voice. Slowly some life returned to his dull eyes. "So," he pondered, "my young friend has come back from the past . . ."

Astonished, he stroked with a dirty hand over my arm, as if to convince himself that I was not an apparition.

Tired and with unspeakable sadness he said: "It is all over, my dear. Only the ruins are left — and the memory of the dead."

His hand drew a large circle, which enclosed far more than the ruins and the few standing houses in our view.

While he drew himself up with effort, the shadow of the old Pötz seemed to flicker. "Here, my child," he said in a tone which sounded like the echo of his former superior irony: "You see the white sheets streaming from all the windows? The white flags?" He started to laugh: "The white flag, my young friend, is the only one on earth for which no government demands from its subjects to defend it with the weapon in hand."

He withdrew into himself again and murmured, lost in thought: "The white flags . . ."